D0935365

Chamberlain and Roosevelt

Chamberlain and Roosevelt

British Foreign Policy and the United States, 1937–1940

William R. Rock

Ohio State University Press: Columbus

LIBRARY OF CONGRESS
Library of Congress Cataloging-in-Publication Data

Rock, William R.
Chamberlain and Roosevelt : British foreign policy and the United States, 1937–1940 / William R. Rock.
p. cm.
Bibliography: p.
Includes index.
ISBN 0–8142–0454–6
1. United States—Foreign relations—1933–1945. 2. Chamberlain, Neville, 1869–1940. 3. Roosevelt, Franklin D. (Franklin Delano), 1882–1945. 4. Great Britain—Foreign relations—1936–1945. 5. United States—Foreign relations—Great Britain. 6. Great Britain—Foreign relations—United States. I. Title.
E806.R725 1988
327.41073—dc19 88–1809
CIP

Printed in the U.S.A.

To
Jenny, Dick, and Lori

I consider the closest possible friendship between the United States of America and ourselves is a matter of vital importance and ought to be the dominating principle of our foreign policy.

Lloyd George to Liddell Hart
April 1929
Liddell Hart, *Memoirs*

The ultimate policy of Britain and the U.S.A. must be identical if civilization is to hold together.

Tweedsmuir to Runciman
March 1, 1937
Runciman Papers

Looking back, the historian of the future will probably wonder why the experiment [Anglo-American cooperation] was not tried many years earlier. Surely the time is ripe now for an epoch-making advance? We are at the commencement in Britain of a new reign that is full of promise, America is in the hands of a President who possesses ideals, great ability and immense power: above all, the world is in desperate need of some move that may save it from disaster.

Admiral Drax to Lady Astor
May 27, 1937
Astor Papers

Such vast issues lie in the hands of these two men, F.D.R. and N.C. We must do everything we can to help keep their minds on parallel lines.

Arthur Murray to Walter Runciman
February 20, 1938
Runciman Papers

Here was the one unexploited reserve [the giant's strength of the United States] which must make itself felt if the world was to be saved.

Anthony Eden
Facing the Dictators

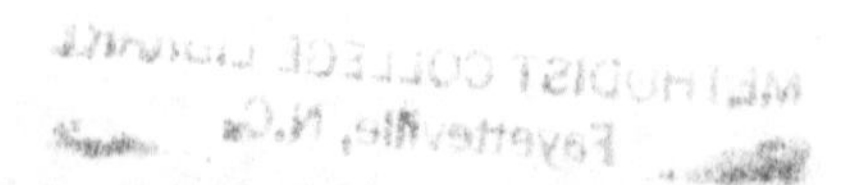

Unless the negative influence of American policy is properly assessed . . . one cannot understand the whole complex of policy that goes under the name of 'appeasement.' "

Max Beloff, "The Special Relationship:
An Anglo-American Myth"

We need education in the obvious, more than investigation of the obscure.

Justice Holmes
quoted in Freedman, *Roosevelt and Frankfurter*

Contents

Preface

THIS STUDY OF British foreign policy and the United States, 1937–40, has both short-term and long-term origins. In the former sense, it has emerged from my career-long interest in, and study of, British appeasement. More particularly, in assessing the motives behind British appeasement for a small book published some years ago (*British Appeasement in the 1930s*), I became curious about the influence that American attitudes and the posture of the United States government had in the formulation and pursuit of appeasement by the British and increasingly convinced that they were a motive force of no small magnitude. Gradually it became clear to me that a full-scale examination of Britain's relations with America in the appeasement era and their relationship to the coming of global war was in order. In a long-term (and much more nebulous) sense, one of my earliest political recollections of a childhood lived in the 1930s was the regular and vigorous berating of the British by my well-meaning grandmother of German extraction for the scandalous and insidious way in which they were gradually dragging the United States into a war in Europe quite against its will—a war in which it had no business and no vital interests. Though a long time gestating, a scholarly examination of the basis and validity of this thesis, widely held by a whole generation of American grandmothers (as well as grandfathers and others) seemed to be in order.

American foreign policy in the 1930s has been examined from various perspectives by numerous scholars of American foreign relations. Indeed, the Franklin D. Roosevelt years have provided a fascination for historians of both foreign and domestic affairs that will not quickly subside.

Likewise, British foreign policy, especially the development of appeasement in relation to the European dictators, has received extensive scholarly attention. But little work had been done, until recently, on Anglo-American relations and particularly Britain's perception of America's posture and policy and the influence it had on British policy-making. In 1975 Ritchie Ovendale published *'Appeasement' and the English-Speaking World: Britain, the United States, the Dominions, and the Policy of 'Appeasement,' 1937–1939*, which deals in intermittent chapters with some of the subject matter encompassed here. But it certainly did not exhaust the topic. Two other books on Anglo-American relations during the same general period have appeared: C. A. MacDonald, *The United States, Britain and Appeasement, 1936–1939* and David Reynolds, *The Creation of the Anglo-American Alliance, 1937–1941: A Study in Competitive Co-operation*. Both make substantial contributions to our understanding of the subject in question. My study has its own special dimensions, including its time frame and the proportion of attention devoted to the various segments thereof, its focus on particular episodes that most clearly reveal the Anglo-American relationship, and its emphasis on personalities and the thoughts and actions of Neville Chamberlain and his associates, which continue to perplex and engross students of history.

Ten years ago Joseph P. Lash published a widely heralded volume entitled *Roosevelt and Churchill, 1939–1941: The Partnership That Saved the West.* His basic thesis is clearly stated in the subtitle of his book; indeed, the relationship that developed between those two men not only makes for fascinating reading (especially for those who still believe that individual personalities can wield a very great influence on the course of historical development), but conveys an aura of genuine inspiration and hope. Pressed to the wall by Hitlerian aggression, they rose to heights of courage and statesmanship that played a very large role in the eventual Allied victory of World War II. But the relationship between Chamberlain and Roosevelt, and their respective nations, just a few years earlier is a very different story. There is very little of the personal attraction, sympathetic understanding, or imaginative statesmanship that characterized the Churchill-Roosevelt relationship. It is much more a story of mutual seclusion, patent excuses, selfish pursuits, and missed opportunities. Indeed, one is tempted to entitle this work "Chamberlain and Roosevelt: The Non-Partnership That Nearly Lost the West." It is not an inspiring story; it is a sad one. It does not convey spirit and hope; instead, it leaves a feeling of discouragement and disappointment. But it must be told, and understood, both for the sake of historical truth and the potential implications of history inherent in it.

In the writing of this study, I have had the kind assistance of many people. In particular, I wish to acknowledge with thanks a year-long Faculty Development Leave granted to me by Bowling Green State University and the travel support awarded to me by the Faculty Research Committee. Personnel at the following libraries and repositories proved very helpful: the Franklin D. Roosevelt Library, Hyde Park, New York; the Library of Congress and the National Archives, Washington, D.C.; the Public Record Office, London; the British Library of Political and Economic Science, London; the National Maritime Museum, Greenwich; the Bodleian Library, Oxford; the Cambridge University Library and the Churchill College Archives, Cambridge; the Birmingham University Library (B. S. Benedikz, head of Special Collections); the Borthwick Institute of Historical Research, York; the Reading University Library (J. A. Edwards, archivist); the Newcastle University Library; the Kent Archives Office, Maidstone; the Scottish Record Office, Edinburgh; and the Bowling Green State University Library, Bowling Green, Ohio.

I owe special thanks to the following institutions and persons for permission to utilize and quote from personal papers as indicated: the University of Birmingham, Neville Chamberlain Papers; the Borthwick Institute of Historical Research (David Smith, director), Halifax Papers; the University of Reading (Michael Bott, keeper of Archives and Manuscripts), Nancy Astor Papers; the Master, Fellows, and Scholars of Churchill College in the University of Cambridge, Hankey Papers and Phipps Papers; the marquess of Lothian, Lothian Papers; Viscount Caldecote, Inskip Papers; and Viscount Simon (who showed special hospitality in inviting me to his home at Topsham, Exeter, Devon), Simon Papers. Multiple efforts to contact the copyright holders of several other sets of papers have been unsuccessful.

For special kindnesses in making my research in London pleasant, I thank Samuel and Sonja Freiman and Andrea and Lena Ferrari. Professor Jane K. Vieth, of Michigan State University, has been a spirited and encouraging critic. Colleagues in the History Department at Bowling Green State University, particularly Gary R. Hess and Bernard Sternsher, have helped in many "little" but important ways. Judith Gilbert has been a splendid typist. For their love, patience, and support over the years, and their readiness to contribute in so many ways to a family climate that encourages the pursuit of creative effort, I am deeply indebted to my wife, Suzanne, and to my sons and daughter, Steve, Anne, and Brian. Since no man is an island, his ideas and efforts are necessarily influenced in positive ways by numerous persons encountered in the normal pursuit of life; and to many such persons, named in my mind alone, I hereby express my gratitude.

CAMERA PRESS LTD.

ASSOCIATED PRESS

I.
The Setting in 1937

ANGLO-AMERICAN RELATIONS over the long span of years have sometimes been characterized by a special spirit of harmony and cooperation; however, they have been equally marred by indifference, suspicion, competition, and hostility.[1] The reasons for this are many and complex, and relate to the evolution of the United States from the status of a British colony to a rival for Britain's position of power and influence in the world after World War I.[2] There have been times, of course, when a close identity of interests—influenced in some degree by cultural, linguistic, or other affinities—has resulted in effective cooperation between the two powers. But it must not be assumed on the basis of the experience of 1940–45 and after that this has always been the norm—the established pattern of Anglo-American relations. Even their seemingly close relationship during World War I is deceptive. Despite the decisive American contribution to the Allied victory over Germany, the United States maintained a certain aloofness from the Anglo-French cause. It was symbolic that President Woodrow Wilson called the United States an "associated," not an "allied," power. His fundamentally moralistic approach to politics implied that America's hands were somehow cleaner than those of the European nations, soiled with sinful traditions like the "balance of power." The British were never quite as offended by this as the French, but it is fair to say that Wilson's ideas never had more than

1. For a good discussion of the "special relationship" idea in broader perspective, see Max Beloff, "The Special Relationship: An Anglo-American Myth," pp. 151–71.

2. Long-term studies of Anglo-American relations include H. G. Nicholas, *The United States and Britain;* H. C. Allen, *Great Britain and the United States: A History of Anglo-American Relations, 1783–1952;* and Arthur C. Turner, *The Unique Partnership: Britain and the United States.*

a mixed reception in Britain. When the United States failed to ratify the Versailles Treaty and join the League of Nations, a potentially important arena of Anglo-American cooperation in the postwar era automatically closed. Indeed, British puzzlement—not to say resentment—over the Senate's crude rejection of the League, after Wilson's insistent campaign at Paris to establish the new world organization as the cornerstone of the peace settlement, was bound to linger for a long time.

In short, the Anglo-American connection in World War I had been just close enough to create as much friction as understanding, and the circumstances of the return to peace did not enhance the potential for growth in the latter area. For one thing, the war had transposed the relative significance of the two powers in the world, although this fact was not at once acknowledged or appreciated on either side. Both nations were set adrift in relation to the rest of the world and to each other. It was widely believed in both countries that the war had been an abnormal disruption of orderly progress, and that a swift return to prewar conditions of "normalcy" was of utmost importance. Further, the quickened rate of change elsewhere in the world, which resulted from the war and caused a natural sense of uncertainty, induced in both peoples an inclination to isolate themselves and not become entangled in developments that they neither understood very clearly nor believed to be vital concerns of theirs.[3] This reversion to isolationism, especially marked in America, was not entirely unexpected. It had characterized the basic American posture on foreign affairs for well over a century, and followed the traditional pattern of British behavior—the historic policy of "splendid isolation"—closely enough to mark no sharp break with the past. In fact, the British found it easier than some other Europeans to comprehend America's outlook precisely because it was not entirely foreign to their own tradition: when the affairs of Europe began to deteriorate rapidly in the 1930s, most British statesmen were excessively skeptical of American intervention and grudgingly accepted her position; conversely, American leaders expected the British to do only what they perceived to be in their own particular interest without any special concern for the good of others.

This is not to say, of course, that there were no significant British and American initiatives in foreign affairs or important Anglo-American contacts in the twenties and early thirties. The United States took the lead in convening the Washington Naval Conference of 1921, and dis-

3. Nicholas, *The U.S. and Britain,* pp. 74–75.

cussions of naval limitation that followed at Geneva in 1927 and London in 1930 were largely Anglo-American affairs (plus Japan) out of which emerged agreement on naval parity among these nations. Certain labors of the League, in which American experts sometimes participated despite Washington's nonmember status, profited from the cooperative efforts of British and American personnel: the Dawes and Young commissions, which reexamined and adjusted the scheme for German reparations payments (in 1924 and 1929, respectively) are examples here. Efforts were made by both governments to oppose Japanese aggression in Manchuria in 1931–32.[4] These failed because of skepticism, incompetence, and shortsightedness on both sides—though in the years that followed, each was inclined to blame the other, thus enhancing doubts in both London and Washington about the other's reliability. The same result emerged from the London Economic Conference of 1933, at which President Franklin Roosevelt's "bombshell" message—rejecting the international stabilization of currencies because it would hamper national policies designed to raise the purchasing power of the people at home by currency regulation—was taken by the British as torpedoing the entire meeting. It was particularly annoying to Neville Chamberlain, chancellor of the Exchequer and leader of the British delegation at the conference. Meantime, mutual recriminations on the subject of German reparations and Allied war debts had come to a head. In the wake of the Great Depression, Britain and other debtor nations had begun to make only token payments to the United States. The scope of economic distress prompted a number of nations, meeting in Lausanne in 1932, to consider a plan for ending reparations with a final lump sum payment *if* the United States would consent to a similar cancellation of war debts. But this was not received favorably in America. Indeed, in 1934 Congress passed the Johnson Act, which prohibited American loans to any government in default on a debt to the United States. Britain then ceased payments altogether, and the war debt issue was gradually submerged in the greater issue of World War II and finally forgotten. Misunderstandings arose between the two powers over differing attitudes toward the World Disarmament Conference (Geneva), German rearmament (and especially Britain's signing of a separate naval agreement with Germany in June 1935), the Italo-Ethiopian war and the imposition of economic sanctions by the League of Nations, the German remilitarization of the Rhineland,

4. For detail see Christopher Thorne, *The Limits of Foreign Policy: The West, the League, and the Far Eastern Crisis of 1931–1933*.

and the Spanish Civil War. There was, by 1937, a legacy of suspicion and frustration in both economic and political relations that was at least as important a factor in Anglo-American relations as any spirit of co-operation or clearly recognized identity of interests.[5]

Neville Chamberlain succeeded Stanley Baldwin as prime minister in May 1937, having served as chancellor of the Exchequer during the previous five years and occupied the role of "heir apparent" for much of Baldwin's last ministry (since June 1935). He had assumed a role of expanding leadership—many saw him as the dominant figure in Baldwin's cabinet—and had become increasingly interested and involved in foreign affairs. Several times he had been seriously considered for the Foreign Ministry, but was deemed too valuable at the Treasury, and was not himself intrigued with the prospect of the move.[6] However tempted he may have been to try to bring some sense of direction to a foreign policy that, in the middle 1930s, was characterized by uncertainty and confusion, he knew the importance of his role in budgetary matters and recognized that his training and experience were largely in the domestic realm. Indeed, it is one of the ironies of history that a man so well prepared to wrestle with pressing domestic issues, upon becoming prime minister, should have devoted his attention so thoroughly to recurrent international crises.

Historians (and others) have long debated the extent to which the influences and experiences of the first fifty years of Chamberlain's life preconditioned his thinking on foreign affairs. These factors cannot, of course, be measured with precision, but a number of them are worthy of mention. Chamberlain sprang from a long line of tradesmen who, in their devotion to civil and religious liberty, along with a sturdy patriotism, were typical of thousands of British families who drew innate strength from their closeness to one of the mainstreams of English thought. His father, Joseph, moved from London to Birmingham as a teenage youth to join his uncle, John Sutton Netterfold, in the manufacture of metal screws. Shrewd and tireless effort resulted in much success;

5. For a fuller description of suspicions and misunderstandings, see Arnold A. Offner, *The Origins of the Second World War: American Foreign Policy and World Politics, 1917–1941,* pp. 110–20, 133–50; and C. A. MacDonald, *The United States, Britain, and Appeasement,* pp. 19–23. As for the war debt issue, by the late 1930s the semiannual American presentation of a bill and a British response to the effect that "we'll have to find a means of solving this problem sometime" had become almost ritualistic.

6. Keith Feiling, *The Life of Neville Chamberlain,* p. 240; Iain Macleod, *Neville Chamberlain,* p. 179.

and Joseph Chamberlain achieved affluence, married well, became involved in civic affairs, and developed interests that ultimately led to a brilliant political career on the national level at the turn of the century—one prominent aspect of which was his crusading effort to promote a settlement of outstanding differences between Britain and Germany. Throughout his political life, Neville was unusually conscious of his father's legacy and was often reminded of it by his two older maiden sisters, with whom he corresponded diligently and at length.

Growing up motherless (after age six) in the relative seclusion of a close family clan, with his prominent father frequently absent on business in London, Neville Chamberlain developed an "accursed shyness" (his term) that he never fully overcame. He attended school at Rugby but did not go on to the university because of an apparent decision made by his father: his elder half-brother Austen was being groomed for a career in politics, so Neville was to go into business. Accordingly, he attended Mason College in Birmingham; took commercial courses, metallurgy, and engineering design; and, after two years, undertook a successful apprenticeship with a firm of public accountants. At age twenty-two, his father sent him to Andros Island in the Bahamas to bolster family fortunes through the operation of a sisal plantation. It was a Spartan six-year ordeal that resulted in failure despite Neville's best efforts: the land and climate were simply not suited for the enterprise. (A few persons have seen his later reliance upon his own judgment and his great tenacity in trying to reach agreement with Adolf Hitler in the late 1930s as an overlearned lesson of the Andros experience.) When he returned to Birmingham in 1897, he purchased a small manufacturing concern (Hoskins and Son) and began the life of a public-spirited businessman, marrying only in 1911. Increasingly involved in civic responsibilities (as a member of numerous municipal committees) and developing special interests in city hospitals and Birmingham University (of which his father was the first chancellor), he showed no particular political ambition; and his election as alderman in 1914 and lord mayor in 1915 seemed to be natural outgrowths of his civic interests. (His extensive experience in business has led some to interpret Chamberlain's approach to foreign affairs as being essentially that of a parsimonious manufacturer trying to keep peace among his customers; and his long involvement in municipal government has been seen by some as a useful explanation for the seeming narrowness of vision that he brought to national affairs.)

His first taste of national politics came in 1917. Through his half-brother Austen (a prominent figure in Lloyd George's wartime coalition), his record of efficient administration in Birmingham came to the prime minister's attention, and he was called to London as director of the Department of National Service. Whether Chamberlain lacked the imaginative qualities necessary to do the job, or Lloyd George failed to provide him the authority and support to do it—the weight of evidence leans in the latter direction—it was a wretched eight-month experience. Mutual recriminations resulted, and each man developed an antipathy for the other that remained for the rest of their lives. This may have indirectly influenced Chamberlain's attitude toward the United States later on. Lloyd George was an outspoken proponent of a British "New Deal" (including a vast program of public works for the purpose of providing employment) and a closer alignment of potential allies as the international situation became more threatening. Although Chamberlain had other reasons for taking a different view of these matters, his longstanding animosity toward Lloyd George certainly reinforced them.

Elected to Parliament in 1918 from the Ladywood district of Birmingham, Chamberlain first took office as postmaster general under Bonar Law in 1922. (Inasmuch as Bonar Law's elevation stood in the way of Austen Chamberlain's hopes for the prime ministership, a painful wound was opened between the Chamberlain brothers that never completely healed.) In rapid order Neville moved to the Ministry of Health, a post well suited to his interests, experience, and well-developed social conscience, then became chancellor of the Exchequer in the first Baldwin government. Choosing to return to the Ministry of Health when the cabinet was reconstructed in late 1924, he compiled there, during the next five years, a record of achievement that is genuinely noteworthy in the social history of the interwar years. He also gradually emerged as an important influence in the ranks of the Conservative party. Meanwhile, Austen had become foreign secretary and had achieved a notable success in the signing of the Locarno Agreements, October 1925, which reduced Germany's bitterness over the outcome of World War I and opened the way for its reemergence as an equal partner in the European family of nations. Sent into opposition by the Labor victory of 1929, Neville devoted the next two years to the Conservative party, serving in turn as chairman of its research department, then as party chairman. A thorough party restructuring resulted in a revitalized organization sensitive to his personal touch; this was significant in the election of 1935, which determined the kind of Parliament he would have behind him when he eventually became prime minister.

As chancellor of the Exchequer, 1932–37, Chamberlain was an orthodox, conservative financier. His first order of business was fiscal revolution in the form of protection, and by the tariff scheme of February 1932, Joseph Chamberlain's cherished dream was fulfilled—by the son set aside from politics and put to an accountant's desk. Neville took an immense amount of pride in that. The Ottawa Agreements (1932), which embodied reciprocal preferential arrangements between Britain and the dominions, contained ideas that were largely of Chamberlain's devising—but that ran directly counter to United States' hopes for free trade. He resented Washington's refusal to accept the cancellation of war debts as a corollary to cancelling German reparations (as proposed by the Lausanne Conference) and was stung by Roosevelt's posture toward the London Economic Conference. Opposed to deficit financing, he insisted on drastic economies in national spending to balance the budget, resisting cuts in the income tax, and refusing to borrow to reduce taxation. Generally, he believed that the nation's economic condition warranted steady, time-tested methods, not wild experimentation; and he clearly attributed Britain's recovery to tariffs, conversion operations, cheap money, balanced budgets, remission of taxation, and the spirit of confidence that grew out of these things. Later on, when the apparent need for heavy expenditures on armaments and defense preparations was growing, it was not surprising that Chamberlain would see things from the vantage point of the Treasury, which worried incessantly that expenditures of the scope essential to prepare the nation for war would undermine the very economic stability of the nation on which its fundamental security rested.[7]

The Europe that Chamberlain confronted upon becoming prime minister was growing tense and combustible. Though momentarily quiescent, Germany was menacing: her introduction of compulsory military service (March 1935) and her remilitarization of the Rhineland (March 1936) constituted flagrant violations of the Versailles Treaty. Waxing ever more confident in the strength of his own position (both at home and in relation to potential national adversaries), Hitler was making threatening gestures in other directions. Mussolini had been on a rampage for several years, invading Abyssinia, defying the League's efforts

7. The paragraphs on Chamberlain's life and career up to 1937 are summarized mainly from William R. Rock, *Neville Chamberlain,* passim. The most recent, fullest, and best biography of Chamberlain is David Dilks, *Neville Chamberlain,* vol. 1: *Pioneering and Reform, 1869–1929.* A second volume covering 1930–40 is expected soon. Two other biographies of note are cited in n. 6, above.

to resist the aggression by means of economic sanctions, and defiantly sending troops and supplies to the Nationalist side in Spain (where civil war had begun in July 1936) despite professed adherence to a nonintervention agreement among the major European powers. Germany and Italy were linked, of course, by affinities of outlook and similar fascist forms of government. A Rome-Berlin agreement of mid-1936 had established their relationship, at least in their eyes, as the "axis" upon which the future of Europe would turn. Britain, on the other hand, was linked with France by common ideals of democracy, freedom, and parliamentary government—although their relationship since 1919 had been anything but close, given their vastly divergent ideas on the implementation of Versailles and what was best for promoting European peace and security.[8] Thus the basic problem, as Chamberlain at length described it, was this:

> Are we to allow these two pairs of nations to go on glowering at one another . . . allowing the feeling . . . to become more and more embittered until at last the barriers are broken down and the conflict begins which many think would mark the end of civilization? Or can we bring them to an understanding of one another's aims and objects, and to such discussion as may lead to a final settlement?[9]

If the four nations could be brought into friendly discussion and to a settlement of their differences, Chamberlain believed that the peace of Europe would be saved for some time to come. He determined to make every effort to reach "what has sometimes been called a general settlement, to arrive at a position . . . when reasonable grievances may be removed, when suspicions may be laid aside, and when confidence may again be restored." This could only be achieved "by a real understanding and effort to meet others' needs," and for that reason, any effort Britain could make to remove legitimate grievances and promote harmony among the nations would bring its own reward, if it made a contribution

8. It is an established fact of diplomatic history that Britain and France approached post-World War I European affairs, especially in relation to Germany, from vastly different perspectives and that the breakdown in Anglo-French cooperation significantly increased the fragility of peace. This was first elaborated in Arnold Wolfers, *Britain and France between Two Wars: Conflicting Strategies of Peace Since Versailles,* and has been examined in detail by many later works. An effective recent study on a crucial segment of the subject is Nicholas Rostow, *Anglo-French Relations, 1934–1936.*

9. Great Britain, *Parliamentary Debates, House of Commons,* Fifth Series (hereafter *Parl. Debs, HC*), 21 February 1938, 332: 64.

to the general welfare.[10] Herein lay the essence, and the motivation, for the policy of appeasement with which his name has become synonymous—and all the other motives that have been attributed to him by a wide range of friends and foes alike were either secondary at best or largely rationalizations concocted after the event to serve a particular purpose.[11]

To be sure, British policymakers were becoming concerned about the disparity between the nation's commitments, on the one hand, and her capabilities, on the other. The prospect of having to confront three potential aggressors (Italy, Germany, and Japan) simultaneously led the Chiefs of Staff Sub-Committee to declare in a secret report of December 1937: "We cannot exaggerate the importance from the point of view of Imperial defence, of any political or international action that can be taken to reduce the number of potential enemies and to gain the support of potential allies."[12] The point was often repeated in varying contexts. Thus it might seem that efforts to appease potential adversaries grew unavoidably from the recognition that Britain needed to extricate herself from a dangerous and untenable position. Some supporters of the policy were no doubt moved by considerations of this kind, and some historians have tended to explain appeasement on the grounds that there was no realistic alternative. But there was a far more positive element in Chamberlain's commitment to the policy. Understanding that policy must depend upon power, he nonetheless saw the basic principle of concessions through strength as a noble concept rooted in the moral and religious traditions of the British people. This policy was further reinforced by a certain cultural sophistication, courage, and common sense, all of which culminated in a special responsibility to "make gentle the life of Europe." Avoidance of war as the highest ambition of statesmanship was a cardinal principle for Chamberlain, who was constantly reinforced in this view by a preoccupation with the "lessons of 1914" and who shared with his countrymen the idea that war in the twentieth century had

10. Ibid., 21 December 1937, 330: 1804–7.

11. For a fuller discussion of motive forces behind appeasement, see William R. Rock, *British Appeasement in the 1930s*, chap. 4. All sorts of objectives have been imputed to Chamberlain, ranging from a calculated effort to gain time until Britain was prepared for war to a vain and desperate effort to preserve the class privileges of the British aristocracy against the rising tide of socialism. Such theories do not hold up under an intensive examination of evidence. They merely complicate and render ulterior motives that were simple, clear, and honorable, however wise the policy may have been.

12. CAB 23/90, 8 December 1937, pp. 265–67.

become the ultimate evil.[13] Thus appeasement, in Chamberlain's view, was not a coward's creed or a treacherous notion advanced alone by stupid men. A large majority of Englishmen seemed to agree with him in 1937.

In pursuing the basic lines of action recommended by the Chiefs of Staff, Chamberlain focused far greater attention upon reducing the number of Britain's potential enemies than upon gaining the support of potential allies. In fact, he saw no reliable allies at hand; and the occasional prodding of political opponents or policy critics for greater effort in this direction only tended to exasperate him. The dismal failure of the League of Nations to respond effectively to critical situations earlier (Manchuria and Abyssinia) had led Chamberlain to acknowledge his total loss of confidence in that organization as a means of promoting security. Labeling the economic sanctions imposed on Italy by the League "the very midsummer of madness"—after it had become clear that they were not working—he initiated Britain's efforts to end them. The familiar problem of French domestic instability (compounded by Anglo-French differences over a wide range of interwar issues that caused a deteriorating national empathy) made France suspect as a steadying force in the European order. Chamberlain and many of his colleagues distrusted the judgment and reliability of French statesmen. Russia was dismissed through an inextricable combination of ideological and practical factors. Bolshevism, with its subversive doctrines of world revolution and socialism, seemed antagonistic and dangerous to traditional British interests; and Chamberlain acknowledged his profound distrust of Russia's motives. Moreover, Russia was weak militarily, unstable politically, and unsound economically—all of these the result of internal travail associated with Stalin's brutal crusade to transform Russian society under the first five-year plans. Further afield, the dominions were extremely cool toward any involvement with Britain in the affairs of Europe and loathe to support her in any situation that did not involve a direct threat to her very existence. That left the United States. But its isolationist sentiment, reinforced by the anti-British press and preoccupation with economic problems arising from the Depression, seemed to rule out all possibility of involvement in European problems. Even should Roosevelt wish for it, it was assumed Congress would never approve.[14]

13. In *Neville Chamberlain and Appeasement: A Study in the Politics of History*, Larry W. Fuchser emphasizes that at almost every moment of important political decision, Chamberlain's mind tended toward the past—what his father would have done and the "lessons" of the Great War.

14. See Rock, *British Appeasement in the 1930s*, pp. 47–51.

None of this was particularly worrisome to Chamberlain, for he was not enamored with alliances in the first place: they had contributed substantially, in his view, to the onset of war in 1914, and he wished to avoid a repetition of those circumstances, especially in the sense of encircling Germany and thus providing Hitler with a pretext for an early war. This made it easy for him to exclude Russia—which he wished to exclude on other grounds as well—from his European calculations. Alliances could result in unwanted entanglements. Certainly Chamberlain wanted no involvement in France's shaky alliance system with some of the smaller states of Eastern Europe. Further, alliances could be costly in a world where nearly every nation was Britain's rival in some dimension; they entailed concessions—perhaps even a high price in economic terms—and forced greater dependence on others. And they might very well be unnecessary. If Germany, as he believed, lacked the economic strength and political cohesion essential for total war, a policy of conciliation that was tempered by firmness might be sufficient to meet the need of the times.[15]

The element of firmness in Chamberlain's policy was to derive primarily from British efforts at rearmament. Chamberlain had early perceived the need for a dual policy: appeasement *and* rearmament. In most of his public pronouncements the two went hand in hand, although appeasement certainly received more emphasis. His was the guiding hand behind three White Papers on defense, 1935–37, in which Britain's need to strengthen her military position was openly recognized, and plans were laid for remedying deficiencies in all three branches of the service. These were modest documents in relation to the nation's later requirements, but they nonetheless reflect an appreciation of the need to improve Britain's military posture; and Chamberlain's role in their development made him as active as anyone in promoting rearmament during those uncertain years.

There were, of course, problems in meeting those needs. The temper of the nation was such that no one crusaded for rearmament. The Labour opposition vehemently denounced it, and concern for its impact on domestic politics was always present. Few Englishmen were yet ready to believe that the nation must prepare for all-out war, and defense was still understood in terms of minimal-deterrent protection. At least equally important was the view that Britain's economic stability was the

15. See David Reynolds, *The Creation of the Anglo-American Alliance, 1937–41: A Study in Competitive Cooperation,* p. 9.

fourth arm of defense, and British policymakers generally agreed that no effort at rearmament should interfere with the normal operations of British industry or threaten the balanced budget, which was seen as the cornerstone of economic stability. The time was not yet right for an emergency commitment to rearmament. Consequently, there was much more talk than actual progress made—at least until 1939. But sensitivity to the need for rearmament and discussion about it was sufficient to permit people like Chamberlain to think of firmness in conjunction with appeasement, although it is clear from hindsight that their perception of Britain's defense needs was grossly deficient.[16]

In view of developing international dangers, and in the absence of strong support from other quarters, it might have seemed reasonable for British policymakers to think about working for closer ties with the United States. Certainly there was a subtle—and growing—number of of common interests that, whatever the differences between the two nations on particular issues, was recognizable to the British. However, their failure to acknowledge those interests may be explained by the interplay of three contradictory emotions: doubt, fear, and hope.

First, there was genuine doubt that reliable support could be gained from America under any circumstances. Its reputation for offering words, not deeds—legendary among British officials—sprang from a broad array of factors ranging from a perception of America's irresponsible behavior in a variety of interwar contexts to a misperception of the American form of government (seen as a fragmented political system in which prejudiced and uninformed public and congressional opinion often immobilized the administration). Reinforcing all this was another popular British view of America as a brash, young, inexperienced, ultrasensitive nation—with an inferiority complex toward Britain—whose people were lacking in culture and sophistication. This perception was unduly nourished by wide British familiarity with American movies, which portrayed primarily the seamier side of American life. This outlook, based upon a pervasive British ignorance of the springs of American behavior and what life in America was really like, and coupled with the American desire to eschew consorting with foreigners, provided no impetus whatsoever for change.

Second, there was fear that American assistance would result in Brit-

16. Rock, *Neville Chamberlain,* pp. 94, 101, 106, 114. For a thorough study of the political and economic aspects of rearmament, see Robert Paul Shay, Jr., *British Rearmament in the Thirties: Profits and Politics.*

ain's displacement by the United States in a wide range of matters, especially economic ones, relating to world leadership. World War I exacerbated the economic rivalry that had been developing between the two nations since at least the turn of the century: the United States became the world's great creditor nation thus supplanting Britain as the world's chief source of investment capital. The early thirties had seen the emergence of divergent economic policies as both nations wrestled with the Depression. The British turned to protectionism within an imperial bloc (the Ottawa Agreements), which the United States was not about to accept quietly. Conversely, Washington pushed to free trade, which prompted London to see Roosevelt as hostile to the British Commonwealth and Secretary of State Cordell Hull— "the American Cobden"—as attempting to restore the world economy of the nineteenth century. Compounded by American insistence upon the payment of war debts and the attainment of naval parity, these developments made it appear to be a genuine threat to Britain's global position. So British leaders, concerned to preserve their nation's position as a great power, were at least as much aware of the costs and dangers of American assistance as the benefits.[17]

Counterbalancing this doubt and fear, however, was an element of hope—hope that America might gradually be educated to world responsibilities, and that it would ultimately respond appropriately and cooperatively when its own vital interests, as well as Britain's, were clearly at stake. America might, for example, lend support to Britain in the closing stages of a tedious negotiation or serve as international mediator. It could coordinate naval activity in the Far East, where Japanese expansionism threatened America's interests at least as much as Britain's. It must certainly come to Britain's assistance with money and munitions, if not with men, in the event of war—and the sooner the better (in comparison with 1914). But America's education could not be rushed. There was little the British could do about that except to rely on the educative power of events, because any active effort to promote such education was sure to result in bitter resentment. This view had long

17. This fear related to military planning too. Basil Liddell Hart writes that in dealing with questions of "limited liability" and "victory" during the twenties and thirties, he had many times pointed out that another unlimited effort like 1914–18 "was bound to end in bankruptcy even if it ended in victory, and result in Britain declining into a poor dependent of the U.S.A." Thus he thought it folly to commit Britain to the aim of total victory if war came. *The Liddell Hart Memoirs*, 2:197.

been taken by Sir Ronald Lindsay, the British ambassador in Washington, and was widely accepted in London.[18]

Franklin Roosevelt had been inaugurated president of the United States in March 1933. Representing the liberal wing of the Democratic party, he was in many ways an unlikely progressive. He had been born into a life of privilege in Dutchess County, New York, and his ancestors on both sides had been men of affairs and social standing for generations. As a young man, he experienced the upbringing common to the sons of country gentlemen: early instruction by tutors, travel abroad with his parents, and attendance at an exclusive preparatory school (Groton, in Massachusetts). An only son whose father was twice the age of his mother, he matured within a highly structured framework with which he apparently learned to cope by keeping many of his thoughts and actions to himself. This attribute carried over into later life. As president, he usually made up his mind quite independently; no associates—and not even his wife—could say with confidence that they really understood the man or grasped his thought processes.

Qualities of leadership and political conviction appeared during three years at Harvard, after which he attended Columbia University Law School and worked without great enthusiasm or distinction on Wall Street. Impelled by a sense of noblesse oblige, and inspired by the example of his cousin Theodore Roosevelt, he sought a career in public service—and at length retraced with striking similarity his cousin's path to the White House. Entrance into politics occurred in 1910, when Democratic leaders in heavily Republican Dutchess County named him their candidate for the state senate. He campaigned with verve against political "bossism" and was elected. His leadership abilities and progressive leanings secured easy reelection in 1912. That same year he became involved in presidential politics as a spokesman for New York progressive Democrats for Woodrow Wilson. His apparent reward was appointment, in March 1913, as assistant secretary of the navy, in which post he served for seven years, expanding upon a lifelong love for the sea. Though he became established in Washington as a promising young Democrat who admired Wilson, it was still surprising when he emerged as the Democratic candidate for vice-president in 1920.

Defeat in the national election did not constitute nearly so drastic a potential setback as did his contracting polio in 1921. Long years were

18. These paragraphs rest heavily on Reynolds, *Creation of the Anglo-American Alliance*, pp. 10–16, in which the factors of doubt, fear, and hope are most effectively identified and analyzed.

spent in efforts at recuperation, but Roosevelt was never able to walk again without the use of leg braces and canes. This did not significantly impede his political career. Maintaining the warm, ebullient, and self-confident attitude, as well as the quick mind that had made him popular initially, he worked within the Democratic party to modernize its structure and to make it more progressive. In short, he remained an important Democratic figure in both state and national politics.

Elected governor of the state of New York in 1928, Roosevelt attracted widespread attention as a moderate progressive seeking to involve the state more fully in projects calculated to improve the lot of the people. This orientation, along with his demonstrated skills as administrator and leader, made him a likely Democratic candidate for the presidency in 1932, a time when domestic problems attending economic collapse preoccupied the nation. His resounding victory over incumbent President Herbert Hoover was followed by the introduction of the "New Deal"—a startling departure in American politics and economics that spawned confusion and criticism, but bolstered the nation's spirit. Domestic affairs remained the first order of business throughout Roosevelt's first term as president. By the beginning of his second term, his party's strength in Congress seemed sufficient to sustain a continuing program of reform. But his attempt at the "court-packing" plan of February 1937 ensnarled Roosevelt in paralyzing political difficulties. A powerful congressional coalition of Republicans and conservative Democrats formed against him, and the impetus of New Deal legislation slowed substantially.[19]

Foreign affairs always interested Roosevelt, and his credentials for active involvement were superior to those of most American presidents. Yet the imprint of his international background and his sophisticated view of the world was uncertain. A faithful follower of Wilson during World War I and a proponent of U.S. membership in the League of Nations as vice-presidential candidate in 1920, he had changed position altogether by the time of his own presidential campaign; and his first inaugural address struck a distinctly isolationist chord. The consummate politician, ever sensitive to the public temper, Roosevelt's change was no doubt due more to his altered perception of American opinion than any sharp intellectual metamorphosis of his own. In this as in so many other matters, it is hard to discern the "real" Roosevelt. It was as if he were

19. Works abound on Roosevelt's early life and career. Notable among them are James McGregor Burns, *Roosevelt: The Lion and the Fox*, and Frank Freidel, *Franklin D. Roosevelt*.

torn between mind and heart, the former embracing internationalist reasoning, the latter feeding, at least periodically, upon the deep roots of isolationism that were so much a part of American history and culture—reinforced by the popular notion of the early 1930s that America had mistakenly forsaken ancient wisdom in 1917 and far from redeeming Europe by her intervention could now only watch that continent losing its soul to communism and fascism. There were specific circumstances during his first term in which an internationalist outlook was visible, but there was enough isolationist sentiment in the president himself to lead him to overestimate the strength and cohesion of the isolationist forces ranged against him. In any case, the limited international agenda of his first term did not go beyond promoting the regional (i.e., hemispheric) influence of the United States and perhaps exploring ways in which the nation might participate in efforts to promote such ends as the interdependence of nations, arms limitation and guarantees against war, and the expansion of international trade.

Historians of American foreign relations have long acknowledged that it is almost impossible to penetrate Roosevelt's reasoning and attitudes, beyond certain generalities; and it is equally difficult to ascertain the extent to which policy was shaped by the president's own mind or significantly influenced by forces outside the White House. No doubt his own personality and outlook account for the ambiguities of his foreign policy as much as any other factor. (This is a major theme in David Reynolds's study; see note 15 above.) Certainly Roosevelt hoped to spare the United States from the scourge of war; but he also hoped, after 1935, to bring American strength to bear against the armed aggression that was spreading round the world. Uncertainty about the means to be employed and the political risks involved surely constrained him. Whenever he did decide to move, he liked to engage in personal diplomacy, feeling that such approaches could somehow promote accommodation more effectively than laborious proceedings through channels.[20]

The State Department was certainly not of one mind about American policy toward Europe or United States relationships with Great Britain. Secretary of State Cordell Hull—a temperate Wilsonian who saw dis-

20. The literature on Roosevelt and foreign policy is extensive. Note in particular Robert Dallek, *Franklin Roosevelt and American Foreign Policy, 1932–1945*, a comprehensive, balanced, fully researched account that is utilized heavily here. Another impressive study is Wayne S. Cole, *Roosevelt and the Isolationists*. Dated but still of great value to this study is William L. Langer and S. Everett Gleason, *The Challenge to Isolation, 1937–1940*. Robert A. Divine analyzes Roosevelt as isolationist, interventionist, realist, and pragmatist in *Roosevelt and World War II*.

armament, free trade, and peaceful change as the foundation stones of world peace—took a dim view of U.S. involvement in European affairs. Suspicious of Britain's intentions, he regarded her system of imperial preference as detrimental to a healthy world economy and harped ceaselessly that world peace depended largely upon expanded world trade. Others in the State Department were divided over the degree to which the existence of the British Empire was essential to American security, as compared with the danger of involving the United States in another war on Britain's side. By early 1938 the leading officials, including Sumner Welles (the undersecretary), Adolf Berle, and Jay Pierrepont Moffat, were wary of Britain and doubted her trustworthiness as an ally. They favored a largely independent policy based upon a limited and realistic conception of America's own particular interests, and saw the United States as a potential neutral arbiter set apart from entanglements in Europe. The opposite view was expressed most effectively by several cabinet members, who found the State Department unduly cautious and who increasingly perceived the emergence of a global struggle between dictatorship and democracy from which the United States could not and should not stand aside. Notable here were Henry Morgenthau, secretary of the treasury, and Harold Ickes, interior secretary. Neither could be called a natural anglophile, but their perception of the drift of world events predisposed them to a considerable degree of Anglo-American cooperation.[21]

As recent scholarship suggests, American opinion toward foreign affairs in the early 1930s might better be described as indifferent rather than intensely isolationist. Consequently there was some room for Roosevelt to maneuver in order to test the possibilities. Improving relationships with Britain and France was high on his list of priorities. If Britain and the United States could achieve a complete identity of political and economic interests, he believed they might assume true leadership in the world. So he early revealed his willingness to discuss the British debt, initiated conversations about it with Ambassador Lindsay, and invited Prime Minister Ramsay MacDonald and former Premier Edouard Herriot (of France) to Washington to discuss fundamental points of monetary and economic policy. Unfortunately, the optimism and good will generated by the latter talks (April 1933) were undermined by Roosevelt's basic determination to keep international economic reform in the

21. Reynolds, *Creation of the Anglo-American Alliance*, pp. 27–29; Offner, *Origins of the Second World War*, pp. 106–10.

background until domestic legislation could be made to work. This promoted his uncooperative stance on the crucial issue of currency stabilization at the London Economic Conference that generated widespread resentment toward the United States. Thereafter, he backed away from efforts at decisive action in foreign affairs and contented himself for a time with expressions of interest in international cooperation. The failure of world disarmament talks at Geneva (spring, 1934), which he had tried to encourage and support in various ways, had two distinct effects: it strengthened Roosevelt's own ambivalence about the extent to which the United States could act effectively to check the world drift toward political and economic turmoil; and it strengthened the hand of those who opposed even symbolic American involvement abroad. By early 1935 the growing threat of war in Europe was grasped by a large number of Americans and began to arouse an isolationist response of sharply increasing proportions. The Senate's rejection of a Roosevelt proposal to seek membership in the World Court (January 1935), which the president had come to believe had wide support, marked a turning point: now the isolationist attitudes usually associated with the thirties more generally came to assume a dominant place in national thinking about foreign affairs. And neutrality legislation, by which Congress hoped to keep the United States out of war by strictly prohibiting all involvement with belligerents, followed shortly thereafter.[22]

Events in Europe in 1935 seemed to convince Roosevelt that America would eventually have to take a stand against Germany. But he was very ambivalent about how to handle American neutrality, the object of much internal debate and animus, and how to deal with the Abyssinian conflict. He certainly wanted to work against Italian aggression, but he was equally wary of stirring up serious internal difficulties over the question of limitations on presidential power in foreign affairs. The upshot of all his maneuvering on these and other issues was that he found no really effective means to serve the cause of peace. In the electoral campaign of 1936, Roosevelt spoke out generally about his hatred of war and spent,

22. Dallek, *Franklin Roosevelt and American Foreign Policy,* pp. 78–97. The Neutrality Act of 1935 empowered the president to prohibit the sale or shipment of arms, munitions, and implements of war to all nations involved in conflict. The law was extended in February 1936, and eleven months later special legislation was passed to deal with the Spanish Civil War. The Neutrality Act of 1937 permitted the president to embargo nonmilitary goods and place all trade on a "cash-and-carry" basis. This would favor the British, with their large navy and merchant fleet, but its primary purpose was to safeguard American neutrality by reducing the risk of replicating the circumstances that had prompted American intervention on the side of Britain in 1917.

by his own account, many hours thinking and planning how war could be kept from the United States. But he made no moves of international significance and avoided any suggestion of involving the United States in commitments abroad. Once the election was over and he had won a resounding victory, the way seemed open for him to make more active efforts for peace. Certainly he received some moving expressions of hope from Europeans that he would take the lead in seeking an effective means of heading off impending disaster. Some emphasized that he was the only statesman capable of doing this. Although his inaugural address ignored foreign policy, early 1937 found him exploring various schemes to save the peace. One of these involved an idea with which he had toyed intermittently for some time, the calling of a conference (probably in Washington) of six or seven major heads of state. Its form and nature were ill defined, but its purpose would be clear enough: to put them all together in one room to iron out all the issues separating them or, falling short of that, to identify clearly the points of disagreement among them. In early March he discussed with Canadian Prime Minister Mackenzie King the idea of a "Permanent Conference on Economic and Social Problems." Nothing specific resulted, but Roosevelt was brainstorming again about international affairs and the preservation of peace. A period similar to the early months of his presidency, when limited foreign policy initiatives were both possible and essential, seemed to have recurred. At the same time, Roosevelt was in the middle of his bitter, all-consuming struggle to enlarge the Supreme Court as a means of preserving New Deal legislation; thus, he was not well situated to seek greater executive control over foreign affairs.[23]

In the context of Anglo-American relations, one is struck by certain similarities between Roosevelt and Neville Chamberlain. Both men were products of prominent families, from which they inherited a strong sense of social responsibility and a certain ambition. Both had attained an early familiarity with other countries and had traveled extensively in Europe and elsewhere. Thus they shared a thoroughly cosmopolitan outlook toward world affairs. Both had close relatives who had been important political figures, from whom they drew inspiration and whom they desired to emulate. For Roosevelt it was his flamboyant cousin, Theodore, whose occupancy of the White House (1901–8) was just one aspect of a genuinely exciting career; for Chamberlain it was his equally flamboyant father, Joseph, a leading figure in Conservative cabinets

23. Ibid., pp. 102–40.

around the turn of the century who had made a special mark as colonial secretary. Their personality traits certainly differed. Roosevelt was far more gregarious and possessed a special talent to influence and manipulate others by force of his personal charm, whereas Chamberlain was shy, reserved, and inclined to rely on the efficiency of his performance to bespeak his competence. But both had what might be called "take charge" dispositions. Roosevelt early saw himself as destined for important political office and carefully calculated the process by which he planned to reach his goal. Chamberlain was less openly ambitious, but often admitted his inability to sit by and tolerate the incompetence of others when he knew clearly what had to be done and how to do it. It was not surprising, then, that both should feel an urge to do something about the deteriorating international situation that posed so dangerous a threat to their own nations and the world at large. That Roosevelt did this somewhat less openly and aggressively than Chamberlain is mainly a reflection of the domestic situation in which they had to work and the relative positions of their nations, historically and geographically, in world affairs.

There was a basic element of appeasement in the approach to continental affairs, and particularly to Germany, common to the thinking of both men. Roosevelt, in fact, had made some subtle moves in that direction before Chamberlain had attained leadership and had formulated his own ideas clearly. One study of the United States, Britain, and appeasement in the latter thirties begins with the assertion: "At the end of 1936 the United States began to use its influence to stimulate appeasement in Europe. The object of American intervention was to secure peace, stability, and the expansion of international trade in the interests of world order and domestic recovery."[24] Roosevelt was concerned about the European drift toward war, sensitive to Germany's demands for economic justice, and convinced that political tensions were closely connected with economic problems—such as Germany's introduction of exchange control and autarky to stimulate recovery and speed rearmament; thus, he sought to learn from German leaders the prospects for a compromise settlement that would satisfy the economic necessities of Germany without resorting to war or making Germany paramount in Europe. He hoped to appeal to German moderates (those who wanted to solve Germany's problems by negotiation, rather than by military action), who might then influence Hitler in the right direction. At the

24. MacDonald, *The United States, Britain, and Appeasement*, p. 1.

same time, he sought to determine Britain's attitude toward these issues both because British cooperation would be essential to the success of a settlement and because the reduction of trade restrictions—one element he believed fundamental to any settlement—applied as much to Britain as it did to Germany. In short, America's interest in expanding international trade was basic to her foreign policy outlook, and an Anglo-American trade agreement would constitute an essential component of economic appeasement.[25]

The response Roosevelt received from London was less than encouraging. Indeed, it is no exaggeration to say that, during the first half of 1937, Britain was the main obstacle to the pursuit of Roosevelt's objective. Not that the British opposed the principle of appeasement or failed to recognize the value of American participation in any settlement. Rather, it was the manner of approach. Whereas America favored reducing economic barriers, and the grievances that arose therefrom, to reduce political tensions and the threats of violence that accompanied them, the British viewed things in just the opposite manner. They favored discussing political issues over considering economic adjustment, arms limitation, or colonial appeasement (colonial concessions of an indefinite kind to which the Cabinet Committee on Foreign Policy agreed in early April). That is, Britain wanted definite political assurances, such as guarantees of European security, as a prelude to other concessions to prevent giving away valuable bargaining chips without any assurance of substantial return or encouraging a dangerous German belief in British weakness.[26] There existed, then, an honest difference of approach to a similar objective, reflecting again the differing needs and perspectives of Washington and London.

The problem was compounded by other factors. Aside from the difficulty of clearly distinguishing economic issues from political issues, Washington wanted to discuss a wide range of European problems—from trade restrictions to disarmament and security—but insisted upon washing its hands of any responsibility for political arrangements that might result. The dilemma of how to assume a position of leadership in relation to Europe, while still maintaining the traditional posture of political noninvolvement in European affairs demanded by American opinion, was still altogether unresolved by American policymakers. It was a huge hurdle to conquer, and was not surmounted until after World

25. For detail see ibid., pp. 4–15.
26. Ibid., pp. 16–18.

War II, when all pretense of political isolation was abandoned in the face of a burgeoning communist threat. During the thirties this policy was a constant source of British suspicion and hesitation.

On the British side, there were many who were unconvinced about the usefulness of the American connection. In addition to the broader question of America's political reliability (its reputation for not following up inspiring words with practical action), there was the deep concern about American economic dominance. The more the Americans emphasized the need for economic change that was not compatible with British thinking—particularly the elimination of trade restrictions—the more the British doubted. Inheriting a protectionist posture from his famous father, who had made an international reputation on the issue a generation earlier, Chamberlain never wavered in his own commitment to a preferential system; it was a kind of glue holding the empire together, and he was quite unready to weaken imperial ties for the sake of American friendship. Many other important persons in the cabinet, in the civil service, business, and finance shared this view. Even Anthony Eden, chief among British leaders who were anxious to cultivate the American relationship, believed that Britain should not be rushed by Roosevelt into unwise concessions.[27]

Meantime, Roosevelt had experienced no greater success with his soundings in Berlin. There was simply no encouraging response about Germany's readiness to discuss such things as economic collaboration and arms limitation. One problem was that most contacts were made through German moderates, since this was the element Roosevelt hoped to strengthen and with whom he hoped to work. But events in Germany suggested that this element was clearly losing favor. Even Hjalmar Schacht, the minister of economics and head of the Reichsbank, abandoned his earlier opposition to autarky in order to preserve his shaky position. By the time Chamberlain became prime minister in Britain, American Ambassador William Dodd in Berlin, always skeptical of a satisfactory agreement with Germany, had reported to Washington that there was "no chance at all" of improving German-American relations. Nor were reports of French soundings in Berlin any more optimistic. A disappointed Roosevelt was left to move the British toward greater cooperation. This would not be easy, for Chamberlain was among those Englishmen who were most skeptical about the value of an American peace initiative and was inclined toward Britain's taking the lead ac-

27. Ibid., pp. 19–22.

cording to her own particular interests, methods, and timing. If Roosevelt were wise, he would let Britain assume the initiative and support British efforts, when called upon, at crucial stages of development.[28]

The course of Roosevelt's policy, and his thinking on it, are difficult to follow. Some American diplomatic historians hold that he made no effort to think out policy systematically and logically but tended to deal with international problems in ad hoc fashion as they arose. He observed himself in September 1937 that American reaction to foreign problems was "on a 24-hour basis." His style of leadership and administrative technique—avoiding friction and conflict with anyone while reserving ultimate decision-making to himself—compounded the problem, as did his desire to keep out of the public record any revelations about the process by which he arrived at personal decisions. Indeed, one can determine what Roosevelt truly believed and supported only by his actions, not by his words. And even here there are inconsistencies and incongruities.[29] His thinking about the British fluctuated. He respected them as the champions of personal and national freedom, but he was also suspicious of them, believing them haughty, capricious, and self-centered; the sentiment prevailing at any particular time depended upon the circumstances of the moment to which he was reacting. In July 1935 he wrote to Ambassador Bingham in London:

> Many years ago I came to the reluctant conclusion that it is a mistake to make advances to the British Government; practical results can be accomplished only when they make advances themselves. They are a funny people and . . . can be counted on when things are going well with them to show a national selfishness towards other nations which makes mutual helpfulness very difficult to accomplish.[30]

Yet by 1937 he had clearly come to believe that some initiative was necessary. It was far from systematic, clearly detailed, and carefully thought out in close consultation with trusted advisers. However, this was simply not Roosevelt's way. The British knew this and were not reassured by it.

Nor were the observations Roosevelt received by way of personal let-

28. Ibid., pp. 23, 26–28.

29. See Warren F. Kimball, *The Most Unsordid Act: Lend-Lease, 1939–1941*, pp. 3–4; Langer and Gleason, *The Challenge to Isolation*, pp. 2–5; Offner, *Origins of the Second World War*, pp. 106–7, 124–32.

30. Roosevelt to Bingham, 11 July 1935, in *Franklin D. Roosevelt and Foreign Affairs*, 2:553–54.

ters from Ambassador Bingham models of consistency. Several months after Roosevelt assumed the presidency, Bingham wrote about a "marked and unmistakable" change for the better in Britain's attitude toward the United States, a change that would lay a foundation "for such cooperation between the British and ourselves as will be helpful to both." This theme was repeated with some regularity thereafter. Nearly a year later he observed that "all thoughtful people here believe that the only hope for peace in the world lies in cooperation between the British and ourselves, and . . . they eagerly desire it." By mid-1935 he was observing that "the British are tending more and more to the view that they must improve their relations with us," but this time he added, "we should leave them entirely alone until they are ready to come to us." In November 1936 he reported "a wide-spread, persistent, increasing feeling" that it was in the British interest to cultivate better relations with the United States. But he saw them as "fumbling" and "jittery," desperate to work out a scheme by which they could tap American credit "when the storm breaks upon them," but which would not cost them anything. And a general review of January 1937 declared that Britain was generating a propaganda drive to convince the United States that the frontier of democracy lay somewhere in the North Sea. The attitude of government officials in daily contacts with the embassy, as well as in public and private hospitality, was marked with "a progressive and almost bewildering friendliness that cannot pass unnoticed." Events would surely force the British at length "to come to us." Presumably, then, America was to wait for British cooperation on her own terms—a curious position in view of Bingham's earlier criticism of London for being "eager to cooperate with us" but only "on their own terms; that is to say . . . we are to seek their cooperation as a favor us."[31] Of course it is difficult to know how much Bingham's letters influenced Roosevelt, if at all.

The course of Chamberlain's policy, and his thinking about it, are considerably easier to follow. Once he had formulated his basic approach to continental diplomacy, he pursued it with unrelenting commitment—quite beyond the point where many would say he should have abandoned it in favor of something different. He was much less constrained, at least for a time, by public opinion, for he was much less at odds with his own people about the role he could play in trying to reduce international

31. Bingham to Roosevelt, 22 May 1933; 8 March 1934; 23 April 1934; 28 June 1936; 13 November 1936; 5 January 1937; ibid., 1:159; 2:17, 80, 543; 3:486.

tension than was Roosevelt. Both the public and private record of his policy endeavors and his thought about them are more revealing.[32] Chamberlain wanted to come to satisfactory terms with Germany. That was his first priority, for if it could be accomplished, Britain's relations with other nations would be much less troublesome and would somehow fall into line. The American role in this was peripheral, supportive at most, but certainly not central. Ironically, the advice he regularly received from the British ambassador in Washington (through the Foreign Office, inasmuch as Lindsay was not in personal touch with Chamberlain the way Bingham was with Roosevelt) was that even though the Americans were difficult people to deal with—apt to lead you up the garden path and then abandon you there—no opportunity should be lost to win their cooperation and establish closer relations with them. Nor should anything be done to discourage them from taking any action they wanted to take, even in their own way. Eden, the foreign secretary, clearly agreed.[33] Again, however, it is not clear how much influence either Lindsay or Eden had on Chamberlain. Events of early 1938 would suggest that it was very little.

Roosevelt's observation about British national selfishness could just as well have been written about the United States by most English leaders. And herein lay a vital difficulty in Anglo-American relations. The need for closer cooperation in the face of developing danger was widely appreciated in both Washington and London, and statements (both public and private) about the peace and security of Europe ultimately depending upon it abounded on both sides of the Atlantic. But selfish interests—along with other factors, such as differing perceptions of objective circumstances and "personality problems" of both an individual and national character—got in the way of achieving meaningful cooperation until the danger to both nations had reached proportions beyond their worst fears in early 1937.

32. There is a full record of cabinet discussions and lengthy weekly letters to his sisters, in which he expressed himself with great candor. The cabinet minutes are in the Public Record Office, London (and also available on microfilm), the personal letters are housed in the Birmingham University Library.

33. See Earl of Avon (Anthony Eden), *The Memoirs of Anthony Eden: Facing the Dictators* (hereafter Eden, *Facing the Dictators*), pp. 595–96.

II. Two "Men of Peace" (1937)

FOREIGN OFFICE DISPATCHES during the first half of 1937 suggest that Roosevelt was making a determined effort to let the British know that he was interested in the general European situation and wished to cooperate with them to help preserve the peace.[1] Ambassador Robert Bingham (on Roosevelt's instructions) told Foreign Secretary Anthony Eden on March 20 that President Roosevelt "had been contemplating some initiative to attempt to better the present international situation." He was not only ready but eager to help and "would be ready to take an initiative" if and when the British thought the moment right. Conversely, the United States would not hesitate to approach Britain anytime it thought the moment opportune. Bingham emphasized that close cooperation between Britain and America "would constitute the best means of averting war."[2] A few days later Sir Robert Lindsay, British ambassador in Washington, in a long dispatch to the Foreign Office discussing the means of retaining American goodwill in the event of a major European crisis—a subject he addressed at the request of Eden—declared that it would be most unwise for Britain to refuse any offer of cooperation that might be extended by the United States. There was, of course, always some danger in dealing with Americans: "They lead you down the garden path until you are committed, and then you suddenly find yourself left all alone." But that could be guarded against by proper caution. He "respectfully but forcefully" submitted that "an American

1. See FO 414/274, January–June 1937.

2. Eden to Lindsay, 20 March 1937, ibid., p. 142. Covering his tracks at a press conference on 2 April, Roosevelt labeled "press inspired" stories circulating to the effect that he was considering "some important move in the international situation." *Complete Presidential Press Conferences of Franklin D. Roosevelt* (hereafter *FDR Press Conferences*), 9:237.

hand is being proferred to us, and it is full of gifts. . . . I earnestly hope that it will be grasped."[3]

Nor did these sentiments emerge without context. One month earlier, Henry Morgenthau, secretary of the treasury, had expressed to Neville Chamberlain, chancellor of the Exchequer—through T. K. Bewley, financial adviser at the British embassy in Washington, and with Roosevelt's approval[4]—his concern that while everyone in America was discussing what the United States should do when war broke out in Europe, no one was discussing whether the United States could do anything to help prevent a war. If Morgenthau could help, he would "die happy" (his phrase); he was inclined to believe that the situation might be saved by some bold initiative by the United States and Britain. He could not think of "anything practical," but perhaps British authorities could suggest something—not necessarily limited to financial matters. Bewley was certain that this message really emanated from Roosevelt, who acted through the Treasury so that he could keep matters in his own hands and, if something could be done, could head off his critics' usual cry of foreign entanglements by tying it up with a popular movement such as a push for currency stabilization.[5]

Chamberlain's reply to Morgenthau, which he had discussed with the prime minister and foreign secretary, expressed warm appreciation for Morgenthau's—and the president's—"earnest desire to find some way in which the United States—possibly in conjunction with the United Kingdom—could help in preventing the outbreak of another war." In view of his later pursuit of appeasement, Chamberlain's further exposition is most interesting: Germany was the main source of Europe's

3. Lindsay to Eden, 22 March 1937, FO 414/274, pp. 172–78; also FO 115/3413. This dispatch was full of shrewd insights concerning America and its attitudes. The United States was compared to "a young lady just launched into society and highly susceptible to a little deference from an older man." Cooperation with Britain would be regarded as a compliment; refusal of cooperation would be a snub.

4. Bewley had carried this message to London. Roosevelt had agreed to bypass regular diplomatic channels and considered sending Bewley on a destroyer, if necessary (Sargent to Lindsay, 16 March 1937, FO 115/4313, File 506).

5. Ibid. Lindsay later confirmed Bewley's explanation of Roosevelt's choice of channels, adding his suspicion that Roosevelt was "bored" by Hull, who was "anything but a practical man." Indeed, the State Department lacked "any real leadership." Lindsay had no practical suggestion for possible U.S. action except that "they should continue to make the greatest possible parade of their sympathies of the democratic ideology, and thereby bring it home to the Germans that an aggression on their part will greatly affect the United States attitude. (Lindsay to Sargent, 30 March 1937, FO 115/3413.) Lindsay and Eden fully agreed on the importance of retaining American good will, i.e., not refusing any offer of cooperation which might be tendered by the United States (Eden, *Facing the Dictators*, pp. 595–98).

fears. It apparently wished to become so strong that no other country would venture to withstand its demands, whether for European or colonial territory. Germany was not likely to agree to any disarmament that would defeat its purpose, and "the only consideration which would influence her to a contrary decision would be the conviction that her efforts to secure superiority of force were doomed to failure by reason of the superior force which would meet her if she attempted aggression." It followed, in the view of the British government, that "the greatest single contribution which the United States could make at the present moment to the preservation of world peace would be the amendment of the existing neutrality legislation." Beyond that, anything America might do to stabilize the position in the Far East would ease Britain's position there and safeguard it against added embarrassment in the event of trouble in Europe. Finally, the conclusion of a commercial agreement with the United States would have "far-reaching effects." Chamberlain hoped this frank exposition would be helpful and trusted that "some form of collaboration may be found possible between our two countries" since he was "profoundly convinced that almost any action common to them both would go far to restore confidence to the world and avert the menace which now threatens it."[6]

Surprisingly, then, in view of this exchange, Chamberlain, after becoming prime minister, failed to follow up on the possibility of a visit by himself or his foreign secretary to Washington to talk with Roosevelt. Norman Davis, Roosevelt's special emissary, who had recently seen both Chamberlain and Eden in London, wrote the prime minister on June 10 that the president "would very much welcome an opportunity to become well acquainted with you and have a frank exchange of views on questions of common interest and concern." He believed that world economic and financial stability, hence peace, depended largely on an enlightened policy of Anglo-American cooperation. Roosevelt realized that any meeting of heads of state for serious discussion was a delicate matter requiring careful planning, and inquired whether Chamberlain thought it preferable for Roosevelt to send someone to London for this purpose or for Chamberlain to come to Washington after Congress adjourned around the middle of September. In the event that the prime minister could not come, Roosevelt wished to know what member of

6. Sargent to Lindsay, 16 March 1937, FO 115/3413, File 506.

the British government Chamberlain would like him to invite in his place.[7]

One week later Bingham reported to Eden, Roosevelt's view that "the international situation was so important that there was clearly the greatest advantage if the P.M. could come [to Washington]." Accordingly, the president had already addressed an invitation to Chamberlain. All this "astonished" Bingham, who had been thinking in terms of an Eden visit to America, and who was "apprehensive" that a visit by Chamberlain would constitute a "very big affair" from which something of material significance would have to result. Both Eden and Bingham believed that Davis might have exaggerated Chamberlain's readiness to visit America; but the invitation from Roosevelt required an answer nonetheless.[8]

Chamberlain sought advice from the Foreign Office and the Board of Trade as to how he should deal with Davis's letter.[9] Oliver Harvey, of the Foreign Office, drafted for Chamberlain's consideration a reply to Davis which emphasized that, in view of his newly assumed responsibilities and attendant anxieties, it would hardly be possible for him to leave England for "some little time to come," and suggested that a visit by Eden would be "extremely helpful and desirable."[10] Oliver Stanley, president of the Board of Trade (which was attempting to discover through diplomatic channels whether there was a basis for formal negotiations with the United States for a reciprocal trade agreement), thought the invitation "should be welcomed, but not for the present actually accepted."[11] In addition, a draft reply prepared by O. S. Cleverly, of the prime minister's staff, emphasized the need for proper timing, better preparation, and fuller information about Germany's posture

7. Davis to Chamberlain, 10 June 1937, PREM 1/261. A month before, Davis and Bingham had discussed with Eden the possibility of his visiting Washington in the autumn. Bingham knew that Roosevelt wanted such an interview very much, and thought it would "contribute greatly to the improvement of Anglo-American relations which were so vital to peace." Both Eden and Lindsay favored such a visit, should a definite invitation be extended. (Eden to Lindsay, 6 May 1937; Lindsay to Eden, 24 May 1937; FO 115/3414, File 1566.) Bingham to Roosevelt, 22 May 1937, President's Secretary's Files (hereafter PSF), Dip. Corres., Box 28. But Roosevelt clearly favored a visit by the prime minister because it would present "an opportunity for a general discussion much less specific than would be the case if Mr. Eden were to come." (Roosevelt to Bingham, 16 July 1937, PSF, Dip. Corres. [Great Britain, 1937–38], Box 25).

8. Eden to Chamberlain, 17 June 1937, PREM 1/261.

9. O. S. Cleverly to J. R. C. Helmore and Oliver Harvey, 21 June 1937, ibid.

10. Draft by Harvey, (n.d.) June 1937, ibid.

11. Helmore to Chamberlain, 22 June 1937, ibid.

(which might usefully be discussed with the president).[12] But Chamberlain's reply to Davis of July 8 was distinctly of his own devising—and indeed is preserved in his own handwriting. He was gratified that the president would welcome an opportunity to meet him, and shared his view "of the immense possibilities of Anglo-American cooperation in restoring stability and peace to the world." But the time for such a meeting was "not yet ripe." Nothing would be more disastrous than a conference that would inevitably attract the utmost publicity but fail to produce "commensurate results." He still hoped that Germany might soon suggest a new date for the visit of the German foreign minister to London—an event that had been scheduled for June but cancelled by Germany on a pretext found in Spain—and that, by providing an indication about the way in which things were moving, would be a useful preliminary to any conversation he might have with the president. So although he stated his earnest desire to take advantage of the president's suggestion "as soon as conditions appear sufficiently favorable to warrant my doing so," for the moment he would simply "keep in close touch" through Ambassadors Bingham and Lindsay.[13]

In a letter to his sister Ida, on July 4, Chamberlain described Roosevelt as "delighted" at Davis's message that the prime minister should like to pay the president a visit that autumn. But unfortunately, Davis had put the initiative on Chamberlain by pressing him to say that nothing would please him more than a visit to Washington, even though he did not see that it was possible. Consequently, he had had to compose "a carefully worded reply saying that a good deal must happen before a meeting would be safe."[14]

Roosevelt's reply to Chamberlain, on July 28, still left matters open. He said that he was pleased to learn that Chamberlain believed a visit to Washington would be desirable "as soon as conditions appear to warrant," and to know of their agreement "as to the importance of Anglo-American cooperation in the promotion of economic stability and peace in the world." He recognized that an early fall visit was not practicable; however, he acknowledged the desirability "of making such progress as is possible on other lines which would have a bearing upon

12. Cleverly to Chamberlain, 1 July 1937, ibid.

13. Chamberlain to Davis, 8 July 1937, ibid. Though he did not say so in this message, Chamberlain believed that the disadvantage of undertaking a visit to America unless the conditions and timing were right applied with equal force to the foreign secretary (unsigned letter from P.M.'s office to Harvey, (n.d.) July 1937, ibid.).

14. Neville to Ida, 4 July 1937, Neville Chamberlain Papers (hereafter NC) 18/1/1010.

the timing of your visit here" and would be glad "to receive any suggestions . . . as to any additional preparatory steps that might be taken . . . to expedite progress towards the goal desired."[15] Chamberlain did not pursue this opening. On a minute from C. G. L. Syers, of his own staff, about a possible follow-up to Roosevelt's reference to "any additional preparatory steps," he wrote: "I don't think it necessary to do anything about suggestions to the President. . . ."[16] Indeed, Chamberlain did not reply directly to Roosevelt for two months. Syers wrote on Chamberlain's behalf to Herschel Johnson, of the U.S. embassy in London (in the absence of Ambassador Bingham), to express thanks for the message.[17] And Chamberlain wrote to his sister Hilda, on August 29, that although contact by correspondence with Roosevelt "may be useful . . . the Americans have a long way to go yet before they become helpful partners in world affairs."[18]

Although Chamberlain first thought that Roosevelt's letter might be regarded as closing the correspondence for the time, on further consideration he was inclined to think that the president might be expecting a reply. In consequence, Cleverly "had a shot at a draft" reply to Roosevelt on September 10. Next day Chamberlain had his own "shot," which was duly passed to Sir Horace Wilson, his chief (though unofficial) foreign policy adviser, for suggestions before transmission to the Foreign Office and Ambassador Lindsay. The letter of September 28 addressed to Roosevelt explained that Chamberlain had deferred a reply until he had returned to London from a holiday in Scotland and gathered up the latest developments there. The situation changed often and rapidly, but Europe was at that moment "less menacing" than it had appeared for some months; "various circumstances have combined to erase the tension and to encourage the friends of peace"—though a cordial resumption of relations with the totalitarian states was, to be sure, a long way off. The Far Eastern situation had justified Britain's worst fears, but he saw little prospect at the present time of being able to improve it by action on the part of the Western powers. "In these circumstances I am afraid that I cannot suggest any way in which the meeting between us

15. Roosevelt to Chamberlain, 28 July 1937, PREM 1/261. The Roosevelt-Chamberlain correspondence may also be found in PSF, Dip. Corres., Box 28.

16. Syers to Prime Minister, 17 August 1937, PREM 1/261.

17. Syers to Johnson, 23 August 1937, ibid.

18. Neville to Hilda, 29 August 1937, NC 18/1/1018. Chamberlain added that he had tried to get the Americans to "come in on China & Japan but they were too frightened of their own people."

could be expedited," which he regretted on personal and official grounds. Thus "we must wait a little longer," all the while watching carefully for "an opportunity of furthering the purpose we both have in view."[19]

Aside from the manner of wording, there were two significant changes in Chamberlain's handwritten draft when compared with the one prepared by Cleverly. The prime minister dropped specific references to recent British contacts with Germany and Italy from which useful results might be hoped, and omitted Cleverly's closing reference to welcoming any assistance that Roosevelt might provide in this connection.[20] From what we now know, it appears that Chamberlain was already intent upon pursuing his unilateral efforts at appeasement in Europe without interference from Roosevelt or anyone else. A letter he wrote to his sister Ida, on August 8, supports that view. With regard to his recent contacts with Italy, he declared:

> I can look back with great satisfaction at the extraordinary relaxation of tension in Europe since I first saw Grandi [the Italian ambassador in London]. Grandi himself says it is 90% due to me and it gives me a sense of the wonderful power that the Premiership gives you. As Ch. of Ex. [chancellor of the Exchequer] I could hardly have moved a pebble; now I have only to raise a finger & the whole face of Europe is changed![21]

It was unfortunate that Roosevelt's invitation to Chamberlain became entangled in issues of diplomatic procedure. Bingham's irritation at "visitors from the United States with stray missions" and his opinion that Davis had "grossly exaggerated the whole matter," perhaps to increase his own authority, were freely expressed at the Foreign Office, which was anything but reassured by it.[22] It is true that the American response to points of political significance raised in Chamberlain's earlier message to Morgenthau was prepared by Cordell Hull, and when Roosevelt's initiative passed into Hull's hands, it mired in the mud of rhetorical generality. Chamberlain's handwritten comment on Hull's rambling

19. Cleverly to Hoyer Millar, 9 September 1937; Chamberlain to Roosevelt, 28 September 1937; PREM 1/261.

20. Cleverly to Chamberlain, 10 September 1937, ibid.

21. Neville to Ida, 8 August 1937, NC 18/1/1015.

22. Troutbeck to Lindsay, 25 June 1937, FO 115/3414, File 1566. Roosevelt at length intervened in the Bingham-Davis issue, wrote to Bingham, and settled the trouble (Lindsay to Eden, 26 July 1937, ibid.). According to Thomas Jones, Chamberlain expressed to Davis a long-standing interest in visiting the United States, but he had never been free to do so (*A Diary with Letters, 1931–1950,* p. 338). Davis apparently concluded that he might now be persuaded.

memorandum of June 1 noted that it was, on first reading, "singularly platitudinous";[23] and the decision reached both at the Exchequer and in the prime minister's office was that this correspondence should now cease.[24] Furthermore, reports from Lindsay about the acute nature of Roosevelt's struggle with Congress over a number of domestic issues, which the ambassador found "unpleasantly reminiscent of the battle Mr. Wilson waged eighteen years ago over the Treaty of Versailles," and which left him feeling "very uneasy," could hardly serve to bolster British confidence in the strength and reliability of the United States.[25] But the American "opening" was there, nonetheless, to be exploited for whatever it might ultimately prove to be worth. That it remained untested was largely the result of British judgment and choice, based upon considerations of general "conditions" and timing.

Chamberlain's late September reply to Roosevelt was followed in little more than a week by a surprising foreign policy pronouncement by the president: his famous October 5 "Quarantine Speech" in Chicago, in which he spoke of the need for positive measures to preserve peace (including the quarantine of aggressors) and hinted at potential American participation in them. The speech was prompted in part, no doubt, by recent aggressive Japanese action against China, but also reflected Roosevelt's growing concern about the more general epidemic of lawlessness abroad in the world and the effects that American isolation would have on other nations. With progress in the implementation of his domestic programs becoming ever more difficult (indeed, politically damaging), the time was right for the president to focus on foreign priorities. He was particularly intrigued by possible courses of action that he might take without incurring the risk of officially declared war. Cutting vital trade with aggressor nations was one idea that had oc-

23. Lindsay to Eden, 1 June 1937, FO 115/3414, File 506; Harvey to Syers, 29 June 1937, PREM 1/261. Marginal Treasury official comments on Hull's memorandum included the following: "a disappointing essay" (R.V.N.H.); "unusually long-winded even for an American. . . . They like exchanging sweet worded nothings" (N.F.W.F.); "typically American" (J.S.) (PREM 1/261, 2–4 July 1937). Hull agrees in his memoirs that the State Department's reply was quite general in tone (*Memoirs of Cordell Hull,* 1:532–33).

24. R.V.N.H. to Fisher, 21 July 1937; Wilson to Fisher and Hopkins, 23 July 1937, PREM 1/261. An innocuous reply from Chamberlain to Hull was sent on 30 July (ibid.; also FO 115/3413, File 506).

25. See, for example, Lindsay to Eden, 19 July 1937, FO 115/3412, File 91. Writing a month later about Roosevelt's efforts to "reform" the Supreme Court, Lindsay feared that a serious constitutional struggle would prevent America from giving to world affairs "the measure of concern that her own interests should properly dictate" (Lindsay to Eden, 16 August 1937, FO 115/3413, File 410).

curred to him—although he later denied that he was necessarily advocating economic sanctions. A number of persons, including Cordell Hull and Norman Davis, had urged Roosevelt to speak out on international cooperation in a large city where isolationism was entrenched; Hull and Davis prepared a draft of the speech for him; Harold Ickes suggested the quarantine analogy in discussing the international situation with Roosevelt before his trip west. The presentation, however, was distinctly Roosevelt's. It was highly suggestive but obviously lacking in specifics.[26]

Both contemporaries and historians have searched in vain for something specific that Roosevelt had in mind when he spoke of "quarantine." The president's mind and method were such that he was most likely exploring possibilities, thinking out loud, attempting to stimulate the thinking of others, and creating a general impression rather than advancing any plan in particular. His answers to questions about the speech posed by reporters at a press conference on October 6 were generally evasive; the president at length said that he was enunciating an attitude, not outlining a program—although "we are looking for a program." There were "a lot of methods in the world that have never been tried yet," and they might be "in a very practical sphere." He wrote to an English friend, Arthur Murray (later Lord Elibank), that he was attempting to fight "a psychology which comes very close to saying 'Peace at any price,'" whereas he believed that the danger of war would be reduced if America used what influence it could to help curb aggressors.[27] Specifically with regard to Britain, Roosevelt declared off the record:

> We will get one or two stories from London which say, "Why doesn't the United States suggest something?" Why should we suggest something? Can't somebody else make a suggestion? We have done an awful lot of suggesting. Every time we enter into some kind of an effort to settle something with our British friends, when we make the suggestion they get 90% and we get 10%. When they make the suggestion it comes out nearer 50–50. Why should we be doing the suggesting?[28]

Chamberlain, for his part, was not much impressed by Roosevelt's

26. Hull, *Memoirs*, 1:544–45; Cole, *Roosevelt and the Isolationists*, pp. 243–46; Dallek, *Franklin Roosevelt and American Foreign Policy*, pp. 147–49; Reynolds, *Creation of the Anglo-American Alliance*, pp. 30–31.

27. *FDR Press Conferences*, 10:247–50; Cole, *Roosevelt and the Isolationists*, p. 246; Viscount Elibank, "Franklin Roosevelt: Friend of Britain," p. 362.

28. *FDR Press Conferences*, 10:249–50.

speech. As he wrote to his sister Hilda, it sounded fierce, but it was contradictory in parts and very vague in essentials. He believed the speech intended to sound out the ground and see how far public opinion was prepared to go, but Roosevelt himself had thought nothing out and had no intention of doing anything that was not perfectly safe. With the two European dictators in a thoroughly nasty temper, Chamberlain emphasized: "Britain simply cannot afford to quarrel with Japan and I very much fear that after a lot of ballyhoo the Americans will somehow fade out & leave us to carry all the blame & the odium." Nor was that all. Chamberlain resented the United States' refusal to make a joint démarche at the very beginning of the Asian dispute when it might have stopped the whole thing. "Now they jump in, without saying a word to us beforehand and without knowing what they mean to do." Britain had been carrying on "some quiet talks" with the Japanese that might have come to something, but of course those were now wrecked, and one effect of Roosevelt's speech might well have been to draw the Germans and Italians much closer to the Japanese. Even so, Chamberlain thought it wise "to give the appearance of believing that R. [Roosevelt] meant much more than in fact he did" because the psychological effect on the "totalitarians" of the idea that they could not count entirely on the United States standing to one side while they ate up the democracies might be useful. But he was moving with extreme caution and had committed himself to "absolutely nothing at all."[29]

In the cabinet meeting of October 6, Chamberlain seemed almost as concerned about the political use to which the opposition parties in Britain might put Roosevelt's declaration as about the meaning and implications of the speech itself. His inclination was simply to refer to it in a speech he was to make at the annual Conservative Conference at Scarborough two days later, saying that Roosevelt's remarks voiced the feelings of people in Britain, and that he welcomed a statement on the sanctity of treaties coming from such a quarter and would await any proposals that might be made. "This would bring out the point that the intentions of the President's speech were not very clear." Eden pressed for some diplomatic action to clarify the American attitude, and Chamberlain agreed that the United States might have to be asked whether,

29. NC 18/1/1023, 9 October 1937. Hilda had written on 7 October that she was "very pleased" with Roosevelt's declaration, and thought Neville must be also. One could not know how far Roosevelt would be supported by public opinion, but it was "refreshing to see an American statesman attempting to form public opinion instead of waiting until he has seen the cat jump" (NC 18/2/1039).

in the event that it favored economic sanctions, it was prepared for the consequences, which might include cooperating in the defense of British possessions in the Far East. Roosevelt "had rather embarrassed the situation," the prime minister said, but he did not underrate the importance of his statement as a warning to the dictators that there was a point beyond which the United States would not permit them to go. So the cabinet approved the inclusion of some reference to Roosevelt's statement in the prime minister's speech at Scarborough, and authorized Eden to "consider appropriate diplomatic action at Washington."[30]

The reserved British response to Roosevelt's speech was not without reason. Following the Marco Polo bridge incident near Peking on July 7, by which Japan had reopened its intermittent campaign of aggression against China,[31] the British had sought American cooperation in approaching the Japanese and Chinese governments, asking them to suspend troop movements and agree that Britain and the United States should advance proposals to resolve the conflict. But Cordell Hull objected to joint action unless backed by force, which neither Britain (he assumed) nor the United States had any thought of employing because it would only exacerbate the situation. The United States had already made clear its preference for parallel, concurrent action. This constituted an interesting reversal of positions since the Manchurian episode of 1931, when the United States had proposed joint representations in Tokyo, but Britain preferred to proceed independently—a British position that had been roundly criticized by various American officials in the intervening years. Eden reported to the cabinet on both July 21 and 28 that he had done his best to keep in close touch with the U.S. government and to promote joint action with it, but to no avail. He therefore proceeded with his own representations to Peking and Tokyo. Chamberlain continued to believe that joint representations were likely to produce more results than simultaneous, parallel ones; but further contacts with Washington produced no change of position.[32]

Late in September, Eden, believing that Britain should take no step without the support of the United States, decided to make another effort at joint Anglo-American intervention in the Far East, and drafted a telegram to Washington declaring British readiness to consider any ac-

30. CAB 23/89, 6 October 1937, pp. 255–58.

31. See Bradford E. Lee, *Britain and the Sino-Japanese War, 1937–1939: A Study in the Dilemmas of British Decline*, pp. 23–26.

32. Eden, *Facing the Dictators*, pp. 602–4; Hull, *Memoirs*, 1:538–39; CAB 23/89, 21 July 1937, 28 July 1937, pp. 40, 73–74.

tion (including, perhaps, an economic boycott) likely to shorten the war if its effectiveness seemed certain. But Chamberlain redrafted the message, to the effect that Britain was not convinced that economic action would be effective, though it would examine the matter further if the United States thought it worth pursuing.[33] Not surprisingly, the State Department did not rise to this bait, suspecting a British tendency to shove the United States to the fore and campaign for action on the notion that the United States was already committed.[34] The matter had rested there until Roosevelt's Chicago speech.

British consternation over the quarantine speech is well reflected in a draft memorandum that Robert Vansittart, permanent under-secretary in the Foreign Office, prepared for the prime minister for possible transmission to Washington. The speech was "a most outspoken condemnation of aggression and all its works, the remedy for which is declared to be 'solidarity' and 'concerted action' on the part of peace-loving nations." Yet the president himself qualified the boldness of his approach by stating that he would adopt every practicable measure to avoid involvement in war. This was "perfectly comprehensible," but Britain was bound to look beyond these qualifications and, through frank consultation, attempt to discover what the United States *might* do. Britain, no less than Roosevelt, advocated solidarity and concerted effort, and "we believe that the possibilities and consequences of the present situation should be explored together in good time." Britain, for its part, would be ready to explore "without any reticences, or maneuvering for position, above all without any desire to embarrass our fellow-explorer." He hoped for information "on this difficult but vital question how, and how far, we are to proceed together."[35]

Chamberlain was concerned about the "apparent inconsistencies" between Roosevelt's words and the attitude of the State Department, which suggested that the president had not thought out the full implications of his speech before he made it or examined all the possible repercussions of the policy he apparently had in mind. In any case, he should be

33. Eden, *Facing the Dictators*, p. 606; *The Moffat Papers: Selections from the Diplomatic Journals of Jay Pierrepont Moffat, 1919–1943*, pp. 152–53; CAB 23/89, 29 September 1937, p. 212.

34. There was recognition on the part of some State Department officials that an understanding with Britain was essential if the Japanese were to be convinced that America could not be absolutely counted out in the Pacific but no decisions followed from this (*Navigating the Rapids, 1918–1971: From the Papers of Adolf A. Berle*, p. 138).

35. PREM 1/314, 8 October 1937, pp. 88–92.

informed at once of certain British conclusions, "lest by further public statements he should commit himself to actions which might prove seriously embarrassing to us." Attention now shifted to a conference under the Nine-Power Treaty, which the United States had intimated it would attend; and it was of utmost importance that the two governments should enter such a conference with the closest understanding. Consequently, he hoped for a frank consultation at the earliest possible moment.[36]

In view of the widely critical—indeed, hostile—public reaction that is usually said to have greeted Roosevelt's speech, it is interesting to note that Ambassador Lindsay in Washington did not see it that way. He sent messages to London reporting its favorable reception by public opinion, then wrote Eden, on October 12, that the speech "might . . . almost appear to have been made in response to the urge of popular feeling [that the nation should abandon isolation in favor of cooperation to preserve the peace of the world]." How much further Roosevelt could lead the country toward cooperation with Europe remained uncertain, but his approach to an objective he had long had at heart was careful and well timed. And American participation in a nine-power conference was, after the speech, "at once inevitable."[37]

In the weeks that followed Roosevelt's Chicago speech, Chamberlain tried, by his own account, to encourage (by his speeches) those sections of American opinion that seemed to welcome Roosevelt's pronouncement. He wished to support any tendency toward a closer understanding and a more complete community of purpose between Britain and America. But he was "very conscious of the difficulties that still had to be overcome by the President before it can be said that he has his people behind him." The Chicago speech signaled Roosevelt's recognition of the need to educate American public opinion, but Chamberlain doubted "whether such education can yet be said to have proceeded very far,"

36. Memorandum by Neville Chamberlain, 9 or 10 October 1937, ibid., pp. 86–87.

37. FO 115/3412, File 91; FO 414/274, pp. 39–42. Several American historians have questioned the traditional interpretation of public reaction to the quarantine speech and Roosevelt's response to it. Among them are Dorothy Borg, who shows that response to the speech was not everywhere hostile, though the administration's judgment may still have been widely governed by sensitivity to the attacks of leading isolationists ("Notes on Roosevelt's 'Quarantine' Speech"); and John M. Haight, who says that the president neither considered public reaction overwhelmingly negative nor retreated immediately from his newly voiced policy ("Roosevelt and the Aftermath of the Quarantine Speech").

and its development would surely take time.[38] He had earlier heard from many sources of a change in American public opinion toward Britain,[39] but he was still generally inclined to count on nothing from the Americans but words.

Roosevelt's quarantine speech coincided with a decision made at Geneva to refer the Far Eastern crisis to the signatories of the Nine-Power Treaty of 1922, which attempted to stabilize the chaotic international and domestic situation of China. Indeed, it was the real genesis of the conference idea. Up to then it appeared that the matter would remain in the hands of the League, but the tone and phrasing of Roosevelt's speech changed things. Britain promptly informed the United States that it considered a nine-power conference essential, and asked whether the Americans would host it in Washington. The United States, for its part, had earlier indicated that it would attend such a conference, if invited. Indeed, Roosevelt was very preoccupied with the threat represented by Japan—though he apparently did not see a way out of the situation any more clearly than State Department officials, who were divided over whether to go easy lest Japan retaliate (mainly against the United States) or to act firmly to preclude later confrontation with a yet stronger Japan. But American officials favored a small European capital as the site for the conference. Norman Davis, "sniffing a conference from afar like a battlehorse," favored London, but Brussels eventually emerged as the American choice. On October 16 the Belgian government sent out invitations "at the request of the British Government and with the approval of the American Government."[40]

Roosevelt's hopes for, and attitudes toward, the conference remain open to debate. Two American historians who have studied the record carefully have come to opposite conclusions. Dorothy Borg believes that the barrage of isolationist criticism that was provoked by Roosevelt's speech prompted the president to instruct the American representative,

38. Letter from Chamberlain to Lord Tweedsmuir, 19 November 1937, PREM 1/229. Cordell Hull saw the quick and violent reaction to the quarantine speech as setting back the government's educational campaign for at least six months (*Memoirs,* 1:546).

39. Neville Chamberlain to Mary Chamberlain, 8 September 1937, NC 1/20/1/77.

40. *Moffat Papers,* pp. 155–57; Hull, *Memoirs,* 1:550; Sumner Welles, *Seven Major Decisions,* p. 25. Some State Department officials feared that even if Japan was "completely downed" by effective sanctions, China would merely fall prey to Russian anarchy (*Moffat Papers,* p. 156). Britain first approached Holland about calling the conference, a move that, in view of the Japanese threat to the Dutch East Indies, seemed to Roosevelt like an act of "an inexperienced schoolboy" (*The Secret Diary of Harold L. Ickes,* 2:228–29).

Norman Davis, to make it clear at every step that the United States would neither take the lead at Brussels nor be made a tail to the British kite.[41] But John Haight contends that Roosevelt was not frightened by the isolationist campaign and saw the Brussels conference as an opportunity to stir Americans (and the rest of mankind) to support law and order. The conference was an important vehicle for implementing the quarantine speech in the Far East by a concerted action with other peace-loving nations.[42] The perspective of Cordell Hull adds another dimension. Almost immediately an effort began among several nations that had accepted Belgium's invitation to push the United States into taking the lead at the conference. Hints came from London and Paris that they would readily go as far as Washington's action in the Far East, but no further, thus throwing responsibility for initiating steps on the United States. Roosevelt suggested to the British that they should neither take the lead nor push the United States to do so, but the smaller countries "should be made to feel their own position and standing." In briefing Davis, Roosevelt stressed the importance of mobilizing moral force in all peace-loving nations, and thought the conference should be prolonged as an agency for educating public opinion and bringing to bear upon Japan all possible moral pressure.[43]

If Roosevelt had something more in mind than peaceful consultation when he delivered his Chicago speech, the State Department was some distance behind him. On the same day the president spoke, Victor Mallet twice telegraphed to the Foreign Office from Washington indicating the State Department's attitude of caution (based, he said, on American neutrality legislation and the determination of the American people not to be drawn into any conflict) and concluding that if the British government saw some plan whereby the United States might cooperate by *pacific methods* (underlined in blue by a Foreign Office official), the United States would no doubt give it careful consideration.[44] But the president's speech did seem to suggest something more, and the apparent contradiction confused the British. Consequently, they "bombarded" [Moffat's term] Washington with questions and memorandums, asking whether the United States was aware of the implications of the presi-

41. "Notes on Roosevelt's 'Quarantine' Speech," p. 433.

42. "Roosevelt and the Aftermath of the Quarantine Speech," p. 252. Haight attaches importance to the selection of Davis as the sole American delegate because Davis believed that the United States should play a positive role in world affairs.

43. Hull, *Memoirs, 1:551–52.*

44. Mallet to Foreign Office, Nos. 324 and 325, 5 October 1937, PREM 1/314, pp. 96–98.

dent's speech and indicating that Britain could be counted on to go as far as America (though in the event of trouble they were so preoccupied with the Spanish and German situations that they could do little east of Singapore).[45]

Chamberlain believed that first the conference must decide upon its objective—stopping the war. Public opinion since Roosevelt's speech appeared to be drifting toward the imposition of economic and financial sanctions upon Japan, but he doubted that China could hold out until sanctions on Japan had taken their toll. China would then be in the same position as Abyssinia in 1936. The use of overwhelming force by Britain and the United States to bring compulsion on Japan was ruled out "in view of the President's words." And any effort to supply China with sufficient weapons and equipment to carry out a successful resistance could be stopped by a Japanese naval blockade unless confronted by superior naval forces. So the British government reluctantly concluded—hoping for the greatest possible "moral effect of a unanimous expression by the conference of its view that to continue the war would be an offence to the conscience of the world"—that the conference should announce its intention to try conciliation before considering any measures of compulsion, and "every effort should be made by the two Governments [Britain and the United States] to damp down & discourage suggestions for an economic boycott in their respective countries."[46]

The issue was thoroughly aired in the cabinet on October 13, with the prime minister reiterating his view that Britain could not contemplate sanctions without a guarantee from the United States that it would face up to all the ensuing consequences—and "even then it was impossible to foresee how long public opinion in America would be prepared to maintain the position." If treated diplomatically, Japan and China might still consent to terms, so he believed that Britain should go to Brussels "in the interests of peace" and not think of compulsion until conciliation had been exhausted. There was general agreement with this view, Eden adding that Britain should not refuse to contemplate sanctions in "the extremely unlikely event of the United States Government being prepared to act on those lines"; Britain should take the risk in such an eventuality and thus avoid the possibility of a later American charge that they could have cleared up the situation but for British unwillingness.[47]

45. *Moffat Papers*, pp. 157–58.

46. Chamberlain Memorandum, undated, but clearly 9 or 10 October 1937, PREM 1/314, pp. 83–85.

47. CAB 23/89. 13 October 1937, pp. 296–302.

One week later Chamberlain told his colleagues that their original apprehensions—lest the United States should urge sanctions without assuming responsibility for the consequences, or, alternatively, lay the blame on Britain for not applying sanctions—had not developed. Consequently, he saw the object of the conference as "appeasement," thus precluding the need to discuss the eventuality of failure or to raise the question of sanctions.[48] As he had reported to his sister Ida earlier, Roosevelt was now saying that the conference should begin with mediation—"which was exactly my idea"—and it was clear that "the Yanks . . . hadn't the remotest intention of touching them [sanctions] with the end of the longest imaginable barge pole" and that "quarantine" only referred to "a possible ultimate ideal!"[49] Yet the cabinet agreed that the Advisory Committee on Trade Relations in Time of War should be instructed to consider what results could be achieved by British and American economic sanctions against Japan.

Thomas Jones, a confidant and adviser of prime ministers who moved unobtrusively in high political circles, aptly summarized the situation: "No-one here seems to know what it is hoped to get out of the Brussels Conference. 'Peace' says the P.M. but how? We shall no doubt start off bravely and tell America that we will go with them all the way they wish to go, but do they want to go beyond Hawaii? Not they."[50] Small wonder that Foreign Secretary Eden approached the conference as "an exercise" from which he expected "no good, except to show the Americans that what they would do, we would do, and to build confidence between us by a repetition of this maxim."[51]

The Brussels conference, which convened on November 3, proved to be an exercise in futility, the course of which would have been humorous had not the stakes involved been so important. The United States, represented by Norman Davis, was gravely concerned lest Britain push America to the forefront and attempt to hide behind its skirts. Conversely, Britain, not knowing how far America might be willing to go, was determined to go only so far as the United States and in general to model her policy on America's. The British seemed convinced that America's interests in the Far East were much greater than their own; the

48. Ibid., 20 October 1937, pp. 345–46.

49. NC 18/1/1024, 16 October 1937. Roosevelt had said in a "fireside" broadcast on 12 October that the purpose of the conference was mediation; and direct British inquiries to the State Department had met with the reply that the question of sanctions did not arise.

50. Jones, *Diary with Letters*, p. 370.

51. Eden, *Facing the Dictators*, pp. 607–8.

Americans were concerned that Britain, being unable to protect her interests in Asia, was trying to maneuver America into pulling her chestnuts from the fire. The Americans made clear from the start their wish to use the conference to educate the American people on the realities of the international situation, in the hope that, should the conference fail because of Japanese obstruction, American public opinion would react and permit the government to do "something more." On the other hand, the British feared that any action which depended upon an upsurge of American opinion would be quite inadequate. The British felt that only if Britain and America stood shoulder to shoulder in joint action could threats of lawlessness in the world be dispelled. But America wanted no part of joint action; independent action on parallel lines was essential from its political point of view. The situation was further complicated by a sharp division of sentiment on both sides. Eden, the chief British delegate (who told Parliament that in order to get the full cooperation on an equal basis of the United States government in an international conference he would travel not only from Geneva to Brussels but from Melbourne to Alaska) was clearly more disposed to positive action and initiative-taking than Chamberlain and the British cabinet would permit; and Norman Davis, widely deemed by his colleagues to be pro-British, was less suspicious and more cooperative toward Britain than either Roosevelt or a number of leading State Department officials. Each side seemed to feel about the other as Hilda Chamberlain wrote her brother about Americans: "Hardly a people to go tiger shooting with."[52]

Eden and Yvon Delbos, the French foreign minister, did what they could to encourage American initiative, the latter urging that only an organized front of the free nations could stop aggression and that only one leader in the world, Roosevelt, could organize such a front. Eden pressed his own government to consider sanctions against Japan should the United States be willing to do so (and got a flat no from Chamberlain), and proclaimed that world peace depended to such an extent upon Anglo-American cooperation that no effort should be spared to consolidate it. At the end of the first week, the two agreed that it was time to consider "how far we would be willing ultimately to go"; they could not remain in Brussels indefinitely. Eden assumed that the United States might have considered stopping all commerce with Japan—an unpopular

52. *Moffat Papers,* pp. 160–66, 170–71; Berle, *Navigating the Rapids,* pp. 141, 146; *The Diplomatic Diaries of Oliver Harvey, 1937–1940 (hereafter Harvey Diaries*), pp. 54–56; Hull, *Memoirs,* 1:553; Eden, *Facing the Dictators,* pp. 609–12; NC 18/2/1043, 4 November 1937.

move in Britain because of the Ethiopian precedent, but one that the government could carry through. He thought that if Britain and America would take a positive stand, the other powers would follow suit, even if reluctantly. But Davis could only reply that public opinion would have to guide any decisions of the American government, and it was still too early to know what it could do; he was not sure, in fact, whether this was better discussed in Brussels or by direct negotiations among the foreign offices. Telegrams from the State Department instructed Davis (in the words of Pierrepont Moffat) "to initiate nothing more than platitudes," and described the country as definitely against any form of pressure on Japan. Consequently, as days passed, Washington seemed less and less inclined to take any action, and Britain remained determined to base its own position on that assumed by America. At length the conference adjourned with nothing more to show for its efforts than a declaration endorsing the principles of the Nine-Power Treaty, reaffirming the interest of all signatory powers in the Far Eastern conflict, and urging the suspension of hostilities.[53] This outcome could scarcely have been in more marked contrast to the Nyon Agreement of September 9, by which nine European powers, led by Britain and France, had initiated a firm and effective system of patrol zones in the Mediterranean to combat a mysterious outbreak of submarine piracy in connection with the Spanish Civil War.

Eden certainly had tried. According to Pierrepont Moffat, he courted the Americans assiduously, and when he saw that they could not "advance up one alley," he was quick to suggest that "we proceed together up another alley." In lieu of something better, the British delegates had sought American participation in a declaration of readiness to offer good offices to the parties in the Far Eastern conflict in order to give the conference a "reasonable excuse" to adjourn its sittings at least until the new initiative had been given a chance to develop. But Davis squarely opposed this as premature, as he did a British suggestion that the conference should give the British and American governments a mandate to offer conciliation if and when they saw fit—though allowing in both instances that such an initiative might be possible later. Not surprisingly then, despite his own hesitant posture (and the insistence of Malcolm MacDonald, dominions secretary, that cordial relations and complete cooperation with the United States delegation had been maintained and

53. *Moffat Papers,* pp. 169–70, 174–83; Eden, *Facing the Dictators,* pp. 612–13; *Harvey Diaries,* p. 58.

the door kept open for some possible future initiative by the two nations), Chamberlain told the cabinet on November 24 that "the main lesson to be drawn [from the conference] was the difficulty of securing effective cooperation from the United States of America."[54]

As the conference ended, Cordell Hull expressed concern about American newspaper articles alleging that if Brussels failed it would be the fault of the Americans. Hull's comments resulted in a promise of British cooperation to combat such statements. But Norman Davis (distressed with the level of support received from Washington and disappointed at the way American opinion had failed to react to Japan's intransigence), felt the American government had only itself to blame for the difficulty it was in—and Roosevelt's unfortunate talk of "quarantine" had constituted the primary basis for misunderstanding. Yet he remained optimistic; perhaps within a month American opinion might develop to a pitch where the American government would be able to take some such action as a declaration of nonrecognition of alterations of the status quo in China and of an intention to withhold any financial assistance to Japanese development schemes in China.[55] But this hardly represented the view of the State Department. As Hull much later explained it, action of a positive nature would have solidified the Japanese people behind the military, and possibly would have led to reprisals and war. America was not prepared for that, "in arms or mind," and would have had to bear the brunt of it in the Pacific. "Our only hope was to keep on good terms with Japan so that, if the right moment came, we should have had the same opportunity for stepping in to end the war as Theodore Roosevelt had had in 1904 [the Russo-Japanese War]."[56]

Perhaps President Roosevelt had initially hoped to move at Brussels. The surprisingly favorable response to his Chicago speech had permitted him to contemplate—at least for a few days—pursuit of a stronger line. Perhaps he initially saw the conference as "an important vehicle for implementing the quarantine speech in the Far East." But things changed quickly. Whatever public enthusiasm was generated at first by the quarantine idea—and certainly there was moral repugnance among all segments of American opinion at the ways of fascist aggressors—it went unsustained in the absence of any clear method for peacefully opposing aggression. Its short-lived appearance was sufficient to stimulate isola-

54. *Moffat Papers*, p. 182; CAB 23/90, 24 November 1937, pp. 173–74, 184–91.
55. CAB 23/90, 24 November 1937, pp. 191–91A; Welles, *Seven Major Decisions*, p. 84.
56. Hull, *Memoirs*, 1:554.

tionists to a greater outcry, which prompted the administration not to arouse American opinion unduly at Brussels and not to permit other nations to push America out in front. A sharp November downturn in the economy, a special congressional session to deal with pressing domestic legislation (which failed to pass anyway), and a suspected business conspiracy that Roosevelt feared was designed to weaken him made it quite unwise for the president to risk a political dogfight over stronger action in Asia. And beneath it all lay the president's perception that an effectively operating democratic system in the United States was essential to combatting fascism abroad, and his realization that he did not have the means to implement genuine quarantine action without the risk of war (as many who supported the quarantine idea seemed to think possible).[57]

More likely, then, Roosevelt decided to use the conference at Brussels as he had used the Pan American Conference at Buenos Aires: the United States would play a public role no greater than that of the smallest state present; but by her presence and attitude of cooperation, she would promote the idea of a common front in which some smaller powers might begin discussions that might ultimately result in unity. Moreover, he would further familiarize the American people with growing fascist dangers and with the idea of cooperation with Britain—something that never had been possible at Geneva inasmuch as the League had many enemies in America.[58] But mobilizing moral sentiment against aggression while eschewing participation in any collective, international action required a magician's touch, and it is not surprising that Roosevelt did not accomplish the trick convincingly. The upshot was ambiguity and hesitation, and the strange anomaly of a president who one year before had received the greatest electoral majority in American history shying away from a course upon which he appeared to believe the safety of the country would ultimately depend.

Eden recognized from the beginning that if neither Britain nor the United States was willing to take the lead at Brussels, it was quite unlikely that the smaller powers would do so in such a serious situation. His readiness—indeed, anxiety—to cooperate fully with America and

57. Haight, "Roosevelt and the Aftermath of the Quarantine Speech," pp. 252–55; Dallek, *Franklin Roosevelt and American Foreign Policy*, pp. 151–53.

58. The latter was the essence of a message Roosevelt sent the British in late October, adding that he hoped Britain would not embarrass the United States at Brussels by rushing ahead, all the while understanding that America did not intend to take the lead (Eden to Lindsay, 28 October 1937, FO 414/274, p. 45).

to "examine any proposition jointly" with her, was clear from the start. Even Sumner Welles later wrote: "The only courageous note that was heard at the conference was sounded by Mr. Eden."[59] But his own initiative was hamstrung by the posture of his government. Chamberlain was adamantly opposed to vigorous action, partly from fear of Japanese retaliation, partly from fear of not having American support in facing the consequences; and his cabinet backed him. In a meeting of November 17, no resolution was reached—or sought—on alternative courses of action posed by Eden; Chamberlain suggested only that the British delegates "take soundings" whether the conference would be willing to nominate Britain and the United States as conciliators, and in the event this proved impossible, Britain might propose to substitute a joint effort by the two countries independently of the conference. As he reported to his sister Hilda a few days later, he had had to subdue the Foreign Office, "which was anxious to finish up the Brussels Conference with more fist-shaking at Japan"; and he had come up with "some alternative suggestions of an ingenious character to meet all the difficulties of saving 19 faces" and was "not without hope that before long we may see negotiations for peace opened."[60]

The evidence available clearly supports Eden's later contention (in his memoirs) that he saw America's strength as "the one unexploited reserve which must make itself felt if the world was to be saved."[61] But there was little he could do immediately after Brussels but to reassure America that Britain "should at all times be ready to examine with the United States Government any action which they might desire should be jointly considered." The situation in the Far East would no doubt grow worse "unless and until it was possible for foreign Powers interested to take effective action" and to "share the risks alike."[62] But neither his own government nor America's was yet prepared for such a course.

The situation did indeed grow worse before more than two weeks had passed. In mid-December an American vessel, the *Panay,* and a British gunboat, the *Ladybird,* operating on the Yangtze River, were struck—apparently quite deliberately—by Japanese bombs. Acting independently and quickly (despite a British request for delay) in order to anticipate an apology from Japan, the United States government sent a note of protest to Tokyo. Eden, feeling keenly that there should be joint

59. Ibid.; Welles, *Seven Major Decisions,* p. 84.
60. CAB 23/90, 17 November 1937, pp. 131–34; NC 18/1/1029, 21 November 1937.
61. Eden, *Facing the Dictators,* p. 356.
62. C. W. Orde to Lindsay, 9 December 1937, FO 115/3415, File G 39.

Anglo-American action in so serious a situation, telegraphed Washington that "if nothing more than apologies were required for the successive and increasing outrages," the Japanese might soon go to lengths requiring truly drastic action, adding that what the British had in mind was that the two governments "might have proceeded for instance with some measures of mobilization to show Japan and the world that we were in earnest." Both he and Chamberlain were dubious (so Eden told the cabinet on December 15) whether America would feel able to adopt any suggestions of this kind, but they nonetheless felt it necessary to inform Washington of what they had in mind. They were considering the possibility of dispatching a battle fleet to Far Eastern waters and earnestly hoped that the United States government would do the same—in which case naval staff conversations should be initiated. Of course, Britain would not act unless America was willing to do so. As the cabinet deliberated, a message arrived from Lindsay in Washington saying that although Roosevelt and Hull had been doing their best to bring American public opinion to realize the situation, "they were not in a position to adopt any measures of the kind now contemplated." Indeed, Hull had remarked that some other event would have to happen before the American government would be prepared to act in the sense Britain had in mind. Chamberlain still thought that some action ought to be taken; it might be asked whether the United States was willing to consider mobilization as a first step. However, he recognized that to act alone was probably beyond the capacity of British forces, and that would make it harder for the United States to cooperate later on. At length it was agreed to ask the British ambassador in Washington how far it would be wise to press the United States government, and a decision was deferred pending his reply.[63]

The British were not without hope. Chamberlain wrote his sister Hilda:

> The unfortunate misfortune on the Yangtze has stirred up the Americans properly. . . . It seems to me just a Heaven sent opportunity and you can bet your bottom dollar I am making the most of it. It is always best & safest to count on *nothing* from the Americans except words, but at this moment they are nearer to "doing something" than I have ever known them. . . .[64]

63. CAB 23/90, 15 December 1937, pp. 297–304.

64. NC 18/1/1032, 17 December 1937. The same day Hilda wrote her brother: ". . . I imagine with all her indignation America will not contemplate joining with us in threats of war and yet if we cannot make them what can we do?" (NC 18/2/1049, 17 December 1937).

The diaries of several of Roosevelt's cabinet members suggest that the president was thinking seriously about taking some action against Japan, perhaps by way of freezing Japanese assets in America or imposing, in cooperation with Britain, a naval blockade.[65] In a conversation with Lindsay, the president plunged right into the issue of a blockade and the question of naval staff conversations with Britain.[66] Shocked and indignant over Japan's behavior, Roosevelt definitely leaned for a time in the direction of "doing something" that would punish the Japanese and restrain them in the future. His assumption continued to be—as in his quarantine thinking—that any action taken would prevent war rather than risk it; but the determination of action that would have the desired effect without risking military consequences was no easy matter. This helped to cool the president's impulse. So did the obvious fact that public opinion was not behind him. The president's indignation was widely shared by the American people, and there were some calls for a strong retaliatory response; but most of them preferred to see preventive measures that would reduce the possibility of a recurrence of the *Panay* episode. Nor did the British remain as bold as they first appeared to be. Chamberlain was alarmed by Roosevelt's nebulous comments (as reported by Lindsay) about economic and military sanctions on the occasion of the next Japanese outrage, and his apparent belief that they could be imposed without running the risk of war. Messages from London to Washington showed little faith in the effects of economic pressure on Japan and implied that the British were saying no to Roosevelt's ideas. Chamberlain's fear that Roosevelt might lead Britain into a joint confrontation with Japan only to abandon her under the impact of isolationist pressures was matched by Roosevelt's sensitivity to the possibility that British diplomacy might unduly entangle the United States in its own affairs. As Hull eventually wrote in his memoirs: "We did not feel . . . that joint action was the solution, or that any show of force on a large scale was possible." When the Japanese apologized and agreed to compensation for damages on December 23, the case was closed.[67]

If Chamberlain and Roosevelt both appear uncertain and ambiguous about their policy positions during 1937, this no doubt accurately reflects the situation. Chamberlain clearly recognized the potential value of the United States in lending weight to the forces of peace, but he did

65. Ickes, *Diary*, 2:274–75; John M. Blum, *From the Morgenthau Diaries*, 1:491–92.

66. Eden, *Facing the Dictators*, p. 618.

67. Hull, *Memoirs*, 1:561–62; MacDonald, *The United States, Britain, and Appeasement*, pp. 55–60; Dallek, *Franklin Roosevelt and American Foreign Policy*, pp. 153–55.

not believe that America could be counted upon to act decisively—or at all—and was so inclined to disregard that possibility that he fully believed that Britain must proceed on her own. Efforts to cajole the United States toward cooperation were probably more bother than they were worth. Roosevelt was clearly aware of the trouble developing in Europe and of the potential contribution that the United States—especially in cooperation with Britain—might make to avert the coming of war. But he was suspicious that the British would "use" America for their own purposes, and was no doubt discouraged by a wide range of isolationist influences. Roosevelt seemed genuinely interested in meeting with Chamberlain to talk things over, but the British were reluctant. On the other hand, the opportunity to demonstrate his seriousness of purpose—suggested by the quarantine speech and made readily available in the Brussels conference—was quickly discarded, despite Britain's unmistakable signal that it would go as far as the United States in any positive action that might be taken.

III. The Roosevelt Initiative of January 1938

EARLY IN DECEMBER 1937, the British cabinet had before it a memorandum comparing Britain's strength with that of certain other nations as of January 1938. This embodied the secret report by the Chiefs of Staff Sub-Committee that emphasized the importance of "any political or international action that can be taken to reduce the numbers of our potential enemies and to gain the support of potential allies." Chamberlain believed that detaching one of the three adversarial powers (Germany, Italy, and Japan) from the other two "could only be done at the cost of concessions which would involve humiliations and disadvantages" to Britain "by destroying the confidence of other nations"; and "no-one would suppose, therefore, that we should try and bribe one of the three nations to leave the other two." On the more positive side—gaining the support of potential allies—the prime minister acknowledged that the United States had the greatest strength; but, he quickly added, "he would be a rash man who based his calculations on help from that quarter."[1] Before many weeks had passed, Chamberlain changed his tone dramatically on the first matter, and potentially important initiatives by the United States were pushed aside.

Chamberlain's pessimism about America's attitude certainly had foundation in the difficulties experienced during British efforts to coordinate Anglo-American attitudes, policies, and actions toward the situation in the Far East. Hopes for a joint show of strength, either by economic or naval power, that might bring Japan to a settlement had

1. CAB 23/90, 8 December 1937, pp. 265–67.

thus far gotten nowhere. In an atmosphere of mutual wariness, occasionally aggravated by difficulties in communication, good intentions were sometimes misrepresented on both sides. Eden believed that Britain's fast-collapsing position in China might soon make vigorous action necessary and hoped to obtain American cooperation in sending naval reinforcements to the Far East. Chamberlain, agreeing that Japan could not be coerced without American support (a view that the Admiralty fully shared), doubted that such an approach to the Americans would be successful; the reply would be that American interests were not sufficient to justify the dispatch of ships and that American public opinion was not much concerned. But Eden persisted, and in late November was authorized to offer the United States naval staff talks as the necessary complement to a joint display of naval force. Ambassador Lindsay's lack of information about Britain's proposed contribution to the joint effort at first left State Department officials suspicious, and they turned the whole thing down. The question was reopened, however, by the *Panay* incident, and the British returned to the call for joint action. Eden informed Washington that Britain would send eight or nine capital ships, with accompanying vessels, if the United States would make at least an equivalent effort.[2]

Roosevelt responded by seeing Lindsay secretly (with Hull present) on December 17 after a White House diplomatic reception. Not impressed with the prospects of mobilization or a demonstration, the president talked about a possible blockade of Japan, to take place after "the next grave outrage," and made two specific proposals: to take part in naval staff conversations, and to consider sending some ships to Singapore and advancing the date of American naval maneuvers from April to January. The first of these, providing more intimate knowledge of England's naval situation, was essential to effective American planning of naval expansion—probably the basic reason (rather than any desire for quick action against Japan) behind the president's thinking.[3] When Roosevelt's proposals were discussed in the cabinet, Eden still preferred "some immediate action as a deterrent to another 'incident.'" And Chamberlain was concerned about Roosevelt's "failure to appreciate the needs of the situation": apparently he was loathe to take action until *after* yet another incident, and was still contemplating the possibility of

2. Lawrence Pratt, "The Anglo-American Naval Conversations on the Far East of January 1938," pp. 746–51.

3. Ibid., pp. 751–53.

sanctions without being ready to back them up by force. Consequently—though the time was right for a move to be made, inasmuch as British prestige was suffering from an "unavoidably passive attitude"—it was seen as a mistake for Britain to send ships to the Far East (save in the event of serious Japanese aggression), and that British efforts should be directed toward "bringing home to President Roosevelt the realities of the situation." Perhaps the impending visit of an American naval officer to London, which had been quickly agreed upon though its purpose was unclear, would facilitate this.[4]

The skeptical reaction of Chamberlain and the cabinet to Roosevelt's suggestions did not provide an auspicious backdrop for conversations with Captain R. E. Ingersoll, director of the War Plans Division of the United States Navy, who visited London for secret staff talks during the first two weeks of 1938. But Eden's hopes were high. He regarded this development of Anglo-American relations, for which he had been working for years, as the first element of encouragement in what was obviously going to be a very difficult year internationally; he felt that he and Chamberlain must do "everything we can privately to encourage the Americans."[5] Perhaps Eden was too eager. In his New Year's Day discussion with Ingersoll, he left the impression that he was more interested in immediate gestures to impress Japan than in long-range planning. And concluding for himself that Ingersoll did not have authority to discuss joint action in the near future, he left London for a holiday in France, all the while continuing his advocacy of Anglo-American cooperation in correspondence with the Foreign Office and the prime minister.[6]

Ingersoll's talks at the Admiralty and elsewhere were friendly and wide-ranging, but they did not resolve the issue of immediate action. After a week of discussion, Ingersoll still believed that the matter could be addressed only after further technical consultation. But the British decided to force the issue. Informing Washington that their own naval preparations were just short of mobilization, London asked whether Roosevelt would declare a state of emergency in present circumstances. Adding that recent incidents at Shanghai might force Britain to announce

4. CAB 23/90, 22 December 1937, pp. 327–29.

5. *Harvey Diaries,* p. 65; Eden to Chamberlain, 31 December 1937, PREM 1/314.

6. Pratt, "The Anglo-American Naval Conversations of January 1938," pp. 754–55. Eden apparently went to France rather than Madeira as originally planned because he recognized that the prime minister was heavy-handed, had no touch for dealing with delicate situations, and might easily upset the Americans for good (*Harvey Diaries,* p. 65).

its preparations, London inquired whether Roosevelt would act in parallel fashion, perhaps dispatching an advance force to Hawaii.[7] Chamberlain's impatience was apparent in a January 9 letter to his sister Hilda:

> I am trying to jolly them [Americans] along with a view to making some sort of joint (or at least "parallel") naval action. They are incredibly slow and have missed innumerable busses. . . . I do wish the Japs would beat up an American or two! But of course the little d——v——ls are too cunning for that, & we may eventually have to act alone & hope the Yanks will follow before it's too late.[8]

Roosevelt's reply of January 10 put the British squarely in a position where they had to decide upon their own willingness to act. The president was prepared to announce that three American cruisers would visit Singapore; to make known, within a few days, that the United States Pacific Fleet was being prepared for action—*if* Britain first announced its own preparations; and, thereafter, would indicate that American maneuvers in the Pacific were being advanced to February. But their anxiety about the situation in Europe now held the British back. Mobilization of the fleet, followed by its dispatch to the Far East, might set in motion a chain reaction with possible repercussions in the Mediterranean. Indeed, an effort to reach a settlement with Italy was now being planned (a move for which the Chiefs of Staff had been pressing for some time), and the absence of the fleet would remove Britain's strongest bargaining card. Consequently, Chamberlain, Admiral Lord Chatfield, and the Foreign Office agreed that it would be unwise to take further action in these circumstances.[9]

The American response to British pressure about action against Japan stopped short of the commitment the British seemed to hope for. But Roosevelt, moving warily while slowly educating American opinion, had not rejected the advance entirely. Indeed, it was Britain that proved unwilling to respond to Roosevelt's schedule of escalatory steps. The British did not appear to grasp Roosevelt's gestating conception of an undeclared war, which issued both from his intellectual interest in Axis military strategies and strong congressional restraints on his war-making

7. *The Diaries of Sir Alexander Cadogan, 1938–1945* (hereafter *Cadogan Diaries*), p. 33; Pratt, "The Anglo-American Naval Conversations of January 1938," pp. 756–57; Orde to Lindsay, 7 January 1938, FO 115/3415, File G-39.

8. NC 18/1/1034.

9. Pratt, "The Anglo-American Naval Conversations of January 1938," p. 757.

authority. They detected instead a naïve belief in blockade without a readiness to back it with force. Perhaps that is what they wanted to see. In a dangerously weak position themselves in Europe and the Mediterranean, they were simply not prepared to undertake serious intervention elsewhere. To send a fleet to the Far East would leave Britain so weak in Europe, Chatfield lamented, that she would be liable to blackmail or worse. So the Chiefs of Staff had concluded that the time for dealing with Japan must await the achievement of stability in Europe through diplomatic approaches to Italy and Germany. This suited Neville Chamberlain just fine.[10]

Before he could proceed with these efforts, however, Chamberlain had to deal with a Roosevelt initiative that brought Anglo-American cooperation on a broader plane to a critical juncture: the president's January 1938 scheme for promoting international cooperation and peace. This episode, often related from a number of perspectives, bears thorough reexamination here because of its crucial place in developing Anglo-American relations.

Alexander Cadogan, permanent under secretary in the Foreign Office, recorded in his diary on January 12: "About 5:15 telegrams began to roll in from Washington—personal messages from Roosevelt to P.M. R. has wild ideas about formulating a world settlement!"[11] The president had set in motion, belatedly and now rather urgently, an idea with which he had toyed, with strong encouragement from Under Secretary of State Sumner Welles, for some months. First envisioned for Armistice Day, 1937, the idea had been held up by the hesitancy of Cordell Hull. But early in the new year, Hull's opposition had weakened, and Welles convinced Roosevelt, who was quite distressed by the progressive deterioration of the world situation and especially the way in which minor states were falling away from democratic ideals and loyalties, that it should be delayed no longer.[12] The president advanced, with utmost secrecy—hoping to derive considerable benefit both at home and abroad from the element of surprise—a two-step plan whereby he would first

10. See ibid., pp. 757–58. An official in the British embassy in Tokyo later wrote about early 1938: "As events proceeded, it became more and more clear that . . . the question of whether or not there would be effective resistance to Japanese expansion would depend entirely on the United States" (Paul Gore-Booth, *With Great Truth and Respect*, p. 82).

11. *Cadogan Diaries*, p. 36. He also noted with regard to the need to handle this quickly: "This is not the way to transact such business!"

12. Welles, *Seven Major Decisions*, pp. 40–41. Welles's version is generally corroborated by many other sources. See Dallek, *Franklin Roosevelt and American Foreign Policy*, pp. 149, 155ff.

consult in Washington with representatives from a number of small governments (Sweden, the Netherlands, Belgium, Switzerland, Hungary, Yugoslavia, Turkey, and three Latin American nations to be selected by the Latin American governments themselves) about: (a) essential and fundamental principles to be observed in international relations; (b) the most effective methods of achieving the limitation and reduction of armaments; (c) methods for promoting equal access to raw materials and other elements necessary to economic life; and (d) the rights and obligations of neutrals, and the laws and customs of warfare whose observance neutrals might be entitled to require. Thereafter, as a second step, the results of their deliberations would be circulated as soon as practicable to all other nations for such action as they might be disposed to take. Reiterating the United States' "traditional policy of freedom from political involvement" and her unwillingness to participate in the determination of political adjustments, Roosevelt nonetheless declared that every kind of adjustment might be more readily arrived at if all nations first agreed upon the principles essential to healthy international relationships. What he sought was a quick and favorable response from Chamberlain before proceeding with the plan according to a quickly evolving timetable.[13]

Two points that were later misconstrued must be clarified. Roosevelt did not propose to call a world conference. The first stage of his plan was to summon a sort of drafting committee of small nations. Thereafter, special proposals devised by the group would be submitted to a large number of other nations for their reactions. This was clearly stated in Roosevelt's message, and the distinction was clearly drawn by Cadogan when he transmitted Roosevelt's message to Chamberlain.[14] Further, it was not Roosevelt's intention to interfere with Chamberlain's efforts to approach the dictators. On the contrary, in pressing the scheme on Roosevelt, Welles thought it "would lend support and impetus" to the British effort; and in conveying Roosevelt's message to the Foreign Office, Lindsay clearly emphasized the president's hope to "give an impulse" to British negotiations with Germany and Italy, and to lend support by taking "valuable parallel action" toward the preservation of peace in the

13. Draft of Roosevelt's message to Chamberlain, left at the British embassy by Welles, 11 January 1938, FO 115/3416, unnumbered file; Lindsay to Foreign Office, 12 January 1938, FO 371/21526, pp. 122–24. Roosevelt planned to inform France, Germany, and Italy (as well as Britain, officially) of the general lines of his scheme on 20 January and to announce the plan to the diplomatic corps at Washington, called to the White House for that purpose, on 22 January.

14. Cadogan to Chamberlain, 12 January 1938, FO 371/21526, pp. 113–14.

only way open to him. But Roosevelt did not want to see the dictators bought off for a time by economic concessions alone, thus creating a situation that would degenerate into a vicious circle. Rather, he wished to assure the achievement of a complete settlement embodying the prospect of permanent security, and his initiative was designed to support that end. Nor had he forgotten the Japanese. If Germany and Italy entered upon serious negotiations, he believed Japan would have to make peace within the terms of the Nine-Power Treaty.[15]

Ambassador Lindsay, to whom Welles had carried Roosevelt's message at the British embassy in order to ensure secrecy, gave the proposal strong endorsement. He shared Roosevelt's view that a combination of disarmament and economic relaxation—the two elements that the president had identified as the core of his scheme—would gain the support of American opinion, which he believed vital to any hope of averting disaster. Lindsay felt that destructive criticism, reservations, or attempts to redefine issues would accomplish little and create a disproportionately bad impression so he urged a quick and cordial acceptance of "this invaluable initiative."[16]

Cadogan's initial reaction (relayed to Chamberlain at Chequers) was mixed. The success of the plan was problematical and the risks considerable; yet Roosevelt should not be discouraged. He certainly had courage—grounded, Cadogan hoped, on something more than ignorance—and "his readiness to enter the arena" was obviously a fact of "first importance." From another perspective, the under secretary noted, concessions made in the interest of peace might be more readily accepted by British opinion if they could be attributed to American prompting.[17] But here the positive reaction ended.

Upon consulting Sir Horace Wilson, on the prime minister's instructions, Cadogan agreed that however desirable it was not to appear to discourage Roosevelt in any way, "it really seemed that he was taking and holding over our heads rather a hasty decision without full light on the situation here." Certainly that was Chamberlain's view when he

15. Welles to Roosevelt, 10 January 1938, *Foreign Relations of the United States: Diplomatic Papers* (hereafter *FRUS*), 1938, 1:116; Lindsay to Foreign Office, 12 January 1938, FO 371/21526, pp. 116–17, 122–24, 127. Welles had argued that in any case the plan would be "productive of practical good" because of its repercussions on the German and Italian people, as well as upon the smaller nations of Europe.

16. Lindsay to Foreign Office, 12 January 1938, FO 371/21526, pp. 125–26. According to Welles, Lindsay told him "with profound emotion" that this was the first hope he had had in more than a year that a new world war could be prevented (Welles, *Seven Major Decisions,* p. 41).

17. Cadogan to Chamberlain, 12 January 1938, FO 371/21526, pp. 113–14.

returned to London on the evening of January 13. Cadogan had meantime drafted a reply that concluded by assuring Roosevelt that if he was "nevertheless determined to proceed with his proposal and to adhere to his timetable," the British would "accord the warmest welcome to his initiative and give it . . . whole-hearted support." But Chamberlain would have none of it. He wished simply to appeal for delay and further consideration in light of his own position. Cadogan recorded in his diary that Wilson was "very anti-Roosevelt" and that Chamberlain "hates R's idea."[18]

Chamberlain's reply of late evening, January 13, explained his hopes for imminent discussions with Italy and Germany and asked the president to consider whether his proposal risked "cutting across" British efforts. He appreciated that Roosevelt's initiative was intended as an action by the United States government parallel to the efforts Britain was making with the Axis powers; but he was concerned lest the Italian and German governments—of whom Britain would have to ask some contribution toward peace—might refuse to continue negotiations on the ground that the subjects under discussion were all merged in the wider problems that Roosevelt intended to address. It would be counterproductive if Roosevelt's action could in fact be used to block progress in directions that Britain had laboriously worked out and for which he now felt the stage "not too unfavorable." Consequently, he asked Roosevelt "to consider holding his hand" while the British tackled "some of the problems piecemeal." He felt that this request would not prejudice the larger effort that the president might be willing to make later.[19]

Chamberlain replied to Roosevelt without consulting anyone else, later citing among his reasons the need for haste (Roosevelt required an answer by January 17) and the need for secrecy (he could not risk telephoning Eden in France). (Indeed, it was Roosevelt's initial desire that the matter be considered only by the prime minister.)[20] He was also influenced no doubt by the strength of his own feeling: the plan was "fantastic & likely to excite the derision of Germany & Italy."[21] As he explained in a separate telegram to Lindsay, he hoped that the president would not find his message disappointing. But it seemed to him that Roosevelt's idea, conceived without full knowledge of all that was going on, "risks upsetting" what the British were attempting to accomplish.

18. Cadogan to Eden, 13 January 1938, ibid., pp. 110A–12; *Cadogan Diaries,* p. 36.
19. Foreign Office to Lindsay, 13 January 1938, FO 371/21526, pp. 128–31.
20. Lindsay to Foreign Office, 12 January 1938, ibid., p. 124.
21. Entry in Chamberlain's diary, 19 February 1938, NC 2/24A.

And there were phrases in Roosevelt's draft (such as those relating to traditional United States freedom from political involvement and the removal of inequities stemming from the settlement of 1919), that caused him "grave misgivings." Chamberlain had long had in mind that Roosevelt might, at some advanced stage, help to clinch an agreement on certain of Europe's problems, but there was a lot of preliminary work that could best be done in London.[22]

Cadogan's report to Eden on "the amazing telegraphic correspondence with Washington," January 13, is interesting from several perspectives. It conveyed the impression that Chamberlain, in appealing to the president "for a little delay and further consideration," had left the decision open; that would depend upon the reply from Washington. Indeed, Eden had not been consulted, Cadogan explained at the prime minister's request, because the reply to Washington "had to be sent off at once in order to give time for the President to give us his reply before Monday." This constituted a beneficent interpretation of Chamberlain's initial reaction. Further, Cadogan now invited Eden to offer his views by telephone, especially his ideas "as to what the decision should be in the event of the Presidential reply being unfavorable."[23] Previously, telephone conversation had been ruled out by the need for secrecy.

Eden had views on the matter, strong ones in fact, and he hurried home to offer them. Met at Folkestone (late morning, January 15) by Cadogan and Oliver Harvey, his private secretary, Eden read the Washington telegrams and at once declared that the president had been snubbed too much. He wanted to see Roosevelt proceed with his plan.[24]

The obvious difference between the prime minister and his foreign secretary was the central issue in their conversation at Chequers on Sunday, January 16. That agreement would be difficult was presaged in their divergent reactions to Lindsay's early reports concerning the reception of Chamberlain's message in Washington. Informed that Welles had said the message would be welcome to the president, that it conveyed "just the kind of information that was desired here," that Roosevelt would not want to interfere if prospects for arresting the deterioration of the international situation were favorable, and that he would probably decide to postpone his initiative, Chamberlain minuted: "This is better than I had hoped for."[25] But Eden was clearly disturbed when Lindsay

22. Chamberlain to Lindsay, 13 January 1938, FO 371/21526, p. 132.

23. Cadogan to Eden, 13 January 1938, ibid., pp. 110A–12.

24. *Cadogan Diaries,* p. 37.

25. Lindsay to Foreign Office, 14 January 1938, FO 371/21526, pp. 109–10; Minute by Chamberlain, 15 January 1938, PREM 1/259, p. 64.

reported, shortly thereafter, a telephone call from Welles, who had just seen the president, that Roosevelt would send a written reply on Monday (January 17), that he would postpone his scheme for a while, and that he was a little disappointed. Indeed, Eden had thereupon sent a message to Lindsay attempting to neutralize what he feared had appeared to Roosevelt as a negative attitude on Britain's part and to hold things open until after his conversation with Chamberlain. This independent action was resented by Chamberlain, who refused to endorse what Eden had said.[26]

The conversation at Chequers resolved nothing. Eden later wrote: "For the first time our relations were seriously at odds." The issue was simple. Eden believed that everything must give way to the primary importance of good relations with Roosevelt and America; Britain would have a much better chance with the dictators if Roosevelt was also dealing with them, and even if the initiative failed, Britain would have gained immeasurably from this American intervention in Europe. Chamberlain, on the other hand, saw the Roosevelt initiative entirely in terms of obstructing his impending talks with the dictators, in which he placed great hope—not shared by Eden. He thought Roosevelt's proposal vague and bound to fail; it was likely to excite the derision of the dictators, who would see in it another attempt of the democratic bloc to put them in the wrong, and thus constitute an excuse for postponing conversations with Britain. The deadlock complete, Eden urged cabinet discussion on so important an issue, and Chamberlain unenthusiastically agreed.[27]

Next morning Eden wrote to Chamberlain agreeing that there were unhappy phrases in Roosevelt's message as well as "a certain danger of confusion" in both the president's method and the United States government's lack of intimate knowledge of European affairs. "But all these things seem to be of minor importance against the significant fact that President Roosevelt, with all the authority of his position which is unique in the world, wishes to help to avert a general war." American collaboration with Britain, public or not, would be of greatest service in steadying the situation generally. Nor did Eden feel that Roosevelt's initiative need necessarily injure British efforts to improve relations with Germany or Italy; rather, "with the world as it is now, it is almost impossible to overestimate the effect which an indication of United States interest in

26. Lindsay to Foreign Office, 15 January 1938, FO 371/21526, p. 106; Eden to Lindsay, 16 January 1938, ibid., p. 104; Eden, *Facing the Dictators,* pp. 627–28.

27. For Eden's account of the Chequers conversation, see *Facing the Dictators,* pp. 628–30; for Chamberlain's, see his diary entry for 19 February 1938, NC 2/24A.

European affairs may be calculated to produce." He understood Chamberlain's fear that the dictators would resent Roosevelt's tone and blast the democracies verbally, but he thought them more likely to conceal their dislike and become more negotiable as a result of their knowledge of Roosevelt's attitude. Roosevelt, Eden reasoned, had to employ methods that were not easy for Britain to endorse in order to obtain public support for what he was doing. This did not betoken disagreement with Britain about the world situation. In sum, Eden was convinced that any British action that deterred Roosevelt from launching his appeal would be "the greatest mistake," and fullest use should be made of any opening in Roosevelt's reply to convince the president of British willingness to give complete support to his proposed initiative.[28] Chamberlain's response to all this was to write at the top of Eden's letter: "Sir H. Wilson to see. There is nothing to be done now but to await the further communication from the President."[29]

In his answer, delivered as promised to Lindsay through Welles, Roosevelt agreed to defer making his proposal for a short while in order that Chamberlain might see what progress he could make in the direct negotiations that he was undertaking. He then confessed a deep concern about Britain's intention to recognize de jure the Italian conquest of Abyssinia, which Chamberlain had cited as a contribution Britain was willing to make toward appeasement. Devoting half his message to this point, Roosevelt noted the profound importance of preserving the sanctity of treaties and international law as well as the serious effect that failure to do so would have on American public opinion, and saw the issue of recognition as a matter affecting all nations that should therefore be dealt with as an integral part of measures for world appeasement. He closed with a request that Chamberlain keep him informed of developments in the negotiations with Germany and Italy.[30]

American concern over the issue of de jure recognition—particularly what it implied for Japan's position in Manchukuo, which had been seized from China a few years before—had been voiced by Welles upon receipt of Chamberlain's message. It had been repeated, in stronger language, to Lindsay by Hull, who emphasized that the effort to interest the American public in broad issues of world affairs was based largely on improving international morality and checking systematic disregard

28. Eden to Chamberlain, 17 January 1938, FO 371/21526, pp. 100–103.

29. Note by Chamberlain, 17 January 1938, PREM 1/259, p. 55.

30. Lindsay to Foreign Office, 18 January 1938, FO 371/21526, pp. 96–98; Welles to Roosevelt, 17 January 1938, *FRUS*, 1938, 1:120–22.

of obligations, and asked specifically that his views be placed before the British government.[31] The recognition issue had immediately caught the attention of Eden, whose reservations about dealing with Italy were strong and long-standing, and he had discussed it pointedly, but unsuccessfully, with Chamberlain at Chequers. Lindsay raised it again in transmitting Roosevelt's message. He was impressed at receiving "this third warning," reporting that Welles's commentary, delivered on Roosevelt's instructions, was even more emphatic than the actual message. Worried about reversing a favorably crystallizing public opinion, the president felt that recognition, given in wrong conditions, would rouse a feeling of disgust, revive old prejudices, and be seen as a corrupt bargain completed in Europe at the expense of interests in the Far East in which the United States was intimately concerned. Should Italy demand recognition as a condition of negotiations, that, Welles said, would constitute "pure blackmail"; and if Britain yielded, unconscionable demands from Germany would soon follow. So in its dealings with the dictators, Lindsay concluded, Britain must have "a particularly tender regard for cases where American interests are in any way concerned."[32]

There were other noteworthy points in the ambassador's message of January 18 (which may have been more descriptive of Roosevelt's reaction than the president's message itself). Roosevelt had left the door open, Lindsay believed; Welles remarked that questions or suggestions would "receive every consideration." And the timetable, laid down for administrative purposes, could be transferred to any later date within reason. Further, Lindsay was "anxious" about Roosevelt's feelings, inferring from the evidence available to him that the "President's disappointment had been distinctly felt."[33] The latter point became an issue in the British deliberations that followed, continued as a subject of debate among principals in the case long afterward, and remains a matter unresolved by historians. More will be said about it later.

Roosevelt's message in hand, Eden set down his views for Chamberlain and sharply delineated the issues at stake. He thought it clear that Roosevelt had been disappointed by Chamberlain's reply and felt strongly against de jure recognition, so to continue to ask him to hold his hand while Britain negotiated with Italy and Germany would be "a grave error." At best, Britain might improve relations with Mussolini—

31. *FRUS*, 1938, 1:133–34; Lindsay to Foreign Office, 17 January 1938, FO 371/21526, p. 99.
32. Lindsay to Foreign Office, 18 January 1938, FO 371/21526, pp. 93–95.
33. Ibid.

though the obstacles to this were great—at the cost of jeopardizing them with Roosevelt. A "still graver danger" was that Roosevelt, disappointed by Britain's failure to support his initiative and critical of its negotiations with Italy, "would withdraw more and more into isolation." The patient efforts of the last six months to build up Anglo-American cooperation would be destroyed—"the greatest possible disaster to the peace of the world." Eden then defined the central issue, demonstrating clearly the extent of his differences with Chamberlain and unmistakably presaging his resignation one month later:

> The decision we have to take seems to me to depend upon the significance which we attach to Anglo-American cooperation. What we have to choose between is Anglo-American cooperation in an attempt to ensure world peace and a piece-meal settlement approached by way of a problematical agreement with Mussolini. If as is clear to me we must choose the former alternative, then it seems that we should reconsider our attitude and strongly support President Roosevelt's initiative.[34]

He did not believe this needed to injure the prospects of negotiations with Germany, which he regarded as more important than those with Italy. In fact, the closer the sympathy and cooperation between the United States and Britain, the stronger would be Britain's position in dealing with Germany. And if Britain supported Roosevelt's initiative, it would be justified in asking modifications in his text.

The foreign secretary delivered his paper personally to 10 Downing Street late that afternoon. According to Eden's account, Chamberlain thought Roosevelt's reply not too bad and wished to persist in asking the president to withhold his initiative while Britain went on with her negotiations, excluding de jure recognition, about which he was still prepared to argue. The prime minister had been greatly influenced by a letter from his sister-in-law, Lady Ivy Chamberlain, in Rome, in reply to one of his own, in which she described a meeting with Count Ciano, the Italian foreign minister, who told her that this was a "psychological" moment and that Mussolini was ready for a settlement with Britain. Skeptical of United States cooperation, Chamberlain thought that Britain must come to a settlement with Italy at all costs. Germany could wait. The deep difference between them now clear to both, Chamberlain and Eden agreed to ventilate the issue further in the Foreign Policy Committee of the cabinet the next afternoon, and Eden recorded in his diary

34. Eden to Chamberlain, 18 January 1938, ibid., pp. 86A–88. The letter communicated to Chamberlain was a revised (toned down) version of an initial draft, preserved in the file cited above.

that night: "I fear that fundamentally the difficulty is that Neville believes that he is a man with a mission to come to terms with the dictators. Indeed, one of his chief objections to Roosevelt's initiative was that with its strong reference to International Law it would greatly irritate the dictator powers." He also began to consider resignation if the cabinet committee would not support Roosevelt's scheme.[35]

The Foreign Policy Committee met "as a matter of urgency" on January 19—and again on January 20 and twice on January 21—to consider the situation that had arisen out of the events of the preceding week. No official records of these meetings have been found,[36] but what transpired is generally clear from other sources. At the first meeting, Chamberlain and Eden explained their respective views and Chamberlain read a draft of a further message to Washington, explaining again his hopes of de jure recognition and asking Roosevelt to use his influence in Rome to advance an Anglo-Italian agreement. The prime minister observed that Roosevelt's announcement would be greeted with laughter in Nazi Germany, where it was not believed that people lived in an anxious world, full of fear, a world in which physical and economic security for the individual were lacking. He criticized the four points on which the president wanted the governments of the world to agree, doubting that the same principles to be followed in international relations would appeal to both Germans and democratic nations. Halifax (lord president), Simon (chancellor of the Exchequer), and Inskip (minister for coordination of defense) were all strongly against Roosevelt's plan, believing that the United States would do nothing practical to help, whereas Britain now had a real chance to reach agreement with the dictators. Eden tried a compromise on the issue of recognition, suggesting that any discussion of it be tied directly to Roosevelt's announcement. But this was not accepted, and Eden at length asked for more time to consider the draft and discuss it with Chamberlain.[37]

35. Eden, *Facing the Dictators,* pp. 635–36. There is nothing in Chamberlain's summarized diary entry of 19 February 1938 to refute Eden's account of this meeting; rather, it generally corroborates it (NC 2/24A).

36. Inside the back cover of CAB 27/622, FPC Minutes, vol. 1, stamped as page 259, the following cabinet office notation appears: "No trace has been found among the records of the Cabinet Office of the summaries of the discussions in the Foreign Policy Committee on 19th–21st January 1938; nor has any trace been found of the Secretary's standard or Official File for this Committee. There is no firm evidence that an official record was made." It is hard to believe that no records were kept, since there are full records for all other FPC meetings, and the secretary to the cabinet, Hankey, was present. But the fate of such records as there may have been is a mystery.

37. Eden, *Facing the Dictators,* pp. 636–38; *Cadogan Diaries,* p. 39; CAB 27/622, 19 January 1938, p. 251. In Eden's view some of his senior cabinet colleagues, "as old-fashioned Conservatives. . . felt little sympathy with Roosevelt whom they regarded as something of a demagogue."

Most of Eden's Foreign Office colleagues shared his view that Britain must let Roosevelt proceed; and Cadogan, who was especially concerned about the consequences should Eden resign over this issue—a possibility that was openly recognized—undertook to draft another telegram. When Eden saw Chamberlain shortly after noon on January 20, the prime minister was thinking in terms of parallel action: Roosevelt would go ahead with his plan while Britain pursued Italy. Eden thought this unrealistic in view of Roosevelt's declared stand on de jure recognition, and said so to the Foreign Policy Committee that afternoon. There the atmosphere had changed, and what resulted seemed, on the face of it, a reversal of Chamberlain's attitude. It was now agreed that Eden should produce three draft telegrams: two to Roosevelt, one withdrawing the request that he consider delaying his initiative, the other explaining Britain's thinking on de jure recognition but agreeing to defer this negotiation; the third to Lindsay seeking, if he thought it possible, modifications in the wording of Roosevelt's appeal. But the following morning, discussion in the committee went badly. Some members liked the drafts, but more did not—including the prime minister, who chafed about their effect on the Italian negotiations. A further redrafting followed, this time by Stanley (president of the Board of Trade) and McDonald (secretary for the dominions). Eden pressed the point about Italian negotiations, and the committee agreed that Britain was not committed to them until she could assess the reception given to Roosevelt's plan. The foreign secretary had apparently won a considerable victory.[38]

Thus a series of telegrams was dispatched to Washington on the evening of January 21. Upon further consideration of the president's proposal and its relationship to British plans, Chamberlain told Roosevelt, he did "not now feel justified" in asking him to delay the announcement of his scheme any longer; he welcomed the initiative and would do his best to contribute to its success. A second message from prime minister to president explained in detail Britain's reasons for contemplating de jure recognition, which he saw as a necessary contribution toward a broader settlement of political—and perhaps eventually economic—problems. It would not be accorded quickly and bore no necessary relationship to Manchukuo, inasmuch as Japan had not asked for recognition there and apparently did not intend to do so.[39] Two other

38. CAB 27/622, 20–21 January 1938, pp. 254–58; Eden, *Facing the Dictators*, pp. 638–41; *Cadogan Diaries*, p. 39; *Harvey Diaries*, pp. 73–77. Cadogan thought Eden had shaken the prime minister; Eden thought Chamberlain was moved, perhaps, by the support given to him by some members of the committee, notably MacDonald and Stanley.

39. Chamberlain to Roosevelt, 21 January 1938, FO 371/21526, pp. 80–83, 86.

telegrams were addressed to Lindsay by Eden, explaining the tightrope Britain was walking in seeking to reduce tension without sacrificing higher ideals, and also in giving the president encouragement to launch his initiative without ignoring criticisms that could be leveled against the substance of it or assuming any element of British responsibility for it: "In all circumstances, we want the President to take his initiative"; but it was quite ambitious and might prove very difficult to pull through.[40]

These telegrams represented a compromise reached after long and tedious discussion. They were less than Eden would have wished. But they were more than Chamberlain would have liked. It now remained to see what Roosevelt's reaction would be.

The president's response was slow in coming. When Lindsay delivered Chamberlain's messages, Welles said the president would be pleased. Welles himself was relieved by British assurances regarding de jure recognition, a bitter pill that London and Washington would have to swallow, but one that Roosevelt wished to include in a general settlement involving world appeasement. But Lindsay's questions about the functions and objects of the ten-power meeting contemplated in Roosevelt's plan; the extent of Roosevelt's appreciation of the difficult task he was undertaking; the potential reactions of the dictators; and the possible modification of wording about postwar inequities and American freedom from political involvement, all seemed, by their very nature, to cast doubt upon Chamberlain's message of approval. The conversation ended with Welles's comment that the president probably would wish to address some questions to the British government and probably would not initiate his plan for a week or more (while the League Council was in session in Geneva). Two days later Welles reported to Lindsay that Roosevelt was "deeply gratified" by the contents of Chamberlain's messages, that there probably would be a further message in writing from the president, and that within the next few days he (Welles) would talk with Lindsay about "further procedure." But when nothing was heard for four more days, Chamberlain asked Lindsay when Roosevelt's reply could be expected; delay would cause problems in planning future action in regard especially to Italian, but also German and Chinese, policy. Roosevelt's verbal response was that the British should "hold back their horses" for a few days yet, and then he expected to have clarified his

40. Eden to Lindsay, 21 January 1938, ibid., pp. 77–79, 84–85.

ideas about when to proceed.[41] Another month would pass before it was clear that Roosevelt's scheme would not be initiated at all.

Roosevelt's decision to set the plan in motion in the first place had been taken somewhat haltingly. He was clearly torn between avoiding impractical interventions in foreign politics and doing something from his widely recognized position of leadership to help save the deteriorating international situation. What he initially sought from Chamberlain was "cordial approval and wholehearted support"—perhaps as a means of bolstering his own confidence in the plan. When it was not at once forthcoming, the president's enthusiasm was no doubt dampened, his hesitation strengthened.

The degree of Roosevelt's disappointment over Chamberlain's initial reply has been much debated and is difficult to measure. Lindsay thought it "distinctly felt," and reported this to London both in writing and by telephone. Eden interpreted Roosevelt's reaction as one of disappointment and was deeply concerned about it—to the point where fear of damage to Anglo-American relations took clear precedence in his mind over the merits of Roosevelt's proposal. The question was frankly weighed in the Foreign Office, where it was generally agreed that Roosevelt must not be turned down, and it played a role in Foreign Policy Committee deliberations. Welles later described Chamberlain's reply as "a douche of cold water." And there is evidence that Roosevelt expended no personal effort on his January 17 reply to Chamberlain; on the draft composed by Welles, the president merely noted: "OK FDR." Chamberlain wrote in his diary some weeks later that this reply constituted "a somewhat sulky acquiescence in postponement." A recent study of Roosevelt's foreign policy declares forthrightly that the president was "sorely disappointed" and took Chamberlain's rebuff as a sign that he placed no great stock in cooperation with the United States. Further, he was "offended by the moral compromise involved in recognizing the fruits of Italian aggression and skeptical of the practical effects of Chamberlain's policy"; on the other hand, some have flatly denied this, including

41. Lindsay to Foreign Office, 22, 24 January, 2 February 1938; Chamberlain to Lindsay, 28 January 1938; ibid., pp. 61, 68–69, 71–76. The only mention of all this in the cabinet meeting of 26 January was Chamberlain's acknowledgment of word from Washington that Roosevelt was gratified with his two messages of 21 January (CAB 23/92, p. 19). But Roosevelt could not have been encouraged about British policy by a 24 January letter from his old and trusted English friend, Arthur Murray, who wrote: "Nothing can alter the bedrock fact that no Agreements will be entered into by Berlin that would serve as a check upon its expansionist policy" (Elibank, "Roosevelt: Friend of Britain," p. 363).

Halifax and Hoare (home secretary). Halifax wrote to Mrs. Neville Chamberlain in May 1948 that when he was in Washington as British ambassador (1941–46) he looked up the file and formed the opinion that "F.D.R. had not in fact been so upset by Neville's reply as was made out at the time and since"; and Roosevelt had, by implication, confirmed this in conversation. Hoare scribbled in his personal notes at the time that Washington did not "blow up" but was "quite happy" when reassured over Abyssinian recognition.[42]

No doubt the crucial question is not merely the degree of Roosevelt's disappointment over Chamberlain's first reaction but the broader sense of doubt and discouragement he must have felt about lending active support of any kind to British efforts in Europe. Hull had long been urging him in another direction: the utilization of financial power and economic measures (especially trade agreements) to reduce international tension. And a January 20 message from Ambassador Bullitt in Paris—with whom he was accustomed to communicating frankly—was hardly encouraging. Predicting that Austria would soon fall into German hands and that France would do nothing but protest feebly, Bullitt thought the idea of a conference in Washington to discuss international law would seem "an escape from reality to the rest of the world. It would be as if in the palmiest days of Al Capone you had summoned a national conference of psychoanalysts to Washington to discuss the psychological causes of crime." Bullitt now thought Roosevelt could do nothing effective in Europe until he had ambassadors in London and Berlin who could discover for him what those governments really wanted.[43] The course of events in succeeding weeks made all this quite uncertain.

Certainly Chamberlain was not disappointed with the postponement of Roosevelt's initiative. He had been persuaded to modify his initial response so as not to rebuff the president too sharply, but he was still dead against Roosevelt's idea. On January 23 he wrote his sister Ida about his "strenuous and anxious endeavors to deal with a bombshell which after a 3000 mile journey suddenly landed in my lap" and had

42. Sumner Welles, *The Time for Decision*, p. 66; Letter from Welles to Roosevelt, 17 January 1938, State Department Manuscripts (hereafter SDM) 740.00/264 1/2; NC 2/24A, 19 February 1938; Dallek, *Franklin Roosevelt and American Foreign Policy*, p. 156; Lord Halifax, *Fullness of Days*, pp. 196–97; Viscount Templewood, *Nine Troubled Years*, pp. 269–75; Halifax to Anne Chamberlain, 13 May 1948, Halifax Papers, A4.410.18.41; Templewood Papers, X:5. Simon recorded in his diary merely that the Foreign Policy Committee was busy all week with a secret message from Roosevelt (Simon Diary, no. 11, 23 January 1938).

43. Lindsay to Foreign Office, 16 January 1938, FO 371/21526, p. 105; Bullitt to Roosevelt, 20 January 1938, PSF, Diplomatic Correspondence, Box 23.

cost him "much time and some very uncomfortable moments." A week later he wrote the following to his sister Hilda: "the bomb . . . hasn't exploded yet and I hope now to surround it with blankets sufficient to prevent its doing any harm." But it had given him "an anxious time and a perilous moment or two." Upon reading Lindsay's account of Welles's explanation that the ten governments to be invited to Washington had been chosen so that every view would be represented and advocated, Chamberlain penciled in the margin: "Except that of the people who matter." When the full cabinet was informed, on January 24, of the exchange of messages with Washington, Chamberlain's comment was largely negative: Roosevelt's "rather preposterous proposals" contained nothing new, but merely set out four old principles that would most likely be unpalatable to the dictators. It is also revealing, perhaps, that in the next two meetings of the Foreign Policy Committee after the January 19–21 uproar over Roosevelt's proposal, there was no further mention of the issue, save for Chamberlain's report that American reaction was "not too bad"; rather, discussion centered almost entirely on the prime minister's new plan for a colonial settlement with Germany.[44]

The fullest explanation of Chamberlain's thinking appears in the memoirs of Sir Samuel Hoare (Lord Templewood), one of Chamberlain's close cabinet colleagues. Against a background of vain British efforts (since World War I, and especially during the 1930s) to gain American cooperation in the face of difficulties that confronted a weakened France and Britain, Hoare explains that "rightly or wrongly" the British government, in early 1938, was "deeply suspicious not indeed of American good intentions, but of American readiness to follow up inspiring words with any practical action." Whatever the president might wish, Congress would never approve any resolute intervention in European affairs; and however great Roosevelt's sympathy for the democracies, nothing suggested that he would risk a conflict with his own isolationists. Chamberlain was thus convinced that American isolationism made effective American action impossible, and that Britain must rely chiefly upon herself in the immediate crisis facing Europe. Indeed,

> it was this conviction more than any other reason that not only made him impatient of American lectures on international conduct, and American reiteration of moral principles, but more than ever forced his mind in the only

44. Neville to Ida, 23 January 1938; Neville to Hilda, 30 January 1938; NC 18/1/1036–37; PREM 1/259, p. 32; CAB 23/92, 24 January 1938, p. 13; CAB 27/623, 24 January and 3 February 1938.

> direction that then seemed likely to avert war, the negotiation of specific, and probably limited, agreements, first with Mussolini, and secondly with Hitler.

He was thus at first perturbed when "the delays and dangers of an ill-prepared international conference seemed likely to destroy his hope of concrete agreements upon specific points." Hoare thus explains not only the basis of Chamberlain's negative reaction to Roosevelt's proposal but suggests quite clearly that American isolationism was a major consideration in the formulation of British appeasement. The point is corroborated by Chamberlain in an extended diary entry on February 19: he had been trying from the first to improve relations with the two "storm centres" of Europe, Rome and Berlin, in part because "the isolationists" in the United States were "so strong & so vocal" that it could not be "depended upon for help if [Britain] should get into trouble."[45]

There were no doubt other factors that influenced Chamberlain's thinking. Skeptical of the "Foreign Office mentality," which seemed to him often unrelated to practical realities and bound by tradition, he had come to rely heavily for advice on Sir Horace Wilson, the civil service chief whose administrative talents had been helpful to Chamberlain in other ministries, but who was not experienced in foreign affairs. Wilson dismissed Roosevelt's initiative as "woolly rubbish" and urged the prime minister to go ahead with his own plans.[46] Chamberlain knew the minds of his closest cabinet colleagues and was confident of their full support. For some time they had been examining schemes for advancing the appeasement of Europe and had pretty well fixed their ideas on how to proceed. Considering the strength of his own commitment to appeasement, Chamberlain naturally resented anything that might interfere with its pursuit. This posture involved some vanity, of which Chamberlain was clearly victim. He had come to believe not only that Britain had a special mission to "make gentle the life of Europe," but also that he was called by Providence, perhaps in fulfillment of family tradition, to lead

45. Templewood, *Nine Troubled Years*, pp. 263–71; NC 2/24A. Other factors mentioned by Chamberlain in explaining his efforts at appeasement were the "terribly weak condition" of France and the burgeoning cost of British rearmament. American historian Basil Rauch later wrote: "It is quite impossible to disprove the contention of Prime Minister Neville Chamberlain that one influence leading him to abandon collective security and turn to appeasement of the dictators was the failure of the United States to help organize a united front" (*Roosevelt. From Munich to Pearl Harbor: A Study in the Creation of Foreign Policy*, p. 21).

46. *Harvey Diaries*, p. 71; Eden, *Facing the Dictators*, p. 640. The cautious Cadogan wrote in his diary about Wilson: "Don't know what he's at or whether he's straight" (*Cadogan Diaries*, p. 39).

the way.[47] He may not have been anti-American, but his attitude toward Americans generally, and Roosevelt in particular, was condescending and arrogant. Inclined to judge plans in the short run, since he was not adept at looking beyond to long-term prospects, he did not appear to look beyond the Roosevelt plan itself (which might well have failed) to salutary consequences that might have sprung from it even in failure.[48]

On the importance of this episode, consensus will never be reached. The assessments of Chamberlain's contemporaries, in writing memoirs later on, were generally correlative to their developing views on appeasement during 1938–39: those who came to oppose the policy tended to see it as a great opportunity for changing the course of events that was tragically missed; those who favored appeasement were inclined to see it as much less crucial. Churchill, for example, writing ten years later, was still "breathless with amazement" at Chamberlain's waving away "the proferred hand stretched out across the Atlantic." Thus was lost "the last frail chance to save the world from tyranny otherwise than by war." Duff Cooper and Macmillan, allowing that the scheme was open to criticism, consider that irrelevant to the needs of the moment. In such a grave situation, Britain should have turned not to the past but to the future, and it could look to no greater friend in trouble than Roosevelt; his intervention in European affairs might have averted the coming war.[49] On the other hand, Halifax labels this view "legend"; and L. S. Amery (later turned Chamberlain critic) declares that the prime minister had no reason to suppose that the president's plan could do anything beyond irritating the dictators without restraining them.[50] The interpretive slants of historians have varied in like manner, depending on their divergent assessments of Chamberlain, Roosevelt, and the dictators.

It is, of course, impossible to know "what might have been." What we do know is that Chamberlain proceeded vigorously with his efforts at appeasement—which ultimately ended in failure. Roosevelt stood aside. Skeptical of appeasement but not wishing to stand in its way, he did not undertake a similar initiative thereafter. Perhaps no comparable opportunity occurred. It also seems likely that Roosevelt, feeling re-

47. See Rock, *British Appeasement in the 1930s*, pp. 28, 56.

48. This assessment of Chamberlain's limited vision is Eden's (*Facing the Dictators*, p. 645), but there is much to support it.

49. Winston S. Churchill, *The Gathering Storm*, pp. 254–55; Alfred Duff Cooper, *Old Men Forget: The Autobiography of Duff Cooper*, p. 210; Harold Macmillan, *Winds of Change, 1914–1939*, pp. 481–82.

50. Halifax, *Fullness of Days*, p. 196; L. S. Amery, *My Political Life*, 3:232.

buffed, inclined further toward the isolationism already characteristic of so many Americans. The possibility of Anglo-American cooperation in the interest of peace, however limited already, dwindled. Roosevelt was content thereafter to stand by and watch while Chamberlain tried to handle things. And Chamberlain liked it that way.[51]

One positive outcome of the episode was agreement between London and Washington to initiate a full and regular exchange of diplomatic information. Proposed by Hull (who was "anxious that the State Department should have the best information on all questions") to Lindsay on January 20, agreement was easily reached since the Foreign Office officials already favored such an exchange.[52] Information would be given in confidence and not communicated to any third party; where British information and opinions were desired, they would be sought in London, and conversely. The flow of information between the two capitals gradually increased in volume and detail in the following months, and this was certainly beneficial to both sides. But it was a modest outcome when weighed against potentialities, especially considering Chamberlain's opinion on Anglo-American relations as expressed to a relative in Boston on January 16:

> I intend to keep on doing everything I can to promote Anglo-American understanding and cooperation. . . . U.S.A. and U.K. in combination represent a force so overwhelming that the mere hint of the possibility of its use is sufficient to make the most powerful dictators pause, and that is why I believe that cooperation between our two countries is the greatest instrument in the world for the preservation of peace.[53]

The precise point at which Roosevelt's proposal died is difficult to say. That it was dealt a stunning blow by Chamberlain's initial reply is beyond question, and it no doubt expired gradually thereafter. It was still being actively worked on in the State Department at the end of

51. There are historians who believe that Roosevelt was as much an appeaser as Chamberlain; see, for example, Donald Watt, "Roosevelt and Chamberlain: Two Appeasers." H. G. Nicholas writes: "There is nothing either in terms of Roosevelt's proposal or elsewhere to suggest that, particularly in relation to Germany, he was much less of an appeaser at the time than Chamberlain" (*The United States and Britain,* p. 88). For an analysis of American relations with Germany, see Arnold A. Offner, *American Appeasement: United States Foreign Policy and Germany, 1933–1938.*

52. Lindsay to Foreign Office, 20 January 1938, PREM 1/259, p. 37. See also Lindsay to Foreign Office, 26 January 1938, and Foreign Office Minute, 27 January 1938, FO 371/21525, pp. 368–71. In a 23 January note to Chamberlain, Wilson cited Hull's request as refuting the idea that the United States government was offended by "our caution on the President's new scheme" (PREM 1/259, p. 36).

53. Feiling, *Life of Neville Chamberlain,* p. 323.

January,[54] and the likelihood that he would proceed with it clearly lingered in British calculations for some time.

There was confusion in the Foreign Office over Roosevelt's "hold back your horses" message, but the president's attitude was interpreted as applying only to his plan and meaning that Britain could proceed with the Italian conversations provided it did not reach a point of committing itself on Abyssinia. Lindsay confirmed this for Eden, who, having minuted that "the time for decision has come," also sought Lindsay's opinion on the extent to which Britain's explanation of her position toward Abyssinia would obviate the ill effect on Anglo-American relations of which Roosevelt had warned. Lindsay described himself as having been "taken aback" by the negative reaction of Welles, Hull, and Roosevelt to the matter of recognition, but he thought they were "laying it on rather thick" in their estimate of public reaction. He thought Britain would have the support of the administration, and that it would do all it could to influence opinion favorably if it adhered to the line of Chamberlain's message. On Lindsay's reply, Cadogan minuted (February 7): "What, meanwhile, has happened to the President's plan, about which there was such a hurry at one time?" And Eden minuted (February 7): "I hope that we have not discouraged the poor President too much." But this hardly bothered Chamberlain, who wrote to his sister Hilda on February 6: "The bomb is still unexploded and there seems little doubt that my prompt action averted what might have been a very awkward and perhaps unfortunate denouement." Now things seemed to be moving in the right direction in Rome, Washington, and Tokyo.[55]

Lindsay heard from Welles on February 9 that Roosevelt had decided to postpone proceeding with his plan in view of events in Germany (major changes in the Foreign Office and the military command) and would await a scheduled speech by Hitler on February 20. Welles also mentioned the impression, held especially by Hull but not by Roosevelt, that the British were not very enthusiastic about the plan, as suggested by their failure to offer any suggestions or amendments in regard to it. He wondered whether this was an indication of apathy. In reporting this to London, Lindsay said he could not tell how the American view of Britain's attitude might affect the final decision to launch the plan. Cadogan's minuted response was twofold: if Roosevelt still had faith in his

54. See Berle, *Navigating the Rapids,* p. 161.

55. Lindsay to Foreign Office, 2 February 1938; Eden to Lindsay, 4 February 1938; Lindsay to Foreign Office, 6 February 1938; FO 371/21526, pp. 56–62; NC 18/1/1038.

plan, it might be better for him to produce it before February 20; the Foreign Office should send Lindsay some material with which to allay American suspicions concerning Britain's attitude, "if only because of the risk that the President may one day say that he was discouraged from taking a useful initiative by the cool reception which we gave to his proposals." He drafted a telegram to Lindsay denying that the British government was lukewarm about the president's plan or wished in any way to discourage it, and explaining that the failure to make any constructive suggestions or amendments was due to the president's indicating his intentions in such broad outline that it was not clear exactly how they would be implemented or what their effect might be. The draft welcomed the president's intention to grapple with these problems and hoped he would launch his plan. But when Eden sought Chamberlain's approval, important revisions resulted. As Harvey wrote in his diary, "there was the usual wrangle with the P.M., who wished to water it down"; and the telegram that went to Lindsay on February 11, to be used as he saw fit, contained no positive endorsement and referred to Britain's understanding that the president "was anxious to present the plan as a purely American initiative." Lindsay emphasized the latter point in his February 12 conversation with Welles:

> . . . A leading characteristic of all United States action [in international affairs] had been that it had been independent or parallel and always a purely American initiative. This was a condition of any American contribution to world affairs which was perfectly understood by His Majesty's Government and it must account for their hesitation in putting forward any constructive suggestions in regard to the President's plan. What was an American proposal must on no account be susceptible to being called an Anglo-American proposal and this was more important at a moment like the present when isolationists [*sic*] element in America were mobilized in great strength and exerting pressures the effect of which could be estimated by the United States Government but not by His Majesty's Government.

Lindsay thus gave Welles a dose of standard American medicine—which Welles accepted while adding his own view that the secrecy of the communication and its necessarily inchoate form provided an opportunity for amendments or suggestions. Chamberlain, for one, liked Lindsay's handling of the matter, penciling on the report of the conversation that came to him on February 13: "This was rather astutely put by R. L."

And the Foreign Office sent Lindsay a special telegram approving his language.[56]

But Lindsay had second thoughts on the matter. Three days later he wired to the Foreign Office his concern about Britain's failure to make suggestions of substance and offered one of his own: it might be suggested that Roosevelt put the conference idea "somewhat into the background" and emphasize the alleviation of tension by direct negotiations between states. He might proclaim his keen concern about the success of conversations already initiated and his anxiety to see other necessary negotiations undertaken without delay. He might even express a willingness to assist them through diplomatic channels and a desire to be kept fully informed so as to assess the usefulness of further proposals and representations. Lindsay did not know whether this would appeal to Roosevelt, but it would cause less outcry in America than his own plan. It was well within the president's constitutional authority and neutral in character, and while it would expose Britain to "stimulative communications" from Roosevelt, it would be "of great value towards appeasement" because of the strong moral influence that America exercised through her vast industrial strength.[57]

Cadogan did not like this idea. It would mean "irresponsible interference in our negotiations"—a special danger for Britain, which was more susceptible than Germany or Italy to United States influence. It would also be full of "involvements" for the president, who seemed to have in mind "a clear clarion call from his mountain-top, addressed to the wicked European countries," but did not want to get mixed up in their discussions. And, of course, Britain did not want to have much of a hand in shaping Roosevelt's action. It was to be his plan, for which he should bear responsibility. The specific reactions of Eden and Chamberlain are not revealed in the documents, but the message to Lindsay on February 18 was drafted by Cadogan, utilized his arguments, and was approved by Eden without change.[58]

56. Lindsay to Foreign Office, 9 February 1938; Foreign Office to Lindsay, 11 February 1938; Lindsay to Foreign Office, 12 February 1938; Foreign Office to Lindsay, 15 February 1938; FO 371/21526, pp. 43–55; Welles Memorandum, 9 February 1938, *FRUS,* 1938, 1:124–25; PREM 1/259, p. 13; *Harvey Diaries,* p. 88; *Cadogan Diaries,* p. 46. Cadogan recorded that Chamberlain didn't like his draft, but Eden managed to retain "just enough."

57. Lindsay to Foreign Office, 15 February 1938, FO 371/21526, pp. 39–42.

58. Minute by Cadogan, 16 February 1938; Eden to Lindsay, 18 February 1938; ibid., pp. 33–34, 37–38. On the copy of Lindsay's dispatch that crossed his desk, Chamberlain had noted: "No doubt the S.S. will consult me about the reply" (PREM 1/259, p. 9).

Meantime, Lindsay had heard from Welles that Roosevelt planned to leave Washington on February 18 for five days at Hyde Park. His "present purpose" was to launch his plan essentially unchanged shortly after his return, irrespective of Hitler's speech. But nine days later—after a cabinet crisis in Britain prompted by Eden's resignation over the opening of negotiations with Italy—Lindsay learned from Welles that the president had "of course" decided to hold his plan in abeyance for the present. It was the opinion of the president "and of every other responsible member of the administration" that the intended procedure of the British government as described in Chamberlain's statements to Parliament, was "entirely right and that present prospects were favourable." Chamberlain's reaction to Lindsay's report was a succinct notation: "This is excellent!"[59]

Some days later (March 7), Welles tried to temper the interpretation of "entirely right" to mean simply that the Roosevelt administration regarded the course and objectives of the British government as wise and hoped they would meet with success. Roosevelt had put his own plan aside, he added, and was content to watch the course of forthcoming conversations. A week after that—by which time Europe had been shaken by the Austrian *Anschluss*—Cadogan minuted: "I think the time has come when all this story [Roosevelt's plan] sh. be entered 'Green'" (meaning filed away quietly and secretly).[60] Thus ended the episode of the Roosevelt initiative of early 1938.

A combination of factors impossible to measure precisely had figured in Roosevelt's abandonment of his proposal. Beyond whatever discouragement he had felt over Chamberlain's initial reaction, compounded by his own subtle reservations about what the proposal could accomplish, the course of events during the weeks in question was intimidating. Word from Bullitt about French political instability and a probable German move against Austria was not encouraging. Hitler's early February reshuffle of the Foreign Office and the army command, by which "moderates" were dismissed and the Führer took control of the military into his own hands, augured ill. Roosevelt recently had learned from former Weimar Chancellor Brüning of a struggle under way within the Nazi system and had been warned that the removal of conservative army leaders would be prelude to a policy of adventure. Equally unsettling

59. Lindsay to Foreign Office, 16 and 25 February, 1938, FO 371/21526, pp. 32, 36; PREM 1/259, p. 5.

60. Lindsay to Foreign Office, 7 March 1938; Cadogan Minute, 15 March 1938; FO 371/21526, pp. 17, 26–27.

was the Eden resignation crisis of late February (see Chapter 4), the outcome of which left many Americans suspicious that some immoral deal with the dictators, perhaps in Britain's interest but at the expense of other nations, was afoot. The basic dimensions of the Chamberlain-Eden rift were known in Washington, where the coldly calculating prime minister (Chamberlain's glacial personality was always a subtle factor against him) was suspected by some—not least in the State Department—as the agent of selfish financial interests that would benefit especially from deals with Berlin and Rome wherein American hopes for free access to raw materials and open world trade would be disregarded. His readiness to recognize Italian Abyssinia reinforced this suspicion; and though he retreated from his initial position, considerable damage had been done. Roosevelt surely felt offended by the moral compromise inherent in Chamberlain's thinking. Divergent American and British political-cultural traditions were involved here. The president's dropping of his plan was also influenced no doubt by anxiety over becoming *too* closely associated with British appeasement. If Chamberlain was skeptical of the practical results of Roosevelt's proposal, so too had the president become skeptical of Chamberlain's planned approach to the dictators. The more he heard of it, the less he liked it, and he no longer wished to be associated with it by initiating a parallel endeavor. Roosevelt was still eager to demonstrate that the United States was not indifferent to the actions of aggressors, and he made pointed remarks denouncing "international gangsters." But the time had come to wait and watch. Langer and Gleason summarized the outlook well in an early study of American diplomacy of the period: Roosevelt and his advisers "sympathized with the British and wished them well in whatever efforts they felt constrained to make in the direction of peaceful adjustment, but there was never any question of approving or supporting their specific policy and certainly no thought of assuming any political or military commitment in connection with it."[61]

61. Langer and Gleason, *The Challenge to Isolation*, pp. 31–32; MacDonald, *The United States, Britain, and Appeasement*, pp. 71–73; Dallek, *Franklin Roosevelt and American Foreign Policy*, p. 157; Offner, *Origins of the Second World War*, p. 123.

IV.
Chamberlain's Italian Initiative and the Anschluss

WHILE THE FINAL DISPOSITION of Roosevelt's plan remained unsettled, Chamberlain was busy launching an initiative of his own: the opening of conversations with Italy, which he regarded as an important step toward the appeasement of Europe. Actually his primary objective was to reach an agreement with Germany, and at the end of 1937 the British cabinet explored in some detail how this might be accomplished. Italy's aggressive actions in Abyssinia and Spain were troublesome, but the reestablishment of cordial Anglo-German relations would neutralize the danger from Italy and significantly reduce her pomposity. Chamberlain had written to his sister the previous July: "If we could only get on terms with the Germans, I would not care a rap for Musso." But when his initial contacts with Germany failed to receive a positive response, Italy loomed larger in his calculations; he began to think about weakening Germany's position by detaching Italy from her, or at least by using Italy's good offices for the purpose of influencing Berlin. Throughout the second half of 1937, Italian conversations had never been very far from his mind, and questions arising in connection with them, especially the recognition of Italian sovereignty over Abyssinia, had received considerable attention. He concluded that conversations must be arranged, and Abyssinian recognition was vital to their success.[1]

Foreign Secretary Anthony Eden had never been more than cautiously

1. Neville to Ida, 4 July 1937, NC 18/1/1010. Chamberlain's interest in, and attitudes toward, Italian conversations are clearly revealed in materials in PREM 1/276 and various letters to his sisters (NC 18/1/1010–31).

lukewarm toward the Italian conversations and was especially troubled by the idea of Abyssinian recognition, though prior to Roosevelt's initiative he was prepared to discuss these possibilities in the seeming absence of better alternatives. But the Roosevelt plan had brought him to a decision, and he told Chamberlain clearly on January 18 that Britain must choose "Anglo-American cooperation in an attempt to ensure world peace" over "a piece-meal settlement approached by way of a problematical agreement with Mussolini." Two weeks later he directly challenged one of the basic premises on which Chamberlain's developing policy rested: the contention of the Chiefs of Staff that Britain might be called upon alone to face three potential enemies and must therefore lose no opportunity to reduce their number. Seeing a tendency to overemphasize the strength and cohesion of potential enemies and to underestimate the potential of Britain and her possible allies, Eden fretted that the Chiefs wanted "to reorientate [Britain's] whole foreign policy and clamber on the bandwagon with the dictators, even though that process meant parting company with France and estranging . . . relations with the United States." As for Italian conversations, "there should be possibilities" once Britain had heard what Roosevelt had to say and had determined her own desiderata.[2]

Again on February 4 Eden provided Chamberlain with the reasoning of Viscount Cranborne, under secretary of state, on these points. Opposed to conversations with Italy on the basis of de jure recognition at that time, partly because he perceived Mussolini to be in a precarious position and thus should not be catered to, Cranborne saw the "first and foremost" consideration to be Britain's relations with the United States. The strongest factor for peace and stability in the world was ever closer cooperation between Britain and America; a platform must be constructed on which they could stand side by side; and the only platform possible at the time was a common interest in the maintenance of international obligations and of a high standard of decency in international life. British recognition of Italy's title to Abyssinia would destroy that. All the arguments in favor of recognition had been used before—for lifting sanctions against Italy in 1936 and for justifying the so-called Gentleman's Agreement (in which both nations disclaimed any desire to modify the status quo with respect to national sovereignty in the Mediterranean area) in 1937. Instead of detaching Italy from Germany as anticipated, the result had been exactly the opposite. Was the same

2. Eden to Chamberlain, 31 January 1938, PREM 1/276.

mistake to be made again? Cranborne asked. It was in pursuit of closer cooperation with the United States, while negotiating with Germany, that Britain must seek the solution to her difficulties.[3]

Eden took up these points once more in a discussion of defense expenditures in the cabinet meeting of February 16. Recalling that Admiral Leahy's description of the situation confronting America was similar to the British Chiefs of Staff appraisal of British dangers, and questioning whether it was possible to reduce the number of Britain's potential enemies (inasmuch as all three powers had ambitions for the fulfillment of which Britain stood in the way). Eden thought that Britain ought to concentrate on courting her friends and finding out what they could do to assist her. But cabinet discussion did not develop in this direction, and there was no reference to Eden's line of thought in the cabinet's conclusions.[4] This clearly suggests that Chamberlain's calculations on appeasement did not involve the United States in any positive way, and that Eden's view had little support in the cabinet. The diary entry of Sir John Simon a few days before told all: Chamberlain was "most anxious" to put Anglo-Italian relations on a better footing—an objective about which the Foreign Office was "not equally enthusiastic." Simon's view, which nearly always coincided with the prime minister's, was that a prompt and friendly understanding with Italy was "of the greatest importance." Britain could not prepare to fight Germany, Japan, and Italy all at once: "Let us at any rate get rid of *one* potential enemy!" And a few days later, Simon recorded: "The P.M. . . . is determined to tolerate no obstacle now."[5]

Chamberlain did not wait around for Roosevelt. Renewed contacts with Mussolini early in February, through his sister-in-law, Ivy, an old acquaintance of the Duce, revealed Italian readiness—indeed, anxiety, in view of Germany's bullying of Austria—to work toward an agreement

3. Eden to Chamberlain, 4 February 1938, ibid. Eden withheld comment on Cranborne's memorandum because he hoped "over the weekend" to set out his own views on "this very vexed question." When he wrote Chamberlain on 8 February, he was particularly concerned about the role Lady Chamberlain was playing in Rome and the impression it would create in Mussolini's mind. He agreed with Cranborne that, in view of the Duce's "extremely uncomfortable position," Britain had nothing to gain by appearing overeager. But he made no mention of relations with the United States, nor did Chamberlain in his reply. He was sorry that his sister-in-law's "unorthodox procedure" had caused Eden apprehension and appreciated Britain's strong position with respect to Italy; but he did not want to give the impression, "in our over-anxiety not to be over-eager," that Britain did not want conversations at all. Eden to Chamberlain; Chamberlain to Eden, 8 February 1938, ibid.

4. CAB 23/92, 16 February 1938, pp. 135–47.

5. Simon Diary, no. 11, 12, 18 February 1938.

with Britain.[6] This was exactly the kind of opportunity that Chamberlain sought, and he pursued it with both determination and an element of reckless abandon. Intent on turning the opportunity to advantage in the cause of appeasement, and seeing it as the last chance with Italy (as the Italians pointedly said it was), he went far to accept the Italian view of things and to agree to negotiations without conditions. He also engaged in questionable tactics to undermine or circumvent the protests of Eden, who maintained that, in the absence of tangible evidence of Italian good faith, neither the timing nor the projected technique of conversations was appropriate. The issue forced to the surface a long-evolving antagonism between Chamberlain and Eden, a contrariety that embraced temperament, outlook, and general political philosophy as well as policy. The upshot was Eden's resignation on February 20, after the issue had come to a head in the cabinet, and Chamberlain's enhanced determination—fortified by the concurrence of most of his colleagues—to proceed with Italian appeasement at once.[7]

Eden's resignation has long been explained by historians primarily in terms of his opposition to the opening of conversations with Italy. Its timing clearly supports the connection, but that was simply the "last straw." Chamberlain's attitude toward the United States and his readiness to disregard it in favor of courting Italy were no doubt more fundamental to Eden's action.[8] It was not simply the fact of conversations with Italy, however distasteful he found them, that troubled Eden; it was what this implied for the nature and direction of British foreign policy more generally. The distinction is necessary in order to help clarify a long-standing ambiguity concerning Eden's attitude toward appeasement. He did not flatly oppose appeasement in principle. His attitudes and actions during the second half of 1937, when there was broad compatibility between him and the prime minister, do not support that view. But Eden saw appeasement as a policy that must be implemented from

6. In an earlier exchange of letters between Chamberlain and Mussolini in July 1937, the Duce had suggested his willingness to discuss all points of difference in Italy's relations with Britain. But there had been no immediate follow-up because of Italian belligerence in Abyssinia and Spain and Chamberlain's "Germany-first" approach to appeasement.

7. For a fuller account, see Rock, *Appeasement on Trial,* pp. 24–31. Eden's resignation brought the validity of appeasement into open public controversy in Britain, to be debated with increasing intensity as long as the policy lasted.

8. Eden wrote in his memoirs years later that "if the whole business [the Roosevelt initiative of January] had not been secret, I should have resigned then and there" (*Facing the Dictators,* p. 642). It is clear from other sources that resignation was openly discussed with Foreign Office colleagues (*Harvey Diaries,* p. 73; *Cadogan Diaries,* p. 40).

a position of strength, and the close association of the United States with British policy would add strength to Britain's bargaining position in a way that nothing else could. Chamberlain, much less able and willing, experientially and temperamentally, to think in terms of power politics, did not calculate the same way. The manner of his approach to Italy suggested a readiness to bargain hastily and from a position of weakness. This Eden could not accept. So the difference that developed between them involved not so much the validity of appeasement as a foreign policy but the circumstances in which the policy should be undertaken and the broader foundation from which its implementation should proceed. Chamberlain did not understand or appreciate the distinctions that Eden made for Britain's bargaining position, especially as they pertained to the United States; nothing previously had forced them to the surface. But the Roosevelt initiative and the Italian conversations, taken together, did so with shocking suddenness—which no doubt explains Chamberlain's surprise (and that of others) at the abruptness with which his differences with Eden erupted as well as the rigidity of the posture that Eden then assumed.

Eden's concern for strengthening Britain's position by closer association with the United States—before the appeasement of Italy (or Germany)—emerged clearly in his statements of February 19–20. In the cabinet debate of February 19, where the crucial vote was taken, one of the grounds on which he adjudged it a bad moment for Italian conversations was that it would anticipate President Roosevelt's statement expected the following week. Further, de jure recognition would create "an impression of scuttle in England and alienation in the United States." The next day, in elaborating his difference of outlook on foreign affairs with the prime minister, he cited as an example Chamberlain's message to Roosevelt on January 13. A mistake had been made; he would have taken a different course. His letter of resignation (February 20), declaring his inability to recommend in Parliament a policy with which he did not agree, made no reference to the United States. Nor did his resignation speech in the Commons (February 21), where mention of the Roosevelt affair was still precluded by the demands of secrecy. But he did assert that his immediate difference with the prime minister was not an isolated issue; rather, the difference had been "fundamental" a few weeks before upon an important matter that did not concern Italy at all.[9] In sum, the American issue was basic to Eden's

9. CAB 23/92, 19, 20 February 1938, pp. 191, 224, 228, 231; Eden to Chamberlain, 20 February 1938, PREM 1/276; *Parl. Debs., HC,* 21 February 1938, 332:45ff. See also Record of Events Connected with Anthony Eden's Resignation, Halifax Papers, A4 410 11.

thought and action. The issue of Italian conversations clinched his position and provided the occasion to resign.

But if Roosevelt's initiative changed things for Eden, it changed nothing for Chamberlain. He did not accept the importance that Eden attached to American cooperation as a means of influencing the European dictators, nor did he believe it possible to obtain that cooperation in any meaningful way. In surveying the international situation in his diary on February 19—prompted to do so by the cabinet crisis, which made it imperative that he set down some observations about what was happening (his first entry since May 30, 1937)—Chamberlain noted: "The U.S.A. has drawn closer to us but the isolationists there are so strong & so vocal that she cannot be depended on for help if we should get into trouble." And he wrote Lord Chatfield a few days later that "it was now or never if we were able to check this drift." It had been a trying ordeal, but the objective had been obtained; and "I think we may look forward to the future now with increased confidence."[10]

Naturally, the Foreign Office acted at once to assure the United States that Eden's resignation did not imply any change in the aims and purposes of British foreign policy. It had been on tactics, not strategy (according to Cadogan), that the prime minister and Eden had disagreed. Rumors that Britain would now come to some agreement with the dictators at any cost were "absolutely nonsensical." No agreement would be entered into that violated the principles that previously had guided British policy and would not result in general appeasement and the preservation of peace.[11]

Official American reaction to Eden's resignation was most subdued. In reporting American press reaction to the Foreign Office on February 23, Lindsay noted that no one in the administration had yet given a public expression of opinion. That did not materially change. An attitude of wait-and-see prevailed. Lindsay himself was at a loss to explain exactly what had happened, and when he sought Welles's reactions on February 25, he got nothing but generalities. Herschel Johnson, chargé in the London embassy, reported confidential Foreign Office information that British policy was now being drastically overhauled, and even responsible officials were not yet sure of the new directions, adding: "It is difficult to escape the conclusion that questions of tactics and

10. NC 2/24 A, 19 February 1938; Chamberlain to Chatfield, 24 February 1938, CHT/3/1 (Chatfield Papers), p. 241. Chamberlain also confided to his diary that it was "really a relief" that the peacemakers in the cabinet had failed to persuade Eden to change his mind.

11. Johnson (London) to Hull, 21 February 1938, SDM 841.00/1324; Minute by Gladwyn Jebb, 23 February 1938, FO 371/21547, pp. 45–46.

procedure are fundamental and that ways and means may themselves very largely determine the results that will be achieved." So wait-and-see was the only practical pose.[12]

One State Department official who was not reticent in private was Pierrepont Moffat, head of the Division of European Affairs. In a memorandum to Hull, he concluded that Chamberlain's decision to "play ball with Hitler and Mussolini" had now reached a concrete stage and was no longer a mere abstraction. He could not recall other instances in recent British history when a cabinet minister was allowed to go while under attack from abroad or when Britain proposed to yield to a country which that very day was attacking her and threatening her empire. Moffat feared serious repercussions on the Continent: France would feel deserted, Italy would take new courage, and the smaller states would feel helpless before the totalitarian juggernaut. "The belief will grow that Britain's interest in principles and in democracy was skin deep—something to be played up when it coincided with Britain's material interests and to be discarded as soon as it no longer served a useful purpose." Hull's own policy, he added, would become more difficult to accomplish in the face of public feeling that Britain had deserted her cause and that the United States should withdraw still more into her own hemisphere.[13]

Two American ambassadors in Europe offered unsettling comment on events in London. Bullitt in Paris reported to Hull that Premier Chautemps and Foreign Minister Delbos were gravely perturbed; they feared that Delbos's policy of revitalizing France's position in eastern Europe had been undermined and the area would now slip into the hands of Germany. Claude Bowers (Madrid) wrote Roosevelt directly that the policy of the "utterly stupid" Chamberlain was "brazenly fascistic." He had betrayed England and democracy shamelessly. On the other hand, American press reaction to Eden's resignation, as reported to London by Lindsay, was mixed and uncertain; in fact, Foreign Office officials

12. Lindsay to Foreign Office, 22 February 1938, FO 371/21547, pp. 42–43; Welles Memorandum, 25 February 1938, *FRUS,* 1938, 1:138–39; Johnson to Welles, 26 February 1938, SDM 841.00/1334. Eden's resignation did not take American officials totally by surprise. Johnson had reported on 15 February confidential information about the divergence of views over Italian conversations and word that Eden had resigned ten days before, only to reconsider under considerable pressure. Johnson to Hull, *FRUS,* 1938, 1:136–37. And Moffat noted that Chamberlain had for many months been out of sympathy with Eden's ideas: "we saw clear proof of that in Brussels" (*Moffat Papers,* p. 190).

13. Moffat to Hull, 21 February 1938, SDM 841.00/1336. Years later Hull recorded simply in his memoirs: "Eden thought as I did on the subject of appeasement" (Hull, *Memoirs,* 1:581).

Beith and Balfour found it unexpectedly moderate—no doubt demonstrating the influence of the isolationists, who were still in a majority.[14] British opinion, of which the State Department was fully informed, was likewise mixed. Churchill thundered in the Commons that millions of Americans had been armed with a means to mock the sincerity of British idealism whereas Americans friendly to Britain were downcast and bewildered. But Arthur Murray, Roosevelt's old friend, wrote the president to back the "realist" attitude of Chamberlain in the Eden embroglio. The impact of such opinion on Roosevelt, Hull, and others is impossible to measure, but the president must have been puzzled by a letter at that moment from Lord Runciman, another English friend, quoting Chamberlain as having said to him sometime before, "There is nothing in the world I so much desire as a closer understanding with the United States and the President."[15] That his diplomatic initiative of the previous month was heard of no more perhaps tells all there is to know.

Roosevelt's private reaction to the circumstances surrounding Eden's resignation was pretty well expressed in a letter to John Cudahy, American minister in Dublin. Cudahy had written the president on March 1 that the real issue in London was whether to enter into a contract with someone who had shown bad faith and repeatedly broken agreements. Chamberlain wanted to treat Mussolini as one whose good faith could be taken at face value; Eden held out for some assurance of performance. The justification for Chamberlain's policy was that the time had not yet come in Britain's rearmament program to risk war. But it was a policy of retreat, which might be fatal in encouraging the dangerous adventures of both Mussolini and Hitler. Roosevelt replied that Cudahy's analysis was the best he had seen. As someone had said to him: "If a Chief of Police makes a deal with the leading gangsters and the deal results in no more hold-ups, that Chief of Police will be called a great man—but if the gangsters do not live up to their word the Chief of Police will go to

14. Bullitt to Hull, 21 February 1938, *FRUS,* 1938, 1:27–28; Bowers to Roosevelt, 20 February 1938, PSF; Spain, Box 54; Lindsay to Foreign Office, 22 February 1938; FO Minutes, 23 February 1938, FO 371/21547, pp. 41–43. See also Lindsay to Foreign Office, 1 March 1938, FO 115/3415, File 112; and Minute by Beith, 11 March 1938, FO 371/21547, p. 49. Lindsay reported that there was not "that almost universal condemnation of policy" that had appeared at the time of the Hoare-Laval proposals. The two most serious syndicated columnists were taking opposite views: Dorothy Thompson wrote about Eden as "the last knight of Europe," but Walter Lippmann saw him as "the knight with the wooden sword."

15. *Parl. Debs, HC,* 22 February 1938, 332:243; Murray to Runciman, 21 February 1938, and Runciman to Roosevelt, 18 February 1938, Runciman Papers, WR 284. For an account of the British debate over Eden's resignation, see Rock, *Appeasement on Trial,* pp. 31–45.

jail." Then came the president's pointed commentary: "Some people are, I think, taking very long chances—don't you?"[16] At the same time, he replied to Bowers that the ascendancy of Chamberlain had been established, and he was evidently taking the position that it was best for the general cause of peace to make a great effort with Italy and Germany, even making concessions such as the recognition of the Ethiopian conquest.

> If he succeeds in establishing reasonable assurance of peace for two or three years to come, even if he has to compromise with principle, he will be hailed as a great leader. If he fails or is asked to give too much and receives too little, public morality will be shot and he will be overthrown. It is impossible to guess. But fundamentally you and I hate compromise with principle.[17]

On March 10, Roosevelt told the cabinet that if Hitler adhered to his reported demands for colonies, a limitation of armaments, and the right to protect German minorities, Eden would be more than justified in his resignation and Britain would find herself in a difficult situation.[18]

Eden's successor at the Foreign Office was Lord Halifax—a man of wide political experience (most recently as lord president, 1937–38), prestige, and irreproachable personal qualities—who was wholly attuned to Chamberlain's thinking. If Eden "was always against negotiations with dictators," as Chamberlain wrote his sister on March 3,[19] Halifax was not; and if Eden perceived unwarranted interference by the prime minister in the conduct of foreign affairs, Halifax did not. Loyal to a fault, and not inclined to resent Chamberlain's personal initiatives, he would make an unusually compatible colleague. A strong supporter of conversations with Italy, his appointment facilitated their opening in Rome, through Lord Perth, the British ambassador there, on March 8.

An important personnel change also occurred at the American embassy in London on March 1. Joseph Kennedy arrived to replace the ailing Robert Bingham as United States ambassador. Roosevelt's reasons for choosing Kennedy a few months before were as diverse as appraisals (both before and after) of Kennedy's qualifications, personal suitability, and record of performance. His generous contributions of time and

16. Cudahy to Roosevelt, 1 March 1938; Roosevelt to Cudahy, 9 March 1938; PSF: Ireland, Box 44.

17. Roosevelt to Bowers, 7 March 1938, PSF: Spain, Box 54.

18. Ickes, *Diary*, 2:333.

19. Neville to Ida, 3 March 1938, NC 1/17/9. Sister Hilda "thought at once" that Chamberlain would choose Halifax as Eden's successor (Hilda to Neville, 21 February 1938, NC 18/2/1060).

money to Roosevelt and the Democratic party, his demonstrated ability as chairman of the Securities Exchange Commission and the Maritime Commission, his acquaintance with leading British economic and political figures, his commonplace opinion of the English as a nation of shopkeepers, and his vigorous campaigning for the post, all figured to some degree in the appointment. In addition, the sometimes unconventional Roosevelt no doubt relished the selection of an Irish Catholic saloon-keeper's son, not likely to be "taken in" by British charm, for a post normally reserved for blue-blooded Brahmins; and some weight must be given to the president's desire to get Kennedy, an intensely ambitious and outspoken man, out of the way in Washington.[20] The latter consideration would limit Kennedy's potential for influence on foreign policy, which was otherwise great in view of Roosevelt's temperamental openness to opinions from outside the professional establishment and his permission—sometimes encouragement—to ambassadors, especially his handpicked men, to report directly to him. As it turned out, Kennedy got on well with both Chamberlain and Halifax, with whom he came to share—at least for a time—a basic foreign policy outlook. But this was not assured from the start. As Rabbi Stephen Wise wrote from London, in reporting to Roosevelt the first impressions Kennedy was making: "These British will hear . . . language from him to which their dainty ears are not accustomed. He must have said some things to the godly Halifax at their first meeting which that plaster saint of 1938 will not speedily forget."[21]

Halifax and Kennedy had barely settled in their new posts when Hitler delivered a rude shock to Europe by invading and annexing Austria. Anglo-American contacts during the *Anschluss* crisis mainly took the form of British reports to Washington on their perception of the situation in central Europe. Lindsay also reported from Washington about American reactions both to Germany's behavior and Britain's response.

Two Halifax telegrams to Lindsay, for the information of Roosevelt, reveal the depth of British disappointment with the course of events in Austria. The first described an interview with German Foreign Minister Ribbentrop on March 10, from which it was apparent that Germany's attitude was anything but conciliatory and constructive. Ribbentrop had said that the most useful contribution Britain could make to the situation in Austria was to influence Chancellor Schuschnigg to cancel a scheduled

20. See Jane K. Vieth, "Joseph P. Kennedy at the Court of St. James's: The Diplomacy of a Boston Irishman"; David E. Koskoff, *Joseph P. Kennedy: A Life and Times*, pp. 114–18.

21. Wise to Roosevelt, 4 March 1938, PSF: Great Britain, Box 29.

plebiscite (clearly designed to forestall a German move to absorb his nation). This suggestion Halifax found "astonishing," and Chamberlain was prompted to lament: " . . . In talking to Ribbentrop I am always overcome by a feeling of helplessness. He is so stupid, so shallow, so self-centered and self-satisfied, so totally devoid of intellectual capacity that he never seems to take in what is said to him." The second telegram frankly admitted that the German action in Austria rendered further negotiation with the Germans impossible, at least for some time to come. Their brutal disregard of any argument but force showed the difficulty of reasoning with them and cast doubt upon the value of agreements reached with them. Britain had protested Germany's action but did not expect it to have any useful result. The world had been presented with a fait accompli that no threat unsupported by force could have averted. And a threat supported by force, if ignored in Berlin, would have plunged Europe into war. In these circumstances, Halifax concluded with disarming candor, he was "bound to confess" the failure of one of the twin efforts that the British had been anxious to make in order to prepare the way for an appeasement, and on account of which President Roosevelt had been asked to postpone his January initiative.[22]

On receiving Halifax's messages, Welles told Lindsay that the president was "revolted" by Germany's behavior. But with the situation in Europe so complicated and obscure, and the president limited by public opinion, it was unlikely that the United States would make any move at the moment. As for Roosevelt's earlier initiative, the opportunity had passed and was not likely to recur. Welles did not say so, but many State Department officials apparently believed that Hitler's action would have its own backfire effect by weakening his relationship with Italy. Moffat recorded that Hull, Herbert Feis (an economic adviser), and he were "about the only three in the building who believe that the Rome-Berlin axis will survive."[23]

There was certainly no encouragement from London for Roosevelt to act in any way. Halifax told the cabinet that Foreign Office officials had wished to insert in his message to Roosevelt a passage saying that there might now be a breathing space, but if the forces of order could not be mobilized, Germany's action would be repeated in Czechoslovakia. But

22. Halifax to Lindsay, 11, 12 March 1938, FO 371/21526, pp. 20–21, 22–23; (also *FRUS,* 1938, 1:130–32); Neville to Hilda, 13 March 1938, NC 18/1/1041.

23. Lindsay to Foreign Office, 12 March 1938, FO 371/21526, p. 19. Cadogan minuted on Lindsay's message: "I think there is clearly nothing to be done on this." Halifax initialed without comment. *Moffat Papers,* p. 192.

he had deleted it because he thought the subject "required further exploration." And Kennedy was convinced that the United States "would be very foolish to try to mix in." The feeling was "almost unanimous among the top side people" that all they wanted from America was for her to stay prosperous and to build a strong navy: "they feel that time will take care of their position with the United States." He did, however, add that sometime (after Chamberlain had made the necessary political offers) Roosevelt would have to make "a world wide gesture and base it completely on an economic stand."[24]

Chamberlain told the cabinet that Hitler's action showed the futility of a country appealing to collective security and observed how fortunate it was for Roosevelt that he had held up the issue of his proposed message. In a letter to his sister next day, he wrote:

> . . . Those wretched Germans. I wished them at the bottom of the sea. . . . It is perfectly evident surely now that force is the only argument Germany understands and that "collective security" cannot offer any prospect of preventing such events until it can show a visible force of overwhelming strength backed by determination to use it. And if that is so, is it not obvious that force and determination are most effectively mobilized by alliances which don't require meetings at Geneva and resolutions by dozens of small nations who have no responsibilities? Heaven knows I don't want to get back to alliances but if Germany continues to behave as she has done lately she may drive us to it.

If the United States figured in his thinking here, he did not indicate it. Further, the prime minister could not refrain from lamenting that had Halifax been at the Foreign Office two months earlier, the *Anschluss* might have been prevented. Then he directed some choice words at Roosevelt: "What a fool Roosevelt would have looked had he launched his precious proposal. What would he have thought of us if we had encouraged him to publish it, as Anthony [Eden] was so eager to do? And how we too would have made ourselves the laughing stock of the world." If it occurred to Chamberlain that Roosevelt's plan might have made a difference in Germany's action, as he clearly believed that earlier conversations with Italy would have done, he did not reveal it.[25]

24. CAB 23/92, 12 March 1938, p. 352; Kennedy to Roosevelt, 11 March 1938, PSF: Great Britain, Box 29.

25. CAB 23/92, 12 March 1938, p. 349; Neville to Hilda, 13 March 1938, NC 18/1/1041. Oliver Harvey, in the Foreign Office, thought that if Roosevelt's plan had been launched in January, the events in Austria would not have occurred, and considered this "perhaps the worst of the P.M.'s blunders" (*Harvey Diaries*, p. 117).

The sudden absorption of Austria into the German Reich, and still more the methods of Hitler in accomplishing it, created in the British government—as Sir John Simon wrote in his diary—"so much alarm that for some days there was widespread uncertainty . . . as to what we should do or say."[26] But with Czechoslovakia quickly emerging as the next focal point of attention and anxious expressions about future British policy emanating from Parliament, press, and public, it was necessary to formulate quickly and announce a policy position toward central Europe. This was agreed upon in a series of Foreign Policy Committee and cabinet meetings, March 18–23, and announced by Chamberlain to the House of Commons on March 24. Vague in certain particulars and negative in general orientation, its basic thrust was clear enough. Under pressure from Britain and France, Czechoslovakia was to come to terms—whatever they might entail—with its disaffected Sudeten German minority, thereby removing another German grievance and smoothing the way for Anglo-German understanding. Rejecting the notion that the European scene had radically changed, eschewing any serious reappraisal of policy and strategy, and proceeding largely without the benefit of considered professional advice from within or consultation abroad, Chamberlain and his colleagues determined not to abandon or modify the policy of appeasement, still essentially untested as a cure for Europe's ills, but to pursue it more assiduously. Thus the British government embarked on the road to Munich. The twists and turns in the next six months of traveling notwithstanding, the destination had been firmly fixed.[27]

In the formulation of Britain's position toward central Europe and Czechoslovakia in particular, the policy and position of the United States was not a factor in open discussion. Indeed, reference to America is conspicuous by its absence from both the Foreign Policy Committee and cabinet minutes, as well as from Chamberlain's correspondence with his sisters—in which he returned very quickly to the idea of dealing again with Germany.[28] It must therefore be assumed that the British

26. Simon Diary, no. 11, 24 March 1938.

27. See Rock, *British Appeasement in the 1930s*, pp. 6–7, and Rock, *Appeasement on Trial*, pp. 60–61. The formulation of this policy is traced in detail in Keith Middlemas, *Diplomacy of Illusion: The British Government and Germany, 1937–39*, pp. 182–97, and Ian Colvin, *The Chamberlain Cabinet*, pp. 106–15.

28. See CAB 23/93, 22, 23 March 1938, and CAB 27/623, 15, 18, 21 March 1938. Chamberlain wrote his sister that helping Czechoslovakia would simply be a pretext for going to war with Germany and he could not think of that in the absence of any reasonable prospect of being able to beat her in a reasonable time. But if he dealt with the Germans again and talked bluntly to them, they might listen. It would at least postpone a crisis and perhaps avert it. NC 18/1/1042, 20 March 1938.

government, convinced that there was nothing it could do to help Czechoslovakia and intent upon giving appeasement a fuller trial, saw no role for the United States in developing European affairs and continued to assume that it could be depended upon for nothing and was therefore best discounted.

Had there been an inclination among the British to take the United States more positively into their calculations, it would have been arrested by Lindsay's reports from Washington. In the period March 16–22, he informed the Foreign Office that the impact of recent European developments on America was only to increase isolationism. There was, to be sure, widespread condemnation of Hitler's action and a certain resurgence of pro-British feeling that sprang from an acknowledged community of interest on broad issues. Further, Hull's speech of March 17 to the National Press Club decried the rising tide of international lawlessness, rejected isolation at any price, and quoted Roosevelt to the effect that there must be positive efforts to preserve peace in which America must play a part. But most sections of the press severely criticized the British government and Chamberlain's "realistic policy," which had already met its first spectacular failure, brought Britain's prestige to its lowest ebb, and moved the country one step nearer to a new world war—all the while thanking God for the Atlantic Ocean. Congress was becoming more independent of the president, critical of his administration, and edgy about an alleged understanding with Britain. Thus, Lindsay wrote: "the Administration is weakened in its power of leadership at the very moment when world events make it important that its authority should be strong." Roosevelt himself was no doubt anxious to carry on the education of public opinion begun at Chicago, but even he had reportedly referred to Chamberlain as "a Wall Street man," one who coldly surveys a situation and deliberately takes his decisions in the manner best calculated to serve his own interests. Although the scoldings to which Britain was being subjected might (in Lindsay's opinion) arise partly from a genuine affection as well as a guilty conscience spawned by America's own "unheroic attitude," this was of limited consolation in the circumstances of the moment.[29]

On the American side, little confidence could be gained from a London embassy dispatch quoting Colonel Ismay, deputy secretary to the Committee on Imperial Defence: the British empire was threatened by a

29. Lindsay to Foreign Office, 18 March 1938, FO 371/21526, p. 9; Lindsay to Halifax, 21, 22 March 1938, FO 414/275, pp. 130–32; FO 115/3415, File 17; FO 115/3416, File 587; Lindsay to Cadogan, 22 March 1938, FO 115/3415, File 112.

coalition of three totalitarian powers; to preserve the empire, this coalition needed to be weakened immediately by detaching one or more of its members; any Englishman who did not cooperate in this policy was unpatriotic and failing in his duty. Chargé Johnson thought this accurately reflected the opinion of the CID and enormously influenced the prime minister. (We now know this to be true on both counts.) No wonder Moffat recorded: "British reaction . . . is, of course, the key to the whole situation and with each day that passes it becomes clearer that England is willing to surrender Eastern Europe to German ambitions."[30]

Roosevelt's first impulse upon hearing of the *Anschluss* was to issue a statement of condemnation, but he withheld it upon the advice of Welles. The State Department was divided in its reaction: one-half was inclined to follow an uncompromising moral line that might eventually involve war on Britain's side, the other half (including Welles) was still hoping to direct matters toward an ultimate conference. The president at length, not wishing to jeopardize "certain political appeasements in Europe" by alienating the Germans altogether, limited Hull to a guarded statement of American opposition to anything that endangered peace and a few guarded measures affecting Austrian trade and facilitating the migration of political refugees from Austria and Germany.[31] But he was not entirely happy with that. In response to a Cudahy letter from Dublin decrying the destruction of Europe's power balance and denouncing Chamberlain's "weak, vacillating, humiliating policy," he wrote:

> Over here there is the same element that exists in London. Unfortunately, it is led by many of your friends and mine. They would really like me to be a Neville Chamberlain—and if I would promise that, the market would go up and they would work positively and actively for the resumption of prosperity. But if that were done, we would only be breeding far more serious trouble four or eight years from now.[32]

Meantime, Chamberlain had recovered his composure and was feeling optimistic again. His letter of March 27 to sister Hilda radiated the week's success: the decisions on Czechoslovakia (in which, he said, military considerations were most important), his policy statement in the

30. Johnson to Hull, 21 March 1938, SDM 841.00/1363; *Moffat Papers,* p. 192.

31. Berle, *Navigating the Rapids,* p. 169; Dallek, *Roosevelt and American Foreign Policy,* p. 158.

32. Cudahy to Roosevelt, 6 April 1938; Roosevelt to Cudahy, 16 April 1938, PSF: Ireland, Box 44.

Commons (he could not remember a speech by a British minister in time of crisis that had won "such universal approval in Europe"), the rallying of his colleagues to his support, and so on. He was cheerful and confident at having "got over another fence." His own buoyant spirit must have appeared in sharp contrast to Lord Tweedsmuir's late March assessment of politics and economics in America, where, he wrote to Chamberlain, there appeared to be "a general break-down of nerve . . . in all classes," the worst sign being that people had stopped abusing the president "as though they felt he was in as bad a hole as they themselves."[33]

Anglo-Italian conversations, which had been under way in Rome since March 8, culminated in a mid-April agreement covering a wide range of conflicting interests and provided that implementation would follow only upon Italian acceptance of a British scheme for evacuating "volunteers" from Spain and fulfillment of a British promise to take the lead at Geneva toward the recognition of Italian Abyssinia. Lord Perth kept the United States informed of developments through William Phillips, the American ambassador in Rome. But there was never any question of Britain's deferring to United States' disapproval of de jure recognition in Abyssinia; that had long been taken by Chamberlain and others as a sine qua non of successful conversations, was fully accepted (however unhappily) by Halifax, and was reaffirmed in the Foreign Policy Committee meeting of March 1, on the condition that agreement was reached on all other outstanding questions between the two governments.[34]

But in entering the conversations with Italy, the British were not unmindful of America's position and sensitivities. Halifax instructed Lindsay to let the United States government know that though the British felt compelled to tackle the improvement of relations with Italy and Germany piecemeal, for any real and lasting betterment of the situation it would doubtless be desirable to seek "some scheme of general cooperation in Europe, both political and economic. If the United States Government could at any time see their way to assist or encourage such a development, that would evidently be of the greatest value." Further,

33. Neville to Hilda, 27 March 1938, NC 18/1/1043; Tweedsmuir to Chamberlain, 26 March 1938, NC 7/11/31/281.

34. Phillips to Hull, 8 March 1938, *FRUS*, 1938, 1:139–41; CAB 27/623, 1 March 1938, p. 126. On an earlier acceptance of de jure recognition as essential to successful negotiations, see for example: Record of a Meeting in the Secretary of State's Room, 10 August 1937, PREM 1/276; Chamberlain's undated notes for a conversation with Eden and Halifax on 25 August 1937, PREM 1/276; Chamberlain to Leo Amery, 15 November 1937, NC 7/2/72.

the United States government would be kept fully informed of the process of negotiations "so that they may, if they will, help us with their advice or criticism, and so that the President may, if he is so disposed, judge whether at any point it might be opportune for him to take independent but correlated action," in which case it was hoped that Britain would be given warning of any initiative that he might contemplate. A rather audacious message in view of Britain's handling of Roosevelt's January proposal, it is not surprising that it generated no particular response aside from Welles's retort that it had taken the British government a good many years to comprehend the truth of what Lindsay was now saying.[35]

As the conversations with Italy drew to a conclusion, Chamberlain wished to see the United States "specially treated" by being notified of the terms of the agreement at the same time as France and the dominions. But the British also had a favor to ask of Roosevelt. Speaking privately to Kennedy, Halifax said how great a help it would be if, when the terms of agreement were made public, the president could say a word in commendation of them as a contribution to peace. And how helpful it would be if he added something about the justification for recognizing facts in Abyssinia, since (for reasons he had never understood) American spokesmen were generally held to be more moral than Englishmen, and consequently anything the president might say on these lines would have effect. In reporting this to Lindsay, Halifax doubted that Roosevelt would do it. But Kennedy tried, assuring Roosevelt through Hull that "Chamberlain and Halifax and the present British government highly regard the influence of the President and yourself throughout the world."[36]

In sending the agreement to Washington on April 15, Halifax repeated his plea, hoping that Roosevelt would share his own and Chamberlain's view that it embodied "a real contribution towards world appeasement," and would thus approve publicly both the agreement and the principles that had inspired it. Welles and the State Department seemed initially

35. Halifax to Lindsay, 3 March 1938, FO 371/21526, pp. 28–31; Welles to Roosevelt, 8 March 1938, *FRUS*, 1938, 1:127–30.

36. CAB 27/623, 29 March 1938, p. 249; Halifax to Lindsay, 6 April 1938, FO 414/275, p. 135; Kennedy to Hull, 6 April 1938, PSF: Great Britain, Box 20. See also CAB 27/623, 7 April 1938, p. 279. If Britain was prepared to blink American objections to Abyssinian recognition, it was equally willing to do so with France. Halifax told the Foreign Policy Committee that France might give "violent opposition" to that provision in the agreement, but the Foreign Office thought it should be disregarded and Britain should proceed at Geneva as though it had obtained France's full concurrence (CAB 27/623, 29 March 1938, p. 249).

sympathetic to the agreement, so Lindsay informed London; Welles, in fact, reportedly said that he could see nothing in it to which the United States government could take exception. Although this reflected the personal position of Welles, supported by Ambassadors Kennedy (London) and Phillips (Rome)—all of whom now believed the opportunity to weaken the Italo-German combination to be the predominant consideration—there was another view. Immediately before the signing of the agreement, Roosevelt had arranged for a congressional resolution asking the administration to name all the nations that had violated treaties with the United States. The inclusion of Italy provided a way for him to reemphasize American opposition to recognizing the Abyssinian conquest. Within the State Department, Hull and Moffat considered it unwise for Washington to identify with British policy; and the concession that Roosevelt ultimately made during Hull's absence from the capital resulted in rumors that the secretary might resign (although it was unlikely that Hull would want to depart and leave an open field for his sometime adversary Welles). Welles at length persuaded the president that silence would seem tantamount to rebuke, that Britain was "on the spot" and deserved to be given moral support. So Roosevelt agreed to say something. But the statement they produced and Roosevelt issued at his press conference on April 19 was tepid and noncommittal. So, in fact, was the manner in which Roosevelt delivered it. When asked by a reporter whether there was any comment on the Anglo-Italian accord, the president responded: "Yes, by Jove, there is. I forgot it. I will see if I can find it. I have a perfectly good comment. Here it is right here." The statement read:

> As this Government has on frequent occasions made it clear, the United States . . . believes in the promotion of world peace through the friendly solution by peaceful negotiation between nations of controversies which may arise between them. It has also urged the promotion of peace through the finding of means for economic appeasement. It does not attempt to pass upon the political features of accords such as that recently reached between Great Britain and Italy, but this Government has seen the conclusion of an agreement with sympathetic interest because it is proof of the value of peaceful negotiations.

The president concluded: "I think that covers it all right."[37]

37. Kennedy to Hull, 15 April 1938, PSF: Great Britain, Box 29; Lindsay to Halifax, 19 April 1938, FO 115/3415, File 135; Hull, *Memoirs,* 1:581–82; Welles to Roosevelt, 18 April 1938, PSF: Great Britain, Box 29; *FDR Press Conferences,* 19 April 1938, 11:321–22; MacDonald, *The United States, Britain, and Appeasement,* pp. 77–78; Dallek, *Franklin Roosevelt and American Foreign Policy,* p. 158.

Roosevelt had not lost his distaste for the recognition of Italian Abyssinia—which, in fact, the United States never extended. But he sympathized with Britain up to a point and felt a certain pressure to help; and the ambiguous statement, cavalierly delivered, was his way of finding a middle ground between rejection and support of appeasement. This left Moffat muttering that "in one breath we praise the British for getting together with the Italians, in the next breath we imply that the Italians are treaty breakers and unworthy to be dealt with on a footing of equality." When the French ambassador sought the meaning of Roosevelt's statement, Welles explained that it was the method of finding the solution in which the president had expressed sympathetic interest, not the contents of the agreement itself. And Roosevelt showed no disposition in the days that followed to dissuade cabinet members from condemning fascism in public speeches, as Welles thought useful. But the net effect of it all, perceptively stated by a recent Roosevelt scholar, was to leave the president "largely immobilized in foreign affairs."[38]

Though perhaps the normal stuff of diplomacy, a few minor issues arose during early 1938 that demonstrated the caution and equivocation that characterized Anglo-American relations. The proposal that President Roosevelt be awarded an honorary degree by London University commanded Foreign Office attention lest it imply that Roosevelt was accepting favors at the hands of the British. When the matter was dropped by the university, Foreign Office officials considered it "a good thing."[39] Likewise, the Foreign Office was deeply concerned about a possible visit of former President Herbert Hoover to England. Though Hoover was "a back number," Roosevelt's feelings about political opponents were "notoriously vindictive," and he might think the British were intentionally embarrassing him. Even Hull's assurance to the contrary was interpreted as possibly showing generosity after the event; and

38. Memorandum by Welles, 20 April 1938, *FRUS*, 1938, 1:148; Dallek, *Franklin Roosevelt and American Foreign Policy*, p. 158. Welles told the Chinese ambassador that although the United States government had long opposed recognition of territory acquired by force, it would "consider the question in its broadest aspect" if it independently reached the conclusion that recognition was an essential part of world appeasement (Memorandum by Welles, 18 April 1938, *FRUS*, 1938, 1:145–46). When Roosevelt was questioned again in his press conference of 10 May about the significance of his statement, he declined further comment (*FDR Press Conferences*, 11:410–11). Ambassador Phillips had written from Rome a few days earlier that what seemed uppermost in the minds of all Italians was a spirit of thankfulness that the past hostile attitude toward England had been allowed to disappear (Phillips to Roosevelt, 5 May 1938, PSF: Italy, Box 32).

39. Foreign Office Minutes, 21 January, 8 February 1938, FO 371/21541, pp. 36–39.

in any case, both the Foreign Office and the American embassy were concerned that the United States press might misinterpret the visit and cause trouble. It was hoped that Hoover would understand the British attitude, although that was of considerably less consequence.[40] When Captain Ingersoll's visit was at length discussed in the press, the Foreign Office News Department, by prearrangement, said only that his purpose was consultation with the Admiralty regarding capital ship construction. Officials worried, lest this give the United States government the impression that Britain was trying to belittle what it was doing for naval cooperation, and sought Lindsay's counsel on the matter.[41] But Henry Morgenthau's prompt and positive response to an "indirect suggestion" from Lindsay that he visit England met with mixed reactions in London. Simon thought the general effect of such a visit would be good, but only if it occurred on "a purely informal footing" and after the signing of the trade agreement then under negotiation; otherwise, it would almost certainly give rise to embarrassing rumors. Lindsay himself retreated in view of Simon's reaction and rumors in Washington that Kennedy would stay in London only a year and that Morgenthau hoped to succeed him. He did not think Morgenthau would make a good ambassador and did not want to encourage his ambition by "promoting a preliminary canter." The whole idea eventually collapsed over failure to find a mutually convenient time for the visit, Simon holding out for "a day or two" in late July or the second half of October and Morgenthau not being able to make those times.[42]

Lindsay was also in doubt about what to make of a foreign affairs debate in the United States Senate on January 31–February 1. The old guard isolationists (led by Senators Lewis, Johnson, and Borah) carried the discussion, complaining about the term "quarantine," deploring Eden's implication (as they interpreted it) of the previous December that Britain and the United States had a working alliance, and lamenting about recent unnamed visitors from Britain spreading propaganda to the effect that only such an alliance could keep peace in the world. This was all pretty discouraging, yet Lindsay saw grounds for hope. The heavy isolationist artillery having been fired, very little resulted. Senator

40. Foreign Office Minutes, 31 January, 3, 12 February 1938, FO 371/21543, pp. 90, 101, 107–8.

41. Foreign Office to Lindsay, 28 January 1938, FO 371/21526, pp. 67, 70.

42. Foreign Office Minutes and Foreign Office-Treasury-Lindsay correspondence, 11 February–22 March 1938, FO 371/21544, pp. 332–48.

Pittman, speaking for the administration, defined American foreign policy "in terms far more liberal than those usually inferred from the historical dicta of George Washington," merely stipulating nonintervention in the domestic relations and in the local affairs of other governments. And this surprising departure from time-honored formulas had passed without criticism. Back in the Foreign Office, J. G. S. Beith (third secretary) found the tone of this debate "extremely hopeful"; Britain had every reason to be pleased so long as Senators Borah and Johnson were not provided further ammunition by unguarded statements from London. But another (unidentifiable) official minuted that the debate showed how dangerous it was for the British "to attempt to interpret the pronouncements of American statesmen and to express any strong or definite opinion on the community of Anglo-United States interests." And Eden could hardly have been reassured by Hull's request for a clarifying comment in response to Borah's remarks—which was supplied.[43]

Of greater long-term importance was the fact that the mutual suspicions and misgivings in Anglo-American relations did not deter the British from exploring the possibility of purchasing military aircraft in the United States. This prospect emerged, at the urging of Lord Swinton, secretary of state for air, at the March 24 meeting of the Committee on Imperial Defence. The cabinet recommended that Swinton's proposal to send a confidential mission to the United States should be reexamined in broader terms of purchasing war materials more generally. But this was deemed a complicating factor by the CID, both because of American neutrality provisions and the need to encourage British production of arms and munitions. So the mission that Swinton arranged to sail during the third week of April was concerned mainly with precise details about, and potential delivery dates of, airplanes. But enthusiasm for this venture was restrained. There was concern in the cabinet that dispatch of the mission, along with the initiation of staff conversations with France and the development of the Sudeten German problem in Czechoslovakia, might alarm and provoke Hitler. Chamberlain played down the mission in his important meetings with the chief French ministers, Daladier and Bonnet, in London, April 28–29, describing its purpose "to investigate

43. Lindsay to Eden, 2 February 1938, FO 414/275, pp. 96–97 (also FO 115/3415, File 35); Foreign Office Minutes, 10 February 1938, FO 371/21525, p. 377; Hull to U.S. Embassy in London, 2 February 1938, SDM 711.41/377A.

the possibility of making use of the American aircraft industry" but not to purchase planes.[44]

Other issues of importance tempered Anglo-American relations during the early part of 1938, including negotiations for a trade agreement, which had been under way for some time, and disputes over the sovereignty of certain Pacific islands. These are treated elsewhere.

44. CAB 2/7 (CID), 24, 31 March 1938; CAB 23/93, 30 March, 13, 27 April 1938, pp. 87–88, 166–67, 202–3; Record of Anglo-French Conversations, 28–29 April 1938, *Documents on British Foreign Policy, 1919–1939,* Third Series (hereafter *B.D.*), 1:203–7. Word of the proposal to purchase airplanes in the United States prompted a strong protest from the chairman of the Society of British Aircraft Constructors Ltd., who saw this as highly detrimental to Britain's own aircraft industry (C. Bruce Gardner to Swinton, 14 April 1938, PREM 1/236).

V.
The Czech Crisis

FOLLOWING THE ANGLO-ITALIAN Agreement, Roosevelt remained immobilized in foreign affairs until the Czech situation began to assume dangerously explosive proportions. Preoccupied with finding a recovery plan for a half-year recession (which had forced several million Americans back into unemployment); defending himself against highly exaggerated charges of dictatorial designs (which arose from congressional discussion of his proposal for reorganizing executive agencies); working hard for new labor laws, an antitrust investigation, and the defeat of conservative Democrats in state primaries, Roosevelt had little time and energy for foreign affairs and certainly did not want to stir up additional problems by any determined involvement in them. He underwent considerable domestic pressure to reform American neutrality laws, especially to repeal the Spanish arms embargo; but despite his sympathy for the Spanish Republic, he refused to take any initiative and supported the scuttling of the Nye resolution—which would have lifted the Spanish embargo—in the Senate Foreign Relations Committee. His concern for Catholic and isolationist votes, as well as a feeling that it was too late to do any good in Spain (and perhaps China as well) and no time to challenge a recalcitrant Congress (which had sharply rebuffed his scheme for reorganization) certainly figured in his thinking. Nor was Secretary Hull anxious to reverse a policy that had kept the United States "out of a European mess" or to assume leadership in European matters that he thought the prerogative of Britain and France. The United States had enough problems to deal with at home and should not be watching for opportunities to meddle in dangerous situations abroad. In any case, he would defer to the president's position.[1]

1. Dallek, *Franklin Roosevelt and American Foreign Policy*, pp. 158–61.

Meantime, there was certainly no encouragement from London for change in America's posture, and when Roosevelt moved modestly to influence things in August and September, the impetus did not come from Britain. In the wake of the *Anschluss,* the British government acknowledged the need for a fresh review of the nation's defense program; and there was considerable sparring in the cabinet over the scope of rearmament—the lines essentially drawn between those (including the service ministers) who favored increased military preparedness and those (including Treasury officials and the prime minister) who saw the nation's economic strength, unendangered by heavy increases in military expenditure, as the first line of defense. The upshot was no important change in the tempo of defense preparation and an undiminished reliance on diplomacy to protect the nation.[2] Put another way, the months that followed the *Anschluss* witnessed an extension of Chamberlain's efforts to appease the dictators in which he envisaged no particular role for the United States. He was certain that American interference in this endeavor would only complicate matters by antagonizing Hitler and Mussolini. Even if American support—mainly of a "moral" variety—were desirable, it was widely accepted by British officials that such support could not be cultivated by British propaganda or obtained by British promptings. It must grow naturally in American minds and hearts in response to the course of events. Whether Chamberlain was influenced more by his confident desire to proceed alone or his conviction that the United States could do nothing useful is moot. These considerations reinforced each other and pointed to the same conclusion.

British policy toward Czechoslovakia having been set by March 24 and French concurrence having been obtained (not without difficulty) during the Daladier-Bonnet visit to London a month later—during which the British persuasively argued Anglo-French inability to defend Czechoslovakia militarily and the impossibility of reestablishing the nation in its current form even in the event of a successful war—it remained only to see what would happen next. Britain's position was ambiguous. Two weeks before, Chamberlain had described for Joseph Kennedy his conviction that Germany did not possess sufficient resources or reserves to go to war, and it knew it. Germany was like a boa constrictor that had eaten a large meal and was now lying back to digest it; thus, he saw no difficulties in the near future. This appraisal was no doubt puzzling

2. Rock, *British Appeasement in the 1930s,* p. 8. The debate over rearmament is described in detail in Shay, *British Rearmament in the Thirties.*

to Washington, which had recently received from Chargé Johnson in London confidential information that Germany would inevitably "settle" the Czech problem as soon as the right psychological moment arrived. The latter view corresponded to the judgment of Assistant Secretary of State George Messersmith, who saw Germany proceeding on a fixed course and a definite policy that could "only mean the gradual disintegration of the British Empire." No concession would satisfy her. Thus Britain's attitude was hard to understand. And equally discouraging was the failure of the American public to grasp the implications of it all—a failure that constituted "the most difficult problem with which [Washington] now [had] to deal."[3]

If Chamberlain really believed there would be no difficulties regarding Czechoslovakia in the near future, he was mistaken. During the third week of May, negotiations between the Czech government and Sudeten German leaders (now known to have been operating under instructions from Berlin, with the ultimate objective of destroying the Czechoslovak state) broke down amid a suddenly deteriorating situation in the Sudetenland and rumors of German troop movements, which made another lightning German coup appear to be impending. The British policy of pressuring Prague could not succeed if Germany refused to wait, and London issued a surprisingly stiff warning to Berlin about the possible consequences of precipitous action. The crisis passed—Germany had not ordered an attack—and Chamberlain wrote his sister what a "d——d close run thing" it was. Convinced that Germany had made all the necessary preparations for a coup and had turned back only upon receiving Britain's warning, he admitted that the incident showed "how utterly untrustworthy and dishonest the German Government is." Beset with gout and thoroughly discouraged, he wondered about the use of his continuing in office, although he did not see anyone who could replace him "without undermining confidence." Ensuing deliberations with his ministers quickly revealed there would be no new direction in British policy. The fitful warning to Germany, issued on impulse, on Halifax's initiative, in a moment of high crisis was qualified in word and discarded in practice before the week was out; and the lesson drawn from the crisis by Chamberlain and his colleagues was not the need hereafter to

3. Kennedy to Hull, 11 April 1938, *FRUS*, 1938, 1:43–44; Johnson to Hull, 22 March 1938, SDM 741.62/258; Memorandum by Messersmith, 18 February 1938, *FRUS*, 1938, 1:19–21.

restrain Hitler by firmness but to do everything necessary to avoid its repetition, since next time the outcome would be worse.[4]

In British deliberations during the May crisis, there was no mention of the United States or Roosevelt; and the president, for his part, remained mute throughout. He was pressed to intercede both by Bullitt and Hugh Wilson, the new American ambassador in Berlin. Bullitt, himself being pressed by a frantic Bonnet, urged an Anglo-French-German-Italian conference (with a United States representative attending) in The Hague, where they would probably decide upon a Czech plebiscite. Even if the Czechs refused, France would be freed from its "desperate moral dilemma" (its reluctance to fight versus its alliance commitment to Czechoslovakia) and there would be no war. He recognized that Roosevelt might be accused of selling out the Czechs, but thought it essential for the sake of peace. Wilson proposed representations in Prague and Berlin in support of "a peaceful solution." Roosevelt did not reply to these proposals. As Robert Dallek has succinctly put it: "Reluctant to counsel appeasement, or to urge anyone else to fight, he remained a detached observer."[5]

This does not mean that Anglo-American relations had worsened. In fact, there were several developments of a positive sort at this juncture. Three "Agreements" signed in late April by Britain and Ireland (settling some long-standing differences between them) were cordially welcomed in the United States, where, Lindsay noted, "the O's and the Macs" were still numerous enough to make politicians find it worthwhile to testify from time to time to their affection for Ireland and their sympathy for Irish aspirations. Chamberlain had met a dozen American newspapermen—"hard-boiled toughs," he called them in a letter to his sister—at a luncheon arranged by the Astors and gave them both a more accurate appreciation of his own personality and better information on the situation in Europe. He did not, however, know whether this would result in "a more accurate account of what we are after." When Lindsay reported Secretary of the Interior Ickes's adamant refusal to sell helium gas to the German Zepplin Corporation, the response of the Foreign Office officials was a resounding "Good for Mr. Ickes!" And they noted with interest—and skepticism—the opinion of James Dunn, political

4. Rock, *British Appeasement in the 1930s,* pp. 8–9; Neville to Hilda, 22 May 1938; Neville to Ida, 28 May 1938; NC 18/1/1053–54.

5. Offner, *American Appeasement,* pp. 249–50; Dallek, *Franklin Roosevelt and American Foreign Policy,* p. 162; *FRUS,* 1938, 1:506–7, 509–15, 519–20.

adviser in the State Department (offered privately to the British military attaché), that in the event of Britain's becoming involved in a serious situation in Europe, the expression of American public opinion would be sufficient to prompt almost immediate United States cooperation. Reports on the efforts of the British mission to America to investigate aircraft purchases, which filtered back to London throughout the month of May, revealed friendly and cooperative receptions by large American firms. Hesitations in the cabinet, ranging from technical questions of construction to the acquisition of suitable bombs and ammunition in the event of war, were met by an important political argument advanced by Halifax: the purchase of American planes, "with its implication that America was behind us," had already had a useful effect in Germany. As a result, in early June the British government signed contracts with two American companies, Lockheed and North American, for 400 aircraft (200 bomber reconnaissance planes and 200 trainer service planes).[6]

None of this, of course, did anything to alter fundamental postures; and there were developments of another kind as well. United States press reaction to the mid-May proceedings at Geneva (where Britain sponsored a proposal by which members of the League were freed to recognize Italian sovereignty over Abyssinia independently at their own discretion) re-echoed the censure of several months before; and Hull declared emphatically that United States policy remained "absolutely unchanged." Walter Lippmann concluded (in a column that Lindsay sent to London and Foreign Office personnel found "worthy of note") that the effect of this was to dispel any impression that the United States was supporting the Chamberlain policy and to render collaboration between Britain and America in world politics less effective than had been anticipated. Some State Department officials derided Britain's urging of the Czechs to be reasonable. As one of them expressed it: "When you want to make the lion lie down with the lamb, there is not much point in beating the lamb." On the British side, all departments of the government (Sir Warren Fisher, head of the Civil Service, informed Kennedy) had been advised to proceed independently on war plans without looking for any support from America. The latter was hardly surprising in view of the cabinet's reluctance to discuss economic collaboration in the event

6. Lindsay to Halifax, 9 May 1938, FO 115/3415, File No. 8; Neville to Ida, 13 May 1938, NC 18/1/1051; FO 371/21547, p. 73; Lindsay to Halifax, 24 May 1938, FO 115/3415, File 112, and FO 371/21526, p. 218; AIR 19/39, May 1938; CAB 23/93, 18, 25 May 1938, pp. 318–19, 360–61.

of war even with France lest it give the impression of being directed against Germany.[7] Churchill's poetic imagery was near the mark when he wrote in *News of the World* (May 15) about the "majestic edifice of Anglo-American friendship" on which "the facing stone has been eaten away by acids in the atmosphere" and the appearance of "cracks in the Pillars which support the mighty dome."

While Czech–Sudeten German negotiations smoldered during June and July, British hopes for appeasement ran strong. Though Halifax alerted the Foreign Policy Committee on June 1 to the probability that German economic influence would penetrate throughout central and southeastern Europe and lead to political domination as well, Chamberlain questioned both this basic premise and the assumption that it was possible for Britain to do something about it. The small countries did not want to be dominated by Germany, yet they were quite prepared to claim that it was about to happen in order to gain concessions from Britain, who must therefore be very careful not to be misled. In the face of a growing belief in the cabinet that a solution of the Czech minority problem would not in itself ensure peace and that Czechoslovakia's pacts of assistance with France and Russia were a source of trouble, Halifax, for his part, began to contemplate readjustments in Czechoslovakia's external relations to meet Germany's professed sensitivities. Here was a new refinement in appeasement, proposing concessions that would greatly strengthen the position of the aggrieved before they had even been requested. But a lack of response from France stymied this idea for a time. Then mid-July brought what Chamberlain called "the most encouraging move from Berlin" that he had heard of to date: a proposal from Hitler, carried to London by his personal adjutant, Captain Fritz Wiedemann, that he send over one of his top men (probably Göring) for unofficial conversations looking toward a comprehensive Anglo-German agreement. Halifax, with Chamberlain's blessing, declared the current moment of tension over Czechoslovakia unpropitious for such a visit, though a Czech settlement, or a German renunciation of force in Czechoslovakia, would certainly change things. But Wiedemann's visit produced nothing; British efforts to follow it up, by way of Anglo-German cooperation in promoting a peaceful settlement in Czechoslovakia, elicited no response from Berlin.[8]

7. Lindsay to Halifax, 19 May 1938, FO 115/3415, File No. 35; 31 May 1938, FO 371/21526, p. 213; Berle, *Navigating the Rapids,* p. 177; Kennedy to Hull, 16 May 1938, SDM 741.62/270; CAB 23/93, 27 April 1938, p. 207.

8. CAB 27/623, 1 June 1938, pp. 284–86; F. S. Northedge, *The Troubled Giant: Britain among the Great Powers, 1916–1939,* pp. 512–13; Neville to Ida, 16 July 1938, NC 18/1/1060.

In mid-July a dangerous breakdown of negotiations occurred in Prague, which prompted Chamberlain to initiate a scheme for mediation that had been under consideration for some weeks. Lord Runciman, a respected English liberal and lord president in Chamberlain's cabinet, was pressed into service—with the quick approval of France and the grudging consent of the Czechs—as an independent conciliator who would hear the facts and arguments and suggest expedients and modifications in the demands of both sides. Chamberlain saw this as a logical step in his plan to reduce the danger points in Europe and promote appeasement. Perhaps no one in authority realized how it would inevitably drag Britain into the forefront of the struggle between Germans and Slavs.[9]

Runciman's appointment was no doubt of interest to Roosevelt. Though he was busy campaigning against conservative opponents in Democratic primaries, he had not ceased to be concerned about European affairs. Already troubled by the course of events in Spain, where the Fascist rebels were winning—though he was unwilling to make any move (such as a lifting of the arms embargo) that might have influenced these events—he was particularly worried over reports that Hitler intended to force his will on the Czechs, even if it meant risking war. Beyond that, the president had established a good personal relationship with Runciman when the latter, as president of the Board of Trade, had visited Washington in January 1937. Runciman had come away believing Roosevelt anxious to maintain a degree of intimacy with the British government to which London should respond in full measure, and in which he might himself play a special role in view of the prominence of economic questions in Anglo-American relations. Roosevelt described Runciman as "a grand fellow" whose visit had "definitely helped things," kept up an intermittent correspondence with him, and may have shared in Runciman's bitter disappointment at Chamberlain's failure to name him to the Exchequer when he formed his first cabinet. Such an appointment would have constituted a potentially important British contact with Roosevelt; but Chamberlain, in naming Sir John Simon, had had other priorities in mind.[10]

When Runciman's mission to Prague was announced, Arthur Murray wrote Chamberlain that the appointment would surely please Roosevelt,

9. Rock, *British Appeasement in the 1930s,* pp. 9–10; Templewood, *Nine Troubled Years,* p. 298.

10. See various letters in the Runciman Papers, WR 284 and 285; Runciman to Baldwin, 8 February 1937, PREM 1/291; Dallek, *Franklin Roosevelt and American Foreign Policy,* p. 162.

and the contact established earlier might now prove helpful. The Foreign Office hoped so; Assistant Under-Secretary Sir Orme Sargent informed the United States embassy in London that it would be "extremely helpful" if Roosevelt "were to feel inclined to find some means of expressing his approval and commendation" of the Runciman mission. But Roosevelt was at that moment on holiday and not easily reached, so the first secretary told Sargent. Runciman himself wrote Roosevelt to explain the "new departure" of the British government firsthand. He felt "about to be set afloat in an open boat in a treacherous ocean" but nonetheless hoped to succeed. Actually, Roosevelt had no desire to comment on Runciman's assignment. Washington remembered all too well that the president's reluctant and lukewarm approval of the Anglo-Italian Agreement a few months before had been used by Chamberlain for partisan political purposes (in implying in Parliament an exaggerated degree of U.S. support for the agreement, presumably to help neutralize lingering criticism from the Eden resignation controversy) and by Halifax for diplomatic purposes (in proposing that the League of Nations free members to make independent decisions about the recognition of Italian Abyssinia). The Americans wanted to make no move that could associate them in any way with schemes to pressure Czechoslovakia. Further, the fallacy of Britain's claim that Runciman could (and would) act wholly independently of British government policy was recognized, and Washington wished to run no risk of being pressured itself to pressure the Czechs in the event they resisted Runciman's "solution"; that would only implicate America in a potential sellout. So Roosevelt chose to maintain his silence on the matter.[11]

There appeared at this juncture a problem for the British that would cause increasing difficulty with the passing of time: how much credence to give to Ambassador Kennedy's views on Anglo-American relations and European affairs generally, and how best to respond to his sometimes dubious or gratuitous personal judgments. Attuned to appeasement for reasons that included personal business ones, and anxious to cultivate the confidence and favor of Chamberlain and his like-minded coterie, Kennedy told Halifax in early May, prior to a summer visit home, that the change of feeling in the United States in the last two months in favor of British policy had been very great. He was going to "rub it in

11. Murray to Runciman, 27 July 1938, Runciman Papers, WR 284; Speaight (for the SSFA) to Lindsay, 2 August 1938, FO 115/3415, File 112; Runciman to Roosevelt, 28 July 1938, PSF: Great Britain, Box 25; MacDonald, *The United States, Britain, and Appeasement,* pp. 90–91.

to them all" in Washington that repeal of the Neutrality law (which would cost them nothing) was the one thing they could do to make Germany think. He returned to London in early July with what Chamberlain described as "the most roseate accounts of the change in American opinion in our favour & of the President's desire to do something to help." As Oliver Harvey (Foreign Office) understood it from Halifax, American opinion, which had earlier regarded Eden as the "second cousin of Jesus Christ," had now come around to a favorable view of the prime minister; Roosevelt, anxious to help whenever he could, intended to send a fleet into the Atlantic and, in event of war, to operate the Neutrality Act so as not to hurt Britain. Harvey doubted the accuracy of all this. Representatives of the American Institute of Foreign Affairs (admittedly a specialist body) had recently expressed to Halifax great misgivings about Chamberlain's attitude, and Eden had been enthusiastically received in a brief Independence Day speech to Americans in London. Nor does it seem that Chamberlain accepted Kennedy's comments at face value either. Appreciative of the ambassador's reports at a time when he needed a "moral uplift"—as much because of troublesome internal politics as external affairs—there is nothing to suggest that he changed his long-term views on American policy. Kennedy's credibility is thrown further into question by his naïve—and futile—summer attempts to visit Germany and achieve some kind of personal diplomatic triumph.[12]

There was little else in Britain's relations with America to suggest a change in outlook. A British proposal to establish an international commission to investigate bombardments resulting in civilian deaths in Spain, in which it was hoped the United States would participate, elicited no support in Washington. Hull told Lindsay that his government was more concerned with bombings in China, where American property was being destroyed; and Halifax reported to the cabinet on several occasions about the "hesitating" or "lukewarm" attitude of the United States that made it difficult for him to proceed with the proposal.[13] Likewise,

12. Halifax to Chamberlain, 6 May 1938, FO 800/328 (Halifax Papers), pp. 101–2; Neville to Hilda, 9 July 1938, NC 18/1/1059; CAB 23/94, 6 July 1938, p. 106; *Harvey Diaries,* p. 160; Kennedy to Hull, 6 July 1938, *FRUS,* 1938, 1:56–57; Offner, *American Appeasement,* pp. 251–54. Sir George Schuster, recently returned from an extensive tour of the United States, personally reported a steady American drift toward better understanding and greater appreciation of British policy to Chamberlain on 27 June. The prime minister took notes in his own hand, but does not appear to have acted on Schuster's suggestion that "if some of those who frequently visited the U.S.A. were called together . . . they might suggest a number of ways in which we could improve our position over there" (NC 7/11/31/240).

13. Welles Memorandum, 6 June 1938; Hull Memorandum, 10 June 1938; *FRUS,* 1938, 1:207–8, 213–14; CAB 23/94, 22, 29 June 1938, pp. 43, 61.

a British scheme for providing financial assistance to China (through a loan against future supplies of wolfram and antimony)—about which Chamberlain had grave misgivings unless the United States would participate—was quietly laid aside when a discreet sounding of Joseph Kennedy evoked the observation that "the British Empire had enough trouble on its hands . . . without gratuitously taking on more"—a view that Halifax reluctantly adjudged to be sound.[14] London had somewhat more success in obtaining an American protest against the Mexican government's confiscation of the (British) Mexican Eagle Company, a move with serious implications for Britain's oil supply. Feeling it vital for Washington to give public indication that it did not endorse the policy of the Cardenas regime, Halifax hesitated to say anything that could be interpreted as an attempt to exercise official influence. So British oil companies sent an unofficial emissary, Sir Thomas Royden, to Washington to see Roosevelt; and Lindsay cautiously raised the issue with Welles. At length (August 22) the United States sent a strongly worded note to Mexico City. But the state of relations between Britain and America is well illustrated in a memorandum that Welles composed when the matter first arose. In reference to a conversation with Lindsay, he recorded: "[the ambassador] made not the slightest suggestion or intimation that the British Government desired to avail itself of our good offices in patching up the quarrel between Great Britain and Mexico, nor did I make any reference as to any disposition on our part to do so."[15] London was afraid to ask, and Washington certainly was not going to volunteer.

There were, of course, some signals on both sides that could possibly be interpreted to betoken more positive things. Hull told the Tennessee Bar Association at Nashville in early June that the current condition of lawlessness was a direct consequence of the drift toward national isolation, that peace through isolation was impossible, and that America was ready to work with other nations in revitalizing international cooperation.[16] Halifax echoed Hull in an address to the Royal Institute of International Affairs on June 21, describing Hull's words of "profound truth" especially applicable to Britain. A *New York Times* article entitled

14. CAB 27/623, 1 June 1938, p. 305; Wilson Minute, PREM 1/303, 28 June 1938, pp. 8–10; CAB 23/94, 6, 13 July 1938, pp. 105–6, 138–42.

15. Halifax to Lindsay, 5 July 1938, FO 115/3415, File 23; Welles Memorandum, 16 May 1938, SDM 740.00/395 1/2.

16. Lindsay to Halifax, 6 June 1938, FO 414/275, p. 166. Foreign Office reaction to the speech was mixed. Beith saw it as a "real contribution," but Holman thought it "the usual stuff" into which Britain should not read too much. Balfour thought it "fireworks—but no more." From his vantage point of detachment, Eden thought it a "remarkable speech"—every word deserving of closest study. FO 371/21526, pp. 246–49; Johnson to Hull, 14 June 1938, SDM 741.00/194.

"A Way of Life"—which emphasized that in any ultimate test of strength the United States would have to be on the side of those nations whose way of life it shared—was read and initialed by Foreign Office personnel right up to Halifax. Earl Winterton, undersecretary in the Home Office, back from the Evian Conference (to consider the problem of emigration from Germany and Austria) told the cabinet on July 20 of statements relating to Roosevelt's concern for the international situation and the cooperative posture of the United States (made in private by Myron Taylor, the American representative) "that were almost of a historic character." Chamberlain declared in the Commons a few days later that relations with the United States had never been better, and Opposition leaders joined in urging a greater measure of cooperation with America. In another way, the obvious deterioration in German-American relations, punctuated by Hull's sharp exchanges with the German ambassador in Washington, seemed to be the sort of thing that might promote better Anglo-American understanding. And a Gallup Poll, which showed that in the event of war 65 percent of the American people would favor Britain and only 3 percent Germany (with 32 percent neutral) brought an element of comfort to Foreign Office personnel.[17] But all this was of dubious value, unrelated as it was to hard issues and specific problems.

As the Czech crisis intensified during August and word reached Washington of extensive German military preparations and Hitler's intentions to use the Nuremberg Party Congress in September to force the issue to a conclusion, both Hull and Roosevelt issued, in well-publicized speeches, warnings against international lawlessness. Both aimed, no doubt, to make some small effect in Berlin—to create a condition of doubt about American policy sufficient to help deter Germany from extreme provocation. Halifax appreciated this fact and noted that if either official could make a further declaration toward the existing danger in central Europe sometime before the Nazi gathering, it might help to restrain Hitler. But the British did not exaggerate the importance of these statements. Foreign Office officials saw their primary usefulness in educating American opinion and understood the need to avoid saying anything that might prompt the isolationists to think that Britain was dragging the United States into the affairs of Europe—which they thought anyway. Hull himself compared them at this point to a drown-

17. Johnson to Hull, 23 June 1938, SDM 741.00/196; FO 371/21526, pp. 271–72; CAB 23/94, 20 July 1938, p. 168; Kennedy to Hull, 26 July 1938, SDM 740.00/431; Memorandum by Hull, 7 July 1938, SDM 711.62/160; FO 371/21526, p. 283.

ing man who in a paroxysm of fear convulsively grapples with his rescuer. Chamberlain and Halifax also knew that the creation of doubt worked both ways, leaving England to wonder as well just what America would do in the event that the worst occurred.[18]

By late August, Roosevelt did begin to look for other devices short of commitments to help the British. Upon his initiative, for example, the Treasury quickly produced a plan for depositing English (and French) gold in the United States—for "safe-keeping" and possible use in purchasing war materials—which the president hoped would produce a positive psychological effect. But his exuberance about the plan was curbed by Hull, who cautioned against getting the American people "up on their toes over the European situation." Furthermore, discussion of the plan coincided with the arrival of diplomatic reports from Europe which suggested that Chamberlain was talking out of various sides of his mouth once more. Roosevelt's ambiguous feelings flip-flopped again; he told Hull and Morgenthau that Chamberlain was "slippery," not to be trusted, and involved again in the game of peace at any price. Indeed, British inquiries about American intentions in case of war raised the old specter of British efforts to pin responsibility for Britain's action on the United States. He decided to do nothing for a time, and American policy again drifted.[19]

Meantime, however, the British had understood from Kennedy that if Britain went to war in support of France, the United States would soon follow. The ambassador believed that Roosevelt had decided "to go in with Chamberlain"; whatever course he desired to adopt, the president would think right. This hardly represented Kennedy's own outlook. A draft speech he was scheduled to make in Scotland on September 2 expressed puzzlement why anybody would want to go to war to save the Czechs. The section was struck in process of clearance by the State Department, and Roosevelt told Morgenthau, "The young man needs his wrists slapped rather hard." At the same time, Halifax learned

18. FO Minutes, 19 August 1938, FO 371/21526, pp. 287, 298; Johnson to Hull, 24 August 1938, *FRUS,* 1938, 1:551; Hull, *Memoirs,* 1:586–89. See also Middlemas, *Diplomacy of Illusion,* p. 285. Pierrepont Moffat describes the creation of doubt in the minds of *both* Germans and British as "the eternal question mark of American foreign policy" (*Moffat Papers,* p. 194).

19. Blum, *From the Morgenthau Diaries,* 1:514–17; Dallek, *Franklin Roosevelt and American Foreign Policy,* pp. 163–64. Roosevelt received words of warning from others as well. Adolf Berle, for example, cautioned him in a personal memorandum on 1 September about reacting too emotionally to Hitler's campaign to revise a situation that was untenable from the beginning, and warned that Halifax's request for continual consultation could easily make the United States "an associate power" before it knew it (Berle, *Navigating the Rapids,* pp. 183–84).

through Ambassador Phipps in Paris of Bullitt's warning that strong anti-German feeling in America did not imply anything with regard to American participation in the event of hostilities.[20] The signals received in London about America were vague, mixed, and uncertain.

Of course, the signals passing from London to Washington were also equivocal. Halifax outlined for Chargé Johnson the issues of morality and self-interest involved in bringing force to bear on behalf of Czechoslovakia. The former were no greater than those involved with Japan in China or Italy in Abyssinia. Aside from forestalling perhaps inevitable war with Germany, fighting for the Czechs against Sudeten Germans would be "most dubious" since Sudeten grievances were very soundly based. Both from private talks with responsible officials and observation of the press, Johnson saw no indication that the government intended to become involved in a war with Germany over the rights of Czechs and Germans in Czechoslovakia. The director of military operations and intelligence at the War Office had put it squarely: the average Englishman, who knew or cared little about Czechoslovakia, would have great difficulty accepting the issue on which war would have to be declared as vital to the country. Yet at nearly the same moment Chamberlain was remarking to Kennedy that a German attack on Czechoslovakia would arouse public opinion and force France and England into the fray.[21] Cabinet discussion reflected similar confusion. Halifax suggested that a German absorption of a portion of Czechoslovakia might arouse American opinion against Germany; Duff Cooper (first lord of the Admiralty) declared that British failure to act in such an instance would result in American discouragement and a lapse into further isolation; and Malcolm MacDonald (secretary of state for colonies) warned that any threat of war would strain the loyalty of the dominions and possibly break up the Commonwealth.[22]

September arrived with everything in flux, but Chamberlain, always seeking alternatives, had come up with another idea of his own. Thinking it "positively horrible" that the fate of hundreds of millions depended on one man (Hitler) who was half-mad, the prime minister had been "racking his brains" (his term)—so he wrote his sister on September 3—

20. Halifax to Lindsay, Phipps to Halifax, 2 September 1938, *B.D.*, 2:212–13, 219; Blum, *From the Morgenthau Diaries*, 1:518; Berle, *Navigating the Rapids*, pp. 182–83.

21. Johnson to Hull, 24 August 1938, PSF, Confidential File, Box 20; Johnson to Hull, 26 August 1938, SDM 740.00/457–58; Kennedy to Hull, 30 August 1938, PSF, Confidential File, Box 20.

22. CAB 23/94, 30 August 1938, pp. 292, 302, 306.

to devise some means of averting a catastrophe. He had thought of one "so unconventional and daring that it rather took Halifax's breath away." But it had been laid aside momentarily in deference to Henderson's view that it should be reserved for use at the eleventh hour. This was the first mention of the idea that the prime minister might fly to Germany to visit Hitler. The dramatic quality of this action at the final moment carefully calculated, no one outside of his closest cabinet colleagues (Halifax, Hoare, and Simon, who soon came to constitute the Cabinet Committee on the Czechoslovak Crisis, or more simply the Inner Cabinet) was informed of the plan.[23] Certainly Roosevelt did not hear of it and his reaction, if he had, can only be conjectured—dubious business in view of his own personal idiosyncracies and the rapidly changing nature of the situation.

In the first two weeks of September, certain moves by Roosevelt showed his preference for a strong stand against Germany. But the crucial difference between making such a stand oneself and urging it upon others must always be borne in mind. He authorized Bullitt to make some strong remarks in a speech at a Paris war memorial; he ignored appeals by Bonnet that he arbitrate the Czechoslovak dispute and ask Hitler not to use force; upon Kennedy's suggestion he diverted two U.S. cruisers to British ports (the *Nashville* to Portland, the *Honolulu* to Gravesend). On September 12 Lindsay reported directly that the president had been "aroused" by Germany's brutal diplomacy, that opinion in Washington favored a strong stand by the British government against German aggression, and that any compromise might bring about a letdown of American friendliness.[24]

There were also factors that pointed in another direction. At a press conference on September 6, Roosevelt expressed—off the record—exasperation that it was difficult to tell much about the international situation because "so many stories that come through . . . are just rumors." State Department dispatches were "darned near as wild" as newspaper stories. Several days later he labeled press speculation that the United States was aligning itself with Britain and France in a "Stop Hitler" bloc as "100 per cent wrong." And when Halifax asked Kennedy again on September 10 what would be America's reaction if Hitler attacked Czechoslovakia, the ambassador had not the slightest idea—"except that

23. Neville to Ida, NC 18/1/1066; Personal Notes, 5–9 September 1938, Templewood Papers, X:3.

24. *Harvey Diaries*, pp. 170, 176; Halifax to Lindsay, 11 September 1938; Lindsay to Halifax, 12 September 1938; *B.D.*, 2:295–96, 301.

we want to keep out of war." When Halifax then inquired—merely for the sake of argument, Kennedy explained to Washington—why Britain should be the defender of democratic ideals rather than the United States, Kennedy told him that the British had made the Czechoslovak incident "part of their business, their allies were connected with the whole affair, and our people just failed to see where we should be involved."[25] All this was no doubt true, but it was hardly the sort of thing to steel British nerve for impending confrontation. Indeed, British cynicism is clearly reflected in the September 12 diary entry of Sir Thomas Inskip, minister for coordination of defense: "All this time anxious looks were directed to U.S.A. hoping something helpful might be said." Although Kennedy had been sympathetic and helpful, "Roosevelt told someone [a French visitor] we could have everything except 'troops and loans.' He ought to have added 'or lethal weapons.'"[26]

Although London took pains to keep Washington well informed about developments in the Czechoslovak crisis, and Chamberlain publicly described American sympathy and friendship as being "particularly precious,"[27] it is fair to say that British strategy, which emerged to meet the crisis, developed without much reference to the United States. The absence of solid signals from Washington, as well as Chamberlain's own determined policy and personality, assured that.

There was sharp division in British inner circles whether to warn Hitler bluntly against the use of force. The cabinet first rejected the idea on the grounds that it was unwise to issue threats unless ready and able to execute them—and of that there was room for doubt. But as reports (including some from moderate Germans) accumulated that Hitler was set to march and that only a dire warning could deter him, a definite public sentiment against surrender arose (particularly in response to the *Times*'s September 7 suggestion that the Sudetenland simply be ceded to Germany). On September 9 agreement was reached on a strongly worded message to Berlin that in the event of war Britain would stand by France. Chamberlain's heart was never in it, however, and when Ambassador Nevile Henderson protested such a warning, on the grounds that it would only provoke Hitler, permission was granted to lay it aside.

25. *FDR Press Conferences,* 12:80–81; *B.D.,* 2:293 (fn.); Kennedy to Hull, 10 September 1938, *FRUS,* 1938, 1:586. Hull was reportedly "much put out" by suggestions that there was a London-Paris-Washington peace axis: "it is becoming a leitmotif with him" (*Moffat Papers,* p. 199).

26. INKP 1 (Inskip Diaries), pp. 8–9.

27. *B.D.,* 2:682.

He realized, the prime minister confided to his sister, that if things went wrong and aggression occurred, there would be many—no doubt including Americans, though he did not say so—who would blame the British government for not having the courage to stop Hitler by telling him that if he used force Britain would at once declare war. But Chamberlain was not about to put the decision as to peace or war into the hands of the ruler of another country, "and a lunatic at that."[28]

On September 13 "things began rattling down to war" (Inskip's expression). Hitler's envenomed speech at the Nuremberg Party Congress the day before, reports of German troop movements, a fresh outbreak of disorders in the Sudetenland (hardly spontaneous), and a pitiable appeal from Paris (September 13) to find some way to keep Hitler from invading Czechoslovakia and thus invoking the French alliance prompted the Inner Cabinet to decide that the time was right for Chamberlain's offer (Plan Z) to visit Hitler. Although it is impossible to weigh the influence of these—and other—factors against Chamberlain's commitment to a peaceful solution, certainly the posture of France was more crucial in British thinking at that moment than that of the United States (and would have been so even had the latter been far more certain). As the crisis had developed in September, Ambassador Phipps in Paris had sent a series of pessimistic letters to Halifax, to the effect that the French government would not fight, the people would not support war, and French ministers would not back up "big" talk with action. Referring to these messages in his diary (September 13), Inskip recorded that Bonnet was "in a state of collapse"; and Daladier, "appalled" at the idea of France's being faced with her obligations to Czechoslovakia, wanted Germany stopped from moving "at all costs" (a remarkable switch of position from the previous week).[29]

Put another way, in view of all the other factors that influenced them, the British did not find America's uncertain position a high priority matter. They did inform Lindsay (leaving it to his discretion whether to tell Roosevelt directly) that in the event of Britain's being involved in

28. *Cadogan Diaries,* pp. 92–96; Colvin, *The Chamberlain Cabinet*, pp. 146–48; Personal Notes, 5–9 September 1938, Templewood Papers, X:3; Neville to Ida, 11 September 1938, NC 18/1/1068.

29. See PHPP 1/20 (Phipps Papers); INKP 1, pp. 9–10. On 20 September Halifax thanked Phipps for these letters, "which have been most useful to me." Phipps was a highly respected diplomat who had earlier (1933–37) served in Berlin, and who had inclined toward the containment of Germany until his views were eroded by his own gloomy assessment of French morale. Chamberlain told a Labour delegation on 17 September that "the real difficulty is the weakness of France" (Hugh Dalton Diary, 19:32).

war, it would be best for her if the U.S. Neutrality Act would not be applied at all. (The Foreign Office was even now concerned to avoid any hint of unwarranted interference in matters of domestic policy.) Chamberlain spoke forthrightly with Kennedy about his hopes and fears immediately after informing the cabinet of his intentions on September 14. And the Foreign Office let it be known that any statement of support from Roosevelt for Chamberlain's action would be welcomed. But this was all peripheral to the central deliberation and action.[30]

There was no American response to the British hint for a statement of support for Chamberlain's action. State Department officials agreed it would be a bad mistake; Pierrepont Moffat reflected this attitude in his personal journal: "Ever since the beginning of the crisis the British have been maneuvering to get us to give advice or to express ourselves . . . with the sole view of throwing responsibility on us in case their ultimate decision is an unpopular one." Hull merely told the press on September 15 that developments were being observed "with the greatest interest," and Roosevelt asked for nothing more. The president, in fact, unburdened himself to the cabinet (September 16) in a sharply critical sense: Chamberlain was for peace at any price, and France would join England in abandoning Czechoslovakia to Hitler's aggression. After this international outrage, they would "wash the blood from their Judas Iscariot hands."[31]

Chamberlain's three dramatic flights to Germany in the second half of September—a trilogy that has come historically to symbolize ap-

30. Halifax to Lindsay, 13 September 1938, FO 371/21548, pp. 108–10; Kennedy to Hull, 14 September 1938, PSF, Diplomatic Correspondence, Box 25; *Moffat Papers,* pp. 202–3; Hull, *Memoirs,* 1:589. Chamberlain told Kennedy that he feared his action might be misunderstood, but the time had come to demonstrate to the world that all his efforts were bent upon preventing war. The greatest danger would be Hitler's request for a plebiscite, thus putting the democracies in a position of standing against democratic principle. But he had two answers for that: Sudeten local autonomy for five years followed by election under international supervision, or, if Hitler wanted action immediately, it could be done at the end of six months. He was prepared "to talk colonies, economics or any other big plan for the peace of the world." He would tell Hitler he had come to formulate a settlement for world policy and that "Czechoslovakia is a small incident in that big cause." If this suggestion was turned down, he would tell Hitler that Britain would fight on the side of the French, who, to be sure, were not anxious to fight and would "throw their hat in the air" when they heard of his plan (Kennedy to Hull, 14 September 1938).

31. *Moffat Papers,* pp. 202–6; Hull, *Memoirs,* 1:589; Ickes, *Diary,* 2:467–68. State Department officials were also unsympathetic to any direct American involvement. When Bullitt telephoned Hull on 13 September that Britain and France were considering a direct three-power conference with Germany and that other powers "would have to come in," Hull, Moffat, and Berle agreed—over a game of croquet—that the United States could add little to such a conference (Berle, *Navigating the Rapids,* p. 184).

peasement—and the policy deliberations in London that surrounded them, have been chronicled fully elsewhere.[32] Here it remains to describe how the United States figured in British deliberations and to show the American role in, and reaction to, what transpired. With regard to the first consideration, the temptation is great to say essentially "not at all," for, tensely preoccupied with a host of other factors and forces, British decision-makers simply did not think much about the United States. In cabinet deliberations, for example, there was no mention of America before September 26, except for two references by Duff Cooper. The first (September 17) noted his fear that a solution to the Czech problem would not settle anything and Hitler might thereafter "make some attempt" on the British Empire in which both France and the United States would stand aside; the second (September 21) involved his suggestion that Hitler should be told that any further demands would result in a British declaration of war, that the United States would come in on her side, and Germany would thus face ultimate defeat. Urging had earlier come—over a period of time and from a variety of quarters (Churchill, Labour leaders, and a few others in Parliament, Duff Cooper in the cabinet, Vansittart in the Foreign Office, and sections of the press that lacked confidence in appeasement)—to draw the United States closer to Britain in order to meet aggression in Europe more effectively. Limited overtures had been made, but so little had been accomplished, and the prospects seemed so meager, that there was no hope among leading officials of substantial or sudden change.[33]

In the meantime, American officials, for their part, were following events closely. In the State Department, where a nearly continuous "death watch" of Europe was in process, it was acknowledged that the sacrifice of British and French prestige would make Germany virtually supreme in Europe, but it was generally agreed that the best thing for the United States to do was to steer clear and keep quiet. Several officials had reviewed the possibility of a presidential call to a general European peace conference, a proposal which had been put before Roosevelt by Leon Jouhaux (a French labor leader and emissary of former Socialist

32. See, for example, Telford Taylor, *Munich: The Price of Peace,* and Middlemas, *Diplomacy of Illusion.*

33. CAB 23/95, 14–25 September 1938, pp. 59–239; Dalton Diary, 17 September 1938, 19:27; Rock, *Appeasement on Trial,* passim. Duff Cooper was more confident of the sympathy and eventual assistance of the United States, and thus more inclined to assign it importance in British decision-making, than most of his colleagues; see, for example, his diary entry for 20 September in *Old Men Forget,* pp. 231–32.

premier Leon Blum), but Roosevelt had shown no particular interest.[34] Even after Chamberlain's second (Godesberg) meeting with Hitler, September 22— at which the Führer rudely rejected Anglo-French agreement to an orderly transfer of the Sudetenland from Czechoslovakia to Germany and threatened military action if his demands for swifter resolution of the problem were not met at once—the consensus remained that the time was not yet ripe for any statement by the president.[35]

Roosevelt watched uneasily behind the scenes. He seemed to accept the State Department viewpoint about steering clear of intervention, but he was wrestling with potentially helpful ideas. He revealed this in striking fashion to Ambassador Lindsay, whom he summoned to the White House for a secret conversation on September 19. In outlining possible outcomes of the crisis, the president indicated his willingness to attend a heads-of-state world conference to try to achieve a general settlement, if called by the western powers and held outside Europe (possibly in the Azores or some other Atlantic island). More stunning still was his thinking about how he might help the western powers if they found themselves forced into war: London and Paris should wage war "purely by blockade and in a defensive manner." They should close their frontiers to Germany, stand on an armed defensive line, and call on other states to cooperate with them. Such resistance on "loftiest humanitarian grounds" would help him persuade Americans to recognize the blockade and—if the allies avoided an actual declaration of war—even to send arms and munitions to them. Indeed, "somehow or other" the United States might ultimately be drawn into the conflict. Lindsay, who surmised that this might have been what Roosevelt had in mind in his "Quarantine Speech" a year before, understandably regarded the president's remarks as momentous.[36]

But Lindsay's message made very little impact in London. At the time

34. There is no evidence of British involvement in this French contact. Roosevelt told Jonhaux that the situation did not seem to warrant an initiative from him, and a call for a conference, if not accepted, might only make the situation worse. He did say, however, that if Britain and France summoned a conference and invited the United States, he was prepared to accept.

35. Berle, *Navigating the Rapids*, pp. 185–86; Moffat Memorandum, 20 September 1938, SDM 740.00/461 1/2; *Moffat Papers*, pp. 207, 211.

36. Lindsay to Halifax, 20 September 1938, *B.D.*, 7:627–29. See Joseph Lash, *Roosevelt and Churchill, 1939–1941: The Partnership That Saved the West*, pp. 25–27. Roosevelt regarded Anglo-French pressure on Czechoslovakia to surrender the Sudetenland a "terrible remorseless sacrifice." He would be the first to cheer if Chamberlain's policy worked, but he thought this virtually impossible. The Czechs would surely fight, and even if they did not, other Nazi demands were sure to follow.

it arrived there, the British were anxiously awaiting Czechoslovakia's acceptance of the Anglo-French plan for the transfer of the Sudetenland—which had come to be regarded in the cabinet as the only way to resolve the Czech problem without war. And the Czechs' initial disposition to balk only heightened the determination of Chamberlain and his inner circle to pressure them to accept. Lindsay prompted Halifax that "it would be useful if you sent me a friendly expression of appreciation" to Roosevelt for his message; and Halifax dutifully telegraphed on the afternoon of September 23—after Chamberlain had experienced Hitler's shocking rejection of the Anglo-French plan at Godesberg the previous day—that Lindsay should convey to the president "my appreciation of his having taken you so far into his confidence." It was difficult to forecast events, but should the British be drawn into a conflict, "the major role would probably be enforcement of blockade, as [the] President foresees." Expressing himself in a way that sounds patronizing in retrospect, Halifax found it "of great encouragement to know that the President [had] been giving thought to these questions."[37] Chamberlain himself did not communicate with Roosevelt.

By September 25, however, Roosevelt reached the conclusion that he could no longer keep silent. The Czechs, to his surprise, had grudgingly agreed in principle to the cession of the Sudetenland, and a war over method and detail made no sense to the president. A cabinet meeting on September 23 generated much concern about the possible repercussions of a European war on the Far East and Latin America, the latter of which was assuredly "close to home." Not only had his suggestion about a defensive war stirred little response in London, his most recent information from American ambassadors indicated that England and France were simply not ready to fight at all. On Sunday morning, September 25, his own ideas still undetermined, Roosevelt asked the State Department to prepare (by evening) a public message for his consideration. Berle and Moffat produced a draft suggesting, instead of a conference, that the president extend his good offices—if invited by all the countries—and definitely hinting at treaty revision to lure Germany. The president himself decided that he wanted to appeal to Hitler, Benes, Chamberlain, and Daladier to keep negotiations going. Welles reworked the draft amid State Department disagreement about including the tender of good offices, some thinking it necessary in order to give substance

37. Ibid., pp. 27–28; Rock, *British Appeasement in the 1930s*, pp. 12–13; Lindsay to Halifax, 21 September 1938; Halifax to Lindsay, 23 September 1938; *B.D.*, 7:630.

to what would otherwise be a mere exhortation, others fearing that the public would confuse good offices with mediation. It was at length left up to the president, who decided to omit the section on the grounds that it was implicit in the rest of the statement.[38]

Telephone messages from Kennedy and Bullitt on September 25 were apparently influential in Roosevelt's decision to act. The latter, who had written the president a few days earlier that Britain and France had mishandled the situation abominably—acting "like little boys doing dirty things behind the barn"—telephoned the urgent advice that Roosevelt should offer to arbitrate. Kennedy, acting on his own initiative, exhorted the president to "consider taking some immediate action." His explanation to Chamberlain about what he had done is poignantly revealing both of the ambassador's belief in his own influence and Chamberlain's disdain for American involvement:

> You remember on my return back from America in the early part of July . . . I told you . . . that among other things the President suggested that if a crisis arose when you thought he could do anything to stave off difficulties you should let me know. This morning at half past two, although not having seen you, I realized that the situation was becoming very bad. I talked to Secretary Hull and told him what I thought of the situation and suggested that the President consider taking some immediate action. A little later the President sent telegrams to Dr. Benes and Herr Hitler.[39]

Roosevelt had extended an offer to help however he could if a crisis arose. A crisis had assumed the most dangerous proportions. Chamberlain had not responded to Roosevelt's offer or even been in contact with him. Staunch commitment to his own perception of things, reinforced by disbelief that Roosevelt could do anything useful, largely account for this, and the president could not have felt encouraged.

38. *Moffat Papers,* pp. 211–12; Ickes, *Diary,* 2:272–74; Dallek, *Franklin Roosevelt and American Foreign Policy,* p. 165. Hull was not convinced that an appeal from Roosevelt would accomplish much and might lead to his classification as an "appeaser." The secretary has written: "Welles kept pushing the President on, while I kept advising him to go slow" (Hull, *Memoirs,* 1:591). Only a display of force, the secretary believed, would deter Hitler (Blum, *From the Morgenthau Diaries,* 1:520).

39. Note by Syers, 26 September 1938, PREM 1/266 A, p. 111; Bullitt to Roosevelt, 20 September 1938, PSF, Diplomatic Correspondence, Box 23; Hull, *Memoirs,* 1:591–92. Kennedy's personal posture struck influential Englishmen differently. Geoffrey Dawson, editor of the *Times,* wrote in his diary that the ambassador "supported all that 'the old man' [Chamberlain] was doing" (John Evelyn Wrench, *Geoffrey Dawson and Our Times,* p. 377). But Undersecretary Cadogan wrote about having to hold Kennedy "at arm's length" since he "makes little secret what he thinks of us!" (*Cadogan Diaries,* p. 103).

Roosevelt's September 26 appeal to Hitler, Benes, Chamberlain, and Daladier to continue negotiations, at a time when their nations were in various stages of mobilization, built upon an assertion that "there is no problem so difficult or so pressing for solution that it cannot be justly solved by the resort to reason rather than by the resort to force," and emphasized the incalculable consequences, the "unspeakable horror," should hostilities break out. "So long as these negotiations continue there remains the hope that reason and the spirit of equity may prevail and that the world may thereby escape the madness of a new resort to war." Once broken off, "reason is banished and force asserts itself. And force produces no solution for the good of humanity." There was no offer to arbitrate; neither Roosevelt nor Hull was prepared to go that far. The tender of good offices was omitted as being too dangerous; and a disengaging statement that "the United States has no political entanglements" was included. What remained was what one disappointed State Department official called "a repetition of the Kellogg-Briand Pact."[40]

Chamberlain's reply of the same day—actually prepared in the Foreign Office and sent off by Halifax—"hailed with gratitude" Roosevelt's "weighty message" and assured the president that the British government was doing its utmost to secure a peaceful solution. But the Roosevelt communication received barely passing mention in the cabinet meeting that day, and the manner of its reporting there left room for misunderstanding. He had received a message from President Roosevelt urging him to "continue negotiations up to the last possible moment in order to arrive at a peaceful settlement," the prime minister reported without further commentary; and the subject did not come up again in the meeting. How had Chamberlain intended Roosevelt's message to be taken by his cabinet colleagues? It is impossible to say. Busy consulting indecisively with French ministers who had come to London, and caught between his own inclinations and growing cabinet objection to accepting Hitler's demands, he had already determined to try still another tack: he would send a special emissary, Sir Horace Wilson, to Hitler in a last desperate move to keep negotiations open. If Hitler refused to consider the proposal that Wilson would carry (the formation of an international body of Czechs, Germans, and British to work out the details of Sudeten transfer) he would be told that France would fight for Czechoslovakia

40. Telegram from Roosevelt to Chamberlain, 26 September 1938, PREM 1/266 A, pp. 101–110; Berle, *Navigating the Rapids*, p. 187.

and that Britain would stand by France. This should satisfy both the desire to keep the door of negotiation open as well as the need to take a stand somewhere.[41]

Roosevelt's message received favorable editorial comment in the British press, and Kennedy reported that "it helped offset a good deal of bitterness that had arisen as a result of the terrific blast from the American newspapers on the question of the betrayal of Czechoslovakia." But in the cabinet meeting of September 27, in which Wilson told of his trip to Berlin, reference to the United States and Roosevelt was again conspicuously absent. Only Duff Cooper mentioned the president's message—in citing factors that weighed against capitulation to Hitler. Chamberlain did propose, through Kennedy, to address the American people directly in his scheduled speech to the British public on the night of September 27. But Welles thought a direct broadcast would be misconstrued as an appeal and Roosevelt agreed. So Chamberlain spoke only to his own people in a radio address carried in America. It was this address that contained his oft-quoted statement: "How horrible, fantastic, incredible it is that we should be digging trenches and trying on gas masks here because of a quarrel in a faraway country between people of whom we know nothing. It seems still more impossible that a quarrel which has already been settled in principle should be the subject of war."[42]

Inclined himself to the reasoning of the latter point, Roosevelt had already undertaken an additional appeal for peace. Hitler's intractable reply to his message had prompted him to solicit Mussolini's help in bringing about a negotiated settlement and to agree to ask other heads of state to make similar appeals to Prague and Berlin. With the help of State Department officials, he prepared another telegram to Hitler in which he added to his earlier appeal for continuing negotiations the suggestion of a conference of all nations directly interested in the controversy at some neutral site (perhaps The Hague) in Europe. The idea had been pressed on him again by Bullitt and Welles. Kennedy was instructed to seek Chamberlain's reaction to the idea of a conference and suggestions about the mechanics of making a direct appeal to

41. Chamberlain to Roosevelt, 26 September 1938, FO 115/3415, File 112; Unsigned Minute, 27 September 1938, PREM 1/266 A, p. 98; CAB 23/95, 26 September 1938, p. 247; Rock, *British Appeasement in the 1930s,* p. 13.

42. Kennedy to Hull, 27 September 1938, *FRUS,* 1938, 1:673; CAB 23/95, 27 September 1938, p. 269; Hull, *Memoirs,* 1:593; Welles Memorandum, 26 September 1938, *FRUS,* 1938, 1:661; Neville Chamberlain, *In Search of Peace,* p. 174.

Hitler—no doubt a concession to Hull's concern about the danger of so bold a step. But the press of events led Roosevelt to proceed without waiting.[43]

Chamberlain likewise proceeded. Just when all hope seemed gone, a message arrived in London from Hitler. A bit more conciliatory than before, the Führer left it to Chamberlain's judgment whether to continue efforts to bring the Czechs to reason at the very last hour. Chamberlain responded with the idea of a five-power conference (including Czechoslovakia), conceived a few days earlier, for which he was ready to go to Germany at once. Hitler agreed, but excluded the Czechs, and the meeting at Munich ensued.[44]

Estimates of Roosevelt's influence in getting Hitler to agree to the conference at Munich have varied, though it certainly was not as important as the influence of Mussolini and the realization that Britain and France would concede to his final demands without the need for force.[45] The British made no official comment on this; Halifax simply expressed on September 29 his thanks for the help that Roosevelt "had given by his intervention during the last two or three days." There is little to suggest that the British expected or requested anything from the United States during the crisis, after the initial bid for a statement of support for Chamberlain's first visit to Germany, though they no doubt hoped for long-term assistance if negotiations failed and the worst occurred. There was no ground on which the British could confidently ask anything of America; and besides, Chamberlain did not have any great interest in this—an attitude that grew out of an uncertain commingling of his perception of practical possibilities and what was desirable. There is evidence, however, that the prime minister did have the United States in mind when, before departing Munich, he sought out Hitler at his apartment and obtained his signature on a short declaration (of Cham-

43. Dallek, *Franklin Roosevelt and American Foreign Policy,* pp. 165–66; Berle, *Navigating the Rapids,* p. 187; *Moffat Papers,* pp. 215–16; Welles Memorandum, 27 September 1938, PSF, Diplomatic Correspondence, Box 23; Welles Memorandum, 27 September 1938, *FRUS,* 1938, 1:678.

44. Rock, *Neville Chamberlain,* p. 154.

45. Other factors often cited include the reticence of German military leaders and the glum reception that Berliners gave to a propaganda march of German troops on 27 September. The German ambassador in Washington, Dieckhoff, cabled Berlin the same day that in the event of war, the United States would side with Britain (*Documents on German Foreign Policy, 1918–1945,* Series D (hereafter *G.D.*), 2:981–82. Five weeks later Chamberlain gave credit (in a private letter to his stepmother) to Mussolini for persuading Hitler to accept negotiations at Munich (Neville to Mary, 5 November 1938, NC 1/20/1/186).

berlain's drafting) that expressed their determination to remove sources of difference and to employ consultation when dealing with future issues of mutual concern. Chamberlain's private parliamentary secretary, Alec Douglas-Home, later explained that his action was deliberately calculated: "If Hitler signed it and kept the bargain, well and good; [but] if he broke it, he would demonstrate to all the world that he was totally cynical and untrustworthy and . . . this would have its value in mobilizing public opinion against him, particularly in America."[46]

Roosevelt, for his part, attempted to exert some influence—by appealing to all parties to continue negotiations—without getting involved directly or making any commitments. Through much of the Sudeten crisis, he had maintained a judicious distance from events, keeping his options open against the unlikely possibility that Chamberlain's efforts would succeed, but taking no chance of being implicated in, or having to assume any responsibility for, what occurred. In this sense he supported the cause of peace by keeping both Britain and Germany guessing—for very different reasons—about what to expect of America. But his generally evasive posture had little apparent effect in Berlin and struck the British as typical American irresponsibility—which might have prompted still greater disgust had they not themselves been using the same tactic on the French. At length the president was forced to deny rumors of American participation in a front against Germany and to follow a course described euphemistically by the State Department as a "policy of non-action." Lacking confidence in Chamberlain, and alarmed at Hitler's behavior, Roosevelt's concern about the "terrible sacrifices" demanded of the Czechs did not extend to encouragement of "vain resistance." He offered neither detailed advice nor personal services. Such influence as he finally used no doubt encouraged the settlement that eventually was made. His famous two-word telegram, "Good Man," sent to Chamberlain (September 28) upon learning of his receipt and acceptance of Hitler's invitation to Munich, probably connoted nothing more than relief that the door of peace was still ajar—though one of Chamberlain's closest colleagues later wrote that of all the expressions of support that Chamberlain received during those dark days, none

46. Halifax to Lindsay, 29 September 1938, *B.D.*, 2:625; Alec Douglas-Home, *The Way the Wind Blows: An Autobiography,* p. 66. In a letter of 2 October to his sister, Chamberlain explained that he arranged the meeting with Hitler about 1 a.m. on 30 September, while they were waiting for draftsmen to complete their work on the Munich Agreement. But he said nothing about his motivation. NC 18/1/1070.

encouraged him so much as Roosevelt's brief message. "What two words could better show his full approval of Chamberlain's efforts?"[47]

The president's immediate reaction to the Munich Agreement was mixed and uncertain. Like so many others, he rejoiced that war had been averted; and he wrote Ambassador Phillips in Rome that he was "not one bit upset over the final result." Yet there are other indications that he seriously doubted whether Munich had solved anything and feared that it was the prelude to war. State Department officials were likewise divided in their reactions, mixed feelings being the general rule.[48] And this extended more broadly to their attitudes toward Britain and her policy in Europe.

47. Reynolds, *Creation of the Anglo-American Alliance,* pp. 33–34; MacDonald, *The United States, Britain, and Appeasement,* pp. 102–4; Roosevelt to Chamberlain, 28 September 1938, PSF, Diplomatic Correspondence, Box 25; Templewood, *Nine Troubled Years,* pp. 325–26. Arnold Offner, historian of American appeasement, holds that "taken in *toto,* Roosevelt's cables of September 26–28 show how strongly he supported appeasement and a conference whose outcome was foregone" (*Origins of the Second World War,* p. 126).

48. See Offner, *Origins of the Second World War,* pp. 126–27; Hull, *Memoirs,* 1:596–97.

VI. Munich Winter

PRECISELY WHAT NEVILLE CHAMBERLAIN believed he had accomplished toward a settlement of major European problems by the Munich agreement is unclear. Conflicting evidence reflects, no doubt, the various moods induced by different circumstances that he encountered—a vacillation between hope and misgiving and ambivalence about where it all might lead. He wrote Maurice Hankey on October 2: "I believe with you that we have at least laid the foundations of a stable peace, though it still remains to build the superstructure." But to his sister Hilda he lamented a short time later: ". . . We are very little nearer to the time when we can put all thoughts of war out of our minds and settle down to make the world a better place." Years thereafter, Halifax still insisted that the prime minister's phrase about "peace in our time" "meant what it said." But Chamberlain's cousin Arthur recalled a letter that his father had received from the prime minister immediately after Munich:

> Neville wrote that he found Hitler unstable, if not mad—that he didn't believe a word he said and that he hoped he had won a year to rearm before Hitler's lust for conquest overtook him. He thought it dangerous for these beliefs to be public knowledge, for that might tempt Hitler to move before we could do anything to protect ourselves. As near as I can remember the last sentence was "Pray God that what I have done will give us time to prepare!"[1]

In any case, nothing that had happened significantly altered his attitudes

1. HNKY (Hankey Papers) 4/30; NC 18/1/1072; Halifax to Editor of the *Times,* 26 October 1948, Halifax Papers, A4.410.19.6; Arthur Chamberlain to Kenneth Humphreys, 2 January 1973, NC 7/6/44.

toward the United States or sharpened his sense of the need to build a closer relationship with it as a hedge against a dangerously dubious future. So the period from Munich to the German conquest of rump Czechoslovakia in mid-March 1939 failed to change the basic British outlook toward America.

Although Roosevelt sent no message to Chamberlain about Munich, he wrote the prime minister within a few days about another matter: "Now that you have established personal contact with Chancellor Hitler, I know that you will be taking up with him from time to time many of the problems which must be resolved in order to bring about . . . [a] new and better order." The German policy of racial persecution, which created a disturbing refugee problem, was one of these, and the president hoped that Chamberlain would find an appropriate opportunity to raise the issue with Hitler. One can only imagine Hitler's likely response—in view of his brutish treatment of Chamberlain during his recent visits to Germany—to British promptings on such a matter; and Chamberlain could have had no illusions about this. Not surprisingly, he agreed with Roosevelt about the problem and hoped that the German government would contribute to its solution, but suggested only that the British and American ambassadors in Berlin might take responsibility for raising the issue there.[2]

A similar rebuff of a potentially greater opportunity occurred a short time later. With the impending conclusion of an Anglo-American trade agreement, which had been in the painful process of negotiation for months, Canadian Prime Minister Mackenzie King cabled Chamberlain that it would be a "great stroke" if he could arrange to "come over" for the signing of the agreement. Roosevelt, with whom he had spoken earlier about this possibility, would be delighted if it could be arranged. "You would receive a great welcome in America the effect of which would be most significant and far-reaching" (by way of demonstrating Anglo-American friendship to the world). Chamberlain's response, delayed by a holiday in Scotland, was not encouraging. He had been thinking over the suggestion, but there were so many "exceptionally important and pressing questions" requiring his attention in London that it would be difficult for him to visit the United States in the near future "even for so important a purpose." Besides, the outcome of the trade negotiations was still in doubt, and it could not be taken for granted that

2. Mrs. Neville Chamberlain to Sir Samuel Hoare, 22 January 1951, Templewood Papers, XIX:11; Roosevelt to Chamberlain and reply, 7 October 1938, FO 414/275, pp. 31–32.

agreement would soon be reached. When agreement was in fact attained shortly thereafter, it made no difference in his outlook. In a message to King of November 11 (initiated and drafted by the Dominions Office and approved by the prime minister), he reiterated that a visit to Washington was "not practicable." The time factor alone would preclude it, and he was planning a trip to Paris two weeks hence. Of course, he appreciated the suggestion.[3]

Chamberlain was simply not concerned with the United States at this juncture. He had other things on his mind. Refusing to accept the judgment that friendly relations with the totalitarian states were impossible, that assurances given to him personally were worthless, and that those states were bent upon European domination—views that were forcefully pressed upon him by a variety of critics in the four-day debate in the House of Commons after Munich—he seemed more determined than ever to see how much further he could push appeasement; and persons who thought differently were troublemakers who should be thrust aside. Any private doubts he may have harbored were not revealed in public, as he met with acrid assurance the nagging doubts of others.[4]

Never one to accept criticism gracefully, his sensitivity was clearly revealed in his reaction to a broadcast speech that Winston Churchill, who had become one of the sharpest critics of appeasement and one of the chief advocates of closer cooperation with America, made to the United States on October 16. Churchill warned of the dangers to peace and freedom and (combatting the notion that since Britain and France had failed to do their duty America could now wash her hands of the whole business) extolled the United States not to wait until British freedom and independence had succumbed to take up the cause alone. Although Lindsay, who had feared lest "such . . . direct . . . propaganda" produce a negative reaction, reported exactly the opposite result (i.e., Churchill's speech "has led to a good deal of serious and objective discussion"), Chamberlain grumbled to his sister that it was "damaging": "the very worst thing you can do with the U.S.A. is to lecture them on

3. King to Chamberlain, 11 October 1938; Chamberlain to King, 24 October, 11 November 1938; Minute from Syers to Chamberlain, 10 November 1938, PREM 1/291.

4. *Parl. Debs., HC*, 3–6 October 1938, 339:32-558. See Rock, *Appeasement on Trial*, pp. 149–55, for an analysis of this debate, which helped restore a sense of balance in Britain and spawned some serious thinking about the broader implications of what had happened at Munich. British historian L. B. Namier later observed about Munich: "The more there was of doubt lurking deeper down, the greater was at first the annoyance and irritation with anyone who dared to give expression to it" ("Munich Survey: A Summing Up," p. 836).

their duty to come to the assistance of the British Empire. Winston's broadcast disconcerted all our friends over there—not least the President himself—and made it practically impossible for them to help." What help he had in mind at that moment is not clear. As for his own upcoming Guildhall speech, which would be broadcast to America, he "would try and get his views across if the papers don't sabotage us in the meantime."[5]

In that address, which constituted a defense and explanation of appeasement and an effort to calm English anxieties, he chose to use a familiar American expression to describe his government as "a go-getter for peace." This reflected his state of mind. Determined not to "go to sleep" now that he was in a position to keep foreign affairs "on the move," and being disinclined to believe disquieting reports about Germany's attitude and intentions (which Halifax presented to the Foreign Policy Committee) the prime minister planned to implement the Anglo-Italian Agreement, to visit Paris (in order to give the French an opportunity to express their gratitude and to strengthen Daladier for the tasks ahead) as a prelude to visiting Rome—and after that, of course, there was no telling what might be possible. He would get no argument from his foreign secretary, who wrote Ambassador Phipps in Paris, November 1, that "one of the chief difficulties of the past" had been the "unreal position" of France in central and eastern Europe, where German dominance was "inevitable for obvious geographical and economic reasons." As for Italy, the British did not expect to detach her from the Axis, but hoped to increase Mussolini's power of maneuver and thus facilitate his resumption of the classic Italian role of balancing between Germany and the Western Powers.[6]

5. *Winston S. Churchill: His Complete Speeches, 1897–1963,* (hereafter *Churchill's Complete Speeches*) 6:6015–17. Lindsay to Halifax, 1 November 1938, FO 115/3415, File 112; Neville to Hilda, 6 November 1938, NC 18/1/1075. One week later Chamberlain wrote his sister Ida that Eden (also a critic of appeasement and firm supporter of closer ties with the United States) was still making his "daily speech" and bidding for support. But he had deliberately abstained from listening to him in the Commons "as I did not want to be provoked into any interruption or retort" (13 November 1938, NC 18/1/1076).

6. Chamberlain, *In Search of Peace,* pp. 229–36; Neville to Hilda, 6 November, 1938, NC 18/1/1075; CAB 27/624, 14 November 1938, pp. 43–44; Halifax to Phipps, 1 November 1938, PHPP (Phipps Papers) 1/21. Halifax added, to be sure, that Britain and France must maintain their positions in western Europe, the Mediterranean, the Near East, and in the colonial empires, as well as developing "the closest possible ties" with the United States. But there could be no assured peace in Europe unless "genuine agreement" was reached with Germany. Kennedy had earlier reported hearing these views from Halifax: there was no sense in Britain's resisting Hitler unless he directly interfered with the dominions; Britain should strengthen itself in the air, then let Hitler do what he liked in central Europe (Kennedy to Hull, 12 October 1938, SDM 741.00/202).

Meantime, in the United States there was no great optimism about what the future might hold. Roosevelt, like Americans generally, shared the immediate relief that peace had prevailed and flirted briefly with the notion that building a more stable world order on free trade, disarmament, and the rule of law might now proceed. Welles declared in a broadcast address, October 3, that the method that had happily averted the outbreak of war might now be used to solve other "tragic controversies" still festering in Europe and Asia. But a sobering effect inevitably accompanied deeper reflection about all that had happened—and how. More potent, therefore, was the growing sentiment, described in Ickes's diary (October 9), that "the Czechoslovak solution was a totally disgraceful thing and the President may want to dissociate himself from too close a connection before he is through with it." Much depended, of course, upon one's estimate of Hitler's aims. Those like Welles, who continued to think that Germany's objectives were limited, still evinced some hope that Nazi extremism might be tempered by greater German participation in a remodeled international system that would include equal economic opportunity for all. Others, like Morgenthau and George Messersmith (assistant secretary of state), distrusted Hitler, spoke openly of his plans for world domination, and favored putting a squeeze on Germany whenever possible—as, for example, by placing a high tariff on German goods and undercutting German trade in Latin America by means of American financial assistance there. Roosevelt now tended toward the latter pole of opinion. If he was not upset initially over Munich, the feeling did not last; and within a few weeks' time he was expressing pained embarrassment about it. Indeed, his own personal attitude was a good barometer of shifting opinion not simply in America but in Britain as well, as the euphoria of release from war subsided and sober reflection suggested frightening implications. Within a few weeks after Munich, Roosevelt had lost any illusions he may have had about the future of appeasement or the mark it had made, and his predominant reaction was that the Czechoslovak "settlement" constituted only a lull in the gathering storm that signaled an imperative need for the democracies to rearm. And if sober reflection alone was not enough to encourage deepening disillusionment, specific developments were. The weeks that followed Munich saw a speech by Hitler at Saarbrücken that was considerably less than conciliatory. There were rumors of diplomatic efforts to tighten the Axis with a view to advancing ultimate designs on the Western Hemisphere, a German trade offensive in South America, and a vicious anti-Semitic pogrom in Germany itself. (The latter was especially important in crystallizing State Department opinion against Germany.) At a pace impossible to trace precisely, Roosevelt came to embrace the view that Germany posed a real, if not immediate, threat to the security of the United States. Beyond his Wilsonian perception that violent change and lawlessness anywhere were inimical to international order, he was also alarmed at the perceived coordination of German and Japanese policies. If Britain and France were subdued, Hitler would likely turn on the United States. He might even attempt an invasion of the Western Hemisphere, if Latin America had been subverted and the British and French fleets neutralized. Thus the president gradually came to envisage the European democracies as America's front line of defense, and his aid-short-of-war disposition began to emerge with greater strength and clarity.[7]

If Munich sprang from necessity born of military weakness, as Roosevelt seemed to believe, then something should be learned from the experience. Feeling no particular confidence that Britain would use the precious months ahead to strengthen her own, and Europe's defenses, Roosevelt began, shortly after Munich, to look for ways to strengthen the will of Britain and France. One way to accomplish this was through a rapid buildup of American air power, both for America's own defense and as a potential way to help Britain and France hold Hitler in check—even, if it came to that, to defeat him without direct American participation. The "galvanizing" event for Roosevelt in this regard may well have been the return of William Bullitt from France to report on the state of Europe. The supreme lesson of Munich for Bullitt (who was greatly influenced by Charles Lindbergh's recent report on the aviation of various nations) was the need for Britain and France to create an air force to match Germany's. But they could not do it alone, and there was no hope for an early reversal of the Neutrality Act. So Bullitt had conceived a plan by which Britain could establish huge aircraft works on the Canadian border at places such as Detroit and draw upon engineers, designers, and skilled workers who would live on the other side. Raw

7. Lindsay to Halifax, 5 October 1938, FO 115/3415, File 112; Ickes, *Diary,* 2:483; Dallek, *Franklin Roosevelt and American Foreign Policy,* p. 171; Burns, *Roosevelt: The Lion and the Fox,* p. 388; Reynolds, *Creation of the Anglo-American Alliance,* pp. 40–41; MacDonald, *The United States, Britain, and Appeasement,* pp. 106ff. Cole, *Roosevelt and the Isolationists,* pp. 298ff., contains a good account of the long gestation of Roosevelt's aid-short-of-war position. The policy was flawed in several ways, misleading Americans about their probable role in a European war, but it was the best the president could do in the circumstances. It enabled him to advance United States preparedness without excessively arousing the isolationists, on the grounds that it was the nation's best hope for staying out of war.

materials and parts of machines could be drawn from all over the United States. The method of financing this was yet to be resolved. It was this subject that Bullitt and Roosevelt discussed at the White House late into the night of October 13. The president apparently made up his mind to push for greatly increased American airplane production; and next day he announced to the press that new world conditions made it imperative to reexamine United States defenses. Within a week planning was under way.

Emphasis on the buildup of air power reflects Roosevelt's assumption (widely held by European military planners in the 1930s as well) that it would be the critical factor in the next war. Assuming a relative stalemate on land and an effective Allied naval blockade of Germany, as Roosevelt seemed to do, the crucial Anglo-French effort would be in the air. Here the United States could be of particular help in supplying the Allies with vital fighting equipment. Of course, the very existence of a powerful air force might serve as a deterrent to further aggression and even promote the cause of a broader settlement. In this sense rearmament had distinct political overtones—a fact of which Roosevelt was very much aware—although it did not imply a particular policy. The president's main concern at this time was not, therefore, balanced rearmament and thorough preparation for war. The idea of sending a large army abroad was not yet part of his thinking; and naval power was subordinated to the needs of the Army Air Force. This was not easily accepted by all sections of the War Department, and bitter internal struggles over priorities lay ahead. But the president's mind was moving. His concept of America's world role still did not embrace its assumption of major responsibility for the preservation of peace or direct participation in another war. But he was beginning to think of it as the "arsenal of democracy" (a term that he used later on) to stiffen the resolve of the British, and possibly the French, on whose shoulders primary responsibility for preserving European peace still rested.[8]

8. Minute of a conversation with Bullitt in Paris, 2 October 1938, HNKY 1/8; Orville H. Bullitt, ed., *For the President: Personal and Secret. Correspondence between Franklin D. Roosevelt and William C. Bullitt*, p. 302; Forrest C. Pogue, *George C. Marshall, Education of a General, 1880–1939*, pp. 321–22; Reynolds, *Creation of the Anglo-American Alliance*, pp. 41–44; MacDonald, *The United States, Britain, and Appeasement*, p. 108. Trusted adviser Bernard Baruch, who had been in Europe at the height of the Czech crisis, told Roosevelt the day before Bullitt's conversation with the president that war was coming and that America must exert a strong rearmament effort (Margaret L. Coit, *Mr. Baruch*, pp. 467–69). On Roosevelt's growing concern for building a powerful United States air force, see the early chapters of John M. Haight, *American Aid to France, 1938–1940*.

Partly at Bullitt's urging, Roosevelt agreed to receive a French mission, headed by Jean Monnet, at Hyde Park on October 18 to discuss the building of aviation plants in Canada, to which American firms could provide basic materials. This was followed by a "proper talk" with Colonel Arthur Murray, the president's old and closest English friend, who was visiting Hyde Park at the time. Murray was commissioned to assure Chamberlain of the president's desire, in the event of hostilities, to help him in every possible way, in particular by placing the industrial resources of America behind him. In the crucial realm of airplane production, he would do his best to provide partly finished basic materials (such as plates for wings, cylinder blocks, steel tubing, wood, and wire) in order to assure an overwhelming superiority over Germany and Italy. Building plants in Britain and transporting basic materials across the Atlantic would also be considered. Murray, however, did not see Chamberlain for nearly two months, whereupon he reported the prime minister deeply grateful for Roosevelt's assurances and heartened by them, but quite uncertain whether a public statement about American resources being marshaled behind Britain would have a deterrent effect upon Hitler.[9] Chamberlain did not take up any of Roosevelt's ideas for further discussion at that time; his mind still was set more upon avoiding hostilities than preparing for them.

American officials were by no means unanimous in their reading of the European situation and the necessities that followed from it in the wake of Munich. But a number shared Roosevelt's new concerns and encouraged him in the direction his thinking had begun to move. Within the cabinet Morgenthau and Ickes were committed to shoring up the democracies and furthering national defense, and Roosevelt often turned for support to the treasury secretary, who believed the United States to be the only country capable of stopping aggression by peaceful means—through the use of financial strength. Morgenthau was excited about Roosevelt's plan to push aircraft production; and a "momentous White House meeting" of November 14 with representatives of the Treasury, Justice, and War departments (including senior army and navy officers) resulted in general support for the president's wish to have large numbers of planes "to sell or lend" to Britain and France. Direct personal letters from ambassadors in Europe who were Roosevelt's close friends reinforced his thinking. Anthony Biddle, in Poland, saw no grounds for

9. Bullitt, *For the President*, pp. 302–3; Elibank, "Roosevelt: Friend of Britain," pp. 365–66; Murray to Roosevelt, 15 December 1938, PSF, Diplomatic Correspondence, Box 29.

believing anything except that Europe was passing through a period of armed truce. An almost power-drunk and overconfident Germany was building a road eastward that would not crumble as Napoleon's had done. Herbert Pell, in Portugal, believed that Chamberlain had bet the future of the British Empire on Hitler's integrity, and he would lose, to which Roosevelt replied: "You are right about the European situation. Our British friends must begin to fish or cut bait." The "dictator threat" was a good deal closer to the United States itself than before. Claude Bowers, in Spain, complained bitterly about Chamberlain and his "notorious anti-American complex." In another vein, several Kennedy speeches, in which he downplayed the challenge of the dictators in a manner not at all commensurate with what the president was now saying, incurred the wrath of even the normally cautious Cordell Hull, who wished that all ambassadors would somehow forgo speech making altogether.[10]

Early November in London found Chamberlain proposing to Parliament the taking of "a further step forward in the policy of appeasement" by implementing the Anglo-Italian Agreement of the previous April. The announced withdrawal of ten thousand Italian troops from Spain, assurances from Mussolini about the future removal of those who remained, and consequently the elimination of the Spanish question as a menace to the peace of Europe were the proffered bases of this proposal. Chamberlain had learned from Ciano a few days after Munich that, unless Britain could give almost immediate assurances about completing the agreement, the Fascist Grand Council would have to take "certain decisions"—meaning a German military alliance. He and Halifax had been ready to act then, but were deterred by the "excited Opposition" in the Commons and the risk of further resignations from the government. The cabinet had approved the proposal without demur on October 26, Chamberlain noting that both Mussolini and Hitler had sent troops to Spain "in the first instance in order to prevent Spain from being Bolshevised" and were now anxious to withdraw them since this danger no longer existed.[11]

10. John M. Blum, *Roosevelt and Morgenthau*, pp. 268, 272; Haight, *American Aid to France*, pp. 58–59; Biddle to Roosevelt, 15 October 1938, PSF, Diplomatic Correspondence, Box 37; *Poland and the Coming of the Second World War: The Diplomatic Papers of A. J. Drexel Biddle, Jr., United States Ambassador to Poland, 1937–1939*, p. 248; Pell to Roosevelt, 21 October 1938, and Roosevelt to Pell, 12 November 1938, PSF, Diplomatic Correspondence, Box 51; *Moffat Papers*, p. 220.

11. Rock, *Appeasement on Trial*, p. 165; Neville to Ida, 9 October 1938, NC 18/1/1071; CAB 23/96, 26 October 1938, pp. 52–53.

There was no consultation with Washington—or anyone else—about this matter. Halifax simply told the cabinet that he intended to inform the United States government of the action Britain was taking; and an explanation was relayed to Roosevelt through Ambassador Lindsay the next day. In elaborating one of a half-dozen considerations advanced by Halifax, Lindsay emphasized the desire to restore to Mussolini the liberty of maneuver and decision necessary if the four-power contact established at Munich was to be maintained and the hope for smoother relations in Europe realized. Welles ventured to say that he did not expect an unfavorable reaction in America, but neither Roosevelt nor anyone else in authority saw fit to comment publicly, no doubt a continuing reflection of the skepticism and annoyance with which the initial Anglo-Italian negotiations had been met some months before.[12]

If Roosevelt hoped to see a strengthening of British will, he must also have been sorely disappointed to hear from Kennedy in late October about Britain's uncertain views on colonial appeasement. Halifax revealed a lingering cabinet willingness to transfer certain colonial areas to Germany—although the basis on which this might be done was the cause of considerable consternation. One idea was to leave it to arbitration, and there was nobody who could arbitrate except the president. It would be a "rotten job," Halifax admitted.[13] Roosevelt no doubt thought so too, and nothing was heard of that idea again.

There were also other issues that served at the time to spur a mutual lack of confidence. When Washington moved in early November to make representations to Japan regarding freedom of navigation on the Yangtze River (in China) up to Hankow, it inquired whether London was prepared to make a parallel representation and what action it would take if the Japanese response was unfavorable. Halifax thought this a significant change in procedure since previous American representations to Japan had been made independently. But Chamberlain doubted that America's proposal of economic pressure would be effective; it might result in a Japanese attack on Hong Kong—and it was quite unclear what action the United States would take in that event. So the best the cabinet would do was to agree that no action was necessary at present. Later on Halifax told Kennedy, off the record, that Britain would do whatever the United States would do, but it would not take the lead in

12. Halifax to Lindsay and Lindsay to Halifax, 27 October 1938, *B.D.*, 3:343–44; Lindsay to Welles, 27 October 1938, FO 115/3415, File 135.

13. Kennedy to Hull, 28 October 1938, *FRUS*, 1938, 1:95–97.

any plan.[14] The old "after you, please" syndrome was still alive and operative to the dissatisfaction of all concerned.

The anti-Semitic pogrom conducted in Germany during the second week of November (during which Jewish property was systematically destroyed and thousands of Jews were arrested and sent to concentration camps) had the effect of producing a strong anti-British (antiappeasement) reaction in the United States, where it was supposed that Britain should have been able to take some effective steps to stop the persecution. Halifax described American public opinion to the cabinet as "now about as critical [of Britain] as it could well be"—although things could be improved if Britain gave a lead in helping the Jews, which would force the United States in turn to take some positive action. The State Department had been expressing the view for some time that Britain was not doing enough to help Jewish refugees from Germany; and Roosevelt had, a few weeks before, asked Justice Felix Frankfurter (of the Supreme Court) to draft for him a message to Chamberlain urging that the "gates of Palestine" be held open as "a significant symbol of hope to Jewry." In the cabinet of October 19, Chamberlain had thought it "not possible to carry this matter further at the moment"; on November 16 there was agreement that Britain must do something, and it was left to a small committee to recommend a course of action.[15]

Roosevelt had quickly decided to take action of another kind: to recall Ambassador Hugh Wilson from Berlin and extend the visitors' permits of some 15,000 German and Austrian refugees then in the United States. When Lindsay asked the president on November 18 how long he meant to keep Wilson at home and he replied gaily (so Lindsay reported) "quite a long time," Lindsay's chief concern was that the United States government not get into a position where it could no longer communicate with Berlin. Roosevelt did not intend a break in relations, he explained, but Wilson would stay in America long enough to make his absence from Germany marked. Beyond this, however, Roosevelt did nothing more to affect the refugee problem at the time; there was too much domestic sentiment against relaxing immigration laws, and other matters were simply more pressing. Nor did Chamberlain. When visiting Paris on November 24, he told French officials that he did not expect assis-

14. CAB 23/96, 9 November 1938, pp. 181–82; Kennedy to Hull, 22 November 1938, SDM 740.00/516.

15. CAB 23/96, 16 November 1938, pp. 221, 225–26; Max Freedman, ed., *Roosevelt and Frankfurter: Their Correspondence, 1928–1945,* p. 463; CAB 23/96, 19 October 1938, pp. 8–9; CAB 27/624, 14 November 1938, pp. 36–43.

tance from the United States in resettling Jewish immigrants. Meantime, Frankfurter was complimenting Roosevelt for "making the Chamberlain Government do its duty in utilizing Palestine," adding: "I've been reading *Hansard,* and the speeches of Chamberlain and Simon and even of Halifax are sickening. How Gladstone and Bryce and Dizzy and Balfour must wince in the other world!" It was still a lot easier to chastise the other fellow than to initiate action oneself.[16]

There were, however, other developments from which a more positive spirit of collaboration might have been expected to emerge. Chief among them was the mid-November signing of the long and tediously negotiated Anglo-American Trade Agreement. It had been clearly recognized in London, at the time the British negotiating team had received its instructions in February 1938 (after nearly a year of preparatory maneuvering on both sides), that the *political* importance of the treaty was nearly as great—if not in fact greater—than the commercial advantages to be gained. While Britain was careful to avoid the impression of entangling America on the political side, Cadogan noted that Washington officials "had been so insistent in their requests for exchange of information on world affairs that there should be no danger of that." He agreed with Frank Ashton-Gwatkin (economic adviser in the Foreign Office) that the impact of signing an agreement might be great enough even to deter Germany for a time from "some act of violence" that it might otherwise commit—though the effect would wear off quickly "when it was seen that this U.K.-U.S. cooperation did not really imply very much." He felt that a high cabinet official, preferably the prime minister, should go to Washington for the signing, and the opportunity should be taken for discussion of "a further program of collaboration" with the United States. Chamberlain and Halifax recognized the political potential too, the former telling the cabinet (July 28) that "the more the impression could be created in Europe that the United Kingdom and the United States were getting together, the less would have to be spent on armaments." Indeed, the cabinet agreed that day to place on record the importance it attached—from a political and international point of view—to the conclusion of an agreement and to authorize British delegates to make further concessions toward that end. And nothing happened thereafter to alter that outlook. Rather, Chamberlain as well as Roosevelt

16. Lindsay to Halifax, 18 November 1938, FO 414/275, p. 49; Record of Anglo-French Conversations, 24 November 1938, *B.D.*, 3:296; Freedman, *Roosevelt and Frankfurter,* p. 466.

acknowledged in the week that followed Munich the heightened political importance of reaching a comprehensive trade agreement.[17]

Yet when the time for signing arrived, it seemed to be anticlimactic. Chamberlain had accepted the Board of Trade's early October position that delay in the negotiations was due to America's pressing for concessions (on tobacco, rice, and hams, for example) that were clearly "impracticable," and it would be mistaken tactics to display too great an anxiety; if Roosevelt really wanted an agreement, he could clear the way at once by ordering American concessions. Vacationing in Scotland, Chamberlain was unwilling to consider returning to London before October 19 for a cabinet meeting on the issue, even though Ambassador Lindsay, bitter and exasperated over American delays and equivocations, was arguing that failure to meet American terms would constitute "a first-class political crime, and our only justification . . . would consist of a multitude of economic factors which could hardly be understood by any but experts." Chamberlain told the cabinet on October 19 that he had never hoped to obtain any great economic or political support from the United States as a result of making an agreement. Rather, the advantages now to be derived were "of a somewhat negative kind"; if no agreement was reached, "hard things would be said" on both sides. The long, hard bargaining, the anxious delays, and the grudging concessions had gradually taken their toll; and when Chamberlain was finally able to tell the cabinet on November 7 that agreement had been reached, he made no comment at all about its potential significance and future benefits. That explorations of possible economic deals with Germany, which would help Britain to avoid unhealthy dependence on the United States, had recently been under way and were still a part of Chamberlain's thinking may help to account for his tepid reaction. The actual signing in Washington on November 17, without the presence of any high-placed official from London, was accompanied only by the usual effusions routinely proffered on such occasions. Halifax saw it a "signal example of what could be achieved when the Governments are animated by mutual good will and a determination to overcome difficulties," and Hull's description was about the same. Even press reaction on both sides of the Atlantic, though generally favorable and cognizant of potential political connotations, was reserved in assessing implications. It was

17. Eden and Stanley to U.K. Delegates, 14 February 1938, FO 414/275, pp. 97–98; Ashton-Gwatkin to Horace Wilson, 14, 16 March 1938, PREM 1/261; Tweedsmuir to Chamberlain, 30 September 1938, and Chamberlain to Mackenzie King, 4 October 1938, PREM 1/291.

simply good that ties had been strengthened between two democratic governments.[18]

Prospects for further improvement of those ties were present in the mid-November revelation of a possible visit by the king and queen to America in 1939. Having earlier heard from Canadian Prime Minister Mackenzie King of a projected royal visit to Canada the following summer, Roosevelt wrote King George VI in late August, inviting him to include the United States as well and noting: "Frankly, I think it would be an excellent thing for Anglo-American relations if you could visit [here]." The king's reply of late October was encouraging, and Lindsay reported that Roosevelt looked forward to the possibility of a visit "with the utmost pleasure." He had no misgivings whatever as to what it might imply about an Anglo-American alliance. Indeed, his eagerness for the visit was evident in the speed and enthusiasm with which he suggested detailed plans. He especially wanted the king to visit Hyde Park; the "simplicity and naturalism" of their meeting there would produce an excellent effect on American opinion and provide an ideal setting for candid and friendly conversation. Lindsay himself believed that only good could come from such a visit and urged acceptance of the invitation as soon as possible.[19]

There was a good deal of Foreign Office minuting in relation to the visit during the last two months of 1938. Taken together, it reveals not only support for the idea but agreement that if His Majesty went to Canada, he must also visit the United States, but also a deep concern that the visit should carefully avoid any hint of a publicity stunt. Chamberlain's personal view is harder to ascertain; there is little to indicate either dislike or enthusiasm for the tour. A succinct "No, Sir" constituted his full reply to a question in the House of Commons about whether he intended to accompany the king, and he gave no answer at all when asked whether he thought it would be a good idea to explain

18. Board of Trade Note on United States Trade Negotiations, 3 October 1938, PREM 1/291; Chamberlain to Tweedsmuir, 7 October 1938, ibid.; Lindsay to Halifax, 8 October 1938, FO 414/275, pp. 32–33; P.M.'s Office Minute, 10 October 1938, PREM 1/291; CAB 23/96, 19 October, 7 November 1938, pp. 20–21, 138; Lindsay to Halifax, 30 November 1938, FO 115/3416, Folder 733. Chamberlain had taken care to confer in advance with some business and labor leaders most likely to criticize the agreement from an economic standpoint (Stanley to Chamberlain, 11 November 1938, PREM 1/291). On the British exploration of possible economic deals with Germany, see MacDonald, *The United States, Britain, and Appeasement,* pp. 109–10.

19. *F.D.R.: His Personal Letters, 1928–1945,* 2:806, 825–26; Lindsay to Foreign Office, 25 October 1938, FO 794/17; Lindsay to Cadogan, 2, 22 November 1938, FO 115/3416, File 1249.

his foreign policy to the New World. That the questions were put by Ellen Wilkinson, a Labour M.P., no doubt tempered his attitude. Roosevelt, for his part, was also noncommittal, responding to the question about whether the prime minister would also come with a simple, "I have no idea."[20]

By this time Chamberlain was preoccupied with some imminent visiting of his own. The effort to improve relations with Italy required the soothing of irritations in Franco-Italian relations, and a visit to Paris would open the way for a January visit to Rome that was very much in his mind at the time (though the official record does not reveal that he mentioned this to the French). Having sought an invitation from Paris, he journeyed there with Halifax on November 24; he regarded the visit, so he told the cabinet, "more in the light of a gesture" and not likely to result in any great diplomatic advances. A "complete identity of ideas" on a wide range of policy issues was achieved, but only after some harsh exchanges over differing perceptions of future requirements and prospects, and grudging French acquiescence in Britain's flexible interpretation of the guarantee to rump Czechoslovakia. Back home in London, Chamberlain complained to his sister that French security officials would not let him ride in an open car. But he had wound the window down and gotten Daladier to tell the chauffeur "to aller doucement so that the people might have some chance of looking at me."[21]

Another prominent visit, of direct and special interest to Anglo-American relations, occurred a few weeks later: Anthony Eden journeyed to the United States, ostensibly to address the National Association of Manufacturers in New York, but certainly for broader purposes. He had been encouraged to go by Joseph Kennedy, who thought he could contribute significantly to improving Britain's image in America; and official approval had been granted by the Foreign Office, which—seeking to combat criticism of the government for neglecting opportunities to maintain contact with America—thought Eden could be trusted to put the British point of view before the American public. In addition to visiting New York, where he spoke of "the gathering storm" and Britain's determination to hold fast to her faith and defend it, he was received (at his request) in Washington, December 13, by President Roosevelt, who (perhaps feeling a bit uncertain how to deal with this prominent but unof-

20. FO 371/21548, pp. 112–224; *FDR Press Conferences,* 12:224.

21. CAB 23/96, 22 November 1938, p. 252; Record of Anglo-French Conversations in Paris, *B.D.,* 3:285–311; Neville to Hilda, 27 November 1938, NC 18/1/1077.

ficial Englishman) insisted that Britain must strengthen its air power and described his intention to increase American armaments, but "gave no glimpse" (as Eden later put it) "of any positive American policy either in the Far East or Europe."[22]

Eden's visit clearly evoked the response in America that Kennedy had hoped for. Victor Mallet, counselor of the British embassy in Washington, called it a "major sensation." Not for many years, he reported to Halifax, had a visitor from abroad excited such interest and enthusiasm. The American public seemed to make Eden its hero because of his championship of democracy and his well-known antipathy to the dictators. Though Eden carefully refrained from criticizing the Chamberlain government, both Roosevelt and Welles had come to see that Britain and its statesmen were "not as flabby as too many Americans had come to believe." Some people were puzzled by Eden's motive for coming, and the really "wise guys" (Mallet's term) suspected another subtle trick of British propaganda. But that idea had been fully exploded. The president was understood to have told Eden how greatly he admired his speeches and how much they had helped Anglo-American understanding; Morgenthau and Postmaster General James Farley, at the Press Club luncheon, were effusive in their praise. Indeed, Mallet wrote privately to Cadogan, Eden's popularity was a bit embarrassing, in contrast with "the less spectacular virtues and physical charms of Mr. Chamberlain and Lord Halifax." It was felt that the British government must be a queer lot if it could dispense with an asset like Eden; and his return to office would bring "a considerable strengthening of admiration [for Britain] in this country."[23]

Nor was Mallet's assessment unusual. Kennedy wired Halifax that Eden had increased Britain's prestige "terrifically." Lord Lothian, touring the United States at the time, wrote to British friends that "Anthony seems to have done very well over here," giving a "first-rate diplomatic performance." He uttered the right phrases, was straightforward and friendly, got on well with the press, did not criticize Chamberlain, made no whines or requests, talked sensibly in private, and even "had a succés with the girls." Lothian's perceptions were of special note since he was the British ambassador-designate, named to replace Ronald Lindsay upon his impending retirement (although this was not yet publicly

22. Earl of Avon (Anthony Eden), *The Memoirs of Anthony Eden: The Reckoning,* pp. 46–48; FO 371/21548, 14 December 1938, pp. 258–59; FO 800/234, 29 November 1938, p. 18.

23. Mallet to Halifax, 14 December 1938, FO 115/3416, File 1577; Mallet to Cadogan, 22 December 1938, FO 371/21548, pp. 271–77.

known). Senator Key Pittman, chairman of the Senate Foreign Relations Committee, was so impressed that he acted to have Eden's New York speech reprinted in the *Congressional Record* of January 4, calling it "one of the ablest expositions of democracy . . . I have ever read." It was "in excellent taste; it was splendidly received throughout the country; in fact . . . I have never known a foreigner coming to our country unofficially who has been more cordially received." Mallet's report of Pittman's views was read by officials in the Foreign Office, who deemed it "proof of Mr. Eden's success," and initialed by Halifax, who sent a copy of "this bouquet" on to Eden. Back in London, Eden too was pleased with his reception in America and encouraged by it. British stocks in the United States were low, he told Oliver Harvey and Harold Nicolson, because Chamberlain's policy was widely regarded as pro-dictator and pro-fascist, and quite serious people imagined that he was in the hands of an insidious "Cliveden Set" (a coterie of prominent appeasement-minded persons who gathered regularly at the Astor country estate by that name). But he felt he had been able to put before American opinion a bigger view of Britain.[24]

Two of those who refused to interpret Eden's visit positively were Neville Chamberlain and his sister Hilda. The prime minister confided that he got a certain satisfaction out of Eden's discomfort at being out of the government. He could not take him back without sacrificing his policy, and besides, Eden would have to proclaim his repentance first—which he doubtless would not do. "It would suit him much better to say that I had come round to his view. But I haven't and I don't mean to!" Hilda replied that it "was quite hopeless about Eden," and that "it was a great pleasure" to be told by someone who had been seeing some Americans that "Eden was a complete 'flop' over there. They expected great things and far from impressing them, they felt a great revulsion of opinion and will think no more of him." And her brother responded that Kennedy, back from America, "gave me the same account of Eden's visit as you had and said that the President had a long talk with him and was totally unable to find out what his policy was or whether he

24. Kennedy to Halifax, 18 December 1938, FO 800/324, p. 19; Lothian to Lady Astor, 27 December 1938, Astor Papers, MS 1416/1/4/57; Jones, *Diary with Letters,* pp. 422–23; Mallet to Halifax, 5 January 1939, FO 371/22823, pp. 30–33; *Harvey Diaries,* pp. 229–30; Harold Nicolson, *Diaries and Letters, 1930–1962,* 1:383. There was another view. Lady Lister Kay telegraphed Halifax that Eden "came in [to America] like a lion and departed like a worm. The pendulum has swung fiercely the other way" (18 December 1938, FO 800/324, p. 20).

had any policy at all."[25] Though allowance must be made for possible variations in Kennedy's reporting, it is nonetheless revealing of Chamberlain's mind-set that he took obvious satisfaction in thinking that Eden had "flopped" in America rather than concerning himself whether he had learned anything of value for British policymakers in his contacts with Roosevelt and others.

Lord Lothian's visit to America (December–February) was notable in several ways: for the repercussions of a conversation with Roosevelt and his observations about the status of American opinion. Before his departure he had asked Maurice Hankey (at Kennedy's suggestion) to prepare for his use a paper on the effect of the collapse of the British Empire on the United States. Hankey had produced a nine-page memorandum that Lothian considered to be "extremely good and just what I wanted." Understandably, it painted a gloomy picture of the situation that would confront America should Britain collapse. France and the French Empire would surely follow, nothing would remain of democracy in Europe, and the process would continue eastward into Asia. Britain's military and naval defenses constituted a "very powerful outpost line," without which it was problematic how long the United States could sustain the principles of liberty and justice against the rising tide of dictatorial lawlessness. The paper concluded that in the present anarchical state of the world, the balance of power lay with America. If adequately armed, she had "only to lift a finger to avert all serious danger of war, as well as the threat to democracy and all ultimate menace to herself." The question for her was "whether one of those rare moments is not at hand when prudence, foresight and self-interest combine in rendering action desirable which may change the history of mankind."[26]

In a White House conversation with Roosevelt early in January, Lothian told the president that the center of gravity in the democratic world was passing from Britain to the United States, which would have to choose whether to take up Britain's role of defending civilization. This defeatist line, as he perceived it, did not set well with Roosevelt; he was willing to give all the help he could, but he expected a much more robust attitude from the British. Ickes wrote in his diary a short time later:

25. Neville to Ida, 12 February 1939, NC 18/1/1085; Hilda to Neville, 16 February 1939, NC 18/2/1111; Neville to Hilda, 19 February 1939, NC 18/1/1806.

26. Paper prepared at request of Lord Lothian, 8 December 1938, HNKY 8/41; Lothian to Hankey, 8 December 1938, HNKY 4/30; Hankey to Phipps, 13 February 1939, HNKY 4/31; also Lothian Papers, GD 40/17/444.

> The President thinks that Great Britain is suffering from an inferiority complex. . . . She is being out-maneuvered at the council table. Her fleet is helpless and she has neglected to build enough airplanes. She has fooled herself with respect to Spain. The wealthy class in England is so afraid of communism . . . that they have thrown themselves into the arms of Nazism and now they don't know which way to turn.

Roosevelt graphically expressed his own disenchantment in a letter to Professor Roger Merriman at Harvard (who had sent the president a letter he had received from eminent historian George Trevelyan defending Munich and British proceedings thereafter, but explaining that Britain would put up "a jolly good fight" if forced to a defensive war to save western Europe):

> I wish the British would stop this "we who are about to die salute thee" attitude. Lord Lothian [who] was here the other day . . . [said] that the British for a thousand years had been the guardians of Anglo-Saxon civilization—that the sceptre or the sword or something like that had dropped from their palsied fingers—that the U.S.A. must snatch it up—that F.D.R. alone could save the world—etc., etc.
>
> I got mad clear through and told him that just so long as he or Britishers like him took that attitude of complete despair, the British would not be worth saving anyway.
>
> What the British need today is a good stiff grog, inducing not only the desire to save civilization but the continued belief that they can do it. In such an event they will have a lot more support from their American cousins, don't you think so?[27]

Roosevelt's letter came to the attention of British officials when Merriman passed it to Trevelyan, who sent it to Halifax. Cadogan thought the whole business "really rather serious," both in terms of Lothian's "dangerous delusion" that he could somehow swing American public opinion and the wisdom of sending him to Washington as ambassador. Halifax agreed it was "troublesome," though perhaps exaggerated in importance, and Chamberlain concurred that "we had better explore the ground further before we send him out in an official capacity." So Cadogan drafted a cable to Lindsay with some questions: Had Lothian talked along these lines elsewhere in the United States? If so, had it

27. See J. R. M. Butler, *Lord Lothian, 1882–1940,* p. 227; Ickes, *Diary,* 2:571; Roosevelt to Merriman, 15 February 1939, FO 794/18 (Lothian Correspondence). Kennedy had sent a copy of the Hankey memorandum to Roosevelt on 19 December (Kennedy to Roosevelt, PSF, Diplomatic Correspondence, Box 29). Whether he saw it before his conversation with Lothian is uncertain. In a letter to his close friend Lady Astor, Lothian gave no hint of presidential displeasure: "I had an hour with the President whose views are entirely sound and means to do everything he can to block or defeat the dictators" (Christopher Sykes, *Nancy: The Life of Lady Astor,* p. 402).

evoked unfavorable comment? Was Roosevelt liable to momentary outbursts, or would the interview with Lothian have made a lasting impression on him? To all of this, Halifax added a question of his own: Should previous appointment plans be reconsidered? Lindsay's reply was reassuring—in a way. The president was not given to outbursts, but he was inclined "to exaggerating what is said to him and what he says in reply." He did not appear to keep lasting impressions of foolish things said to him. And since Lindsay had received no unfavorable reactions to Lothian's private conversations elsewhere, he believed the whole business could be safely disregarded—unless there was reason to think this was "one of those discreet unofficial actions which . . . Governments sometimes take in order to forestall suggestion of a person as Ambassador." This last possibility made Cadogan still more uneasy; Halifax and Chamberlain agreed that Lindsay should take "further soundings," including an informal talk with the president. And that is where the matter rested when the attention of all was suddenly diverted by German action against Czechoslovakia in mid-March.[28]

Lothian's observations about the status of American opinion, which he freely shared with friends in England, especially Lady Astor, were guardedly optimistic. Although noting at first that most Americans whom he encountered did not yet realize how what might happen in Europe would affect the United States itself, there was certainly a deepening realization of importance of the international situation. Munich had made a strong impression, shaking the United States out of its "Baldwinite complacency." Roosevelt was taking a stronger line against fascism everywhere, and the public was beginning to listen as it had not done before. America was beginning to think out her future in the world, although the only conclusion reached thus far was "more armaments." Though the United States was still strongly isolationist and Britain was "off its pedestal" for not going to the rescue of Czechoslovakia, the situation was nonetheless "cheering" in view of the growing realization that America's security was intertwined with that of Britain and France.

28. Trevelyan to Halifax, 25 February 1939; Cadogan to Halifax, 1 March 1939; Halifax to Chamberlain, 2 March 1939; Chamberlain to Cadogan, 3 March 1939; Cadogan to Lindsay, 3 March 1939; Lindsay to Cadogan, 8 March 1939; Cadogan Minute, 9 March 1939; Hoyar Millar to Cadogan, 14 March 1939; Cadogan to Lindsay, 17 March 1939; FO 794/18. The disgust of several Foreign Office officials was recorded in their diaries. Cadogan wrote about "that booby Lothian" who had "fairly put his foot in it" (*Cadogan Diaries*, p. 154). Harvey recorded his hope that the appointment to Washington of "that conceited ass" was now dead (*Harvey Diaries*, pp. 258–59).

Indeed, Lothian felt it "quite clear that the real struggle is going to be between the U.S.A. and Hitler."[29]

Other January observations about American opinion that attracted considerable Foreign Office attention were those of Victor Mallet (counselor in the Washington embassy) who pointed out the general tendency among Americans to assume that British efforts for preparedness were feeble and half-hearted, and who argued that Britain would earn much greater respect if it were clearly shown that it was working hard to make up for past deficiencies. "The American has a great belief in self-help and it would be fatal if the idea gained ground here that we were doing all too little to help ourselves and just sitting down and hoping that America would help us when the time of our trial came." Paralleling Roosevelt's concern as expressed to Professor Merriman, Mallet's letter was favorably reviewed by a number of Foreign Office officials, who agreed that self-depreciation must give way to a more positive presentation of facts. The American looking at Europe must see (as counselor David Scott put it) not "an indiscriminate dog-fight and a welter of power politics but rather the simple clear-cut issue of 'liberty (with a capital L) versus Tyranny.'" Only then would he realize America's common cause with Britain—a cause founded on spiritual values and ideals, whatever the immediate issue might be. The nature of the minutes that Mallet's letter evoked clearly indicates that Foreign Office personnel were deeply concerned about the position of the United States and the condition of opinion there. But this concern did not extend to the prime minister's office to any meaningful degree.[30]

Foreign Office personnel—and others—might have taken some encouragement from Roosevelt's annual January message to Congress, delivered at a time when the president was disturbed about a Francoist offensive in Spain that threatened to vanquish the republic. Carefully choosing words to convey his realization that appeasement had only postponed, not prevented, a major European war, while at the same time avoiding provocation of the isolationists, he warned that philosophies of force were loose in the world that threatened the tenets of faith and humanity basic to the American way of life. No nation was safe when aggression occurred anywhere, and God-fearing democracies could not

29. Lothian to Lady Astor, 21, 27 December 1938, 5, 18 January 1939, Astor Papers, MS 1416/1/4/57-58; Lothian to Lady Cecil Kerr, 18 January 1939, Lothian Papers, GD 40/17/470; Jones, *Diary with Letters,* pp. 422–23.

30. Mallet to Scott, 26 January 1939, and Foreign Office Minutes, 7–8 February 1939, FO 371/22827, pp. 324–30.

"forever let pass, without effective protests, acts of aggression against sister nations." Hinting cryptically at methods short of war, "stronger and more effective than mere words," that would bring home to aggressor governments the sentiments of the American people, he specifically criticized existing neutrality legislation, which had the effect of encouraging aggressors. The instinct for self-preservation, he chided, should suggest something better than that. Thus Roosevelt placed the issue of neutrality revision, which would no doubt require an extensive degree of public support, on the national agenda. But he did not follow up his stirring words with specific ideas for action, and Congress remained slow to accept his advice. Only disturbing events in Czechoslovakia two months later would get the neutrality issue moving—slowly—in another direction. Reporting the speech to London, Mallet observed that the president's emphasis on defense organization and preparedness was an indication of his disquiet as well as his appreciation of the need to educate the people away from isolationism. But, he added, there were signs of alarm in Congress and the press at the hint of action rather than words, and it would take the country sometime to be educated "up to such a revolutionary point of view."[31]

Chamberlain, at the moment, was thinking more in terms of expanding appeasement by a visit to Rome. Bothered by criticism but determined to push on with the policy he knew to be right (so he wrote his sister), he wanted to improve his relationship with Mussolini and secure his good offices in Berlin. Perhaps the Duce could dissuade Hitler from carrying out some "mad dog act," he told his cabinet colleagues. There was also, no doubt, a lingering hope to wean Mussolini from the Axis. Ambassador Phillips, in Rome, wrote Roosevelt that the visit was "a good move," a compliment to the Italians, who love compliments above all things. But by most accounts Chamberlain's visit (with Halifax) on January 11–13 accomplished nothing. Conversations were rambling and indecisive, the depth of Mussolini's interest perhaps attested by his decision to skip the farewell banquet in favor of a skiing party. The Duce refused to discuss Hitler's future intentions. Chamberlain found this disappointing—until he decided that it reflected credit on Mussolini's character. But Chamberlain believed the visit had strengthened the cause of peace, attaching considerable importance to the exuberant welcome he received from the Italian people. And Phillips wrote Roosevelt that

31. Divine, *Roosevelt and World War II*, p. 25; Langer and Gleason, *The Challenge to Isolation*, pp. 46–48; Mallet to Halifax, 6, 10 January 1939, FO 414/276, pp. 5–11.

the result was "a pleasanter atmosphere."[32] There is no record of the president's reaction.

Ambassador Bullitt, in Paris, was considerably less sanguine than Phillips. He began to worry that Chamberlain might get together with Hitler over Italian claims on France and pressure Paris for concessions in the interest of peace just as he had pressured Czechoslovakia earlier. The British ambassador in Paris (Phipps) had vehemently denied this, but Bullitt reminded Roosevelt that the British had always found it easy to sacrifice the interests of other people, adding: "You may find yourself, before another couple of months have passed, wishing to request Mr. Chamberlain quietly not to behave like a S.O.B."[33]

There is nothing to suggest that Chamberlain's mind was running in that direction. In fact, he was busy wrestling with troublesome evidence that the appeasement of Germany was further than ever from realization. Word of Hitler's intense dissatisfaction with Munich, his brutal treatment of rump Czechoslovakia, his sarcastic public references to British "umbrella-carrying types," and a mid-December report of German planning for a surprise air attack on London, all pointed ominously toward this conclusion. Then the third week of January brought alarming reports of an impending German attack on Holland, which stirred the British to seek closer contact with Washington. Halifax's first thought, in the event of a German quarrel with the Dutch, was to be ready with some form of arbitration. It would probably have no effect, but if rejected would give a better *locus standi* for British intervention. "If the United States were ready to nominate an arbitrator, that might be of greatest importance." In any case, Roosevelt should be taken fully into Britain's confidence and told of all her apprehensions and intentions. When the Foreign Policy Committee discussed the ideas on January 23, Robert Vansittart—seldom included in this committee's deliberations despite his official status as chief diplomatic adviser—insisted, and won agreement, that Roosevelt be asked to make some announcement on the subject before Hitler's scheduled speech to the Reichstag on January 30. Oliver Stanley proposed inquiring of Roosevelt whether he would agree to appoint an arbitrator if the necessity arose; but Hoare thought that premature, and Chamberlain doubted that Hitler would regard the

32. Neville to Ida, 4 December 1938, 8 January 1939, NC 18/1/1078, 1081; CAB 23/96, 21 December 1938, pp. 428–30; Freedman, *Roosevelt and Frankfurter,* p. 472; Phillips to Roosevelt, 5, 20 January 1939, PSF, Diplomatic Correspondence, Box 32; Rock, *British Appeasement in the 1930s,* p. 16.

33. Bullitt to Roosevelt, 1 February 1939, PSF, Diplomatic Correspondence, Box 23.

United States as a neutral country anyway. The question of whether to inform the United States that Britain would intervene should Germany invade Holland was left unsettled pending advice about Britain's strategic interests from the Chiefs of Staff Sub-Committee.[34]

The message that went from Halifax to Washington next day detailed the disquieting reports of Hitler's mood and intentions and possible measures to counteract them. It pointedly referred to the "relations of confidence" between the British and American governments that prompted the former to state frankly its apprehensions and the measures it felt able to take, adding: "It would, of course, be a great help . . . if the President had any further suggestions to make." And if he were "disposed to take an occasion for any public announcement"—possibly concurrent with Chamberlain's scheduled Birmingham speech on January 28—"it might be the more valuable if he were to do so before January 30." The tone of this message was clearly one of great anxiety and distrust of Hitler. Chargé Johnson, in London, explained it to Hull in terms of Britain's acute consciousness that British-French armed forces were not equal to German-Italian armed forces, compounded by growing criticism of Britain's rearmament program—"an issue the Government will have to meet." The cabinet was informed of government action the following day.[35]

Word from Washington on January 27 was discouraging. Hull told Mallet ("in his usual cryptic and circumlocutory manner," according to Mallet's account) that he and Roosevelt were anxious to help, but the president felt it essential for reasons of internal politics to proceed with great caution. He was wary of going too far ahead of public opinion and thus losing control of Congress, which would be essential if the anticipated crisis arose. Nor did he want to raise false hopes or cause misunderstandings at home or abroad. Consequently, Mallet reported, with the isolationists full of fight and many critics accusing the president of being unduly alarmist, Roosevelt was not likely to send Chamberlain any specific message, make any definite suggestion, or issue any public statement. Hull's version of the conversation centered on informing Mal-

34. Rock, *British Appeasement in the 1930s*, p. 16; Halifax Memorandum, 19 January 1939, CAB 27/627, p. 177; CAB 27/624, 23 January 1939, pp. 107–10, 118. Chamberlain wrote in his diary, 22 January: "Three successive days of almost continuous rain are as depressing as the state of international affairs" (NC 2/26).

35. Halifax to Mallet, 24 January 1939, *B.D.*, 4:4–6 (also *FRUS*, 1939, 1:2–6); Johnson to Hull, 24 January 1939, SDM 740.00/548; CAB 23/97, 25 January 1939, pp. 72–73. See also *Cadogan Diaries*, p. 144.

let that the United States, alert to the possibility of war in Europe, was preparing plans for defense and security, as well as policies to promote peace, accordingly. He chose not to detail these matters and risk misinterpretation or distortion by "outsiders, critics, or commentators." But the end result was the same.[36]

The British were not entirely deterred, however. The chiefs of staff had decided that Britain must regard a German attack on Holland as a direct challenge to her own security, to be met by war *if* Holland chose to resist—reinforcing, in the process, the view that "the ultimate outcome . . . might well depend upon the intervention of other Powers, in particular the United States of America." The Foreign Policy Committee endorsed their conclusion and Halifax promptly informed Washington. (The full cabinet concurred a few days later.) At the same time, Cadogan relayed to Chargé Johnson a copy of Chamberlain's Birmingham speech, in which he proposed to declare that peace could only be endangered by a demand to dominate the world by force—which demand both he and the president of the United States, in his New Year's message, had already declared the democracies must inevitably resist.[37]

Meantime, Washington seemed silent. The cabinet discussed the European situation on January 27, but the question of support for Britain was not directly confronted. Indeed, one cabinet member (Ickes), in recording the meeting, thought Roosevelt "altogether too prone" to decide important questions alone or with individual cabinet officers. Mallet had learned (from a "highly reliable visitor" to the White House) that Roosevelt and the State Department expected not so much a German invasion of Holland but mobilization on the Dutch frontier and demands for part of the Dutch East Indies, with the object of humiliating Britain and promoting a defensive alliance with Japan through an offer of spoils. But Roosevelt was not sitting idle. To the Senate Military Affairs Committee, called to the White House on January 31, he made an unusually full and frank statement about his perception of the threatening world situation and the dangers therein to America. Painting an alarming picture of German-Italian-Japanese intentions to strive for world domination, the president described as America's first line of defense in Europe the continued independent existence of some twenty nations that he

36. Mallet to Halifax, 27 January 1939, *B.D.*, 4:27, 29; Hull Memorandum, 27 January 1939, SDM 740.00/548.

37. CAB 27/624, 26 January 1939, p. 157; Halifax to Mallet, 28 January 1939, *B.D.*, 4:40; Johnson to Hull, 28 January 1939, SDM 740.00/559. For the Birmingham speech, see Chamberlain, *In Search of Peace*, pp. 249–57.

listed by name. He then developed what in a wholly different context of American foreign relations many years later would be called a "domino theory." If Britain, France, and other European states tried to block Hitler's next moves, the outcome was problematic. If Europe fell to the Axis, Africa would automatically follow, then Central and South America—until the United States would be dangerously encircled. Believing, as he did, that the crucial element in Europe's defense was air power, he explained his past behavior relative to Anglo-French needs and urged planning for the mass production of American airplanes to assist other nations (particularly the British and French) to preserve their independence, which he now thought literally threatened. To maintain the independence of these nations by sending them everything they could pay for—that was the foreign policy of the United States. No doubt by way of assuaging senatorial anxieties and suspicions, Roosevelt concluded that the sending of an American army to Europe again was "about the last thing this country should do." Despite his plea for confidentiality, so as not to frighten the American people, word of this meeting was leaked to the press. Mallet reported it to London, and Halifax mentioned it with some satisfaction to the cabinet on February 1. But there erupted a veritable volcano of isolationist criticism, exacerbated by exaggerated reports that Roosevelt had said that America's frontier was on the Rhine. A bitterly angered president spoke to a press conference several days later about "deliberate misrepresentations" of what he had said and insisted that American policy had not changed and would not change. With the ground thus shaking ominously, the British were left bewildered, wondering what to make of it all.[38]

The circumstances of the moment were not conducive to clarification. An unfortunate incident lay in the background of the January 31 meeting, Roosevelt's unusual candor there, and the criticism he experienced as a result of it: the crash of a Douglas bomber in California with a French military observer aboard brought to public attention the presence of a French air mission in America to purchase planes. This created a "very considerable sensation" and "brought isolationist sentiment out in force again," Mallet reported to Halifax. And Roosevelt's press conference did not "damp down the storm." It was the president's secret

38. Ickes, *Diary,* 2:568–69; Mallet to Halifax, 30 January 1939, *B.D.,* 6:51–52; Mallet to Halifax, 1 February 1939, FO 414/276, p. 19; CAB 23/97, 1 February 1939, p. 101. See Dallek, *Franklin Roosevelt and American Foreign Policy,* p. 181. Cole, *Roosevelt and the Isolationists,* pp. 304–9, contains a full account both of Roosevelt's statements to the Senate committee and the reaction of leading isolationist senators to them.

method, not his actual policy, which was the primary object of attack. Most Americans shared his sympathy with the democratic powers, but they were nervous about being committed too hastily to a line of action in Europe. Ten days later criticism was still ringing in Congress, Mallet reported, the situation so serious that no further sessions of the Senate Military Affairs Committee had been held in order to give time for tempers to cool.[39] Actually, Mallet's accounts understated the bitterness of the controversy and the ill will that it generated.

Meantime, Bullitt had learned from Roosevelt (by telephone) that he did not speak of the United States frontier as being in France or on the Rhine, as was widely reported; but he did say that the French army was America's first line of defense, and anything he could do to strengthen it was all to the good. Bullitt's account of the president's language to Phipps and Hankey in Paris on February 6 struck Hankey as being so similar to that which he had used in the paper he had prepared for Lothian that he believed himself to be "the unconscious promoter of this line of thought in the President's mind." He later produced for Phipps a copy of his paper with certain passages marked in red to support his contention.[40] Lothian's point had perhaps been made at the White House after all.

In any case, the German threat to Holland blew over. Hitler's speech to the Reichstag was less threatening than had been expected, and the rumors of German troop movements went unconfirmed. Halifax continued to keep Roosevelt informed, utilizing both the British chargé in Washington and the American chargé in London to transmit messages. Britain would treat a German attack on Switzerland in the same way as an attack on Holland. France would consider an attack on Holland to be cause for war. Belgium would remain noncommitted. The French were pushing the British to adopt conscription. The British were proposing an extension of staff conversations with France. Halifax told the cabinet on February 8 that Roosevelt's recent pronouncement (reference unclear), synchronizing with Chamberlain's speech in the Commons, had had a very valuable effect in Germany. And Chamberlain told Kennedy that "America's action psychologically," along with Britain's "tremendous amounts for defense," had had a definite effect and "may do the trick." Kennedy, for his part, reported that all the important persons

39. Mallet to Halifax, 3, 7, 16 February 1939, FO 414/276, pp. 23–25, 30–31.

40. Phipps to Halifax, 6 February 1939, PHPP 1/22l; Hankey to Phipps, 13 February 1939, HNKY 4/31. Phipps wrote Hankey on 21 February that he was glad Roosevelt had taken Hankey's views, as expressed to him by Lothian, "so to heart" (ibid.).

to whom he had recently talked believed that Britain was "on its way," that the problem of last September, when it had to do things it would rather not have done, was gone. And "the psychology resulting from what the United States has done is a determining factor in the peace of mind that exists at the moment."[41] What a startling change of outlook from just a month before!

But the month that preceded the German seizure of Prague was one in which official British optimism, especially that of Chamberlain and a few close colleagues, but not Halifax and the Foreign Office, ran high. No doubt partly contrived in hopes of creating confidence by talking it into being, it was in any case not the sort of stuff to reassure American officials about Britain's sense of realism and seriousness of purpose, especially since it conflicted with intelligence reports being received in Washington. Welles informed Lindsay in mid-February of "gloomy news" about Axis military preparations that suggested the possibility of a crisis, even war, by the end of March. Roosevelt, off for a cruise with the United States fleet, had told the press before departing that he might have to return to Washington unexpectedly. But the information in Lindsay's message to London, sent for evaluation to Admiral Sir Hugh Sinclair (head of the British Intelligence Service) was adjudged to involve "alarmist rumors put forward by Jews and Bolshevists for their own ends," and the reply to Washington downplayed any imminent danger. A secret message of March 1 explained in detail why the British government believed that Hitler had abandoned, at least for a time, the idea of precipitating a crisis.[42]

In the binge of euphoria, so evident in Chamberlain's letters to his sisters, the attitude of the United States government appears as one of four or five factors (also including apparent progress in Anglo-German economic relations and advances in British rearmament, especially defensive preparations) upon which the new optimism was founded. But references to its form and nature were certainly mixed and equivocal. The prime minister wrote his sister that Hitler must have noticed Roosevelt's message to Congress approving the French purchase of airplanes, a move that he believed to be deliberately timed—"an ingenious way of conveying a hint to Berlin." Further, he had heard that the Nazis were

41. Halifax to Mallet, 7, 17 February 1939, *B.D.*, 4:83–85, 114–15; CAB 23/97, 8 February 1939, pp. 208–9; Kennedy to Hull, 17, 20 February 1939, SDM 740.00/588–89; Hull to Roosevelt, 21 February 1939, PSF, Diplomatic Correspondence, Box 29.

42. Rock, *British Appeasement in the 1930s*, pp. 17–18; Sidney Aster, *1939: The Making of the Second World War*, p. 53; Welles Memorandum, 1 March 1939, SDM 740.00/597 1/2.

bothered about the Anglo-American Trade Agreement, in which they suspected secret military clauses. Some days later he wrote that "Roosevelt is saying Heaven knows what but anyhow something disagreeable to dictators and there is an uneasy feeling [in Germany] that in case of trouble it would not take much to bring U.S. in on the side of the democracies." To Tweedsmuir he wrote of being struck with several evidences of veering public opinion in the United States; highly critical of Munich, Americans now seemed to be developing a greater understanding and appreciation of British policy. (Kennedy had, in fact, returned to London from America reporting that American opinion was moving "in the right direction," but warning Chamberlain and Halifax that Britain should not ask for anything or speak as if it could count on the United States. Indeed, on the whole question of Anglo-American relations, he advised that the less said the better.) Again to his sister, Chamberlain wrote that although he was glad to hear that Roosevelt was cutting short his holiday on account of disturbing rumors about the intentions of the dictators, "I myself am going about with a lighter heart than I have had for many a long day. All the information I get seems to point in the direction of peace and . . . I believe we have at last got on top of the dictators." This effusion at length led sister Ida to proclaim: "I see the Chamberlain legend growing every day and feel that you will soon have to cast your ring into the sea to placate the envious gods."[43]

The climax of this euphoria came in Hoare's address in Chelsea, March 10, in which, at Chamberlain's urging, he cited the possible imminence of a "golden age." Five men in Europe, working together and "blessed in their efforts" by the president of the United States, "might in an incredibly short space of time transform the whole history of the world" and make themselves "the eternal benefactors of the human race." The day before, Chamberlain had assured an assemblage of correspondents that Europe was settling down to a period of tranquility,

43. Halifax to Lindsay, 27 February 1939, *B.D.*, 4:159–61; Welles Memorandum, 1 March 1939, SDM 740.00/597 1/2; Neville to Ida, 28 January 1939, NC 18/1/1083; Neville to Hilda, 5 February 1939, NC 18/1/1084; Chamberlain to Tweedsmuir, 7 February 1939, NC 7/11/32/281; Chamberlain to Lindsay, 17 February 1939, FO 414/276, p. 25; Neville to Hilda, 19 February 1939, NC 18/1/1086; Ida to Neville, 9 March 1939, NC 18/2/1114. Chamberlain even talked on 12 February of reports that Germany was seeking "for some means of approaching us without the danger of a snub" (Neville to Ida, NC 18/1/1085). In his letter of 19 February, he made note of some "exquisitely funny" American commentaries on his Birmingham speech. One man wrote:

> If you think there's any credit doo [*sic*] him Now's the time to tell it to him 'Cause he cannot smell the flowers when he's dead.

Said Chamberlain: "I laughed over this till my tears fairly overflowed."

and expressed hope for early progress in disarmament. This was too much even for Halifax, who rebuked him for talk that would not "do good in Germany at this moment." And a chastened Chamberlain promised to consult his foreign secretary beforehand the next time correspondents asked about foreign affairs. But his optimism—and self-confidence—were in no way diminished. "I know I can save this country and I do not believe that anyone else can," he wrote to Ida March 12. He wanted a few more years in which to do it, and the reports that he was receiving suggested that he would get them. As for the Conservative critics of his policy, some of whom had earlier parted company with him (Churchill, Eden, Duff Cooper, and others): "All the prodigal sons are fairly besieging the parental door," conceding in one way or another that the prime minister was right.[44]

During the Munich winter, a variety of other matters arose in Anglo-American relations the impact of which is hard to assess, but that are deserving of mention here—with no claim to priority of importance. Indeed, none may be especially significant in influencing relations between the two countries, save in a cumulative way; but some are doubtless indicative of the nature of the relationship that existed.

Though distracted from Asian affairs by the growing pressure of events in Europe, both Britain and the United States remained anxious and uneasy about the tensions that continued to develop there as a result of Japan's remorseless campaign against China. Both nations recognized, in their contacts with the other, the increasing need for governments whose interests were threatened by Japan to take concerted action in their defense. And both expressed interest in hearing of any conclusions the other had reached about the possibility of effective action. In mid-December the idea of enlisting German influence in helping to settle the Far Eastern problem (since "powerful sections" in Germany were disgruntled by the decline of German trade in China) emerged within the Foreign Office. Indeed, one official (R. Howe) believed that such Anglo-German cooperation could be represented as "one of the first-fruits of

44. Speech on "The World's Greatest Opportunity," Templewood Papers, X:6; Halifax to Chamberlain and reply, 10–11 March 1939, NC 7/11/32/111–12; Neville to Ida, 12 March 1939, NC 18/1/1089. In an earlier speech at Swansea, 26 January, Hoare had derided as "jitterbugs" those who "sit listening to all the hot music of the scares and alarms waiting helplessly for the crash which according to them will destroy us all" (Templewood Papers, X:6). A gleeful Chamberlain thought it "a most admirable speech" and sent Hoare a pencil drawing of an ugly, wriggling worm with big eyes and a pin sticking through it that he labeled: "Specimen of jitterbug from the Hoare Collection" (ibid., X:4).

the Munich Agreement." Cadogan scotched the idea quickly—*unless* the cooperation and consent of the United States was obtained. Effective retaliation against Japan depended on it, and "we are discussing, or about to discuss, that with them now."[45]

But discussion did not proceed successfully. Nearly a month later—acknowledging that London had been approached in early November and that a reply was overdue—Halifax submitted to Chamberlain a long draft message to Washington about possible economic retaliation against Japan. He doubted its feasibility but considered it "of great political importance . . . that the Americans should not again have the fun of saying what they would have done if only we had not stood in the way." The draft thus set forth in detail some of the difficulties and asked whether the United States had any definite proposals to make. London would be glad to examine them with a view to possible parallel action—on the understanding, of course, that they would have to be referred to the dominions and the governments of India and Burma, on whom the greatest loss of trade would fall; and that it would also be necessary for all governments concerned to consider what contributions to the common defense each would be prepared to guarantee in the face of Japanese countermeasures. Chamberlain thought the draft "evidently commits us to nothing and I therefore see no reason to object to its despatch. [But] I shall be very surprised if we draw the badger." Actually, there was no badger to draw. American policymakers did considerable thinking about measures that might retard Japan's aggression, but that was about as far as it went. The State Department disliked proposals for economic sanctions and wished to avoid any action unless it involved a comprehensive retaliatory program and was backed, possibly, by fleet maneuvers—in any case, something sufficient to demonstrate that America really meant business. After the November announcement of Japan's New Order, the State Department considered trade and credit reprisals against Tokyo for its disregard of American rights and interests in China. But those interests hardly warranted risking armed conflict under existing circumstances. Nor was there pressure from Roosevelt. Though thoroughly annoyed by Japan's behavior and ambitions, he too had little desire to threaten her to the point of risking danger when his attention was increasingly focused on the primary problem of Europe. Thus Mallet reported that the United States government, like the British, was loathe

45. Howe Memorandum and Cadogan Minute, 14 December 1938, FO 800/396. See also Lindsay to Halifax, 1 December 1938, *B.D.*, 8:278–79.

to pursue an adventurous course in its dealings with Japan. The British may not have trusted American proposals anyway—as was the case in Simon's response to the idea of pressuring Japan by refusing to purchase Japanese gold: it would not be effective and might be dangerous. Japan would sell her gold to Italy, who would then sell it to the United States or Britain. And "it would be dangerous to get the U.S.A. started on a policy of refusing to buy gold, for once started on it they might extend the practice unduly." Small wonder that Cadogan minuted on March 1 that economic cooperation against Japan was unlikely.[46]

A corollary to the issue of economic retaliation against Japan was the question of extending a loan to China—in the form of a £3 million contribution to the Chinese currency stabilization fund. The issue received regular mention in British cabinet meetings between November and February. Halifax, who believed such a loan to be the only concrete action Britain could take to help China, thought it important to know where the United States stood and sought authorization, November 30, to approach Washington about a joint loan. Chamberlain did not think Britain should proceed alone (the position in Europe was too unstable); but if the United States would join in, that would greatly strengthen Britain's inclination to go ahead. American authorities, in turn, inquired what else the British had done for China, and at length took up the view that America's aid was already considerably ahead of Britain's. Roosevelt was reported to doubt the constitutionality of a currency loan without congressional approval, which the Treasury Department considered out of the question. He preferred to support China by silver purchases and export credits. So the United States was prepared to take parallel and simultaneous, but not identical, action, which Welles told Mallet would have the same psychological effect on Japan as both nations giving a currency loan. The British found the American posture "somewhat vague" and continued to press for a clarification of exactly what would constitute America's parallel action. This engendered State Department alarm that an announcement in Parliament of simultaneous and parallel action would cause difficulties with American isolationists. Halifax was at length forced to concede that the United States government was "most unwilling to appear to be acting in collusion with us"; Kennedy (who earlier had warned that the British Empire already had quite enough

46. Halifax to Chamberlain, 9 January 1939, PREM 1/314, pp. 50–57; Halifax to Mallet, 23 January 1939, *B.D.*, 8:411–14; Mallet to Halifax, 9 February 1939, ibid., pp. 450–51; Simon to Chamberlain, 14 February 1939, PREM 1/314, p. 42; *Cadogan Diaries*, p. 153; Offner, *Origins of the Second World War*, pp. 156–58.

trouble on its hands without taking on more) countered that American public opinion would be "shocked" if it knew how much the government had already done for China; and the British cabinet eventually decided that it was safe to proceed alone without fear of provoking retaliation by Japan.[47]

The perennial question of the repayment of Britain's war debt to America arose again, not in acute form but in a mildly bothersome way. Some months earlier (February 1938), Lindsay had described for Welles a striking change of attitude that he had observed in high official circles in London. Whereas the government previously had been utterly unwilling to discuss the possibility of debt negotiations, there was now an active interest in the matter "from Mr. Chamberlain down." Welles in turn observed a few months later that if Roosevelt won the forthcoming election, the period immediately thereafter would be (in view of the president's objective views on the question) a most favorable time for Britain to make an offer. But Foreign Office officials were unconvinced. There was doubt that American opinion would permit compromise, and though a gesture to show that Britain had not written off the whole thing might be beneficial, the form of the gesture and the opportunity for making it would be (in Cadogan's words) "mighty hard to determine." Chamberlain was asked in the Commons on November 24 whether he now would initiate negotiations in an effort to reach a final settlement. His response was noncommittal. There followed in December the usual semiannual notification of debts due and payable; but Lindsay's routine assurance that the British government would be "willing to reopen discussions on the subject whenever circumstances are such as to warrant the hope that a satisfactory result might be reached" was all that followed. By then the Foreign Office had decided that the timing of a gesture was almost as important as the gesture itself—and any gesture at that juncture would only be interpreted in the United States as an attempt to buy American friendship at a moment when Britain needed it. Further, there was doubt in London that Washington wanted a settlement, since that would remove Britain from "listing" under the Johnson Act (which prohibited loans to countries owing war debts); it would make it possible for her to borrow from the United States, and thus permit her possibly to entangle America further in Eu-

47. CAB 23/96, 30 November, 14, 21 December 1938, pp. 296–302, 378–79, 421–24; CAB 23/97, 18 January, 1, 8, 15 February 1939, pp. 13–16, 105–6, 198, 256, 297–300; Mallet to Halifax, 11 December 1938, *B.D.*, 8:310–11; Mallet to Simon, 11 January 1939, ibid., p. 385; CAB 53/10, 23 November 1938, pp. 22–25.

rope's problems. And the American press, Mallet reported, did not seem interested in the matter.[48]

The Anglo-American controversy over the control of, and rights in, certain Pacific islands continued intermittently during the Munich winter. Notes were exchanged during November on the establishment of joint control over Canton and Enderbury Islands, but disputed points of detail were not easily or quickly resolved. The British agreed to suspend their earlier claim to the right to colonize Canton and to keep a permanent British administrator there, but thereafter became concerned that the United States intended to "force the issue" in regard to Gardner, Hull, and Sydney Islands. They moved to consolidate their position on both Hull and Christmas Islands (needed for a trans-Pacific airline)—prepared if necessary to go to arbitration over Christmas Island but willing to share Hull with the United States "only in the last resort." They also pondered an American suggestion that the whole question of the status and use of all the islands should be discussed in conference, with one possible solution being to accept United States sovereignty over Canton and Enderbury, with Britain keeping Hull and Christmas Islands.[49] The controversy engendered may not, in retrospect, seem very important in relation to other issues confronting both governments at the time. And that is precisely the point: it caused irritation out of proportion to its relative importance and was just one more factor delaying the development of trust and cooperation that the broader course of events increasingly seemed to require.

The same thing may be said of issues relating to ambassadorial representation on both sides. The British, who had been sometimes disconcerted by the brash and abrasive Kennedy almost from the moment of his arrival in London, were increasingly puzzled by his mercurial outlook and pronouncements. His commitment to appeasement was strong, and that assisted British officials of similar views to overlook his personal idiosyncracies to some degree. But as it became ever more apparent that his outlook rested upon a conviction that Britain was "over the hill" and no longer able to play her traditional power role in the world, their

48. Welles Memorandum, 28 February 1938, SDM 841.00/1352; Lindsay to Halifax, 11 July 1938, FO 115/3416, File 463; Foreign Office Minutes, 21 July 1938, FO 371/21545, pp. 245–46; Foreign Office Note, 24 November 1938, ibid., pp. 280–81; Welles to Lindsay and reply, 1, 13 December 1938, FO 115/3416, File 968; Mallet to Halifax, 21 December 1938, ibid., File 463; Foreign Office Minutes, 2 March 1939, FO 371/22829, pp. 94–95; FO 371/21545, passim.

49. FO 115/3416, File 177; FO 115/3417, File 91; Mallet's Annual Report, FO 371/22832, pp. 28–33.

patience sometimes wavered. He had once astonished Halifax by telling him that he did not care for the post of ambassador; he felt better in America where he was "as independent as a hog on ice." Understandably, British officials became progressively unsure how to evaluate his advice and his interpretation of things back home, sometimes falling into the natural pattern of accepting it at face value when it suited their own purposes, but viewing it skeptically when it did not. Chamberlain was mildly disturbed by Kennedy's long holiday absence in America (early December to mid-February), thinking, as Cadogan recorded it, that "it might be a good thing for . . . [his] own education to resume his contact here"—apart from the fact that what he must know from his consultation with Roosevelt and others "would be of value." But upon his return, the Foreign Office found his views on economic appeasement as a means of seeking rapprochement with Germany untenable. And Cadogan recorded with some disgust: "After his resumption of contact with the U.S., I can hardly understand a word he says. It's a different language."[50]

On the British side, the issue was different but nonetheless tedious. Sir Ronald Lindsay having made known, some months before, his wish to retire early in 1939, British officials at length had settled upon Lord Lothian as his successor. There was from the start a question about his association with the "Cliveden Set," which Lindsay himself had raised with London while writing to Lothian that there was no one else he could "so enthusiastically welcome" to the post. Lothian officially had been tapped by the time he visited America—although the effective date of his takeover had been set back so that Lindsay would remain to handle the upcoming visit to America of the king and queen, and Lothian had been permitted to withdraw his acceptance temporarily so as to avoid awkward questions. Roosevelt's reaction to Lothian's White House visit in January, once it became known in London, threw British officials into a quandary whether the appointment ought to be withdrawn altogether—especially since numerous other persons (including Vansittart, Leith-Ross, Grigg, Lytton, Chatfield, Tweedsmuir, Eden, and Cadogan) had been mentioned earlier as possible choices. There is little evidence of consultation with American officials, although Tweedsmuir volunteered to Chamberlain that he knew Roosevelt considered the appoint-

50. See *The Diaries of Sir Robert Bruce Lockhart,* 1:411; Cadogan Minute, 7 February 1939, FO 371/22827, pp. 294–95; Foreign Office Minutes, 20 February 1939, FO 371/22829, pp. 85–86; *Cadogan Diaries,* p. 151.

ment "enormously important" and did not believe that a career diplomat was the proper choice at the time. The issue remained unsettled, causing no little anxiety on the British side, until well into the spring of 1939.[51]

In addition to the tedious matters that exacerbated Anglo-American relations in varying degrees during the Munich winter, there were also lost opportunities that might have helped turn things in a more positive direction. Most obvious among them was the failure to capitalize on the signing of the Anglo-American Trade Agreement. Its conclusion had long been understood on both sides to carry important political implications far beyond its value in promoting trade, and others had so recognized it, too. Canadian Prime Minister Mackenzie King, for example, telegraphed Chamberlain on September 30, reminding him of his own view (of a year before) that such an agreement would be "a major contribution towards the future peace of the world" and urging a quick conclusion to the negotiations. But they had dragged on so long and had been characterized by such stubborn and sometimes petty haggling that the governments themselves—to say nothing of the general public—had lost confidence in the meaning and impact of agreement. To be sure, press reaction (including trade papers) in both nations was generally favorable. But initial expressions of satisfaction were followed by a quick descent of the whole matter into near-oblivion. Apparently many Englishmen shared Cadogan's view: "Unfortunately, the Americans are the spiritual heirs of the Dutch [in things commercial], and open their mouths rather wide." And many Americans were wary of what the wily English might try to pull next.[52]

The severe deterioration in American-German relations after Munich might have been expected to affect Anglo-American relations positively, at least indirectly. Welles spoke sharply with the German ambassador in Washington on November 1 about American dissatisfaction with certain German policies and behavior, especially the persecution of religious groups and press attacks on the United States. Again on December 21—

51. See Lindsay Correspondence, 27 October–21 November 1938, FO 794/17; Halifax to Lothian, 22 November 1938, FO 794/18; Lindsay to Lothian, 30 November 1938, Lothian Papers, GD 40/17/369; *Cadogan Diaries*, pp. 78, 82–83, 90, 110, 122, 130; Tweedsmuir to Chamberlain, 23 January 1939, NC 7/11/32/280; Lothian Correspondence, 10–25 March 1939. FO 794/18. On the positive side, two papers on "Britain and America," undated but apparently written by Lothian during the Munich winter, show a keen appreciation of the Anglo-American community of interest and the need for the two democracies to stand together in the developing world crisis (Lothian Papers, GD 40/17/444).

52. King to Chamberlain, 30 September 1938, PREM 1/291; Lindsay to Halifax, 30 November 1938, FO 414/275, p. 64, and FO 115/3416, Folder 733; *Cadogan Diaries*, p. 119.

in statements to which Roosevelt gave emphatic approval—he rebutted the German chargé's protests about remarks Secretary Ickes had made by telling him bluntly that recent German policies had profoundly shocked and confounded American public opinion. By late February 1939, the German ambassador to London, von Dirksen, was complaining to Halifax about almost weekly utterances of the president, which had convinced Germany that in the event of war the United States would come to the aid of Britain and France not in two years or even two months, but in two days. Thus a suspension of German armament production, about which Halifax had inquired, was unthinkable. Indeed, in an ironic twist, Bullitt reported von Dirksen's hope that Britain might assist in improving German-American relations.[53] But none of this was consciously used to affect Anglo-American relations materially. The British were still afraid to make any move that might be construed as suggestive; the Americans were still loathe to consider anything that might smack of "cooperation" with Britain or "entanglement" in her affairs.

The contact established between Chamberlain and Roosevelt through their mutual friend Arthur Murray bore no particular fruit either in the months that followed Munich. When Murray finally carried Roosevelt's message of October 21 to Chamberlain (through Halifax) in mid-December, the foreign secretary first lamented that he had "failed to ride him [Murray] off seeing you," then allowed that a meeting would be worthwhile. It was duly arranged at the House of Commons on December 14. Murray provided notes of his conversation with Roosevelt; they revealed a simple, friendly, candid assessment of how the president might help in the event of hostilities and how the scope of his aid might vary in different circumstances. At the top of these notes, Chamberlain wrote: "To be carefully preserved. Note formula on 2d page which may be used." Murray then reported to Roosevelt that the prime minister had "derived a real feeling of encouragement from the messages and tokens of your sympathetic attitude, and from the sense of friendly contact with yourself that these messages and tokens brought." Whether

53. Welles Memorandum, 1 November 1938, *FRUS*, 1938, 2:446–51; Welles Memorandum, 21 December 1938, SDM 711.62/176 1/2; Halifax to Henderson, 22 February 1939, *B.D.*, 4:139; Kennedy to Hull, 23 February 1939, SDM 740.00/592; Bullitt to Hull, 27 February 1939, SDM 711.62/235. Additional problems in German-American relations included the German persecution of Jews, unsatisfactory trade relations, the American refusal to sell helium to Germany, the participation of German nationals in the German-American Bund, disagreement on treaty provisions affecting naturalization and dual nationality, and difficulties arising from the German annexation of Austria (see *FRUS*, 1938, 2:355–515).

that was Chamberlain's real reaction or Murray's interpretation of it for Roosevelt is uncertain. But nothing followed. At Chamberlain's suggestion, Murray called a few days later on Kingsley Wood, minister for Air, who promised to have Roosevelt's message "very carefully examined from every appropriate angle." And there the matter languished until May. Roosevelt wrote to Murray later that he was glad to hear that Murray's talk with Chamberlain "helped him to realize my real friendship for him." And Murray relayed this to Chamberlain, explaining: "I thought I would just let you know this."[54] What emerges from this exchange is an impression that Roosevelt was skeptical that Chamberlain realized his friendship and that Chamberlain still doubted whether it mattered.

The latter seems corroborated by Chamberlain's response in the House of Commons, February 7, to a question about whether he would consider the advisability of visiting Roosevelt as a continuation of his recent visits to national leaders. In a reply that he himself drafted, he said that his visits to other countries "have in all cases been in connection with special circumstances"; and although he would gladly extend them, his absence from the country for more than a brief interval would cause "a good deal of inconvenience which it is desirable to avoid." The Foreign Office quickly assured Washington that the British government was not responsible for the question, and the answer given was not to be read as a hint, or as calling for any sort of notice on the part of the U.S. authorities.[55] There was, in short, a lot of defensive maneuvering over what, in retrospect, appears to have been a very good question—even though asked by Geoffrey Mander, an outspoken critic of the Chamberlain government. The United States still played no substantial role in Chamberlain's calculations.

54. Halifax to Chamberlain, 9 December 1938, PREM 1/367; Notes of conversations between Roosevelt and Murray at Hyde Park, 16–24 October 1938, ibid.; Murray to Roosevelt, 20 December 1938, and reply, 19 January 1939, PSF, Diplomatic Correspondence, Box 29; Elibank, "Roosevelt: Friend of Britain," p. 367; Murray to Chamberlain, 1 February 1939, PREM 1/367.

55. Foreign Office Minutes, 7 February 1939, FO 371/22827, pp. 68, 73.

VII.
From Prague to the Outbreak of War

THE SHOCK ADMINISTERED TO Europe and the world in general, and to Britain and Chamberlain in particular, by the sudden German conquest of rump Czechoslovakia in mid-March 1939 and the British response during the first few weeks thereafter have been described in other places and need only be reviewed in outline here. Although stunned and dismayed, the prime minister's first reaction was to treat the event lightly. Czechoslovakia had disintegrated through "internal disruption," he told the House of Commons on March 15, thus freeing the British government from any obligation to her: the spirit of Munich had been violated, to be sure, but Britain should not be deflected from its course (appeasement) because of that; the object that it had in mind was "of too great significance to the happiness of mankind" to be given up lightly or set aside. This provoked fierce criticism and a pitch of anger rarely seen in the Commons. The press reflected an explosion of public dissatisfaction and this—reinforced by potential insurrection in the Conservative party, pressure from the Foreign Office, service chiefs, and sections of the cabinet, and "fuller information" about what had happened—led Chamberlain, speaking at Birmingham (on March 17) to concede that it was impossible to negotiate with Germany "on the old basis" any longer and to declare his readiness to resist domination of the world by force.[1]

Two weeks of frantic diplomatic activity followed, impelled by the course of events and a Parliamentary and popular demand for new initiatives. The British first sought suggestions from Paris, Moscow, War-

1. Rock, *Appeasement on Trial*, pp. 203–13; Rock, *British Appeasement in the 1930s*, pp. 18–19.

saw, Ankara, Athens, and Belgrade—most of whom looked in turn to Britain for a lead. Russia's proposal for an immediate conference, perhaps in Bucharest, to discuss common action was rejected by the British in favor of Chamberlain's "bold and startling" scheme (his own description) to associate France, Russia, and Poland with Britain in a declaration of immediate consultation on measures of common resistance in the event that the independence of any other European nation was threatened. But Poland refused such association with Russia and, forced to choose between them, the British chose Poland, believed to be the more formidable military ally. (Chamberlain and Halifax apparently decided and the cabinet acquiesced.) What at length emerged, on March 31, was the unilateral guarantee of Polish independence, an improvisation born of intense and unrelenting pressure on Chamberlain to "do something," and impelled by a rash of reports that Poland was the next—and imminent—object of German aggression.[2]

Consultation with the United States played almost no part in Britain's calculations during these trying weeks, nor was it openly discussed in decision-making circles. There was little reason to believe that British inquiries would have been welcomed in Washington, where the view that Britain must demonstrate her own "backbone" to inspire others to courage still prevailed. But America figured in Britain's actions in several ways: it was kept fully informed of major developments, and the effect of various actions (or the failure to act) on American opinion was taken into account. The latter was early evident in the cabinet's weighing, on March 15, whether to recall the British ambassador from Berlin. Halifax did not feel strongly on the matter, but he was "reluctant to allow public opinion in the United States or in South-eastern Europe to think that [the British] were inert." A mild enough position, it was not surprising when seen in relation to the fact that, aside from War Secretary Hore-Belisha's concern about the takeover of non-Germans and a new *Drang nach Osten*, there was little cabinet appreciation of the broader meaning of what had happened. State Department officials also debated whether to break relations with Germany. One consideration was the wish to avoid exciting hopes in Britain—and France—that (as Berle recorded it) "in case of ultimates we would go to war." It was pretty well decided within a week to maintain relations but to decline to recognize the seizure of Czechoslovakia. Amidst it all, the State Department was "get-

2. Ibid.

ting to the boiling point," and the president apparently felt the same way.[3]

Halifax's concern about American opinion was spurred by Kennedy's suggestion on March 17 that one American reaction to the events in Czechoslovakia might be a growth of anti-British sentiment—on the grounds that these disturbing crises could be avoided if the western European democracies would only set their minds to it. But the foreign secretary believed that Chamberlain's speech at Birmingham would make it clear that Britain had no illusions about the issues that were now at stake. The two agreed that the most useful contribution that Roosevelt could make at the moment was to initiate revision of the United States Neutrality Act. The president did in fact announce (at a press conference that day) his intention to begin drawing up a program for revision,[4] but its actual accomplishment was still some months away.

At the British cabinet meeting of March 18, a much fuller realization of what was now at stake in Europe (i.e., German domination) emerged, and there was general agreement on the need to get in touch with Britain's potential allies to consider mutual action. There were, however, only two passing references to the United States: Halifax's report that Kennedy, in "warmly approving" Chamberlain's speech, had noted that it carried the connotation that Britain would not submit to further aggressive action on Germany's part; and a question whether Ambassador Henderson's recall from Berlin was "on the same footing" as the withdrawal of the American ambassador. But since Halifax had no information on the latter, he could not say. Halifax reported to Lindsay, Kennedy's view that American public opinion was moving faster than he had expected in the direction Roosevelt was leading it, and was in fact in advance of his own position. But precisely what this implied is unclear from the message. Kennedy in turn related Halifax's opinion that Britain would fight if Hitler entered Romania (the Romanian ambassador in London had reported a German ultimatum to his country) and his own view that resistance to this by Chamberlain would cause a break with the foreign secretary. Word of the threat to Romania, and subsequent information that threw doubt upon it, was sent directly to Roosevelt by Halifax.[5]

3. CAB 23/98, 15 March 1939, p. 13; Berle, *Navigating the Rapids,* pp. 200–201. Berle also concluded that whatever America did, she would have to do it alone. Britain could not be trusted; she was "frightened and unfrank." And he added: "No one here has any illusions that the German Napoleonic machine will not extend itself almost indefinitely; and I suppose this is the year."

4. Halifax to Lindsay, 17 March 1939, *B.D.,* 4:364–66.

5. CAB 23/98, 18 March 1939, pp. 45–50; Halifax to Lindsay, 18 March 1939, *B.D.,* 4:380;

At the cabinet meeting on March 20, which confirmed agreement to seek a declaration of consultation with France, Russia, and Poland, Chamberlain received approval to address a private letter to Mussolini, "the only person who could put the brake on Hitler." He hoped to drive a wedge between the Axis partners—for which Halifax thought that Britain would be willing to pay a large price. Halifax's query to Kennedy about America's point of view toward Italy raised an old and sensitive issue. The one thing necessary to work something out, Kennedy said, would be recognition of Abyssinia—hardly an issue to raise in the wake of American disgust over German aggression in Czechoslovakia. Halifax received a similar warning through Duff Cooper, reporting the views of a "highly intelligent" French newspaperman just returned from four months in America: if Britain and France found themselves at war, the United States would come to their assistance *only* if it were an ideological war, a war based on moral principles. If Italy were on their side, the United States would not stir but would see it only as another move in the dirty game of European politics. Halifax found this "interesting," though he hoped to find a way of inducing Italy to adopt a different position without forfeiting American sympathy and possible cooperation. Ambassador Davies, in Brussels, thought that Roosevelt could again (as before Munich) contribute to securing peace by influencing Mussolini's decision. He suggested an eight-point message and offered to arrange to have the Italian ambassador in Brussels, an old war buddy of Mussolini's, sound out Rome informally. But this unpromising foray went no further.[6]

Whatever Chamberlain had in mind for Italy and the United States, it did not involve a conference. Receiving a deputation from the National Peace Council on March 20, he was urged to take, "in consultation with the President of the United States," the necessary steps to secure the holding of a conference, open to all nations, to remedy economic and political conditions likely to lead to war. The timing was certainly wrong, but Chamberlain had not been thinking in this direction anyway. When the deputation's first request for a meeting had arrived some weeks before, he noted for his secretary: "The 1st April would seem a more

---

Kennedy to Hull, 18 March 1939, SDM 940.00/360; Halifax to Roosevelt, 20 March 1939, ibid., 740.00/651 1/2; Lindsay to Welles, 21 March 1939, FO 115/3418, File 321.

6. CAB 23/98, 20 March 1939, p. 84; Kennedy to Hull, 20 March 1939, SDM 740.00/638; Duff Cooper to Halifax, 22 March 1939, FO 800/315, pp. 57–58; Davies to Hull, 21 March 1939, SDM 740.00/646.

suitable day on which to receive such a deputation but since it is well known that I suffer fools gladly perhaps you might give them March 20." Several weeks later he was asked in the House of Commons whether he would consider an approach to the United States government on the possibility of summoning a conference. He did not believe that the time for that had arrived, and his response to a question whether he had been in communication with Roosevelt about this was a crisp "No, Sir, but I shall do so when I think it will be useful."[7]

A more promising line of American support, however indirect, seemed to open up on March 21 when Kennedy reacted "enthusiastically" (so Halifax told the cabinet) to the suggestion that it would be useful to Britain if, in the event of trouble, part of the United States fleet could be sent to Honolulu, thus permitting the British navy to concentrate its strength elsewhere. Lord Chatfield, minister for coordination of defense, found Kennedy somewhat less enthusiastic and unprepared to discuss the matter beyond saying that he intended to propose that the United States fleet be brought to a state of preparedness. But the ambassador did relay Halifax's suggestion to Hull, along with Chatfield's view of how important such a move would be.[8] More would be heard of this later.

Whether Roosevelt could move at all was problematical; Lindsay informed London that the president was deeply involved in controversy with his critics in Congress over two matters fundamental to his foreign policy: rearmament and neutrality revision. It was uncertain whether he could wield sufficient influence to get his way. This was hardly grounds for British encouragement. Conversely, American officials were not heartened by Britain's initial diplomatic moves after March 15. The inquiry to various capitals about their attitude in the event of German aggression against Romania and the proposal for a declaration of consultation seemed, as Pierrepont Moffat put it, "curiously inept." Nor

7. PREM 1/320, 9, 24 February, 20 March 1939.

8. CAB 23/98, 22 March 1939, p. 97; Kennedy to Hull, 22 March 1939. SDM 740.00/647 1/2. A few days later, Churchill sent Chamberlain and Chatfield a "Memorandum on Sea-Power, 1939" in which he emphasized that nothing that happened in the Far East should divert Britain's primary attention from Europe; that British naval action in Asia, in the event that Japan joined a hostile coalition, would depend entirely upon America's coming in against Japan; and that there would be no harm in sounding out the United States about her attitude toward a Japanese threat to Australia. Chatfield agreed on nearly every point and wrote to Chamberlain: "If . . . we have the United States Fleet at Honolulu our position will at once become much easier." Churchill's Memorandum, 27 March; Chatfield to Chamberlain, 30 March; Chatfield to Churchill, 3 April 1939; CHT/6/4, pp. 16, 22–28.

was it reassuring for the State Department to hear from Ambassador Anthony Biddle, in Warsaw (who heard it from Robert Hudson, British under secretary of foreign trade), that the British government had decided upon the Dardenelles as the place where Britain would defend its own interests against Hitler's eastward drive—although London acknowledged that abandoning the central and eastern European states might alienate American public opinion and, ambiguously, hoped that those states would stand their ground in the reasonable expectation of support from Paris and London. British sensitivity to American feeling was also revealed when Halifax, referring to a possible Anglo-Polish secret agreement of consultation, suggested to Lindsay that he might wish to paraphrase the term "secret agreement" when communicating with the State Department about it.[9]

The British government's movement from the idea of securing a four-power declaration of consultation to a more immediate, decisive action was impelled in part by the pressure of events: Germany's seizure of Memel on March 22, its unilateral assumption of responsibility for the "protection" of Slovakia, and its submission to Warsaw of "generous" proposals for a settlement of the Danzig and Corridor problems (the Poles at once rejected them), which made a Polish crisis appear imminent. It was powerfully reinforced by widespread and insistent agitation in the press for more vigorous action to meet the emergency and a growing feeling that "something" must be done to stem the German tide.[10] The frequency of messages from Halifax to Roosevelt summarizing the situation as it developed, and the gravity of their tone, reveal an anxiety that the president be fully informed and a clear desire for American understanding. But there was no hint of an appeal for help. Nothing in British cabinet discussions, where the only mention of the United States pertained to the potential effect of British actions on American opinion, pointed in that direction. Nor did three important meetings of the Foreign Policy Committee, in which there was no reference to the United States at all. Hoare's belief in the importance of Russia was evident, but Chamberlain and Halifax were dubious of that.[11]

Halifax's message of March 29 must have been of special interest to

9. Lindsay to Halifax, 22 March 1939, FO 414/276, p. 36; *Moffat Papers*, pp. 234–35; Biddle to Hull, 22 March 1939, SDM 740.00/657; Halifax to Lindsay, 24 March 1939, *B.D.*, 4:495–96.

10. See Rock, *Appeasement on Trial*, pp. 221–29.

11. See messages from Halifax to Roosevelt, 21–29 March 1939, PSF, Diplomatic Correspondence, Box 25, or FO 115/3418, File 321; CAB 23/98, 29, 30, 31 March 1939; CAB 27/624, 27–31 March 1939.

American officials for its unequivocal reading of the implications of Prague. That event "clearly revealed Germany's intentions," he declared; it was her purpose to extend control over other countries in central and eastern Europe, gradually neutralizing them, depriving them of their power of resistance, and incorporating them into the German economic system. That accomplished, "the way will have been prepared for an attack upon the Western European Powers."[12] His conversion from appeasement seemed to be complete, a change in which, as later events would show, he was, if not distinctly ahead of the prime minister, certainly more resolute.

Insofar as American opinion influenced Halifax's thinking, this conversion was reinforced by a Walter Lippmann column sent by Lindsay, describing the American public as no longer neutral in thought and subject to an explosion of feeling at any spectacular act of violence by the dictators. Lippmann also warned that another Munich would undermine all of this and added that the European democracies could expect assistance only insofar as they first showed a readiness to help themselves. Foreign Office reaction was mixed, but David Scott concurred that any compromise with the dictators over fundamental principle or moral issue would do Britain "untold harm" in the United States. And Cadogan's lament that Americans were "frightfully keen" that Britain should "fight for the right" while evading the issue of what they might do was met by Vansittart's assertion that they would "not only talk but do a great deal, and do it quickly, if we have no more Munichs. . . . Anyhow it is our only chance."[13]

Roosevelt's state of mind at the time is revealed in his March 25–26 conversation with Sir Arthur Willert, an old English journalist friend—notes of which Halifax thought important enough to circulate to the Foreign Policy Committee. Depressed about Europe and believing the odds for war in 1939 to be fifty-fifty, Roosevelt cited a reliable source that had Hitler moving against eastern Europe in 1939, France in 1940, Britain shortly thereafter, and then (with the help of Japan) the United States. This was fantastic, of course, but it showed the sort of man the

12. Lindsay to Hull, 29 March 1939, FO 115/3418, File 321. Halifax was earlier perceived by American Chargé Johnson as feeling that the continued threat of the Nazi regime to the spiritual values of civilization was a greater menace than a world war (Johnson to Hull, 17 March 1939, SDM 740/628). Chamberlain's disillusionment with Hitler is clearly revealed in a letter to his sister Ida on 26 March (NC 18/1/1091).

13. Lindsay to Halifax, 23 March 1939, FO 115/3417, File 43; Foreign Office Minutes, 31 March–9 April 1939, FO 371/22829, pp. 160–61.

world was up against. He spoke of what he was doing to help Britain (warning the dictators that if they challenged it, they would have to reckon with a "maximum of hostility" from the United States) and what he would like to do if war came (assisting Britain economically and patroling the seas with the American fleet). Critical of Britain's failure to adopt conscription and to counter Germany's tactics of intimidation with some of her own, he related the trouble he was having with American public opinion and what he was doing to educate it. "Things are moving here," he said. "But if only you British would give me a lead." In a fuller account of this conversation, written years later, Willert added that Roosevelt was still indignant at Chamberlain's refusal to accept his aid in dealing with the dictators the year before and "bitter about appeasement." He had no use for Chamberlain, Simon, or Hoare, and was generally impatient with the British lack of statesmanship. But he was nonetheless ready himself "to make another effort." Indeed, Willert got the impression that Roosevelt "would welcome circumstances, or perhaps even help to bring them about, which would enable him to persuade his countrymen that the best way to save themselves from Hitler would be to fight him."[14]

One of the things that Roosevelt and the State Department could do was to press the case for revising the Neutrality Act, which had been the subject of intermittent concern for some time. Basically unhappy with neutrality legislation from the outset, the president did not believe that it had contributed to the cause of peace; rather, it tended to encourage aggression by restricting aid to the victim. Both the Spanish Civil War and the Sino-Japanese War had demonstrated this clearly. He had spoken to this issue in his January State of the Union message, but thereafter saw no way to overcome staunch opposition in Congress, overheated as it was by the "frontier on the Rhine" episode, and also in view of his weakened influence there as a result of the November

14. Foreign Policy Committee Memorandum, 20 April 1939, CAB 27/627, pp. 216–17; Sir Arthur Willert, *Washington and Other Memories*, pp. 214–19. Willert summarized his view of American opinion at the time as follows: "What the Americans wanted was a Britain that would, with France, take the lead in ringing Germany around by countries so strongly armed and combined that Hitler would think twice before continuing his program of acquisition by bluff. Few of them envisaged the possibility of their supporting such an organization actively. . . . I used to feel that we British were looked upon very much as the police force is looked upon by the inhabitants of the peaceful part of a gangster-ridden community: it must be strong enough to keep their quarter safe from the gangsters." Yet he allowed that everywhere in America there was appreciation of what the Nazi menace could mean to the world and he never returned to England without being ashamed of the contrast between American apperception and British apathy. Ibid., pp. 209–10.

elections. Further, reports from various quarters in Europe (including some American embassies) during February and early March suggested a diminished danger and thereby lessened the urgency for tangling with a hostile Congress over neutrality revision. But Hitler's action in Prague offended American opinion, raised feelings in the White House and State Department to new levels of exasperation, and helped galvanize support for change. Within a week an opinion poll revealed two-thirds of the American people ready to sell war materials to Britain and France in the event of conflict with Germany and Italy. Roosevelt at once took up the cause of neutrality revision again, and on March 20 Senator Pittman, with strong administration encouragement, introduced a revised bill that would eliminate the mandatory arms embargo and make all trade cash-and-carry. Roosevelt favored full repeal since the cash-and-carry plan would still not help the Chinese (it was too late to help Republican Spain), and authorized Hull and Welles to reveal his position to key congressional leaders. He also instructed Welles to draft a radio address in which he would emphasize that America's remaining at peace itself depended heavily upon its willingness and ability to provide assistance to other victims of attack. But he was soon forced to reduce his offensive, confronted by committee resistance even to the cash-and-carry plan and Pittman's warning that repeal was simply impossible. The president and public opinion were both ahead of Congress on this issue, and Roosevelt had no real choice but to wait. Ambassador Lindsay perceived the prospects rightly, informing London that the bill would require extensive amendment to be workable and would generate much debate before it became law.[15] Six more months of tortuous discussion and the outbreak of war in Europe were in fact required before revision of America's neutrality legislation was ultimately attained.

A lead of the sort that Roosevelt sought from the British was embodied in the guarantee to Poland, announced in the House of Commons on March 31. The process of British decision-making that led to the guarantee was inherently untidy, set as it was in circumstances of crisis where speed seemed essential. There is little evidence of direct American influence, although it was not entirely lacking. Bullitt (Paris) told British Ambassador Eric Phipps on March 27 that Roosevelt, with whom he was in frequent telephone contact, was "plunged into gloom as to the

15. Dallek, *Franklin Roosevelt and American Foreign Policy,* pp. 183–84; Ovendale, *"Appeasement" and the English Speaking World,* p. 234; Lindsay to Halifax, 23 March 1939. FO 414/276, p. 37. A full account of the tortuous discussion over the next six months appears in Cole, *Roosevelt and the Isolationists,* pp. 310–30.

future," and related, "on the very best authority," the same estimate of Hitler's intentions that Roosevelt had given to Willert. Though he considered Bullitt "on the whole a lightweight," Phipps found him so convinced of the truth of his story that he felt duty-bound to pass it on. Such a message no doubt reinforced the burgeoning British conviction that something drastic had to be done. Further, a draft telegram, approved by the cabinet on March 30, instructing Phipps to sound out the French about a simultaneous guarantee to Poland suggests quite clearly that information from the American ambassador in Warsaw (Biddle), relayed by Kennedy, was a prominent factor in Britain's decision for the guarantee: Ribbentrop, exultant over the Memel coup, was pressing Hitler for immediate action against Poland, arguing that Britain and France would not support her, thereby alienating American opinion. Cabinet discussion involved only an unclear reference to the wisdom of declaring Polish independence a vital British interest in view of public opinion in America.[16]

When informed in advance of Chamberlain's projected statement on Poland (Kennedy telephoned information from Halifax), Roosevelt thought it excellent and believed it would have "a very great effect." The United States would consider that war was imminent, but there was no particular harm in that. The president's reaction was in striking contrast to that of Kennedy, whom Cadogan found "very tiresome" in holding that the declaration would be regarded in America as a "subterfuge." But Kennedy promised to do his best with his "beastly newsmen," and in conveying Roosevelt's reaction to Halifax a short time later, he noted that press messages being dispatched to America were "all very good." A State Department release, prepared by Moffat for Welles, declared the most significant element in the guarantee to be Chamberlain's committing Britain to positive action in eastern Europe, which it was never willing to consider before. It had been Britain's policy for centuries to block any power that threatened to gain mastery over the European continent, and its present action showed that it considered Germany to be close to obtaining such a position. Taken together, these statements would seem to indicate that the guarantee both offered a British lead and relieved the pressure of criticism leveled at the president for being unduly alarmist.[17]

16. Phipps to Halifax, 28 March 1939, PHPP 1/22; CAB 23/98, 30 March 1939, pp. 171, 179–80.

17. Halifax to Lindsay, 31 March 1939, FO 414/276, p. 37; *Cadogan Diaries*, p. 167; *Moffat Papers*, pp. 237–38; MacDonald, *The United States, Britain, and Appeasement*, p. 147. See also Neville to Hilda, 3 April 1939, NC 18/1/1092.

The British guarantee attracted widespread attention in the United States, where popular and press reactions were "definitely favorable," Lindsay reported to London. British motives in making plain to Hitler that he would not be allowed to pursue aggression further were generally appreciated, although there was an undercurrent of feeling that the decision might better have been taken earlier and doubt that Anglo-French efforts to restrain Hitler could now succeed. There was also an underlying suspicion that British pledges might be diluted or forgotten. Any such action, Lindsay warned, would have an extremely unfavorable effect on public opinion.[18]

Chamberlain referred to these same issues in a letter to his sister on April 3. Convinced that his timing was right, and believing that Hitler had received a "definite check" that would "enormously affect his prestige," he explained that Britain retained the right to judge whether Polish independence was threatened.[19] The latter assertion, compared with the actual wording of the guarantee, contained the possibility of precisely the kind of hedging that Lindsay was concerned about. Halifax was less sanguine about the setback to Hitler. Indeed, he found Hitler's speech at Wilhelmshaven (April 4) not at all reassuring—and had this view communicated directly to Roosevelt. His information showed Hitler "infuriated" with Britain for its efforts to organize a common resistance against him.[20]

Though Chamberlain described the Polish guarantee in the Commons, on April 3, as "a portent ... so momentous that ... it will have a chapter to itself when the history books come to be written," exactly what it portended for the future development of British policy was quite uncertain. The prime minister did not yet regard war as inevitable and could not believe that his efforts for peace would "not even yet bear fruit." Conversations with the Polish foreign minister, Colonel Joseph Beck, in London, April 4–6—of which Roosevelt was confidentially informed—resulted in agreement to transform the British guarantee into a reciprocal pact for mutual defense, but Beck sidestepped suggestions that Poland should conclude a similar alliance with Romania or associate in any way with Russia. Chamberlain shared his views on Russia, whom he regarded as "a very unreliable friend with very little capacity for

18. Lindsay to Halifax, 4 April 1939, FO 414/296, pp. 37–38.

19. Neville to Hilda, 3 April 1939, NC 18/1/1092.

20. Halifax to Lindsay, 5 April 1939, FO 414/276, p. 38; Lindsay to Hull, 6 April 1939, SDM 740.00/887 1/2.

active assistance but an enormous irritative power on others."[21]

The uncertain direction of British policy was readily perceived on the American side. "We do not know . . . the real designs of British policy," Adolf Berle, of the State Department, recorded on April 2, but any real cooperation between Britain and Russia seemed out of the question. The guarantee to Poland was "not so violent a commitment as it may at first seem," Ambassador Cudahy (Ireland) wrote to Roosevelt April 3—though morally it meant that Britain had at last decided to make a stand. Kennedy reported a discussion with Chamberlain (April 4) about "leaving a door open to Hitler" in case he decided he did not want to fight—a doorway that possibly the United States alone could provide. Chamberlain recognized the psychological importance of having Hitler believe that America was definitely on the side of the democracies.[22]

As the British Parliament and press accorded hearty approval to the Polish guarantee, there was also a potent accompanying sentiment that it was only a first step in organizing the forces of Europe against aggression. The *Manchester Guardian*'s (April 1) view that the government must quickly pass from its "interim policy" to the "final scheme" was widely echoed; and Chamberlain himself acknowledged on April 3 that "the matter could not end where it stands today": if domination of the world by force was indeed the intention of the German government, Poland would not be the only country endangered; and Britain could not confine herself to "a single case which after all might not be the case in point." But occasion to extend the guarantee policy occurred much sooner than expected. On April 7 (Good Friday), Mussolini took his turn at jolting Europe; Italian forces invaded Albania without a word of warning. A gravely disillusioned Chamberlain, who only days before had solicited the Duce's aid in establishing trust and ensuring peace, wrote to his sister with his freezing gift of understatement: "I am afraid that such faith as I ever had in the assurances of dictators is rapidly being whittled away." Yet confronted with the German danger, and consonant with the role he had cast for Italy, he downplayed the Italian threat, refusing to denounce the Anglo-Italian agreement and assuming

21. Rock, *British Appeasement in the 1930s*, pp. 19–20; Rock, *Appeasement on Trial*, pp. 237–38. In a letter to his sister, Chamberlain complained about the "hysterical passion of the Opposition . . . who have a pathetic belief that in Russia is the key to our salvation" (Neville to Ida, 9 April 1939, NC 18/1/1093). Kennedy wired Hull that the British did not think Russia could be of any help outside its own borders and that they were going to try to get along without it (6 April 1939, SDM 740.00/741).

22. Berle, *Navigating the Rapids*, p. 208; Cudahy to Roosevelt, PSF, Diplomatic Correspondence, Box 44; Kennedy to Hull, 4 April 1939, SDM 740.00/736.

an attitude that drew into question his presumed conversion to a stronger line. But this was short-lived. Pressured by a storm of protest in the British press, distressing reports from British envoys in Greece and Turkey, the urging of Halifax and Churchill, and alarms from Daladier (who feared an Italo-German offensive from the North Sea to Egypt), Chamberlain and the cabinet moved quickly toward the extension of a guarantee to Greece. That Romania was also included in the pledges in the House of Commons, April 13, was largely the result of French insistence that Britain and France together should guarantee both countries.[23]

American influence in the extension of British guarantees to Greece and Romania was largely indirect. Hull had publicly deprecated the "additional threat" to peace, which it would be shortsighted to ignore. And Kennedy had told the Foreign Office that a firm British declaration in support of Greece "would be greatly valued" in the United States, where Britain's failure to denounce the Anglo-Italian agreement might be taken as continuing credence in the assurances of Mussolini. It was, in fact, the effects on American opinion that concerned the British most. The Foreign Office had taken serious note of Lindsay's recent warning: David Scott emphasized the need to avoid compromise with the totalitarian states over a question of moral principle. Would America "think it only decent of us to start a European war at once" over Albania? Cadogan queried sardonically. Vansittart replied forthrightly: it would expect "some very strong protest," and Britain should live up to its expectations. This would produce a violent reaction in Italy, but "it is better to think first of America, who may help us, and very secondarily of Italy, who has now cast herself for the almost certain part of foe." Halifax read the exchange without comment, but he carried these views into a cabinet discussion. Sensitive to the possibility that "public opinion in certain countries, such as America," would hold Britain's posture as one of brave words with "less heroic" action, he noted (in support of acting with France to guarantee Romania) that if Britain went to war to prevent European domination by Germany or Italy, it was better to do so "before there was any loss of morale in the Balkans or in the United States."[24]

23. Rock, *Neville Chamberlain*, pp. 179–80; Rock, *Appeasement on Trial*, pp. 238–43.

24. Lindsay to Halifax, 9 April 1939, FO 414/276, p. 38; Ingram to Lindsay, 11 April 1939, FO 115/3418, File 321; Foreign Office Minutes, 6–8 April 1939, FO 371/22829, pp. 209–10; CAB 23/98, 8, 13 April 1939, pp. 243, 297. Yet Kennedy found Halifax "strangely optimistic," leaving the ambassador to wonder whether his judgment was based on information that the United States did not have (Kennedy to Hull, 11 April 1939, SDM 740.00/774).

In his statement to the House of Lords on April 14, Halifax said that the judgment of the British government of Italian action in Albania was shared by "the overwhelming mass of opinion" in Britain, in most of Europe, and by the United States of America. Subsequent U.S. press reports—implying a closer link between Britain and America than actually existed—greatly disturbed Chamberlain, who had purposely avoided any reference to the United States in his own address in the Commons the day before.[25] Yet a closer link of sorts seemed to be developing. Several weeks before, Halifax had asked Kennedy—half jokingly, according to Cadogan's diary—whether the United States would consider transferring its fleet from the Atlantic (where it had been moved in January partly in connection with the World's Fair in New York City) back to the Pacific at the right psychological moment. Britain had promised Australia to send a fleet to Singapore, but was now unable to spare the vessels from European waters. Independently, Bullitt had suggested a similar move to Washington—reflecting Daladier's concern about the possible transfer of British ships from the Mediterranean. Roosevelt was sympathetic to the idea. The right moment had come by April 11; the British reminded Washington that the move would be "a gesture of value," and the sooner it was done the better. On April 15 Roosevelt ordered the fleet back to the Pacific.[26]

Daily dispatches from Bullitt during the second week of April emphasized the gravity of the situation in Europe. He pictured Britain, France, and Poland facing war in the near future "under desperate circumstances"; relayed Bonnet's impression that "it was five minutes before twelve"; and reported Daladier's disgust with Chamberlain—whom he thought misled or criminally weak. Lindsay expressed to Hull in terms "hardly recordable" his chagrin and disgust over the unpredictable behavior of the dictators and the nervousness and fear that it caused. Moffat recorded his opinion that the time was rapidly approaching when the president would want to make some sort of personal move. Roosevelt himself later wrote to a friend about these days: "Never in my life have I seen things moving in the world with more cross currents or greater velocity." Accordingly, the president sought to assist in restraining the dictators. Emphasizing (in press conferences on April 8 and 11) the dangers of aggression to America itself and the need to abandon "paper

25. Kennedy to Hull, 14 April 1939, SDM 711.14/441.

26. Hull, *Memoirs,* 1:630; *Cadogan Diaries,* p. 172; Bullitt to Hull, 11 April 1939, SDM 740.00/770; Halifax to Lindsay, 11 April 1939, FO 115/3418, File 321.

guarantees of immunity" in favor of support for Britain and France, Roosevelt elaborated these ideas in a Pan American Day address on April 14. Peace and security, he declared, depended upon the dictators giving up their dreams of conquest and abandoning the methods used by Huns and Vandals fifteen hundred years ago. The narrowing of the oceans increasingly involved America in the customs and actions of the Old World, "whether we like it or not. . . . We, too, have a stake in world affairs."[27] That evening he made his strongest move. He addressed identical messages to Hitler and Mussolini, made public next day, in which he described the fear of war in which millions of people were living and which was a "definite concern" to the people of the United States; stressed the inevitable "common ruin" that would result if reversion to the threat of arms continued; reviewed the recent loss of independence by three nations in Europe, one in Africa, and the occupation of a vast segment of China by Japan; cited reports ("which we trust are not true") of further acts of aggression being contemplated; and, acting as a friendly mediator, solicited an assurance of nonaggression against thirty-one nations, explicitly named, for a period of at least ten years and preferably twenty-five. In return for the latter, the United States would seek reciprocal assurances from the nations named and would promote and participate in conferences on "two essential problems": disarmament and trade. Separate political discussions might also be undertaken by those governments other than the United States that were directly interested. The "heads of great governments" were directly responsible for the fate of humanity, Roosevelt concluded, so he hoped for positive replies.[28]

Roosevelt's appeal was essentially of his own devising. Precisely what he had in mind in addressing it to Hitler and Mussolini is difficult to say. It is possible to see in his action a return to a formula for appeasement, offering as it did a potential conference solution to the problems of trade and disarmament, once the threat of aggression had been laid aside. But there is more reason to believe that the message was intended as an offensive thrust calculated to put Hitler on the defensive, perhaps even to discredit him with his own people, as well as with other peoples around the world. The president's sentiments were probably still divided. He clearly understood the dictators to be two madmen who respected

27. Bullitt to Hull, 9, 10, 11 April 1939, SDM 740.00/754 759, 772; Hull Memorandum, 11 April 1939, SDM 740.00/899; *Moffat Papers,* p. 239; Dallek, *Franklin Roosevelt and American Foreign Policy,* pp. 184–85, 568.

28. Roosevelt to Hitler and Mussolini, 14 April 1939, SDM 740.00/817A, 817B.

force and force alone (as Henry Wallace reminded him). But the urge toward peace was exceedingly great. Roosevelt must have realized the possibilities of limiting political risk by combining an anti-Nazi initiative with a stated readiness to don the mantle of a mediator. He doubted the initiative would succeed, quoting the odds to Morgenthau as one in five. But even failure should be helpful in clarifying for people everywhere, and especially in America, the nature and objectives of the dictators and, perhaps, in advancing the cause of neutrality revision.[29]

Roosevelt's message took Chamberlain totally by surprise. But his reaction was positive. He wrote his sister from Chequers that the president's appeal, "very skillfully framed," had put the dictators into "a tight corner"; and—though they would no doubt "refuse to play"—world, particularly American, opinion would be further consolidated against them and their own people would be disappointed and alarmed. The official British press communiqué endorsed the president's estimate of the international situation, warmly welcomed his "statesmanlike initiative," and believed that it offered a "real opportunity" of averting the catastrophe that threatened Europe. It did not, of course, reveal the cynicism of the Foreign Office News Department, which wondered how promises of nonaggression from Hitler were any longer of value.[30]

Aside from Germany and Italy, where it was greeted with contempt, Roosevelt's appeal met with a favorable response nearly everywhere. Kennedy reported Englishmen generally to be "overwhelmingly grateful": ". . . This appeal must have filled every British family with an admiration for, and a gratitude to, the President as intimate as if he were their own national leader." Lindsay thought it "the last trump card"—a sound future guide for all peacefully disposed nations. The press was uniformly satisfied that the United States had stepped into a bolder position against aggression. Halifax was gratified by the implicit assurance that if attempts to secure changes by force were abandoned, the United States would cooperate with European nations in securing change by negotiation. And Chamberlain expressed to Kennedy his ap-

29. The idea of the appeal may have come from Bullitt, and Welles drafted the final version; but it certainly carried Roosevelt's personal touch. See Hull, *Memoirs,* 1:620; *Moffat Papers,* pp. 239–40; Julius W. Pratt, *Cordell Hull, 1933–1944,* 1:307–8. For differing assessments of Roosevelt's motives, see Offner, *Origins of the Second World War,* pp. 128–29, and MacDonald, *The United States, Britain, and Appeasement,* pp. 150–51. MacDonald presents evidence that Carl Goerdeler, a leading member of the anti-Nazi opposition in Germany, was instrumental in persuading Roosevelt (indirectly) to act in an effort to divide the German people from Hitler.

30. Neville to Hilda, 15 April 1939, NC 18/1/1094; Press communiqué, 15 April 1939, *B.D.,* 5:218; Aster, *1939,* pp. 222–23; Hull, *Memoirs,* 1:620.

preciation for the president's appeal—although unlike many other heads of state, he sent no personal message to Roosevelt.[31]

Chamberlain (whom Kennedy thought to have failed noticeably, in a physical sense, during the week just past) was at the moment starkly preoccupied with other things; Mussolini's behavior, though far from showing that British policy had been wrong (so he wrote his sister), enabled his critics to mock him publicly and weaken his authority in the country. Clearly bothered by what he saw as partisan personal attacks in the House of Commons, he confessed to feeling "very dispirited and very lonely." Debate in the Commons, as well as a crescendo arising from wide sections of the press, were pushing the government toward negotiations with Russia in order to elicit aid in a peace front against aggression. This ran squarely counter to Chamberlain's basic instincts, distrustful as he was of Russia's motives and skeptical of its political stability and military value. There was also increasing pressure to introduce conscription (which Chamberlain disliked) and to establish a Ministry of Supply as signs of Britain's awakening to reality and seriousness of purpose. Altogether, various forces were pushing the prime minister in precisely the opposite direction to which his whole policy and purpose had been calculated to flow. On every count he was forced to concede before the month of April was out.[32]

There was no open support or objection from the Americans to Britain's opening of talks with Russia. One can only assume that Roosevelt accepted the idea and wished the British well. Ambassadors Biddle (Warsaw) and Davies (Brussels) certainly thought an agreement would be useful. Davies, in fact, offered to go to Moscow (he had earlier been ambassador there) to move it along—an offer declined by Hull and Roosevelt in view of its great potential for misconstruction and possible adverse effect on pending neutrality revision.[33] On the matter of British conscription, American sentiment was more pronounced. Roosevelt thought it absolutely essential, Bullitt informed Phipps—and before April 28, when Hitler was scheduled to speak. He could not understand how Britain could hesitate when peace might very well depend upon it.

31. Kennedy to Hull, 16, 17 April 1939, SDM 740.00/827, 890, 908; Hull Memorandum, 17 April 1939, SDM 740.00/1012; Johnson to Hull, 22 April 1939, SDM 740.00/1274.

32. Kennedy to Hull, 17 April 1939, SDM 740.00/908; Neville to Hilda, 15 April 1939, NC 18/1/1094; Rock, *Chamberlain,* pp. 180–83.

33. Biddle to Roosevelt, 7 April 1939, PSF, Diplomatic Correspondence, Box 37; Davies to Hull, Hull to Davies, 18 April 1939, SDM 740.00/934. See Langer and Gleason, *The Challenge to Isolation,* pp. 128–29.

Indeed, the president (through Bullitt) urged French socialist leader Leon Blum to do what he could to ameliorate British labor opposition, which Chamberlain had identified as a major stumbling block. (Blum's response was an article in *Le Populaire.*) Army Chief of Staff Sir Henry Pownall acknowledged that from every side—"even America!"—came the plea that if Britain really meant business, it must "put on conscription." Chamberlain told the cabinet on April 24 of "great pressure" for conscription from France and the United States. When the measure was adopted in London, Moffat, of the State Department, labeled it "the biggest news throughout 1938 or 1939." But American satisfaction must have been tempered by word that Chamberlain was sending Sir Nevile Henderson back to his ambassadorial post in Berlin in advance of the announcement in order to soften the blow, and planned to hint that Britain would welcome a resumption of the interrupted trade talks with Germany.[34]

While awaiting the dictators' replies to Roosevelt's message, British officials were concerned in various ways with American opinion. Lindsay's report on U.S. reaction showed that the president's appeal was generally accepted as justified in the interest of preserving peace, but it was unlikely to accomplish much; and after the first day or two, there was surprisingly little comment. Foreign Office personnel pondered Roosevelt's query (to Willert several weeks before) as to why Britain let Germany have a monopoly on intimidation. Cadogan wondered whether it was not now time to "make more boast of our Air Force increase," and Halifax thought the issue worth referring to the Foreign Policy Committee. They also wrestled with the sticky question of how to deal with Italy. Still tempted to seek her detachment from the Axis, they recognized that success would, in the event of war, undermine the one condition on which the British believed American assistance most likely: that it be an ideological war based on moral principle. Roosevelt himself would do everything he could to support Britain (and France), but there was always the nagging question of Congress, in which the president's prestige was diminished as a result of domestic squabbling. Special interest focused on a long report from R. H. Bruce Lockhart, recently returned from an extended lecture tour in America: American interest in the European situation was now "feverish" (Roosevelt had "worked

34. Phipps to Halifax, 20 April 1939, *B.D.*, 5:251–52 (also PHPP 1/22); Dalton Diary, 10 May 1939, 20:56; *Chief of Staff: The Diaries of Lieutenant-General Sir Henry Pownall*, 1:199; CAB 23/99, 24 April 1939, p. 8; *Moffat Papers*, p. 240; Kennedy to Hull, 21 April 1939, SDM 740.00/1084.

a miracle" in making Americans Europe-conscious), and Anglo-American relations were better than ever before; but between the president's program of preparing Americans to play their part in an eventual armed clash between democracy and aggressive totalitarianism and its realization "there is a wide gulf which has still to be crossed."[35]

During the third week of April 1939, Lord Lothian's appointment as successor to Sir Ronald Lindsay as British ambassador in Washington was formalized. Earlier British concern that Lothian had compromised himself in his December interview with Roosevelt dissipated when the president assured Lindsay in late March that there could be no possible difficulty about Lothian's nomination. To be sure, Lothian had once believed in a policy of appeasing Germany; but he had later changed his views, and the president did not hold his earlier outlook against him. Nor did Roosevelt make any reference to the December conversation. Accordingly, formal *agrément,* sought on April 15, was forthcoming at once, and Lothian's appointment was announced a few days later. American press reaction was uniformly favorable; Lothian was recognized as a man of intelligence who knew America well and received a certain amount of credit for having the wisdom to change his mind about Hitler.[36] But it is doubtful that anyone on either side of the Atlantic anticipated the crucial role he would play in Anglo-American relations once he had assumed the embassy in August and World War II had begun.

In a lighter vein, Anglo-American (as well as French) cooperation—so difficult to come by on certain issues of state—was achieved at this juncture on one matter: not to subscribe to a fiftieth birthday present for Hitler sponsored by a member of the diplomatic corps in Berlin. But the sending of a birthday message was another matter, for national customs differed. The cabinet at length agreed to send a message congratulating Hitler, but omitting the customary wishes for his health and welfare.[37]

Mussolini proclaimed his indifference to "press campaigns . . . or Messiah-like messages" and labeled the idea of a ten-year guarantee

35. Lindsay to Halifax, 20 April 1939, FO 414/276, p. 41; Foreign Office Minutes, 19, 21, 26 April 1939, FO 371/22829, pp. 216–17, 219–20, 228–30, 231–55.

36. Lindsay to Halifax, 28 March 1939, FO 794/18; Lindsay to Hull, Hull to Lindsay, 17, 18 April 1939, FO 115/3419, File 940; Derick to Harvey, 25–27 April 1939, FO 794/18.

37. CAB 23/98, 19 April 1939, pp. 319–20.

against aggression "absurd"; and Hitler, inclined at first to ignore a message from "so contemptible a creature" as Roosevelt, decided to use his Reichstag speech on April 28 as a forum for reply. His sarcastic ridicule directed at the president denied that any of the states that Roosevelt had listed felt threatened by Germany (he claimed to have asked them all, and all replied negatively); still, he would gladly give assurance to any nation, including the United States, that asked for it. He did not intend to provoke a war, he asserted; German actions, indistinguishable from those pursued in self-interest by other powers, were merely correcting past wrongs. So all that Roosevelt achieved by his effort was the "clearer conscience" (as he had described it to the press on April 15) that sprang from doing what he could to save humanity from war.[38] Whether his appeal would have some subtle effect remained to be seen.

There was no significant Anglo-American sharing of reactions to the outcome. Each side drew its own conclusions and resumed its independent course—though each thought the situation momentarily improved. Chamberlain, though allowing that one could no longer feel any confidence in Hitler, was satisfied that the Führer did not find the time favorable for a new challenge. He expected more periods of acute anxiety, but believed that every passing month without war made it less likely. His inclination was to approach Mussolini again; it might be possible "to give the Axis another twist" and this might be "the best way of keeping Master Hitler quiet." The British press saw no justification for a relaxation of defense measures, but found it difficult to come to any clear interpretation of Hitler's speech. Churchill, in a broadcast address to the United States in which he extolled Roosevelt's service to the cause of peace and appealed for "no diminution of the influence which the United States is exercising for the common good," said that Hitler's speech showed "a certain improvement on any he has made before." Lord Hankey, secretary to the cabinet, a Chamberlain disciple, and confidant of many people, felt that the odds no longer favored the dictators, "especially in view of Roosevelt's attitude, which tends toward restoring the balance of power—the only real basis of peace. . . ."[39] On the American side, the State Department (as Moffat explained it) felt that Roosevelt's message had provided an opportunity "for certain curative forces

38. Dallek, *Franklin Roosevelt and American Foreign Policy,* p. 186; *FDR Press Conferences,* 13:270.

39. Neville to Hilda, 29 April 1939, NC 18/1/1096; Kennedy to Hull, 29 April 1939, SDM 740.00/1228; *Churchill's Complete Speeches,* 6:6116; Hankey to Bickersteth, 29 April 1939, HNKY 4/31.

to come into play" and would work as a leaven for other constructive developments. The American military attaché in London sensed a "definite pause in whatever action was to follow that of Italy in Albania" and foresaw no more *coups-de-force* until Germany and Italy had reevaluated the situation thoroughly. Even Roosevelt and Hull, at a cabinet meeting on May 12, seemed to feel that chances of avoiding war were improved. The president doubted that Hitler would want to go to a test of strength with the new alliances that were forming.[40]

For his own part, Roosevelt concluded that the most effective thing he could do after his rebuff by the dictators was to revive his efforts at changing the Neutrality Law. Already the subject of numerous starts and retreats, progress had been slow to nonexistent; and at that particular moment, revision seemed further away than ever. Eschewing direct involvement insofar as possible, lest he stir the hostility of an already recalcitrant Congress (unduly sensitive to a suspected presidential usurpation of power), he worked behind the scenes to accomplish what he could. Early in April the Senate Foreign Relations Committee had begun to conduct public hearings on a resolution (introduced, upon administration urging, by its chairman, Senator Pittman) that would have left many provisions of earlier neutrality legislation intact while repealing the arms embargo and extending cash-and-carry. But things had not gone well. The opening testimony of former Secretary of State Henry Stimson, who frankly opposed isolationism, seemed only to spur the opponents of revision to new efforts. Pittman tried at length to arrange for testimony by Cordell Hull, but the secretary's insistence that it be given in closed executive session, along with Pittman's dislike of the statement that Hull (after arduous State Department drafting) proposed to make, created an impasse. Roosevelt saw no practical way to break it, and efforts to work through the Foreign Relations Committee broke down. Thereupon he turned to the House Foreign Affairs Committee, urging upon its chairman, Democratic Congressman Sol Bloom (New York), and other House leaders the view that repeal would help prevent war in Europe and, if war developed, would reduce the chances of an Axis victory. The president's efforts were stimulated by word from Bullitt on May 10 that Ribbentrop was known by the British to be goading Hitler with the argument that Germany could fight Britain and France without risk because they could not obtain military supplies from the

40. Moffat Memorandum, 1 May 1939, SDM 740.00/1433; Chynoweth to the Department of State, 4 May 1939, SDM 740.00/1554; Ickes, *Diary*, 2:634–35.

United States, and he was citing the neutrality debate in Congress as evidence. Thus Britain considered it of the highest importance that neutrality revision be accomplished quickly to undercut Ribbentrop's argument.[41]

Roosevelt's campaign in the several months that followed, and the nature of the resistance he encountered (mainly in Congress, not in the State Department, where it was understood that existing legislation was an incitement to Hitler to go to war), have been chronicled effectively elsewhere.[42] The picture that emerges shows the president, strongly supported by Hull, attempting nearly everything in his power to move revision along, but encountering insurmountable obstacles at every turn. It was not simply isolationist sentiment that caused him trouble. Partisan politics and past political resentments within his own party played a part. Roosevelt carefully calculated his tactics so as to raise the least suspicion possible. He sought to reassure Congressmen by declaring that he had no intention of sending American troops to Europe. He remained flexible on the precise terms of revised legislation that he would find acceptable. When stymied in the Senate committee, he turned to the House committee; and when stymied in the House, which actually produced a bill in late June and then destroyed its essence by attaching the confusing Vorys Amendment (which embargoed "arms and ammunition" but not "implements of war"), he turned back to the Senate. At one point of high exasperation, he asked the attorney general how far he could go in ignoring the existing act, but he did not pursue that inquiry very far. At various other times, he convened Senate leaders at the White House to solicit their support; bargained (with Senator Pittman) to back a silver-mining subsidy, which he clearly disliked, in order to win committee votes for neutrality reform; and he publicly appealed to Senate leadership to override the Foreign Relations Committee's mid-July decision, by a 12 to 11 vote, to lay aside the issue of revision altogether until the next session of Congress. Angry and discouraged when this appeal failed, he lamented to Morgenthau that statues of certain senators ought to be erected in Berlin, and subsequently told assembled newsmen that he had "practically no power" to make an American effort to prevent a war from breaking out. Roosevelt's attitude of ur-

41. Dallek, *Franklin Roosevelt and American Foreign Policy,* p. 187; Cole, *Roosevelt and the Isolationists,* pp. 313–14; Bullitt to Hull, 10 May 1939, SDM 740.00/1416; Hull, *Memoirs,* 1:646.

42. See, in particular, Cole, *Roosevelt and the Isolationists,* pp. 312–19; and Dallek, *Franklin Roosevelt and American Foreign Policy,* pp. 187–92. Also see the chapter on "Neutrality Disaster" in Hull, *Memoirs,* 1:641–53.

gency throughout was based on what is now known to have been a faulty assumption: that repeal of the arms embargo would have a signal effect upon Hitler and help to restrain him from further acts of aggression. Actually, Hitler had very little respect for, or concern about, the United States, and his scheming in eastern Europe turned upon other factors. But Roosevelt was not alone in his conviction; it was widely shared both at home and abroad.

The British were among those who believed that an early change in the neutrality provisions was the most effective measure that the United States could take at that time to build up resistance to Germany and Italy. They followed the course of developments very closely. Embassy officials in Washington sent numerous detailed reports to London, where certain conclusions were drawn from what was observed. The British had long understood that the issue did not turn on its own merits alone but was deeply enmeshed in such things as partisan politics, constitutional questions, and personal reactions to Roosevelt and the "style" of his presidency. Early in 1939 the British embasssy in Washington had reported a debate on the "American Forum of the Air" in which Senators Pittman and Taft had laid out the basic viewpoints of the opposing sides, the widely respected Taft arguing that "no one had ever before suggested that a single nation should range over the world like a knight errant protecting democracy and the ideals of good faith and tilting like Don Quixote against the windmills of fascism," and warning that the United States might "go in" on the side of France and England because they were democracies only to find before they were through that they were communist or fascist. A month later Lindsay outlined for the Foreign Office three schools of thought on neutrality legislation and surmised that "final legislation will be postponed to the last moment." The day before Roosevelt addressed his appeal to the dictators, Lindsay reported the results of a recent Gallup Poll that indicated that 66 percent of American voters were in favor of supplying war materials to Britain and France, whereas the figure had been 55 percent a month before and only 34 percent before Munich. This seemed to augur well. But the following weeks found him reporting that the Senate was "very divided" and debate would be "almost certainly protracted." Detailed dispatches to the Foreign Office during May indicated very little progress in congressional debate, but made it clear that Roosevelt and Hull were doing the best they could. By mid-June, Lindsay was expressing doubt that new legislation could be passed by the scheduled adjournment of Congress in mid-July.[43] Taken together, these reports (and many others of a similar nature not cited here) gave the British little encouragement in formulating their own policy positions. A momentarily disheartened Chamberlain wrote in his diary on May 19: "Our only hope, it seems to me, lies in Roosevelt and the U.S.A. But unfortunately they are so unready themselves that they can do little to help us now while preaching at Hitler is not likely to be effective."[44]

Nor did the British feel that they could do anything to influence the situation in America. On the contrary, nearly all the advice they received from persons knowledgeable about America, as well as their own conclusions drawn from the evidence, made it seem essential to avoid saying or doing anything that might smack of an effort to sway American opinion. The reactions of Foreign Office personnel, in early May, to a private letter on Anglo-American relations (handed to First Secretary Gladwyn Jebb and circulated widely) illustrate this clearly. The letter made the point that United States opinion must be left to take care of itself, free from British efforts at propaganda; and Britain must not be heartened into expecting too much from America. Up to that moment, American opinion held that the British government was "too hesitant, too lacking in firmness." This had recently begun to change with the apparent shift in Chamberlain's attitude, and would gradually take care of itself if the new attitude was maintained. Foreign Office officials (Beith, Perowne, Balfour, Scott) all thought this a fair appreciation of the situation and acknowledged the need to let American opinion evolve on its own, influenced only by "outside events" (i.e., the actions of the dictators themselves). Scott put it succinctly: "There is only one safe rule in this matter and that is not to speak of Anglo-United States relations at all." If British policy rested on a basis of morality, and actions corresponded with words, the assurance of American support would increase; Vansittart, Cadogan, and Halifax all took note. Similarly, an inquiry from the Admiralty about the wisdom of representations in Washington on particulars of neutrality legislation was adjudged inadvisable by the Foreign Office. "The European situation is so critical," Perowne wrote, "that it is clearly necessary to refrain from any action

43. Mallet to Halifax, 25 January 1939, FO 414/276, pp. 20–21; Lindsay to Halifax, 21 February 1939; ibid., p. 26; Lindsay to Halifax, 14 April 1939, FO 115/3418, File 229; Lindsay to Halifax, 2 May 1939, FO 414/276, pp. 43–44; Lindsay to Halifax, 23 May 1939, ibid., p. 50; Lindsay to Halifax, 29 May 1939, ibid., pp. 52–53; Lindsay to Halifax, 16 June 1939, ibid., p. 57.

44. NC 2/24A.

which . . . could . . . not fail to embarrass President Roosevelt, who . . . is already doing what he can to assist in a matter which is primarily . . . a problem of the United States domestic policy."[45] This basic point of view was reiterated in a variety of circumstances by many British officials, including the prime minister—and was, in fact, closely adhered to—during the summer months of 1939.

Concern for the condition of American opinion, long of interest to the British, increased from April 1939 onward. Reports that came from Lindsay were examined carefully and often prompted extensive Foreign Office commentary. They showed Americans—even in the Middle West and South—no longer indifferent to European affairs and surprisingly alert to the danger of war. Increasingly anxious to support the democracies, they were equally anxious to keep out of war themselves. Believing, after Munich, that Britain was defeatist and that there was nothing to support, Americans had responded positively to the more decisive British policy of recent weeks. Lindsay felt that the more decisively this lead was given, the more certain it was that United States opinion would follow it. Still, there was much apprehension that Britain might weaken in its determination to resist lawless aggression. With all this in mind, Lindsay ventured on May 8 to make some suggestions concerning ultimate objectives if Britain were forced into war. These, he believed, would be crucially important in influencing American opinion. And the Foreign Office began to think about "roughing out" something that would provide what was "needed from the point of view of opinion in the U.S." But any reference to the United States would have to be "rather anodyne" and the impression of intending to influence American opinion carefully avoided. The balance was "delicately poised" (Scott's words) and it was more than ever important that Britain should give no handle to the isolationists by saying anything that could be construed as an attempt to entangle the United States.[46]

During the first week of June, there occurred in Washington an event of great potential magnitude in Anglo-American relations: a visit by King George VI and Queen Elizabeth. When the possibility had arisen months before, as a side trip to the royal couple's visit to Canada,

45. Foreign Office Minutes, 2–11 May 1939, FO 371/22829, pp. 273–77, 281–85; Perowne to Lindsay, 9 May 1939, FO 115/3418, File 299. The British embassy did make an informal inquiry at the State Department mainly from a legal point of view.

46. Lindsay to Halifax, 8 May 1939, FO 414/276, p. 46; Foreign Office Minutes, 9–12, 19–20, 24–25 May 1939, FO 371/22830, pp. 37, 63–64, 69.

Roosevelt had been immediately enthusiastic about it, and his enthusiasm never waned. He took an extensive personal hand in the preparations for the visit and carried it through in the gracious, hospitable manner of which he was so capable.

The king was at first inclined to take a British minister with him, and Halifax was reported (in early March) to be anxious for the opportunity to talk with Roosevelt and Hull. But Roosevelt thought the presence of a political minister would "excite a lot of talk about an alliance" and divert public interest from the king to political matters, precisely what he wished to avoid. Tweedsmuir, in Canada, also strongly advised against an accompanying cabinet minister because it would cause "a lot of suspicion" in the United States. So it was quickly settled that Their Majesties would travel alone.[47]

Of the various exchanges that occurred in advance of the visit, one of the most interesting is the 37-page brief prepared by F. R. Hoyar Millar, of the British embassy in Washington, as background information for the king. It poignantly reflected the embassy's perception of America in May 1939, fully endorsed by the Foreign Office in London. It began with some words about the president. With all his gifts, he was not a good administrator. He did not choose good advisers, was unmethodical in his work and mercurial in temperament, and liked to show off before subordinates. He tried to do himself many things that were better left to administrators, with the result that "all his laws are in a mess"—and rather than working to put them in order he sought instead for "new fields to conquer." But he was extremely friendly, as were nearly all the State, War, and Navy department personnel with whom the embassy had to work.

As for foreign affairs, the entire country was "engrossed" in the European crisis. Emotionally, American sympathies were all with the democracies. The president, with admirable courage, had frequently warned of the Nazi peril, urged the importance of military preparedness, and had to a surprising degree succeeded in educating the people "in a new school of thought on foreign affairs." But politically there was much neutral thought: Americans simply wished to avoid involvement in another war. Remote from danger themselves, they just did not understand why Britain failed to face up to it more boldly. There were some who

47. Welles to Roosevelt, 4 March 1939, PSF, Diplomatic Correspondence, Box 25; Lindsay to Halifax, 10 March 1939, FO 800/324, pp. 25–26; Chamberlain to Mackenzie King, 29 March 1939, ibid., pp. 30–32; Tweedsmuir to Chamberlain, 11 March 1939, NC 7/11/32/282. There was never any question of Chamberlain's accompanying the king.

actively disliked Britain (the result of war debts, Irish grievances, inferiority complexes, and so on), but this was not heard half so much in Congress or the press as it once was. Indeed, it was common to hear the view that if Britain were involved in war, America would be bound to come in, and soon—an emotional realization that a Nazi world would not be tolerable. Yet American opinion was "not without hesitations amounting almost to suspicion." Dreadful reproaches in the past (over Abyssinia, Austria, and Czechoslovakia) had given way to "a great and satisfactory change" as a result of Britain's stand since Prague. But there was still distrust that Britain "may rat again." So the more forcefully it stood up to the dictators, the more it would be applauded by Americans, who would not, however, give much thought to the state of British armaments nor would they pledge action of their own in advance of any contingency, preferring to say: "Open your mouth and shut your eyes and see what I will give you." Concluding with some "pointers and pitfalls," Hoyar Millar advised: on no account should it be assumed that the United States was "coming in on our side" or have any obligation in that regard. Nor was it wise to criticize anything in America, even if invited to do so. Better to be dull than amusing. Yet, Americans were the most hospitable people in the world, and all they asked in return was that the guest enjoy himself and show it.[48]

The royal visit to the United States, following a three-week tour of Canada, was brief indeed: two crowded days (June 8–9) in Washington, a quick stopover at the New York World's Fair, and a day with President Roosevelt at his country home in Hyde Park, New York. By all accounts the president and the king established a warm rapport almost at once, making the sojourn at Hyde Park, which the intuitive Roosevelt had sensed would appeal to the king, all the more important as an opportunity to discuss mutual concerns in private. Amid a schedule of relaxed, informal entertaining (including a picnic replete with that native American delicacy, the hot dog), they had two long conversations about the international situation, the apparent drift toward war, and the way it affected their respective countries. The president spoke frankly about the security of the Western Hemisphere and how he hoped to assist Britain, within his constitutional limitations, in the event of war; the king explained with equal candor his perception of Britain's situation in Europe. The king was charmed by Roosevelt, telling Mackenzie King, also present at Hyde Park, that he had never met a person with whom

48. Hoyar Miller to Halifax, 23 May 1939, FO 115/3419, File 943; also FO 371/22800, pp. 302–36.

he felt freer in talking and whom he enjoyed more, and inquiring: "Why don't any Ministers talk with me as the President did tonight?" And well he might have been pleased, for aside from the personal charm, Roosevelt's ideas contained in embryo the future Bases-for-Destroyers deal and the Lend-Lease Agreement, so vital to Britain in the war that was to come. Roosevelt too was impressed by the king and shared with him a genuine sense of friendship and accord.[49]

By even the most stringent standards, the royal visit to the United States was a huge success. For all their frontier egalitarianism, Americans were generally caught up in the sentimentality associated with British royalty—and all the more so since the king and queen showed themselves to be gracious, thoughtful, and downright human. As Tweedsmuir put it in a letter to Chamberlain, there was "immense popular interest and a real kindliness towards two most attractive young people." The dispatches that Lindsay sent to London rang with triumph. There were dense crowds everywhere, he wrote on June 12; "the enthusiasm of these people has passed all expectations and is, indeed, unprecedented." The visit had made a "profound impression on the whole country"; it had deepened and fixed feelings of friendship that would not wear off. If war were to come, the popular surge of opinion would mollify at once the unfavorable aspects of existing neutrality legislation. Again a few days later, he referred to the "astonishing enthusiasm" with which the king and queen were greeted everywhere, describing as a "striking feature" of the American reaction the warmth of the welcome even by newspapers in the traditionally isolationist Middle West. By June 20 he acknowledged that Henry Stimson, "a wise and prudent man," had warned him against overestimating the effects of the visit and thinking that Britain now had America politically "in the bag"; but this did not detract a bit from the importance of the results in Lindsay's view. Anglo-American relations were governed by psychological factors and by emotions to a greater extent than the relations between any other countries, and emotions had been "stirred to their very roots." Indeed, the political significance of the visit was frankly and fairly recognized by most American newspapers (the *Chicago Tribune* and Hearst-controlled journals notwithstanding). The impression created "has been deep and has extended to the broadest stratum of the population."[50]

49. John W. Wheeler-Bennett, *King George VI: His Life and Reign*, pp. 381–92. A good account of the visit emphasizing things other than affairs of state may be found in Eleanor Roosevelt, *This I Remember*, pp. 183–98.

50. Tweedsmuir to Chamberlain, 19 June 1939, NC 7/11/32/283; Lindsay to Halifax, 12, 16, 20, 22 June 1939, FO 414/276, pp. 54–68.

The precise effect of the visit on Anglo-American relations is, of course, impossible to measure. Years later Eleanor Roosevelt wrote that the president had extended the invitation largely because, "believing that we all might soon be engaged in a life and death struggle, in which Great Britain would be our first linc of defense, he hoped that the visit would create a bond of friendship between the people of the two countries." Although there was always in America a certain amount of criticism and superficial ill feeling toward the British, he thought that in time of danger "something deeper [relating to their common heritage and ideas] comes to the surface." The royal visit, he hoped, would be a reminder of this deep bond.[51] And it no doubt was—in a subtle and long-term sense. At the moment however, it was difficult to discover direct, tangible effect. There was no sudden change in American attitudes toward neutrality revision or foreign policy generally. And Foreign Office personnel thought it essential to qualify Lindsay's categorical statement about the effects of the visit not wearing off. Chamberlain, for his part, showed no special interest in learning anything political from it and made no particular attempt to discover shifting forces on which he might capitalize. Although he expressed to Kennedy his pleasure over the warm American reception and paid tribute to Roosevelt for his efforts to save the world from war, there is no evidence that he sought the king's impressions about Roosevelt and the problems he was facing (in which Tweedsmuir had found the king "profoundly interested"). His account to his sister of visiting Buckingham Palace, June 25, for the "homecoming" stated only that the king and queen "gossiped away in great spirits about their journey for a long time. . . ." Between King George VI and Roosevelt, however, a simple and personal friendship was established that continued, and grew, in the following years.[52]

Meanwhile, the British (and French) negotiations with Russia were going poorly. Britain's early proposals, vague and guarded, were met by specific Soviet demands; and when the British moved cautiously toward concession, the Soviets raised their requirements or introduced new issues. Chamberlain was wary, and often disheartened, throughout. His personal letters continued to reflect his deep distrust of the Russians and his doubt that a deal with them would be of any value. Even the Foreign Office, where the constraints of power politics and the danger of a Rus-

51. E. Roosevelt, *This I Remember,* pp. 183–84.

52. Kennedy to Hull, 9 June 1939, SDM 740.00/1684; Foreign Office Minutes, 12 June 1939, FO 371/22800, p. 342; Tweedsmuir to Chamberlain, 19 June 1939, NC 7/11/32/283; Neville to Ida, 25 June 1939, NC 18/1/1104; Wheeler-Bennett, *King George VI,* p. 503.

sian deal with Germany were realistically understood, showed no great interest in a Russian agreement, Kennedy reported to Washington (May 19). But the British persisted, spurred largely by intensifying pressure at home (in Parliament and press).[53]

In Anglo-Russian maneuvering the United States played no direct role. Kennedy reported with some regularity on the opinions—mostly negative—of officials with whom he spoke, but these reports prompted no specific response. On one occasion late in May, the ambassador told Halifax that the British were "completely right" in going as far as they had to avoid a breakdown in the negotiations (which he thought would have been "disastrous"), but he apparently spoke entirely on his own. Bullitt's dispatches from Paris pictured the French as much more anxious than the British to reach an agreement and convinced that London must be pushed. But no push came from Washington, and Bullitt's own advice seemed to work in the opposite direction. In the cabinet on June 7, Halifax cited Bullitt's opinion, reported by Phipps (that an agreement with Britain was important to Russia, but that Britain would not get it if she gave the impression of "running after" the Russians), as an argument against sending a British minister to Russia to facilitate the negotiations. Chamberlain accepted the argument, telling his sister that sending a minister (or a former minister: Eden had "foolishly" volunteered) to Moscow "would be the worst of tactics with a hard bargainer like Molotoff." Anyway, the Chiefs of Staff did not believe that Russia's help would be the deciding factor in any war, "especially when we consider what the attitude of the United States is likely to be."[54]

In mid-June Britain and the United States concluded modest barter arrangements which, though successful in outcome, revealed the attitude of hard bargaining that still prevailed between the two countries. Several months before, the United States had proposed a direct exchange of cotton and wheat for British rubber and tin, for the purpose of stockpiling strategic materials in case of war. Concerned lest such a transaction unbalance their rubber market, the British moved cautiously.

53. See, for example, Neville to Hilda, 14 May 1939; Neville to Ida, 21 May 1939; Neville to Hilda, 28 May 1939; Neville to Ida, 10 June 1939, NC 18/1/1099–1102; Kennedy to Hull, 19 May 1939, SDM 740.00/1547. British opinion and policy in the Anglo-French-Russian negotiations have been described elsewhere; see, for example, Colvin, *The Chamberlain Cabinet*, pp. 199–216; Rock, *Appeasement on Trial*, pp. 251–94; A. J. P. Taylor, *Englishmen and Others*, pp. 157–67.

54. Kennedy to Hull, 16 May 1939, SDM 740.00/1501; Halifax to Lindsay, 25 May 1939, FO 414/276, p. 50; Bullitt to Hull, 15 May 1939, SDM 740.00/1478; Phipps to Halifax, 6 June 1939, *B.D.*, 5:775; CAB 23/99, 7 June 1939, p. 303; Neville to Ida, 10 June 1939, NC 18/1/1102; Stanhope to Halifax, 19 May 1939, PREM 1/409, p. 146.

Kennedy called on Halifax to emphasize the great importance attached to the scheme by Roosevelt himself, and asked that Chamberlain be told directly of the American hope for an early decision, "having regard to the great political value which such a plan possessed." A month later Kennedy was back at the Foreign Office urging quick and generous action; the president's personal policy was involved, and failure to clinch matters swiftly would be a great mistake. The issue warranted cabinet consideration on June 14 and 21. The United States had originally hoped for the sale of one million cotton bales; Britain had offered to take one-half that amount; Kennedy thought 650,000 bales would "do the trick"; and the cabinet agreed to 600,000. Chamberlain thought in terms of a definite *quid pro quo,* such as a modification of American neutrality legislation for any increase over 500,000; but he doubted that it could be obtained and conceded that it would be unfortunate if the proceedings broke down or proceeded "in a grudging spirit," particularly at that time. So he favored an increase to 650,000 bales. The following week the president of the Board of Trade (Oliver Stanley) reported that Kennedy was pressing for an alteration in the terms of the deal that would give the United States a $600,000 advantage, on the grounds that the price of cotton had recently risen. On merit, Stanley thought the concession should be refused; American cotton prices were "fictitious," deliberately maintained by the government above the world price. But he brought the matter to the cabinet "in view . . . of the importance of our relations with the United States." It was left to determination by a small group of ministers, and agreement was reached on June 23. Kennedy described the proceedings as "tiresome and difficult" and was relieved to see them concluded. The British no doubt felt the same way.[55]

But this was mild in comparison to the tedium of Anglo-American contacts about a disturbing turn of events in the Far East, where an aggressive Japanese army was engaged in provocative activities, pressuring the International Settlement at Shanghai, blockading British (and French) concessions at Tientsin, subjecting British nationals to extreme indignities, and threatening American rights and interests in a broadening zone of military operations. This campaign, designed to exploit the European crisis to force cessation of Western aid to the Chinese Nationalist Government and to oust foreign interests from Japan's projected Greater East Asia Co-Prosperity Sphere, began in earnest during

55. Halifax to Lindsay, 27 April, 25 May, 7 June 1939, FO 414/276, pp. 42, 50, 51; CAB 23/99, 14 June 1939, pp. 366–68; CAB 23/100, 21 June 1939, pp. 30–31; Hull, *Memoirs,* 1:625.

the second half of June. Their mutual interests again endangered, the question of Anglo-American cooperation to defend those interests quickly emerged once more.

The threat to British interests in the Far East had never been far from the minds of policymakers in London. Indeed, it is clear that, as the German and Italian threat unfolded in Europe, the British were preoccupied with the Japanese danger in Asia to a degree not generally appreciated elsewhere; they were determined to do everything possible to avoid a war against all three powers simultaneously. In mid-April the CID studied the dispatch of a fleet to the Far East in the event of war with Japan, irrespective of the situation in the Mediterranean. It concluded there were so many variables that could not be assessed that it was impossible to say how soon (after Japanese "intervention") a fleet could be sent and what its size might be. One of those variables was the attitude of the United States, whose action (such as a movement of its fleet to Hawaii) would have a profound effect on Japan and might give Britain room to maneuver. Cadogan did not yet wish to sound Washington officially, but he wrote Lindsay that he would be "glad to know" what the American reaction to a Japanese attack on Singapore or Australia would be.[56] This set the tone for what was to follow during June, July, and August 1939. The British sought cautiously but earnestly to determine what they might expect by way of American support in the Pacific—largely without success.

The Japanese action at Tientsin gave special point to the British concern about America's position. With the Foreign Office talking retaliation, and Chamberlain viewing sanctions as useless unless backed by force, the minister for coordination of defense (Lord Chatfield) prepared in mid-June, upon the prime minister's instructions, a memorandum on the "Situation in the Far East" that declared: "It will be obvious to the Chiefs of Staff that the attitude of the United States of America may be a dominating factor." And the chiefs of staff concluded: "When all is said and done . . . the decisive consideration . . . is the attitude of the United States." Without its active support, Britain could undertake economic measures against Japan only by concentrating in the Far East a fleet sufficiently strong to meet the whole Japanese navy; with it, the situation would be "completely altered" and reinforcement of the China fleet by two capital ships to cooperate with the Americans "would be a

56. CID Paper, 19 April 1939, PREM 1/309, p. 12; Cadogan to Lindsay, 17 April 1939, FO 115/3417, File G 70, Part 2.

proper strategic measure." Without active American cooperation, it would not be justifiable, in view of the existing international situation, to take any avoidable action that might lead to hostilities with Japan. Chamberlain drew the moral—perhaps too simply—in a letter to his sister: "If the Americans would come in with us of course it would all be over directly. But I am sure they won't." Despondent over the new crisis and this inability to "make any progress anywhere," he was (so he wrote Ambassador Phipps) "more than ever conscious of the danger of quarreling with all the strongest military Powers at once!"[57]

A telegram had been dispatched to Washington seeking general reactions to the situation. Early indications were not encouraging. Roosevelt told the press on June 19 that the United States government was gravely disturbed, would watch the situation closely, and would be guided by events. But that was all. Kennedy thought the British should regard this statement as "eminently satisfactory." The president did not want to make representations in Tokyo before the British ambassador there (Sir Robert Craigie) had seen the Japanese foreign minister, presumably about opening negotiations. Reading the evidence accordingly, the Foreign Policy Committee, in discussions on June 19 and 20, assumed both that what Britain could do depended heavily upon America and that America's position was altogether uncertain. Whether Japanese military retaliation against Britain would be sufficient to endanger American interests to the point of influencing American action was carefully canvassed, but there was simply no certainty on this point either; and the committee was left with nowhere to go. Halifax's description of the situation provides a perfect example of the "after you" British and American postures with respect to Japan. The foreign secretary had told Kennedy that Britain was making "certain suggestions" to the Japanese government, and it would be well if the United States would make "some previous approach" to Tokyo as a sort of conditioning maneuver. But Kennedy thought it better if, once the British had made their approach, they could "return to the charge and see whether the United States Government were prepared to take further action." Again Chamberlain concluded that with America's position uncertain and Britain able to

57. Chatfield Memorandum, 16 June 1939, CAB 53/11, p. 122; COS 928, 16 June 1939, CAB 53/50, pp. 205–8; Neville to Hilda, 17 June 1939, NC 18/1/1103; Chamberlain to Phipps, 19 June 1939, PHPP 3/1. Chamberlain wrote Walter Runciman, who had warned him in a personal letter that war against Japan without full American support would be disastrous, that the Foreign Office had "changed their tune so it looks easier" (Runciman to Chamberlain and reply, 19 June 1939, Runciman Papers, WR 284).

send an effective fleet to the Far East only at the cost of abandoning her naval position in the Mediterranean, every effort should be made to negotiate an early settlement of the dispute at Tientsin. Halifax observed one more time that the stark choice (between relinquishing Britain's position in the Far East and jeopardizing her position in the Mediterranean) might be avoided if the United States was prepared to act. And Inskip (now dominions secretary) thought America might be more inclined to act if Britain considered sending a substantial fleet to the Far East. But there the matter rested.[58]

In the cabinet, June 21, Chamberlain reiterated that none of the suggestions made for easing the situation at Tientsin "would be really effective unless we had the cooperation of the United States of America." And the French agreed. To a question about possible Russian assistance, Chamberlain replied that the position of the United States was more important. A primary problem deterring America was now openly acknowledged: the difficulty of assisting Britain in Asia without jeopardizing impending neutrality revision. Yet a few weeks later, when cabinet discussion turned to American neutrality legislation, Halifax assessed the prospect for amendment "extremely unfavorable." And this was "unfortunate" since Washington's reason for being unable to help Britain "in several matters" was that to do so would prejudice the passage of amending legislation.[59] The British could not help feeling let down on this count.

The State Department's perception of things is revealed in the diary of Adolf Berle (June 21): "The British were pressing heavily for an indication that we were going to do something . . . , presumably associate ourselves with them, or more likely get out a little in front." The irony of this was great since in 1931, when Stimson had sought British support in protesting the seizure of Manchuria, they had "left him flat." In any case, American military chiefs believed that "we must not get pushed into the front line trench by the British." The chances of this were slim. Though long sympathetic in principle to determined action against Japan, Roosevelt and Hull had for some months been very cautious in their reactions to Tokyo's provocations. They had issued protests but had carefully avoided threats. The consequences of stronger action were thought to be too risky, especially in view of the growing danger in

58. Halifax to Chamberlain, 19 June 1939, PREM 1/316, p. 83; CAB 27/625, 19, 20 June 1939, pp. 144–66, 168–75.

59. CAB 23/100, 21 June, 12 July 1939, pp. 12, 155.

Europe. Neutrality reform would be jeopardized by renewed accusations of foreign entanglement, and the Japanese advocates of alliance with Germany (the issue was known to be under debate in Tokyo) would be strengthened. Some in Washington already feared that the Japanese action at Tientsin was part of a coordinated plot, to be followed shortly by a German thrust in Europe that would touch off another perilous crisis. What the situation seemed to require was some means of warning the Japanese firmly, without threatening them directly or backing them into a corner. Another month would pass before Roosevelt found a means (abrogation of a commercial treaty) that he thought appropriate. It was insufficient to help the foundering British. When the British chiefs of staff summarized the situation again on June 24, they recorded that the attitude of the United States, whose active intervention on the side of Britain would have "such a profound effect on the situation," remained doubtful. This led the CID to conclude that Britain must negotiate with Japan at the risk of further damage to her Far Eastern interests, for the one factor that might have redressed the balance, the naval cooperation of the United States, plainly would not be forthcoming. An exasperated Chamberlain privately began to blame the Foreign Office for "so rashly" landing Britain in "this mess" in the Far East.[60]

In these circumstances Lindsay's message from Washington on June 26 could only add to British irritation. In describing the American attitude as "always less isolationist" toward Asian issues than European ones, it pointedly warned against "anything that could be construed as a return to . . . appeasement as that policy is interpreted here." Halifax dutifully told the cabinet that American opinion would be strongly opposed to any British concessions on "wider issues," and that Washington (so he had heard from Kennedy) was using its influence discreetly behind the scenes (he did not say how). But it is easy to see how Foreign Office personnel would lament: "It is precisely lack of support from the U.S. that is forcing us to pursue a policy of appeasement . . . for perhaps longer than we would otherwise wish."[61]

Chamberlain was pressed to explain the situation by a deputation from the National Council of Labour on June 28. Again he declared

60. Berle, *Navigating the Rapids*, p. 228; Dallek, *Franklin Roosevelt and American Foreign Policy*, pp. 194–95; MacDonald, *The United States, Britain, and Appeasement*, pp. 159ff.; Offner, *Origins of the Second World War*, pp. 158–59; CAB 53/50, 24 June 1939, p. 228; Minutes of CID Meeting, 26 June 1939, PREM 1/314; Neville to Ida, 25 June 1939, NC 18/1/1104.

61. Lindsay to Halifax, 26 June 1939, *B.D.*, 9:227; CAB 23/100, 28 June 1939, p. 38; Foreign Office Minute, 22 July 1939, FO 371/22830, p. 158.

that "the key to the problem lay in the U.S.A.," hamstrung by the critical issue of neutrality legislation. If compelled to retaliate against Japan, Britain "could do nothing effective without American help." To send to the Far East a British fleet capable of holding the Japanese would denude the Mediterranean and offer a great temptation to Hitler. Further, Kennedy had said that Britain's policy was "completely right" and that the Americans were doing all they could to help behind the scenes (by cautioning the Japanese). American sensitivity had been heightened by French Foreign Minister Bonnet's recent speech proclaiming that if the Americans would clearly say the United States would be in the war from the first day, it would not begin. In any case, Chamberlain said, experience showed that the sure way to lose the Americans was to run after them too hard. He had emphasized the same point in a CID meeting several days before.[62]

Weighing heavily on the minds of British policymakers was the considered opinion of the chiefs of staff: Britain's plans should be based on the assumption that France was its only certain major ally; sooner or later Germany, Italy, and Japan would all be ranged against it; and consequently, its vital interests would be threatened in three theaters. ". . . We cannot be as strong as we would like to be in all these theaters simultaneously. The problem therefore resolves itself into one of priority." With a tactical retreat in order, formal talks with Japan were initiated late in June, and British policy faced up to the task of walking the tightrope between making concessions that would smack of abandoning China and avoiding a breakdown of negotiations.[63]

As the talks proceeded in Tokyo, the British continued their efforts to gain American support in specific matters. During the second week of July, for example, they inquired whether Washington was prepared to act with them when currency issues were raised. The negative American reply related currency issues to administrative control of the British Concession at Tientsin, and Welles told Lindsay frankly that American participation in the Tientsin discussions would provide too much of a handle to the isolationists. Halifax informed the cabinet on July 12 that he did not know what had happened to a "proposed wider statement" by Cordell Hull; and while he undertook to inquire about it, he was reduced one week later to saying that the attitude of the United States

62. Notes of a Conversation, 28, 30 June 1939, PREM 1/325; Dalton Diary, 28 June 1939, 20:75–76; Minutes of CID Meeting, 26 June 1939, PREM 1/314, p. 28.

63. Report by the Chiefs-of-Staff Sub-Committee, June 1939, PREM 1/314, pp. 35–36.

government "had not been very helpful"—an observation repeated laconically on later occasions. Meantime, on the issue of economic restrictions, he was careful not to assume a position that would prohibit Britain from following a lead, should the Americans decide to give one.[64]

On July 24 the British signed an agreement with Japan (the Craigie-Arita declaration) recognizing the latter's special position in China, including responsibility for law and order in areas that it occupied. Something of a blow to British prestige, although it did not change the situation very much, it was followed two days later by an American denunciation of the 1911 trade treaty with Japan. Apprehensive over the effects of the Craigie-Arita agreement on America's position in China, Roosevelt had been under growing congressional and public pressure to take some kind of action against Japan. The abrogation of a commercial treaty would warn the Japanese about a possible loss of essential American supplies, blunt the failure of neutrality revision, and meet the growing public feeling against Japan without running any substantial risk. The Japanese were taken quite by surprise. So were the British. Halifax told the CID that there had been no consultation with Britain: "if we had known of it earlier, it might have led us to take a different line." It could have a "salutary effect" upon Japan, and would necessitate reexamination of the Foreign Office view that the best procedure for securing American cooperation (in exercising economic pressure on Japan) was to decide upon some definite action and put it into operation, if possible, before American support was sought. Chamberlain wrote his sister that the conversations in Tokyo should be aided by Roosevelt's action, but it "would have been still more helpful if it had come earlier."[65]

By early August, Britain's position in the Far East was causing Halifax more anxiety, so he told the cabinet, than its position in any other part of the world. The Japanese were raising matters of general policy, and the British might have to break with them on these wider issues. The French had adopted a helpful line (refusing to concur in any agreement on which they had not been consulted); but the attitude of the United States was "much less precise," and he was trying to obtain clarification. Chamberlain, for his part, had seemed to give up trying. He told the House of Commons (July 31) that although the general objectives of the

64. CAB 23/100, 12, 19, 26 July 1939, pp. 151–52, 188, 227; Lindsay to Halifax, 15, 16 July 1939, *B.D.*, 9:283–84; Halifax to Stanley, 13 July 1939, PREM 1/314, p. 18.

65. W. N. Medlicott, *British Foreign Policy since Versailles, 1919–1963*, p. 167; Dallek, *Franklin Roosevelt and American Foreign Policy*, p. 195; Hull, *Memoirs*, 1:635; CAB 2/9, 27 July 1939, pp. 81–82; Neville to Hilda, 30 July 1939, NC 18/1/1110.

British and American governments were "closely similar . . . it does not follow that each of us must necessarily do exactly the same thing as the other. We may find that different methods are appropriate in different cases." Still, he placed "utmost importance" on collaboration where it was possible and would keep Washington informed "of all we are doing or are about to do." In any case, the need for Britain to take up a definite position itself before consulting America was now widely accepted. It was agreed in the cabinet on August 2 to withhold from Washington a report by the Advisory Committee on Trade Questions in Time of War (relative to economic measures designed to restrain Japan from further action inimical to British interest in the Far East) until the British themselves had reached a decision about it. On the currency issue, the French advised avoiding the impression of trying to interest the United States government in an aspect of a problem in which it had already said it had no interest. The Foreign Office embraced this counsel: "if there is to be a real chance of American cooperation, the United States Government will only offer such cooperation at some stage when they see we have made a stand ourselves." Halifax expressed to Chamberlain his concern about "asking the Americans to do something to help us before we have shown that we can stand up for ourselves." Washington no doubt felt it had helped by denouncing the commercial treaty, and for Britain to ask for further assistance at that stage seemed "unlikely to produce a useful result." Consequently, Britain should proceed on its own, and if negotiations broke down, it would be on good ground with public opinion and "in particular . . . [might] hope for warm approval in America." Thereafter, the British informed the Japanese that they could not conclude a bilateral agreement on larger economic issues because other governments were also concerned, and Washington was reportedly pleased with this posture.[66] That is where matters stood when developments in Europe suddenly assumed central importance again.

European concerns, of course, were never far from British minds. German moves in particular were carefully watched. There were moments of hope and times of despair. Chamberlain indulged in some curious thinking about Hitler, who knew very well (the prime minister believed) that Britain meant business, but did not know "whether we

66. CAB 23/100, 2, 22 August 1939, pp. 279–80, 304–5, 322; Johnson to Hull, 2 August 1939, SDM 741.00/250; Halifax to Phipps, 6 August 1939; Halifax to Lindsay, 13 August 1939; Halifax to Campbell, 15 August 1939; Halifax to Chamberlain, 16 August 1939; PREM 1/316, pp. 10–11, 41–42, 46–49, 51–52.

mean to attack him as soon as we are strong enough." Fear of attack would naturally lead him to opt for an early war while Britain was not fully prepared, so Chamberlain was "trying to get the truth conveyed" to him. There seemed at the time to be no practicable solution to the Danzig question short of war, but if the dictators would have "a modicum of patience," a way could no doubt be found both to meet German claims and safeguard Poland's independence and economic security. He was, in fact, thinking of asking Mussolini to appeal for a yearlong truce "to let the temperature cool down." Aware of his declining popularity at home, he hoped to "have long enough to see my policy through" and still believed he could steer the nation "through the next few years out of the war zone into peace and reconstruction."[67] In all of this, there was no apparent role for the United States.

Increasingly embittered by the attacks of his critics (Winston Churchill and Sir Archibald Sinclair, in particular), Chamberlain viewed foreign policy in close conjunction with domestic partisan politics, and his letters to his sisters reveal an intense concern to beat down his adversaries and to demonstrate that he was right. "Winston & Co. never seem to realize," he wrote, that "the longer the war is put off the less likely it is to come at all, as we go on perfecting our defenses and building up the defenses of our Allies." Furthermore,

> You don't need offensive forces sufficient to win a smashing victory. What you want are defensive forces sufficiently strong to make it impossible for the other side to win except at such a cost as to make it not worth while. That is what we are doing and though at present the German feeling is [that] it is not worth while *yet*, they will presently come to realize that it never *will* be worth while. Then we can talk.[68]

This line of thinking dominated Chamberlain's outlook as long as he remained in office, and it tempered, at least indirectly, his attitudes toward the United States and any role it might play either in preserving peace or winning a war.

In weighing alternative possibilities, the cabinet was, of course, con-

67. Neville to Hilda, 15 July 1939, NC 18/1/1107.

68. Neville to Ida, 23 July 1939; Neville to Hilda, 30 July 1939; NC 18/1/1108, 1110. Chamberlain was inclined to accept the view of the *Times* (5 August) that the next general election would be fought mainly around the personality of the prime minister; and "if the contest is to be about me, I should like the biggest majority I can get" (Neville to Ida, 5 August 1939, NC 18/1/1111). The interrelationship between British foreign policy and domestic politics is a primary theme in Maurice Cowling, *The Impact of Hitler: British Politics and British Policy, 1933–1940*.

cerned about Britain's financial position in the event of a long war. Here the role of the United States would be crucial, and a circulated secret "Note on the Financial Situation" held that "unless, when the time comes the United States are prepared to lend or to give us money as required, the prospects for a long war are becoming exceedingly grim." Richard Hopkins, second secretary of the treasury, who had been called for consultation, explained that Britain's primary need would be a share of American production at no cost. Halifax believed that when the war had continued for some time the attitude of the United States would be sufficiently favorable to enable Britain to win. Hopkins replied that he could not assume unlimited American resources and discussion ended inconclusively.[69]

The establishment of certainties was not advanced by the Washington embassy's annual record of leading personalities, which Lindsay sent to London in early August. Notable for its poignant sketches, it described President Roosevelt as "a baffling character" who was "extremely sensitive to public opinion." He probably knew more about what went on in America than any previous president, and his power of leadership was "almost miraculous"; but his ability as a statesman was open to question. Hull and Welles fared all right in their appraisals, save for a reference to the latter's vanity and ambition, but most Senators (including Borah and Pittman) did not do well. And Bullitt, known to have the president's ear, was deemed "no friend of Great Britain."[70]

As August progressed, several prominent unofficial Englishmen tried, through public speeches, to improve America's understanding of Britain and the situation it confronted. In a broadcast to the United States from London, August 8, Churchill described, as only he could do, the hush of suspense and fear that had fallen across Europe as German and Italian armies crunched the gravel of the parade grounds and their neighbors wondered anxiously who would be the next victim of attack. All the "working and creative forces of the world," he averred, must get on with the task of making it impossible for the life of mankind to depend upon the caprice of a single man (Hitler). In personal appearances Baldwin, visiting the United States, addressed the World Congress on Education for Democracy at Columbia University, August 16, and spoke at Carnegie Hall next day. Newsreels showed him dramatically declaring that a democrat must be willing to work for, and to die for, his ideals.

69. CAB 23/100, 5 July 1939, pp. 120, 129, 138–40.
70. FO 414/276, 4 August 1939, pp. 84–116.

Ambassador Lindsay thought this "excellent publicity," and a Foreign Office minute labeled Baldwin's efforts "a classic example of how to state our case in the U.S."[71] But appeals of this sort were soon overwhelmed by threats of force—and war.

The German-Polish crisis over Danzig, which had been brewing for some months, came swiftly to a head in August, and danger of imminent war was sharply intensified by the shocking conclusion of a Nazi-Soviet nonaggression pact on August 22. Surprisingly unperturbed by this startling turn of events—reflecting no doubt his disbelief in the value of Russian assistance and the fact that he had by now come to expect anything of Hitler—Chamberlain seemed, in fact, somehow strengthened by it. He wrote at once to Hitler that the Nazi-Soviet agreement, whatever its nature, did not alter Britain's obligation to Poland, and he reaffirmed that position in the House of Commons on August 24. If Britain was forced to embark upon a struggle of untold misery, it would be fighting not for the "political future of a far-away city in a foreign land" but for principles of justice and freedom. Parliament and press were staunchly behind him, determined that Britain's pledge should be honored.[72]

In the days that followed, Chamberlain bent his efforts to persuade the Germans and Poles to negotiate. He approved an agreement of mutual assistance with Poland, sent messages to Berlin and Warsaw, dispatched a special emissary (Sir Horace Wilson) to Hitler, and tolerated the behind-the-scenes maneuvering of Birger Dahlerus, a Swedish manufacturer, who carried unofficial messages from Göring to Halifax and back. He clearly hoped that war could still be averted but realized the need for standing firm. Writing to his sister on August 27, Chamberlain compared himself to "a man driving a clumsy coach over a narrow crooked road along the face of a precipice." Sometimes his heartbeat stopped for minutes until he somehow rounded the next corner and found himself still on the track. Hitler's proposals did not constitute an offer of a peaceful solution to the Polish difficulty, he explained; rather, they brushed Poland aside as a matter to be settled by Germany, and after that (if Britain did not interfere) the Führer would make a splendid offer of a German-English alliance. Chamberlain believed this prospect had come upon Hitler with new force in view of the ease with which

71. *Churchill's Complete Speeches,* 6:6149–51; Lindsay to Halifax, 22 August 1939, FO 115/3420, File 1283; Foreign Office Minute, 30 August 1939, FO 371/22834, p. 294.

72. Rock, *Chamberlain,* pp. 189–90.

he achieved the Russian agreement, and in his excitement he had almost forgotten Poland. "The mentality of that extraordinary man would be incredible to anyone who had not seen and talked with him." And yet—every hour that passed without catastrophe added its mite to the slowly accumulating antiwar forces, and he recalled the motto on his calendar several days before: "The tide turns at the low as well as at the high level."[73]

The British government took special care to keep Washington fully informed of the messages passing among heads of state during these trying days, but once again, American influence played very little role in British thinking. Halifax was reportedly attracted to an idea put forth in a High Commissioners meeting that Roosevelt should make a broad international appeal for a conference to resolve outstanding problems. But he was also reported to be doubtful whether Hitler was really open to reason; and the idea did not develop. There is nothing to suggest that Chamberlain thought about turning to Roosevelt in any diplomatic way. The one personal letter that he addressed to the president during the last week of August asked Roosevelt to authorize release to Britain of details of the Norden bombsight, which the British air attaché had been unable to acquire. Even in this instance, Lindsay was given the option of not delivering the letter if he could get the necessary information "without flying so high." Kennedy, influenced by Wilson, had telephoned Welles on August 24 that the one thing Britain wanted from the United States was pressure on the Poles. In view of their obligations to Warsaw, the British could not apply it themselves, but Washington could. This message, which reflected the panicky feeling of Wilson and Kennedy rather than a considered request from London, did extensive harm to the British cause in Washington. The State Department saw it as meaning (as Moffat put it) "that they wanted us to assume the responsibility for a new Munich and do their dirty work for them." The idea got no support "from the President . . . down."[74]

Meantime, Roosevelt, wishing to be sure that he had done all he could to prevent a war, undertook several initiatives of his own. Washington

73. Ibid.; Neville to Hilda, 27 August 1939, NC 18/1/1115.

74. See FO 115/3418, File 321, 25 August–1 September 1939; INKP 2, 25 August 1939, pp. 16–18; Halifax to Lindsay, 25 August 1939, FO 115/3418, File G 202; *Moffat Papers*, p. 253. Moffat's notes of 25–30 August reflect his feeling that appeasement was in the air again; that the British were not being entirely frank with Washington; and that they were acting unrealistically in relation to German psychology (ibid., pp. 254–58). Ickes's *Diary* reeks with disdain for Chamberlain's "fumbling ineptitude" (2:703–5).

was not surprised by the Nazi-Soviet pact; indeed, the State Department had known of the German-Russian contacts almost from the beginning and had subtly tried to alert the British without jeopardizing its source of information. Nor did Roosevelt think that Russia would have given substantial aid to Britain had those two nations reached agreement. But he recognized the new face that the Nazi-Soviet pact put upon things and tried to counteract it. On August 23, he addressed a letter to King Victor Emmanuel of Italy, asking him to exert his influence on behalf of peace. Next day he sent appeals to Hitler and President Moscicki of Poland, suggesting a settlement of differences through direct negotiation, arbitration, or conciliation, and expressed his willingness to serve as a mediator under certain conditions (that each agreed to respect the other's independence and territorial integrity). Neither Roosevelt nor the State Department was sanguine about what this might accomplish; Adolf Berle observed that the messages had "all that quality of naïveté which is the prerogative alone of the United States" and would have "about the same effect as a valentine sent to somebody's mother-in-law out of season." But it was important domestically in helping to clarify for Americans where the responsibility for any war must lie, in making it easier for Roosevelt to pursue a pro-Allied policy in the future, and, in a broader symbolic sense, in leaving "no stone unturned" that might preserve the peace. (Two weeks earlier Washington had advised Warsaw that, in the interest of public opinion, it was of highest importance that the first act of a military nature should not be taken by Poland. The British were not officially informed of this though they quickly learned by roundabout means.) When President Moscicki at once declared his readiness for negotiation or conciliation, Roosevelt sent (August 25) still another message for Hitler, stating that countless lives could yet be saved if he would agree to the pacific means of settlement accepted by Poland. This was clearly designed to "put the bee on Germany"—which had not been done in August 1914. Thereafter, Roosevelt waited upon events. There was one personal message to Chamberlain, a letter of August 31 explaining that existing legislation precluded release of details about the Norden bombsight; but he would study the matter further and consider granting the request "either under present conditions or under such new conditions as may arise."[75]

75. Dallek, *Franklin Roosevelt and American Foreign Policy,* pp. 196–97; Charles E. Bohlen, *Witness to History, 1929–1969,* pp. 69ff.; Roosevelt to Murray, 24 August 1939, PSF, Diplomatic Correspondence, Box 29; Berle, *Navigating the Rapids,* pp. 242–43; Troutbeck Minute, 12 August 1939, *B.D.,* 6:678; Roosevelt to Chamberlain, 31 August 1939, PSF, Diplomatic Correspondence, Box 25.

The British did not know in advance of Roosevelt's appeals; Halifax learned from the press of his letter to the king of Italy, and telegraphed Ambassador Loraine in Rome to inform Ciano of this, if he thought it useful. The message was repeated two days later in relation to Roosevelt's letters to Hitler. British anxiety about Italian sensitivities sprang no doubt from assurances received from Rome on August 23 that Italy would not join Germany if Hitler made war—which Mussolini and Ciano were anxious to keep absolutely confidential. Britain's advice to Warsaw (August 25) was that it could not lose anything by a favorable response to Roosevelt's appeal; whereas Dalherus counseled London (August 28) that Britain's reply to Hitler should contain no reference to the Roosevelt "plan." The lack of meaningful Anglo-American communication—to say nothing of cooperation—is reflected in the absence of any substantial reference to America in meetings of the British cabinet, save for the adoption of recommendations for opening a British purchasing mission in the United States (and Canada), which had been in the process of development for some months.[76]

Hitler was just not interested in a freely negotiated settlement with Poland. His cruel and uncompromising behavior during the last few days of August made this clear beyond question, and when the Polish government failed to meet his preposterous demands, the German army opened its assault at dawn, September 1. There followed a two-day period in which Chamberlain and Halifax temporized in honoring Britain's guarantee to Poland—impeded in part by a reluctant France but also tempted by projected schemes for "negotiation." But a near revolt in both the cabinet and the House of Commons forced a declaration of war on Germany on September 3.[77]

In those hectic hours, described by various participants as the most trying in their experience, the United States was barely present in British

76. Halifax to Loraine, 24, 26 August 1939, *B.D.*, 7:199, 263; CAB 23/100, 24 August 1939, p. 364; Halifax to Kennard, 25 August 1939, *B.D.*, 7:226; Ogilvie-Forbes to Halifax, 28 August 1939, ibid., p. 321; CAB 23/100, 28 August 1939, pp. 415–16. That recommendations on the establishment of a British purchasing mission in America should be prepared for submission to the cabinet had been agreed upon in the CID on 29 June (CAB 2/9, pp. 49–50).

77. See Rock, *Appeasement on Trial,* pp. 311–29; and Rock, *Neville Chamberlain,* pp. 191–92. That Chamberlain and Halifax toyed with the idea of trying to negotiate with Germany again is evidenced in various sources. Among the most telling, heretofore uncited, are the diaries or papers of three cabinet ministers: Simon Diary, no. 16, 2 September 1939; David Euan Wallace Diary, c. 495, 2 September 1939; Templewood Papers, X:5, 2 September 1939. Halifax had earlier agreed with Wallace on the folly of accepting any terms that did not effectively mean the end of the Hitler regime (Wallace Diary, c. 495, 31 August 1939). But he seems to have wavered, momentarily at least.

minds. Ambassador Lothian, in Washington, was instructed on September 1 to ask the United States government to undertake the protection of British persons, property, and interests in Germany in the event of war, and Washington consented. This was a routine matter that had been decided in London three months earlier. And a CID subcommittee agreed upon a policy not to bomb civilians, in deference to an appeal to that effect issued by President Roosevelt.[78] But British minds were focused elsewhere, fixed upon central Europe where the war they had ardently hoped to avoid had now to be confronted.

78. Lothian to Hull, Hull to Lothian, 1 September 1939, FO 115/3420, File 1437; Cadogan to Chamberlain, 22 May 1939, PREM 1/372; INKP 2, 1 September 1939, p. 31.

VIII.
The First Four Months of War

THE OUTBREAK OF WAR in Europe did not result in any sudden improvement in Anglo-American relations. Suspicion of Britain's resolve to face up squarely to the new and grim responsibility that it had assumed was widely felt on the western side of the Atlantic. To be sure, Britain had finally grasped the nettle—at least in principle—and saw the need to confront and block potential German domination of the Continent. But up to the final moment, high American officials had little faith that Chamberlain would not again "turn his hand from the plow"; and the feeling of doubt persisted—not without reason—long after the declaration of war. On the other hand, America's seeming obsession to stay clear of the conflict, however understandable it might be, was seen in England as offering little hope of meaningful aid in the struggle now begun. Indeed, there was serious question in Britain whether American intervention of any sort was really desired. There certainly was no wish to repeat the performance of 1919, when the United States had dominated the peacemaking, only to withdraw and leave Europe to its fate. Chamberlain's early thinking reveals both a basis for American apprehension and uncertainty about the dimensions of potential American aid. He did not hope for a military victory, he confided to his sister on September 10, but a collapse of the German home front. For that it was necessary to convince the Germans that they could not win; how, he did not say. The United States might, at the right moment, be of help in this—but again he did not explain.[1] His reasoning on these points unfolded only with time; but the hope of bringing the war to an end

1. Ickes, *Diary*, 2:713; *The War Diary of Breckinridge Long*, p. 1; Neville to Ida, 10 September 1939, NC 18/1/1116.

without decisive victory in the field remained central to his outlook as long as he remained prime minister. It is no doubt fair to say that neither British nor Americans had, at that juncture, a clear appreciation of what World War II was ultimately to become, and this affected their attitudes toward each other.

On the same day that Britain declared war on Germany, Roosevelt broadcast to the American people an unequivocal pledge to try to keep the country out of the conflict; it was, Moffat recorded, "a much needed speech." The president also issued neutrality proclamations as required by international law and the act of 1937. He "felt very badly" about having to do this, Norman Davis told Lord Lothian, the new British ambassador, when every fiber of his being sympathized with Britain and France. But he could not afford to give the isolationists grounds for saying he was disobeying the law. And the best way for getting the 1937 act repealed was to demonstrate to public opinion how its enforcement denied needed supplies to Britain and France. Kennedy, in turn, reported high officials in London "depressed beyond words" that it was necessary for the United States to revert to its old neutrality law. There was a widespread feeling that although America talked a lot about her sympathies, when it came to action it only gave assistance to Britain's enemy. Roosevelt no doubt understood this, and wrote to Chamberlain on September 11:

> I need not tell you that you have been very much in my thoughts during these difficult days and further that I hope you will at all times feel free to write me personally and outside of diplomatic procedure about any problems as they arise.
>
> I hope and believe that we shall repeal the embargo within the next month and this is definitely a part of the Administration policy.

But the letter, sent by diplomatic pouch, did not arrive in London until October 3, when Kennedy sent it along to Chamberlain with the simple message: "I take the pleasure in enclosing a letter addressed to you from the President."[2] Chamberlain was in no hurry to reply.

Simultaneously, Roosevelt wrote to Winston Churchill, who had just been named first lord of the admiralty, inviting him "to keep in touch personally with anything you want me to know about." Thus began, tentatively and cautiously, a notable correspondence that would assume

2. *Moffat Papers*, p. 262; Lothian to Halifax, 5 September 1939, FO 800/324, p. 48; Kennedy to Roosevelt, 10 September 1939, PSF, Diplomatic Correspondence, Box 29; Roosevelt to Chamberlain, 11 September 1939, PREM 1/366.

great importance after Churchill replaced Chamberlain as prime minister in May 1940. The two men were not old friends or political compatriots. They had met only once, in London in 1918. But Roosevelt was keenly aware of Churchill's reputation as a staunch opponent of Nazism and recognized the importance of naval policy in the war at hand. Beyond that, personal contact was a basic factor in Roosevelt's political technique, the means by which he obtained "inside" knowledge of situations and persons and exercised his own exceptional power of persuasion. He had not been able to develop a close relationship with Neville Chamberlain, whose personality and technique were vastly different from his own. The president's closest British friends (men like Murray and Willert) were in some ways dated (he knew them in Washington during World War I) and not at the center of British political life; so the need for a new and different point of contact, of the right personality type and close to the center of power, was certainly clear to him. The outbreak of war increased the urgency for this and Churchill's elevation to cabinet office provided the opportunity. This is not to say that Roosevelt intended to operate behind Chamberlain's back, but he wanted to be in touch with a leading personage whose temperament and outlook were more compatible with his own. Churchill, for his part, immediately recognized the great potential value in the president's approach to him and accepted the proffered hand at once. Keeping Chamberlain informed of the messages he sent (eight in all over the first eight months of the war), he nurtured the liaison carefully until it at length assumed an importance no doubt beyond what even he foresaw in September 1939.[3]

Although it was not at once apparent, an Englishman much to Roosevelt's liking—partly because he understood Americans and liked them—had recently arrived in Washington as the new British ambassador. Lord Lothian had replaced Sir Ronald Lindsay a few days before the war began. An assistant to David Lloyd George at the Paris Peace Conference, he had long felt a measure of personal guilt for Versailles and during the mid-1930s had persisted in the view that Hitler was a protest against the evils of the treaty, not an aggressive dictator who would push the world into war. But he had come to recognize his error and was by the end of 1938 (as Felix Frankfurter wrote Roosevelt) "as hot against Hitler as any of us." The personification of informality,

3. For a good analysis, see Reynolds, *Creation of the Anglo-American Alliance*, pp. 86–87. Lash, *Roosevelt and Churchill*, details the development of this relationship. See also Warren F. Kimball, "Churchill and Roosevelt: The Personal Equation"; and James Leutze, "The Secret of the Churchill-Roosevelt Correspondence: September 1939–May 1940."

especially when contrasted with his dignified, old-school predecessor, he brought a freshness and vitality to the Anglo-American diplomatic relationship at a time when it was sorely needed. Skeptical State Department officials were gradually won over by his charm, intelligence, and good sense; and the outpouring of praise for his work, upon his untimely death in office in December 1940, was entirely beyond the demands of formality and protocol.[4]

When Lothian presented his credentials at the White House on August 30, Roosevelt dispensed with the usual formalities and talked privately for an hour and a half. His most serious concern at that point was that nothing should permit American opinion to form the conclusion that Hitler was successfully cajoling Britain (and France) into pressuring Poland to abandon vital interests. Germany had no right to demand that a Polish representative hurry to Berlin to be treated like Schuschnigg and Hacha.[5] Lothian found "certainly nothing neutral" about the president's attitudes, his observations ranging over ways in which America could help Britain in the event of hostilities, especially by getting all the American republics to join in patrolling the western half of the Atlantic, thus relieving strain on Britain's navy and assuring safe transport of food and war materials to Halifax, Nova Scotia, whence they could be conveyed to Europe in Allied ships. He hoped and expected Congress to revoke the Neutrality Act, and if hostilities could be represented only as police action, he might be able to circumvent it altogether. If Japan became hostile again, he had two more methods of pressure "in the locker": sending aircraft carriers and bombers to the Aleutian Islands and moving the American fleet to Hawaii.[6]

Encouraging as Lothian found Roosevelt's comments, he was not misled by them. Alert to the president's need to move within the boundaries circumscribed by American opinion, he wrote to Halifax a few days

4. Freedman, *Roosevelt and Frankfurter*, p. 472; Grace Tully, *F.D.R.: My Boss*, pp. 298–99. Lothian told an audience in London, July 1939, that he had often visited the United States, "and I always feel fifteen years younger when I land in New York" (*The American Speeches of Lord Lothian, July 1939 to December 1940*, p. xlii). Hull later described Lothian as "unexcelled as an ambassador"; he was "virtually a perfect diplomatic representative" (*Memoirs*, 1:674). For details on Lothian's life and career, see Butler, *Lord Lothian*.

5. The reference was to Hitler's browbeating, at Berchtesgaden, of the Austrian prime minister in February 1938 and the Czechoslovak president, in Berlin, in March 1939.

6. Lothian to Halifax, 31 August 1939, *B.D.*, 7:428–29; also FO 414/276, pp. 121–22, 126–27. Lothian wrote Lady Astor that Roosevelt "wanted to know about everybody and everything. We got on very well." As he left the White House, a black kitten appeared at his feet. He took it onto his shoulder and played with it briefly. This was photographed and reproduced all over the country, so he was at once adjudged "human." Astor Papers, MS 1416/1/4/58.

later about the "tremendous debate" that was going on in the public mind about what America's future policy should be. Although it was widely recognized that a peaceful world could not be organized without American cooperation, the general distortion of post-World War I history (especially the view that America had been tricked into the war by Wall Street finance and Anglo-French propaganda, and the tendency to attribute the return of war to the follies and machinations of the rest of the world) was a "huge problem." It was "obviously going to take a long time to reeducate 130 million people into a truer perspective"—which they could only accomplish themselves through a realization that their own vital interests were in danger.[7] This set the tone of Lothian's ambassadorship and established an approach to American opinion from which he did not depart. The Americans must be aided and encouraged in every way possible to achieve their own understanding of the extent to which American interests were intimately bound to those of Britain. Having come to believe that the future approach to Anglo-American relations would be "strategic rather than political," Lothian set his course accordingly.[8]

He needed to be sure, of course, that the view of the war that he urged in Washington corresponded closely with that which prevailed in London. To this end, he initiated in mid-September personal correspondence with Halifax, Hoare, Churchill, and Chatfield in which he gave his own diagnosis of the situation confronting Britain; he explained the line that he was taking with people to whom he could speak frankly, asked for his correspondents' reactions, and sought from them facts and arguments that would help to bring the "real situation" home to America. The mass of Americans, Lothian believed, instinctively felt that Hitler was the mortal enemy of all that they stood for; but obsessed by the desire to keep out of war, their moral preparedness was about at the level of Britain's in the Baldwin era. The ambassador viewed the outcome of the war as hinging on two things: maintaining control of the seas and

7. Lothian to Halifax, 5 September 1939, FO 800/324, pp. 49–50.

8. Lothian was encouraged in this view by B. H. Liddell Hart, the eminent if controversial British military authority, who had urged him some weeks before, in a conversation sought by Lothian, to emphasize in Washington the strategic dangers to America of a Nazi conquest of Europe, the subsequent extension of German air and submarine bases to the Atlantic islands, perhaps even Central and South America, and a combined German-Japanese menace in the Pacific (*Liddell Hart Memoirs,* 2:248). Admiral Sir Dudley Pound had written Lothian that America's early entry into the war would provide greater security to American trade than neutrality because it would expedite the rounding up of enemy vessels attacking shipping (Pound to Lothian, 20 August 1939, FO 800/397).

destroying the machine industry of Germany. In the long run, the United States held the critical cards in both respects. Its fleet could make the Pacific secure; its machine industry could produce the munitions and bombers (from a base safe from attack) that would eventually be decisive against Germany and Italy.[9]

All replied to Lothian promptly. In addressing war projections (how things *might* go), Halifax noted the difficulty of formulating clear objectives. Britain was fighting for "intangibles and imponderables"—to show Hitler's latest adventure a failure and a disaster so that the German people would not "allow themselves to be led into such errors again." He could well understand how difficult it was for Americans to get a clear conception. It had only been February last that Britain, "on the fringe of this mad continent," had assured France unconditionally of her assistance against unprovoked aggression, and "we cannot expect . . . the United States to evolve quicker than we did." He thought it "*most* valuable" that the United States should send some ships to Penang or Singapore to help keep things quiet in the Pacific. Hoare doubted that Americans realized the magnitude of the task, and the attendant risks, that Britain had undertaken. If Anglo-American civilization were to continue, they would have to give what help they could, both moral and economic, "or we may both be destroyed." In particular, America must supply machine tools—and quickly. "It would be a frightening episode in history if the American nation, having so freely urged upon Great Britain her moral duties to intervene in Europe, were, now that we are committed to a life and death struggle, actually to deny the munitions and supplies which we can pay for and take," Churchill observed while seeking extended latitude in enforcing blockade and contraband control. The result might be the complete triumph of Hitler in Europe and the disappearance of Britain as an independent power—hardly an outcome in accord with American interests. Sharing Halifax's understanding of American reluctance to become involved in the war, Chatfield also recognized the importance of supplies from America, as well as its assistance at sea (the "safest quarter" in which to enlist American aid). But Chatfield was somewhat less anxious than the others, thinking Germany disunited and Hitler faced with growing popular discontent.[10]

Lothian had also written to Chamberlain conjecturing about the fu-

9. Lothian to Halifax, Hoare, Churchill, and Chatfield, 15 September 1939, FO 800/324, pp. 53–55; FO 800/397; Templewood Papers, XI:5; CHT/6/2, pp. 116–19.

10. Halifax to Lothian, 27 September 1939; Hoare to Lothian, 26 September 1939; Churchill to Lothian, 25 September; Chatfield to Lothian, 26 September 1939; FO 800/397.

ture of American neutrality. The prime minister's reply revealed again his basic approach to the war and the role that the United States might play:

> To my mind the thing to aim at is to convince the German people that whatever happens they cannot in the long run win the war and that they have to face a gradually increasing restriction on their normal life. If that can be done I should hope for a crack in the German home front and of course nothing would contribute to it so much as the certainty that the resources of the U.S.A. were being mobilized against them.

Chamberlain hoped for the assurance of American support as a means of cracking German morale, but he had not begun to think of its utilization in pursuit of a military effort. He related to his sister his feeling that the war would come to an early end: "There is such a widespread desire to avoid war and it is so deeply rooted that it surely must find expression somehow."[11]

Chamberlain's letter to his sister (September 10) is notable in two other regards. It gives substantial evidence that the British delay in declaring war was influenced by secret communications with Göring and Hitler, through an intermediary, and conference proposals put forth by Mussolini. The former, Chamberlain said, "looked promising at one time." He did not believe that Hitler was engaging in mere deception; rather, the Führer worked seriously at proposals "which to his one-track mind seemed almost fabulously generous." But then some "brainstorm took possession of him," and he could not stop the machine he had set in motion. Mussolini's proposals were "a perfectly genuine attempt to stop war." These observations are pertinent here for what they reveal about the nature of Chamberlain's thinking and the bases on which he constructed his hope for an abbreviated war. Chamberlain also revealed, in contrast to his prewar sentiment, that he no longer felt indispensable in the prime ministership. Half a dozen people could take his place now, and he did not see that he had "any particular part to play" until it came to discussing peace terms. Yet, he was thinking about a visit to Paris to see Daladier, for "the moment for a mildly spectacular move on my part has come." He was no doubt quickly disabused of the feeling that he was expendable by his wife, Annie, who flatly rejected the notion. His imagination, judgment, and purpose were possessed by no one else,

11. Lothian to Chamberlain, 5 September 1939; Chamberlain to Lothian, 15 September 1939; FO 800/397. Neville to Ida, 10 September 1939, NC 18/1/1116.

she wrote to her husband's sister, and though it tore her heart that he should have to bear the burden of wartime leadership, "I rejoice for the sake of this country—and other countries that he is at the helm."[12]

A very different impression of Chamberlain emerged from another quarter at that moment and found its way to Roosevelt. Daladier, who spoke with the prime minister on September 12, thought him a broken man who had passed from middle age to decrepitude. He would be useful for a while, representing as he did as typical an Englishman as anyone in the pages of Dickens; but before the war could be won, he would have to be replaced by a more vigorous person.[13]

Daladier was said to be shocked by the cynical selfishness of Chamberlain's attitude toward the German bombardment of Poland and his refusal to join with France in bombing military objectives in Germany—reportedly for fear of offending American opinion. Ironically, Churchill had given the same explanation for Britain's failure to undertake aerial activity against Germany to the Polish ambassador in London some days before but, when pressed by Raczynski, had shifted ground and said that it stemmed from France's fear of retaliatory action. Yet in writing to Chamberlain on September 10, Churchill cited American opinion as a major factor weighing against a British initiative. Leaflet bombing (the dropping of propaganda leaflets designed to undermine the will to fight of the German people) had already begun and was reportedly producing a poor impression in America and among neutrals generally. But Chamberlain thought it had great virtue and was determined that it should continue.[14]

The fact of the matter was that during the early days of war, mixed and uncertain signals emanated from all around. The British, like the French, divided among themselves on how to pursue the war, were also confused in their reading of America's posture—no doubt in part because of the confusion and ambiguity that attended America's position. It was widely felt in Britain that the United States expected it to do its "duty"; but the British also anticipated that, once Germany had reduced Poland and offered peace to Britain, there would be considerable pres-

12. Neville to Ida, 10 September 1939, NC 18/1/1116; Annie to Hilda, 13 September 1939, NC 18/1/1117. For a statement concerning Mrs. Chamberlain's influence on her husband, see Rock, *Neville Chamberlain,* pp. 36–37.

13. Bullitt, *For the President,* pp. 370–71.

14. Ibid.; *Biddle Papers,* p. 108; Churchill to Chamberlain, NC 7/9/47; INKP 2, pp. 45, 51, 64. See also Waclaw Jedrzejewicz, ed., *Diplomat in Paris, 1936–1939: Papers and Memoirs of Juliusz Lukasiewicz, Ambassador of Poland,* pp. 302–4.

sure from Washington to negotiate. The war cabinet, impelled by German propaganda that the war in Poland was almost over and all that prevented peace was the attitude of Britain, had decided on September 9 to base its policy on the assumption that the war would last for three years or more. But Chamberlain refused to amplify the bare announcement of this decision, even when American press correspondents evidenced doubt that Britain meant to go the whole way. Further, the need for substantial American assistance if the war were to be won militarily was everywhere recognized in Britain; but there was great uncertainty whether, and how, the Americans might see fit to help.[15]

Some of the uncertainty about America stemmed from the attitudes of Ambassador Kennedy. His prewar devotion to appeasement (whatever its reasons) gave way to a pronounced defeatism once the war had begun. Never one to hide his opinions, he offered them freely to everyone from the king on down. And the disgust that his views engendered in many leading Englishmen was compounded by the smoldering suspicion that Kennedy saw nearly everything in international relations from the vantage point of his own personal investments. By mid-September, Lothian thought it essential—from evidence he had in Washington!—that Chamberlain should "state emphatically" to Kennedy, Britain's determination to see the war through. Chamberlain told the cabinet, after meeting with the ambassador, that Kennedy "had taken a most gloomy view of the situation." He did not believe that Congress would modify neutrality legislation and thought the recent action of Russia in moving into eastern Poland would throw American public opinion into the arms of the isolationists. Yet several days before, Halifax had found Kennedy "pretty confident" that Roosevelt would succeed in changing the neutrality regulations. He had even suggested that when the British got in real difficulty, the right course for the United States would be to *give* them supplies (a hint of later lend-lease) to avoid piling up debts that could never be paid. Generally, however, the pessimism tended to predominate. Even Roosevelt was exasperated. "Joe Kennedy . . . always will be an appeaser," he told Morgenthau; "he's just a pain in the neck to me." Some British officials thought Kennedy anxious to "prepare the stage for Roosevelt" to arrange a compromise peace, whether the president wished it that way or not.[16]

15. See INKP 2, 9 September 1939, p. 44; Findlater Stewart to Horace Wilson, 10 September 1939, PREM 1/377.

16. *Cadogan Diaries*, p. 215; Lothian to Halifax, 14 September 1939, FO 800/324, p. 52; CAB 65/1, 19 September 1939, p. 116; Halifax to Lothian, 14 September 1939, FO 414/276,

Kennedy's talk about Britain being badly thrashed in the war was the subject of spirited comment in the Foreign Office toward the end of September. The problem widely recognized, the question was what to do about it. Gage thought a complaint to the embassy or to Lothian in Washington "might . . . make him shut up," but in that case British officials would not know what he was thinking or telling the American government. Perowne recognized the "manifest disadvantages in this kind of talk," but thought it might help to jog Americans out of their wishful thinking that Britain and France were necessarily going to win. The only way to stop such talk, Scott believed, was to show Kennedy he was wrong: ". . . Primarily interested in the financial side of things he cannot, poor man, see the imponderabilia which, in a war like this, will be decisive." Balfour dismissed him as "an ambitious man who . . . is always thinking of his future. . . . an Irish American . . . naturally predisposed to twist the lion's tail . . . when the animal appears to be in 'one hell of a jam'!" Cadogan had the last word: if the talk continued, he would ask Lothian to "drop a hint in the proper quarter." Kennedy was not entitled to abuse his privileged position in London by expressing defeatist opinions when and where he liked. Halifax agreed.[17]

Halifax talked with Kennedy on September 25. Believing that any British reference to war aims should be very general in character (and that the maintenance of discreet silence on the subject of American intervention was essential to the revision of neutrality legislation), Kennedy also declared that American opinion would be greatly affected by the action of Russia—which it considered "a much greater potential disturber of world peace" than Germany. Halifax, in contrast, interpreted Russian action as useful to Britain in blocking Germany's eastern ambitions. Kennedy asked for a statement about the effect on America if Britain and France were defeated, and Halifax agreed "to get something of the sort prepared." Overall, the foreign secretary found Kennedy's attitude "more robust" than reports had led him to suspect. But Kennedy did not say the same of Halifax, reporting instead a laconic interview which suggested that the British were not intent on fighting and incapable of realizing the consequences of the Russian development.[18]

---

p. 130; Blum, *From the Morgenthau Diaries,* 2:102; Templewood Papers, XI:2 (10 September 1939).

17. Foreign Office Minutes, 20–27 September 1939, FO 371/22827, pp. 306–11. There was clearly a concern among Foreign Office officials that Kennedy's financial interests colored his views unduly; see Foreign Office Minutes, 27 September–2 October 1939, ibid., pp. 313–14. Lothian was alerted to the situation, but not asked to take action, on 3 October (FO 371/22827, p. 315).

18. Halifax to Lothian, 25 September 1939, FO 414/276, p. 132; INKP 2 (28 September

This same general sentiment appeared in a letter that Kennedy sent to Roosevelt at the end of September. British officials were described as uncertain and confused about what they were fighting for. The restoration of Poland was being nudged gently but firmly into obscurity, and the destruction of Germany might simply open the way for communism in central Europe. Britain was fighting essentially for her possessions and her place in the sun, just as she had often done in the past, and the government was hamstrung in any effort at peace (so Simon was said to have told him) by the British people themselves, who were determined to go on. It was unlikely that Chamberlain could survive a serious reversal, but there was no adequate replacement in the parliamentary ranks—certainly not Halifax or Churchill.[19]

It is understandable how Kennedy could sense uncertainty about British war objectives. Seeing no possibility of Hitler's scoring a major success in the West, which was vital to the spirits of his people and to influencing neutrals, Chamberlain was in no hurry to commit himself to conditions. Tweedsmuir's warning (from Canada) that America might still be in doubt about Britain's earnestness, and his appeal for a specific statement of the causes for which Britain was fighting—emphasizing the gravity of the situation and its determination to see it through—did not move the prime minister at all. He did not think it practical to enumerate objectives (aside from redeeming Europe from the recurring fear of German aggression) before the war could be brought to an end. And he still did not believe "that holocausts are required to gain the victory, while they are certainly liable to lose us the peace." Britain might still prevail without bloodshed by convincing the Germans that they could not win. This course, he admitted, was "rather more difficult than a ding-dong fight" if Britain were to hold together its home front, the dominions, and the United States. But he was determined "to go for what I believe to be . . . right . . . and risk the consequences."[20]

1939), pp. 63–64; *War Diary of Breckinridge Long* (26 September 1939), p. 20. Inskip's diary corroborates the contrasting Anglo-American responses to Russian action. The American outlook generally was "very black," but the British were "almost cheerful." The Foreign Office believed that Germany would be hindered, not helped, inasmuch as Russia would use supplies in maintaining her own army that would otherwise be available for Germany (INKP 2 [20 September 1939], p. 54).

19. Kennedy to Roosevelt, 30 September 1939, PSF, Diplomatic Correspondence, Box 29.

20. Neville to Hilda, 17 September 1939, NC 18/1/1121; Tweedsmuir to Chamberlain, 19 September 1939, NC 7/11/32/287; Chamberlain to Tweedsmuir, 25 September 1939, NC 7/11/32/288; Neville to Ida, 23 September, 1939, NC 18/1/1122. Chamberlain wrote to his sister that he had not yet found Churchill very helpful. He was merely talking a lot and constantly writing him letters, no doubt "for the purpose of quotation in the Book that he will write hereafter."

In addition to considerations of European diplomacy, Chamberlain was no doubt influenced by the consensus among British officials that there should be no propaganda of any kind directed toward America—a view to which Tweedsmuir and Lothian had both subscribed. Americans were "so used to the pernicious system of political lobbying," Lothian wrote Halifax, "that they are particularly ready to suspect all and sundry of attempting to use undue influence." The British were considered to be especially adept at the subtlest arts of propaganda and capable of luring innocent Americans into their traps. Yet there was, as Lothian acknowledged, a still greater danger: the emergence of a view that Britain was just biding her time preparatory to another Munich at the expense of Poland. The antidote for this was full publicity from London about everything Britain was thinking and doing. But British publicity had thus far failed to convey a picture of the nation as competent, effective, vibrant, knowing where it wanted to go and the kind of peace it sought to achieve.[21]

One of the things that the British were thinking about—although, of course, not publicly—was the prospect of material and financial assistance from the United States in the event of a long war. The war cabinet quickly approved (September 7) a proposal by the minister of supply to initiate the establishment of a purchasing mission in New York. Roosevelt agreed, asking only that British personnel visit Canada first to avoid undue political suspicion. The war cabinet also weighed a suggestion that Britain might be able to raise loans in America indirectly through the intermediary of the Canadian and Australian governments (not subject to the ban imposed by the Johnson Act). But it was dismissed as bad psychology to attempt such a subterfuge; rather it was decided that Britain should put its cards on the table and ask Washington to deal with the matter directly. A few days later, Churchill urged the purchase of destroyers from the United States as soon as possible—the first suggestion of a famous deal that was consummated some months later. Amid cabinet discussion of expanding the air force and army

21. Tweedsmuir to Macmillan, 11 September 1939, NC 7/11/32/284; Tweedsmuir to Lothian, 12 September 1939, Lothian Papers, GD 40/17/405; Lothian to Tweedsmuir, 13 September 1939, FO 800/397; Chamberlain to Macmillan, 22 September 1939, NC 7/11/32/286; Lothian to Halifax, 22 September 1939, FO 414/276, p. 135; Lothian to Halifax, 28 September 1939, FO 115/3419, File 585. The diary entry of Adolf Berle, 13 September, relative to a meeting with Sir William Wiseman, recently assigned to aid Lothian in interpreting British opinion to America and vice versa, attests to Lothian's point: "The history of our past English 'interpretations' was a history of half-truths, broken faith, intrigue . . . and everything that goes with it" (*Navigating the Rapids*, p. 254).

through a three-year plan, Simon expounded a Treasury calculation showing the devastating effect of such an effort on Britain's dollar reserves, since it would entail an immense buying of machine tools from America. But the threat of eventual bankruptcy only supported the view that, if the war were a long one, American financial aid would be essential. Acting to protect the dollar reserve, the war cabinet agreed on September 20 to halt the purchase of leaf tobacco from the United States, to restrict the purchase of fruit to minimum requirements, and to bargain with American film interests for a reduction of royalties. Essential moves in British eyes, such actions quickly irritated the sensitivities of American financial interests.[22]

In the meantime, a minor incident that sprang from good American intentions had irritated British feeling. With the approval of Roosevelt and the cabinet, Secretary of the Treasury Morgenthau had seen Lothian and offered to "buy" the *Queen Mary* as credit against the war debt (with the idea of using it to bring back Americans stranded in Europe and eventually returning it to Britain at the end of the war). This "queer proposal," as Lothian called it, genuinely intended to be helpful, struck the British as clumsy American exploitation of their predicament. Roosevelt was "horrified" (Lothian's term) when he realized the British reaction and annulled the proposal at once; but the sticky little episode revealed a great deal about British feelings: war debts still rankled, and doubts about American motivation persisted.[23]

The British were also uneasy about what to expect from America in the Far East. With war under way in Europe, they did not want to run the risk of war with Japan at the same time. Consequently, London was disposed to follow Tokyo's "friendly advice" that British garrisons be withdrawn from China. It would, however, reconsider depending upon Washington's attitude and willingness to contribute to preserving common interests. Washington was reluctant to take a firm position—although by the end of September it emerged that Britain would not withdraw. By that time, however, Cadogan had come to complain: "Americans evidently won't take any 'commitment' but will nevertheless

22. CAB 65/1, 7, 12, 18, 20 September 1939, pp. 47, 78, 108, 121; FO 371/22834, pp. 306–10, 313–14; Simon Diary, no. 16 (23 September 1939).

23. Lothian to Halifax, 8 September 1939, FO 800/397 (also FO 800/324, p. 51); Blum, *From the Morgenthau Diaries*, pp. 96–97. A similar proposal to "buy" the *Normandie* was made to France and met with the same reaction. It had apparently been Hull's suggestion to handle the matter in Washington: Bullitt (in Paris) would tell everybody; Kennedy (in London) would claim all the credit.

blame us if we clear out." His lament was clearly representative of the view of many British officials, who long thereafter suffered the dilemma of avoiding all provocation toward Japan while at the same time giving the United States no opportunity to accuse them of growing soft toward the Japanese.[24]

As the war proceeded through its second month, Chamberlain's basic outlook toward it remained unchanged. Replying to Roosevelt's letter of September 11 on October 4 (it had taken that long for it to reach him), Chamberlain reiterated his belief that

> we shall win, not by a complete and spectacular military victory, which is unlikely under modern conditions, but by convincing the Germans that they cannot win. Once they have arrived at that conclusion, I do not believe they can withstand our relentless pressure, for they have not started this war with the enthusiasm or the confidence of 1914.
>
> I believe they are already halfway to this conviction and I cannot doubt that the attitude of the United States of America, due to your personal efforts, has had a notable influence in this direction. If the embargo is repealed this month, I am convinced that the effect on German morale will be devastating.[25]

To his sister he wrote a few days later: "My policy continues to be the same. Hold on tight. Keep up the economic pressure, push on with munitions production and military preparations with utmost energy. Take no offensive unless Hitler begins it." If Britain could stick to this policy, he reckoned that it would "win the war by the Spring." Aware of military opinion which held that Hitler could not afford such an outcome and would attack the Maginot Line, he nonetheless doubted German confidence "to venture on the great war unless they are forced into it by action on our part."[26]

Chamberlain manifestly loathed the war. Even the sinking of German subs gave him an "uncomfortable feeling"; if they called at British ports in peacetime, "we should probably say what good fellows the officers and men were." But killing was required "just to satisfy that accursed madman [Hitler]. I wish he could burn in Hell for as many years as he is costing lives." The Führer was clearly "quite abnormal," convinced

24. Hull, *Memoirs,* 1:717–22; *Cadogan Diaries,* p. 217. See CAB 65/1, 17 October 1939, pp. 273–74.

25. Chamberlain to Roosevelt, 4 October 1939, PREM 1/366. Chamberlain drafted this letter himself.

26. Neville to Ida, 8 October 1939, NC 18/1/1124. See also Neville to Hilda, 1 October 1939, NC 18/1/1123.

at any given moment that the attainment of one particular object would satisfy him, then shortly afterward concentrating just as intensely on something else. But he had made military blunders of "first magnitude": signing the agreement with Russia, provoking France to mobilize, and causing Britain to send troops to the Continent. "Now he has got himself into a complete jam and doesn't know what to do next and if we can hold firm he is done."[27]

This sort of thinking was no doubt encouraged by German "peace offers" that arrived in various forms in London. These included a direct effort by Hitler (during the first week of October) to persuade the British and French to call off their war against a Germany that had no particular quarrel with them, to acknowledge that the future of Poland was solely a German-Russian matter, and to get on with discussions about international trade, a reduction of armaments, and other problems of mutual interest. In the absence of *acts* to prove the sincerity of the German desire for peace, the British showed no interest. In formulating this position, leading ministers agreed that all these matters could have been discussed in a friendly spirit several months before, if President Roosevelt's invitation to a conference had been accepted. Germany had chosen instead to proceed with the ferocious onslaught against Poland. And as for suggestions that all matters of dispute should be settled by a neutral body consisting of Belgium, Holland, the Scandinavian countries, and the United States, Roosevelt had given no indication that he was willing to attempt anything of the kind. American officials had, in fact, discussed at length—and rejected—the idea of initiating any peace effort. It could only benefit Hitler and discourage the Allies. If Britain and France accepted, they would have to agree to most of Hitler's demands; if they refused, they would be blamed for rejecting peace.[28]

The British were, of course, much interested in American opinion generally, reported faithfully by Lothian and followed closely by government officials in London. By the first week of October, Lothian saw "the real issue" coming to the front: Americans were beginning to realize that their own peace and security depended upon the victory of the Allies and that supplies of armaments were essential to assist in the struggle against Nazism. But there was also a general fear of being drawn into the war and suspicion that Roosevelt was too pro-Ally. Some "faint-

27. Neville to Hilda, 15 October 1939, NC 18/1/1125; Neville to Arthur Chamberlain, 25 October 1939, NC 7/6/29.

28. Langer and Gleason, *The Challenge to Isolation*, pp. 246–58; PREM 1/395 (8 October 1939); Simon Diary, no. 16 (13 October 1939); Hull, *Memoirs*, 1:711.

hearts" believed that Britain could not win and had better make peace—although no one seriously suggested it could be done with the present German regime. There was a feeling in intellectual circles that British aims needed sharper definition, and many believed, like Hoover, that Britain could win without American aid. An accompanying report from the British consul-general in San Francisco was downright glum about the fickleness of Americans and their inability to grasp the issues at stake, which he attributed to "terror in a nation caught unprepared . . . by a calamity of which they discern, but refuse to admit, the enormous significance to themselves." Chamberlain's rejection of Hitler's "peace proposal" won general American approval, Lothian reported on October 16, but there was some disappointment that the prime minister did not set forth a more positive statement of Britain's aims. There was no support for the idea that Roosevelt might mediate, owing to distrust of Hitler and the risks of American involvement.[29]

Against this backdrop, Lothian prepared a major address to the Pilgrim Club at the Hotel Plaza, New York, on October 25. Heeding established procedure, recently reinforced by the advice of Professor Thomas North Whitehead, of Harvard (esteemed by the embassy), Lothian spoke frankly about the war but made no attempt to influence Americans directly, leaving them instead to arrive at their own conclusions in their own good time. Britain was fighting for the vital principles of civilization, he declared, and no stable peace was possible until freedom was restored to all the peoples of Europe and the threat of aggression eliminated. Inviting Americans to think about the kind of world they wished to see created at the end of the war, Lothian came closest to being suggestive in saying that the United States would certainly have its own contribution to make to the solution of this great problem. Privately, Lothian was quite unsure of the direction that American opinion and policy would take. He confided to a friend that, after the wave of keeping-out-of-the-war-at-any-price sentiment had faded, the American spirit would be more aggressive; but this could well be neutralized by the presidential election campaign of the following year unless the dangers of the international situation forced themselves on public attention. And to another he wrote that the predominant American feeling was "one of boredom that the tremendous drama of unlimited aerial war in Europe which they had been educated to expect is apparently not going to come off."[30]

29. Lothian to Halifax, 5, 10, 16 October 1939, FO 414/276, pp. 136, 141, 145.
30. Lothian, *American Speeches*, pp. 4–16; Lothian to Halifax, 27 October 1939, FO 115/

Boredom was not, however, an apt description of sentiment in Washington, at least in reference to one particular issue, from late September until early November. The intensely controversial matter of repealing American neutrality legislation had reemerged to center stage. (Long a smoldering issue, as shown in the previous chapter, it figured prominently in British efforts to avoid the impression of trying to influence America, lest that provoke a backlash detrimental to the cause of repeal itself.) In reporting to London (in late July) the failure of Roosevelt's efforts (in a White House conference with congressional leaders July 18) to spur action on neutrality modification, Lindsay had noted the president's disposition to call a special session of Congress to confront the issue, should war break out in Europe before the end of the year. That is what occurred. Nor did Roosevelt require the urging—of Bullitt, Kennedy (relaying the view of Hoare-Belisha, British secretary of state for war), and others—that was, in fact, forthcoming during the first two weeks of September. He and Hull had reached a decision on the need to annul the embargo nearly a year before, and the only remaining question was how to accomplish it. German action in Poland and reports of ultimate Nazi designs against America had their effect on congressional sentiment, and the way was opened for Roosevelt to move, despite an effective isolationist radio campaign, the widespread fear of American involvement, and the danger that partisan politics would falsely skew the debate. To counter the latter, Roosevelt continually emphasized bipartisanship and his determination to keep the country out of war. According to Hull, he genuinely believed that new legislation would offer a better chance of staying out than the old: if the Allies won, America could remain at peace; but if Germany emerged victorious, there was every likelihood that the United States would have to fight.[31]

The president called a special congressional session to begin on September 21.[32] Three days before its convening, Lothian found him

---

3420, File 1786; FO 414/276, pp. 141–44; Lothian to Garvin, 1 November 1939, Lothian Papers, GD 40/17/401; Lothian to Boothby, 3 November 1939, Lothian Papers, GD 40/17/399. See also Lothian to Lady Astor, 27 October 1939, Astor Papers, MS 1416/1/4/58.

31. Lindsay to Halifax, 27 July 1939, FO 414/276, p. 82; Bullitt, *For the President,* pp. 373–74; Hull, *Memoirs,* 1:684, 693; Dallek, *Franklin Roosevelt and American Foreign Policy,* pp. 200–201.

32. Excellent accounts of both the immediate background of the special congressional session and the course of developments therein appear in Cole, *Roosevelt and the Isolationists,* pp. 320–30; and Dallek, *Franklin Roosevelt and American Foreign Policy,* pp. 199–205. The following paragraphs dealing with these matters rest substantially on these accounts. See also Hull, *Memoirs,* 1:682–84, 693–97.

"very confident" about getting the embargo removed, adding: "There is no doubt that he is not neutral about Hitler and Hitlerism!"[33] Indeed, his desire to aid the Allies was clearly understood in government circles, but this could not be admitted openly lest it unduly provoke still-powerful isolationist opinion. Among the president's bases for hope was the fact that he had laid the groundwork well. Having promised American neutrality in a "Fireside Chat" (September 3), he nonetheless declared that he did not expect of the American people neutrality of mind or conscience: "Even a neutral has a right to take account of facts." In the following days, he conferred individually with House and Senate leaders to get their perspectives on political alignments and joined Hull in briefing legislators with up-to-date information that might help influence their thinking. He resisted initial pressures for substantial increases in national defense forces and for rapid industrial mobilization lest they agitate suspicion. When, on September 14, isolationist Senator Borah broadcast his view that neutrality revision was designed to aid one side in the war and would surely result in U.S. involvement, Alf Landon and Frank Knox, the Republican presidential and vice-presidential candidates in 1936, were ready by White House prearrangement to counter Borah's statements to the press. At a meeting of fifteen Democratic and Republican leaders at the White House on September 20, from which the more outspoken Senate isolationists were excluded, Roosevelt was unusually effective in leading the discussion in the direction he wished it to go. He spoke of the need to forget partisanship, of the seriousness of developments in Europe, of his desire to sustain the economy, and of the need for a "new" kind of neutrality based upon "the fundamental principles of international law." Discrediting isolationist opponents by associating them with Germany and the Communist party (a tactic he used with some frequency), he pressed for flexible neutrality legislation free of rigid provisions that by their very nature could draw America into war. He spoke mainly about the kinds of revision that could be accomplished quickly, not the ideal of full repeal that would probably involve months of debating. No doubt recalling his bitter experience with the Military Affairs Committee the previous January, he had the assembled leaders agree to a statement for the press, to be released by the White House, that emphasized the objective of keeping the United States

33. Lothian to Lady Astor, 18 September 1939, Astor Papers, MS 1416/1/4/58. Lothian told Lady Astor in the same letter: "I am getting to know all the State Department people, by degrees. You could not want a nicer crowd."

neutral and out of war and said nothing about aiding victims of aggression.

In convening the special session, Roosevelt reviewed recent international crises and his futile efforts to aid in averting war, his long-standing interest in neutrality reform, and the economic advantages to be gained from embargo repeal. But the heart of the message dealt with assuring peace at home. Anticipating the critics who would say that embargo repeal would draw America closer to war, he declared his "deep and unalterable conviction, based on years of experience as a worker in the field of international peace, that by the repeal of the embargo the United States will more probably remain at peace than if the law remains as it stands today." Repeal of the embargo and the sale of goods on a cash-and-carry basis would, in combination with measures prohibiting American merchant vessels from entering war zones and extending war credits to belligerents, constitute a program "better calculated than any other means to keep us out of war." It was a moving, if not entirely forthright, performance. Thereafter, at Senator Pittman's insistence, the president left the initiative to the Foreign Relations Committee. His own actions while the debate was in progress were carefully calculated to avoid creating any suspicion that neutrality change was a step toward involvement in the war. "I am almost literally walking on eggs," he wrote Lord Tweedsmuir in asking postponement of his request to "slip down inconspicuously" to Hyde Park. Determined to do nothing that might jeopardize a favorable outcome, he was for the moment, "saying nothing, seeing nothing, and hearing nothing."

"The repeal debate is 'on,'" Lothian wrote to Lady Astor in late September. "The President is confident of victory and that he will then be able to put American machine industry behind the allies." Roosevelt's optimism must have shown behind the scenes. Lothian had reported to the Foreign Office the president's saying to him, "We shall come right in before long." But it was recognized in London, as Labour leader Hugh Dalton recorded after a talk with Under-Secretary Butler at the Foreign Office, that "this was rather typical of the President's way of speaking loosely and optimistically in private conversation." Halifax told the war cabinet (September 25), anxiously watching events in America, that he had no definite information on the projected duration of the neutrality debate, but the discussion might well last for five or six weeks. His estimate was nearly correct.[34]

34. Lothian to Lady Astor, 29 September 1939, ibid.; Dalton Diary, 21:62; CAB 65/1, 25 September 1939, p. 145.

The opponents of neutrality revision did not give up easily. A few prominent isolationists (Senators Taft [Ohio], Barbour [New Jersey], and Norris [Nebraska] among them) grudgingly conceded that removal of the arms embargo was not calculated to increase America's chances of getting into the war and followed the president on the issue. But most of the leading isolationists continued to fight neutrality revision with undiminished conviction and determination. Against the proponents of repeal (who denied that it would involve the United States in war and contended that the existing embargo only helped the Axis and discouraged the expansion of munitions factories essential to national defense) the isolationists insisted that repeal would constitute an "unneutral" attempt to aid the Allies and be a definite step toward war. Some spiced their arguments by questioning whether Allied motives involved a defense of democracy so much as the maintenance of power and empire. Senator Vandenberg, of Michigan, had a different twist. He hated nazism and communism as thoroughly as anyone, but disbelieved that the United States could stop these movements in Europe without committing everything it had to the task. There was no middle ground; it was all or nothing. Outside Congress, Colonel Lindbergh made strong noninterventionist addresses and began to establish himself as a formidable Roosevelt adversary. Daily newspapers around the country gave front-page coverage to the debate, and for a few weeks, national interest ran high. Then arguments became repetitive, and people appeared to have made up their minds. But the outcome was still uncertain. White House and Senate mail ran heavily against repeal, but public opinion polls pointed in the opposite direction.

When the vote was taken, neutrality revision was approved by substantial margins in both the Senate on October 27 and in the House on November 2. Had the issues of embargo repeal (on which opinion was seriously divided) and cash-and-carry (which most Congressmen favored) been separated, the outcome might have been different, but an attempt at separation had failed in the Senate in mid-October. Actually, Roosevelt had not been as subdued behind the scenes as he had implied to Tweedsmuir. Taking nothing for granted, he utilized both public and private ploys to head off an isolationist filibuster, to counter contentions that embargo repeal after war had begun would be an "unneutral" violation of international law (an issue raised by some prominent jurists), to alleviate the animosities of political opponents (by freely conceding their honorable motives), to undermine comparisons with 1917, and generally to promote the outcome that he wanted. In the end, the shock associated with the onset of war was no doubt the most compelling factor in influencing Congress, but Roosevelt certainly made things easier by his wise tactics, his restrained manner, and his readiness to accept a cash-and-carry policy determined by Congress itself (thus allaying fears of expanded presidential power). It was an important victory, and from that time forward isolationists were unable to defeat any presidential aid-short-of-war proposal voted upon in Congress. Nevertheless, there was a tinge of bitterness in the administration's rejoicing. As Hull explained later, he could not help feeling that the victory would have been far more effective for the cause of the peace-loving nations if it could have been gained earlier.

The "great development" in Washington prompted Chamberlain to write Roosevelt, on November 8, a note of thanks and congratulation. Repeal of the arms embargo not only signaled an assurance that Britain and France could draw on the great reservoir of American resources; it was also a "profound moral encouragement." Its effect on German morale would be devastating. British satisfaction was all the greater, Chamberlain noted, because "we realize to what an extent we owe it to your personal efforts and good will." However, one may wonder just how important Chamberlain considered it all—at least in any tangible sense. There was no mention of the matter in his weekly letters to his sisters throughout October, while congressional debate was under way, or in his letter of November 5, which elaborated again his hunch that the war would be over before spring—not by German defeat in the field but by the realization that they could not win "and that it isn't worth their while to go on getting thinner and poorer" when they might have instant relief without giving up anything they really cared about. A great many Germans, he explained, were already "near that position," and their number was increasing. To be sure, Hitler and his entourage would have to go—with the possible exception of Göring, who might have "some ornamental position in a transition government." But once rid of the Nazis, he did not expect serious difficulty in Germany over Poland, Czechoslovakia, Jews, disarmament, and the like. The "real trouble" was much more likely to come from the French, who, as a rule, were "very wooden on these matters" and did "not easily learn from past mistakes."[35]

Lothian's report to London on the reaction of American opinion to

35. Chamberlain to Roosevelt, 8 November 1939, PREM 1/366; Neville to Ida, 5 November 1939, NC 18/1/1129.

neutrality change conveyed a mixed impression. He saw "two clear-cut decisions of the American people": they wanted the Allies to win and would make available American resources of every kind on a cash-and-carry basis, but they were determined to keep out of the war themselves until exposed to a direct threat to their own vital interests. In explaining that the war was not yet viewed as a well-defined ideological struggle, that issue having been muddled by the loss of Russia from the democratic side, Lothian derided "the Left Wing idealists who haunt the universities and fill the columns of the more highbrow periodicals" and who salve their guilty consciences over American fear of involvement by accusing Britain of forcing Russia into the arms of Hitler and being interested only in preserving the existing social order. But he did not believe they carried weight in Congress or the country at large. To Lady Astor, some days later, he wrote in words suggestive of Chamberlain's outlook: "The general opinion here is that Hitler has been put into a cage from which he won't be able to escape," although "this end is a long way off." People were already beginning to discuss the possible bases for a peace.[36]

The change in American neutrality legislation did not result in any sudden increase in the placing of British orders in the United States. Although leadership of the New York branch of the newly established British Purchasing Mission had been assumed by the highly respected Arthur Purvis (who had both the skill and the reputation essential to swift and confident transactions), several problems detained the British, among them the need to conserve their dollar balances, and reservations about the quality of certain American goods. In late October, Simon had placed before the war cabinet a memorandum dealing with the difficulty of obtaining U.S. dollar exchange and proposing sharp restrictions on nonessential imports such as apples, tobacco, lard, and films. The need to avoid an expected outcry from American commercial interests before neutrality revision had been accomplished was clearly recognized, and it was not until mid-November that the British began to declare their position in Washington. Halifax instructed Lothian to explain that impending restrictions were being undertaken "with the greatest regret" and intended no discrimination "other than what is forced upon us by the exigencies of war." Even so, Kennedy warned that every restriction was liable to leave behind a pocket of discontent detrimental to Britain if a time should come when it needed further assis-

36. Lothian to Halifax, 9 November 1939, FO 414/276, pp. 151–52; Lothian to Lady Astor, 18 November 1939, Astor Papers, MS 1416/1/4/58.

tance from the United States.[37] To be sure, the restriction of nonessential imports might have been expected to result in an increase of military-related orders from America. But the attitude of uncertainty about the war that prevailed in Britain seemed to make the conservation of total dollar balances for a later time, when a real emergency might be upon it, the wisest course of action. Writing to Bullitt in late November, Roosevelt lamented about the monetary-purchasing matter: ". . . The dear British and French Governments are failing, as usual, to be definite between themselves and to be definite to me."[38]

At the time American neutrality legislation was changed, the British secretary of state for Air, Kingsley Wood, was considering the purchase of certain types of aircraft from the United States. But telling the war cabinet that the aircraft industry in America was small and comparatively undeveloped, he warned against expecting "other than very limited quantities." In cabinet discussion Simon recalled that the mission sent to America in 1938 had reported that American planes were not very good and quite expensive. Since the French had a smaller air force than the British, but more gold, it was more appropriate for them to buy American aircraft. Purchasing from Italy was also being considered, but there were disadvantages of raw material availability and expense. On balance, it was better to buy in America, although "political considerations might intervene." The latter comment was not explained but suggests that diplomatic considerations related to the lingering hope of wooing Italy still held a high priority—at least in Simon's mind.[39]

Over the following month, however, aircraft orders totaling $110 million were in fact placed in America or approved by the cabinet. In seeking cabinet concurrence, both Kingsley Wood and Simon noted the formidable financial problems that such orders presented. But there was a need to insure against the risk that Britain's production might be impeded by the destruction of its factories, and Chamberlain thought that such purchases might help shorten the war, thus precluding the long-range buying of machine tools and related equipment. Yet expected dates

37. Hull, *Memoirs*, 1:700; Tweedsmuir to Chamberlain, 16 October 1939, NC 7/11/32/289; CAB 65/1, 20 October 1939, pp. 298–99; Halifax to Lothian, 11 November 1939, FO 414/276, p. 147; CAB 65/2, 28 November 1939.

38. Roosevelt to Bullitt, 27 November 1939, PSF, Diplomatic Correspondence, Box 23. According to Hull, "Britain was still making geography the cornerstone of her preparedness" (*Memoirs*, 1:700).

39. CAB 65/4, 7 November 1939, p. 42; CAB 65/2, 7 November 1939, p. 55. Tweedsmuir had written to Chamberlain on 2 November: "I am afraid some of us may be disappointed as to America's capacity to produce rapidly—especially airplanes" (NC 7/11/32/290).

of delivery for various types of aircraft varied widely, some beginning in February 1940, others not beginning until more than a year thereafter.[40] Aircraft aside, it was not until May 1940 that Britain began to place large orders for arms in the United States.

Though not at once foreseen, there arose a problem over the delivery of military aircraft purchased in the United States, in view of a State Department ruling (in interpreting neutrality law) that they could not be delivered to the buyer by air. One solution was to fly the planes to Canada for purposes of testing or demonstration, then transfer them to the buyer. Still more novel was an arrangement to fly planes destined for Britain to Sweetgrass, Montana, site of a vast natural landing ground adjacent to the Canadian border, stop the engines, haul the planes across the imaginary frontier, and let Canadian pilots fly them away. Heavy winter snows would constitute a special problem, but the procedure could be utilized at other frontier points as needed. Likewise, flying boats would be transferred to Canadian pilots beyond the three-mile limit.[41]

Another important factor that deterred the British, of course, was the troubling uncertainty about the future directions of the war and especially the way in which the prime minister viewed things. Chamberlain continued to believe that attack in the West was not coming and that a new peace offensive was likely—although he did admit at length to his sister on December 3 (after hearing that German morale was hardening and that Goebbels was successfully making the German people believe that Britain was the implacable enemy) that he was "beginning to wonder whether we shall do any good with them [the Germans] unless they first get a real hard punch in the stomach." Contrary views had precious little forum for expression. Chamberlain dominated the war cabinet so that members were seldom asked to express opinions unless obviously required to do so on account of their special connection with subjects on papers under discussion. Further, he was still enmeshed in partisan—and personal—politics of a debilitating sort. He found the House of Commons "more and more ill-tempered and unreasonable," expressed in private his anxiety to "get rid of it" (meaning adjournment), and exuded relief when it was not in session. Increasingly annoyed at criticism of the government by Englishmen generally, and especially by the

40. CAB 65/2, 9 December 1939, pp. 248–49. British orders for aircraft included 600 Harvard trainers, 200 Lockheed Hudson reconnaissance planes, 200 Lockheed Hudson 32A machines, 50 P.B.Y. 4 long-range flying boats, 120 Republic fighters, and 300 Douglas light attack bombers.

41. Lothian to Halifax, 22 December 1939, FO 115/3420, File 1887.

press, he took obvious delight in stories such as one that Lord Beaverbrook brought back from a visit with Roosevelt in Washington: "This Chamberlain was a very clever fellow," the president had reportedly said; he had so persistently understated his case and harped on his desire for a reasonable peace that everyone now believed him to be a genuine, straightforward peacemaker. A speech to the Junior Carlton Club—admittedly a partisan political group—clearly lacked a balanced appreciation of circumstances as they were developing. Declaring the Axis breaking (and his critics confounded), Chamberlain implied that the government's policy had been carefully planned and executed at every stage and that Britain had entered the war fully prepared. Deriding the Labour party for its refusal to "come in," he nevertheless pronounced the government better off without it. Hardly a speech designed to promote a firm national resolve and internal harmony for a great war effort, it left even so ardent a Chamberlain supporter as Lady Astor chagrined. "The whole thing was so obviously lacking in statesmanship, uplift, or vision of any kind, it really got me down for a moment," she wrote Lord Lothian. It was meant to be a fighting speech, but its effect on her was to make her wish—at least momentarily—that Churchill were prime minister. "Still reeling at the speech" some days later, she was beginning to think that Chamberlain was too old, too narrow for national leadership.[42]

At the same time, Chamberlain's perception of the situation could hardly benefit from the substance of intelligence reports on Germany's probable intentions such as the one Halifax presented to the cabinet on December 1. Pointing to "considerable friction and difficulty" in the coordination of the German High Command, it allowed that Hitler possessed powers exercised in World War I by Hindenburg and Ludendorff combined; but the Führer was "unable to make up his mind." And his chief assistant, Keitel, was "a second-rate man." The result was "endless conferences from which very little emerged." This "lack of decision in high quarters," including Göring's refusal to launch an air attack on Britain unless full use of the army was made simultaneously, had spread a feeling of depression in the army that had even reached the divisional commands. And there was widespread fear of civil uprisings in Germany if heavy air attacks were made by the Allies on German towns, which

42. Neville to Ida, 22 October 1939; Neville to Hilda, 28 October 1939; Neville to Ida, 3 December 1939; NC 18/1/1126, 1128, 1133A; Lord Chatfield, *It Might Happen Again,* p. 180; Wallace Diary, C. 495, 24 October 1939; Lady Astor to Lothian, 23, 27 November 1939, Astor Papers, MS 1416, MS 1416/1/4/58.

was considered inevitable if the German air force were to start bombing England.[43] No wonder Chamberlain possessed an inadequate sense of urgency!

But aside from intelligence reports, there is a personality factor that must also be taken into account. Corroborated by many sources, there is (in the David Margesson Papers) a "candid portrait" of Chamberlain, of unknown authorship but clearly written at this point in time, that summarizes this factor very well: "A man does not easily alter his fundamental conceptions of human nature as he approaches his seventieth year, and Neville Chamberlain is more than usually tenacious of his views and unreceptive to the views of others." He makes up his mind with extraordinary rapidity, and having once made it up he never alters it. The lengthiest exposition of opinions that do not agree with his, never have the slightest effect on his judgment. In his own cabinet, his is the only will that ever prevails. Once he has given his own opinion, there is no more to be said.[44] What Chamberlain believed about the "good" Germans refusing to support Hitler and the possibility of concluding the war without decisive military action has already been indicated. The tenacity with which he believed it seemed unshakable.

Early in November, Lothian sent another round of letters to Halifax, Hoare, and Chatfield (explaining how he saw the prospective development of the war and the essentials for eventual peace) and seeking their reactions. He felt sure that Roosevelt and "other leading Americans" would soon begin to talk with him about possible bases for ending the war, which might otherwise soon engulf them. In his own view, the prospects for an early peace depended essentially upon the United States; if it and other democratic neutrals would "throw their weight" behind the Allies, Germany could probably be convinced that victory was permanently out of reach and some sort of negotiated peace might be possible. Security thereafter would involve a new form of *Pax Britannica* in which the United States would not promise to go to war but would adopt a unilateral policy of standing behind the Allied system to the point where nobody would dream of challenging it. "Fundamentally right" about the need to curb the unlimited ambitions of the militarists

43. CAB 65/4, 1 December 1939, pp. 127–28.

44. MRGN 1/5 (David Margesson Correspondence). This "candid portrait" was written to explain the "remarkable fact" that a prime minister who had had to come before the House of Commons so often to admit his astonishment, disappointment, or frustration could still retain the confidence of a majority of his countrymen and remain the most popular statesmen in the land. David Margesson was the government chief whip during Chamberlain's prime ministership.

in the Far East, America would take the lead in that area, Britain in Europe, and each would stand behind the other. Thus, he concluded, "the key to a stable world peace is the willingness of the United States to commit [it]self to some degree of obligation—not to sending boys to die in Europe, but to putting [its] vast power and resources into the diplomatic scale behind world stability." Roosevelt already wanted to do this, Lothian said, but he needed public support; "something could certainly be done to prepare the ground." He stopped short of specific suggestions.[45]

Halifax and Hoare readily agreed on the importance of America's role as Lothian outlined it, especially in regard to providing future security. Hoare wrote: ". . . Whether in the East or in the West, the ultimate future of peace will depend to a great extent upon the U.S.A., and the more concrete can be their influence on the side of it, the sooner the war will be over and the firmer the peace will be established." But Halifax could not but wonder "how far the United States would go in helping to guarantee our security." If its support stopped short of war, "where is our security?" In the Far East, Britain had done its best to keep in step with the United States and had not been unsuccessful—"though it may be that this view is not wholly shared in America!" Chatfield was skeptical about American opinion. Though he could not exactly blame them (they were, after all "hard-headed businessmen"), Americans "will indeed fight the battle for freedom and democracy to the last Briton, but save their own skins!" It was odd how they could look on the war as an internal European affair and still fear the consequences of Britain's losing. If they ever came in, it would not be out of moral sympathy but in their own self-interest. Yet, he admitted, America was not unlike other nations in this regard. In the Far East, the United States must not ask Britain to take unfair risks unless it was willing to share the consequences—which thus far it had not been willing to do. Overall, Americans should not be critical of Britain: "We are fighting for her and her civilization and world interests. Can she not admit this openly to the world?" Embargo repeal went some distance to give Britain moral support—"*almost* far enough."[46] Throughout this correspondence the importance of America's future role was recognized, but there

45. Lothian to Halifax, Hoare, and Chatfield, 3 November 1939, FO 800/324, pp. 97–107; Templewood Papers, XI:5, CHT/6/2, pp. 152–62.

46. Halifax to Lothian, 6 December 1939, FO 800/324, p. 112; Hoare to Lothian, 21 November 1939, Templewood Papers, X:5; Chatfield to Lothian, 27 November 1939, CHT/6/2, pp. 163–68.

was vagueness about its nature and uncertainty about what in fact could be expected. Meantime, Lothian, in a series of public addresses (including the occasion of the deposit of the Magna Carta in the Library of Congress for safekeeping), spoke mainly about the threat of totalitarianism and the value of freedom, and carefully avoided challenging America head-on.[47]

On the American side, Ambassador Kennedy did not help the situation. Long convinced that Britain would lose a war with Germany, he was reportedly prepared to "sell 100 Polands down the river any day than risk the life of a British soldier or the loss of a British pound." Bankruptcy and defeat became obsessions. His outlook was that Hitler and the Nazis could not have lasted forever and that there was bound to be a change in regime in Germany one day if Britain had only let her alone. In the unexpected event of a German defeat, he dreaded the appearance of a new social order—communism—in central Europe. Consequently, he pressed the British to seek peace by diplomatic means, prompting a lecture from Halifax to the effect that it was not a matter of "diplomatic ingenuity" but the untrustworthiness of the present German government. But Kennedy, Halifax recorded, "did not seem to agree" with this view. Their exchange generated additional observations in the Foreign Office, Balfour minuting that if Britain concluded peace before Nazism was defeated, as Kennedy—no doubt "thinking of his pocket"—wished, Britain would be vehemently accused in America of "selling democracy down the ocean." And Harvey, in noting the ambassador's defeatist propaganda, wrote: "I'm afraid he thinks only of his wealth and how capitalism will suffer if the war should last long." Even so, Kennedy wrote to Roosevelt, November 3: "Make no mistake, there is a very definite undercurrent in this country [Britain] for peace." It would make itself felt by pressure on the government to set forth definite war aims, "because the group who are anxious for peace feel that when those aims are set forth it will be apparent . . . that they are fighting for something they probably never can attain."[48] This was part of Kennedy's continuing effort to encourage Roosevelt to initiate some kind of peace move.

Roosevelt was, in fact, feeling his own way along. Generally pessi-

47. Lothian, *American Speeches*, pp. 1–46.

48. Minute by Charles Peake, F.O. News Dept., 12 October 1939, FO 371/22827, p. 317; Halifax to Lothian, 31 October 1939, FO 414/276, p. 144; Balfour Minute, 1 November 1939, FO 371/22830, p. 182; *Harvey Diaries*, p. 326; Kennedy to Roosevelt, 3 November 1939, PSF, Diplomatic Correspondence, Box 29.

mistic about the international situation, he nonetheless believed that the French and British had more stamina than the Germans, whose morale would eventually crack. The war might bring forth strong leadership in Britain, he wrote to Kennedy, for the British people seemed to be slowly but surely discarding their "muddle through" attitude of the past. He did not think the British need fear the rise of communism in Germany, as the ambassador did; it was not in keeping with German tradition and upbringing. His aversion to a mediated settlement that would leave the Nazis in power and enhance the strength of their position was clear in his rejection of all suggestions that he take the lead in attempting to arrange a negotiated peace. (Such suggestions came not only from Kennedy but from Göring in Berlin, King Leopold in Brussels, and others—though certainly not from any official Englishman.) Prepared to consider mediating if officially asked by the governments involved, he was certain that the time had not yet arrived for that. From a private talk with the president in mid-December, Lothian concluded that "he evidently hopes that before his time is up he may be able to intervene as a kind of umpire." But the timing and circumstances of such a move were moot.[49]

One of his great difficulties, Roosevelt told Lothian, was to get the American people to understand the tremendous risks to themselves in this war. If Britain should lose—and his military advisers were by no means certain that she would not—the United States would be faced with "intolerable difficulties." It would be helpful, the president suggested, if the British could emphasize their commitment to self-government, if Halifax could point out publicly that Britain had abandoned her empire-building of earlier centuries and had "long ago learnt the lesson that the only foundation for a stable international system was national autonomy." One most convincing approach to the American public was to admit the errors of the past while pointing to a change of heart in the present—adding that Germany was trying to force the world back to methods that had been discarded by the United States in the Monroe system and by Britain, at least in principle, in the modern Commonwealth. This hammering on a theme (the error of empire), which would later in the war cause considerable irritation in Anglo-American relations, was not appreciated in London. Chamberlain wrote a marginal comment on Lothian's letter rejecting the admitting of past errors, and Vansittart (at the Foreign Office) labeled it "simply lunacy." "What jam

49. Ickes, *Diary,* 3:37; Roosevelt to Kennedy, 30 October 1939, *F.D.R.: His Personal Letters,* 2:950; Lothian to Halifax, 14 December 1939, FO 800/397.

for German propaganda," he wrote to Halifax, and for all the American isolationists, who, having goaded Britain for cowardice in the past, had now "taken refuge in the pavilion lavatory."[50]

The uncertain condition of American opinion remained, of course, a matter of continuing interest and concern to British officials. In an effort to blunt reproaches for not setting forth specific terms of peace, Chamberlain declared in a broadcast of November 27 that Britain's aim was to defeat the German force and spirit; that accomplished, attention could be turned to building a new Europe that would settle its problems in good will, reduce trade barriers, and limit armies. Intended for the American public as well as the British, it met wide approval in the United States, Lothian wrote the prime minister. But Americans had been so "mis-educated" about their reasons for entering the last war and eschewing international cooperation thereafter, he added, that it was difficult for them to see any clear purpose in the war except the necessity of resisting both Hitlerism and communism. Once they began to see a picture of a "new and better world" such as Chamberlain began to outline, they would be more disposed to take "an active and constructive part." Chamberlain, in turn, described the American audience as "the most critical one can have," despite the sympathy that it felt for the Allied cause.[51]

An exchange about American opinion among Foreign Office personnel was spurred by a report from the Netherlands minister that Roosevelt had intimated to Berlin that any violation of Dutch neutrality might exercise "an immediate and unforeseen influence on American policy." "Nobody, not even Mr. Roosevelt, can foretell with any certainty how American opinion, ever unpredictable, will react to any particular set of circumstances," David Scott minuted. A German attack on Holland would cause a "wave of horror and indignation" that might result in further legislation to permit the Allies to purchase war supplies on credit, and destructive air bombardments on Britain that dangerously diminished its aircraft production might result in a relaxation of laws and regulations appearing to limit the amount of armaments America could supply to Britain. But American opinion, insensitive to the idea of the indivisibility of war, would not support a declaration of war except in the event of a "spectacular, defiant, and insulting" German act that

50. Lothian to Halifax, 14 December 1939, FO 800/397; Vansittart to Halifax, 31 December 1939, FO 800/324, p. 119.

51. Feiling, *Chamberlain,* p. 425; Lothian to Chamberlain, 28 November 1939, NC 7/11/32/170 A; Chamberlain to Lothian, 9 December 1939, FO 800/397.

everyone would immediately recognize as a threat to American vital interests. Cadogan thought this interpretation of the president's warning "probably about correct," and Halifax initialed it without comment. Here, then, was another nice, vague Rooseveltian phrase that could mean almost anything and should not be overinterpreted.[52]

Halifax drew to the cabinet's attention reports that the continued sinking of British ships by mines was having a depressing effect on American opinion, as were accounts that British and French aircraft production was still inferior to Germany's and failing to gain ground. Lothian's suggested antidote, if the demands of military secrecy would permit, was the giving of full information on the arrival of British shipping in British ports and aircraft production to United States correspondents in London, and Halifax was authorized by the cabinet to examine this possibility. But additional reports from Washington in mid-December made the cause seem less than hopeful. In reminding London of the danger of believing that America would automatically remain strongly pro-Ally, Lothian described the emergence of two contradictory shades of opinion. The absence of dramatic Allied victories or exploits, along with British merchant shipping losses, were promoting a view that Britain was really losing the war. But there was also a growing impression that Hitler, blundering in the pact with Russia, had already lost the war—to Russia if not to the democracies. So the United States could comfortably remain aloof. The result was "a certain resentment at the Allied treatment of American trade." The detention of American ships in contraband control ports, irritating interruptions of ordinary facilities for telephoning and cabling about business affairs, introduction of the Navicert system (see below), and the reduction of certain British purchases (tobacco, apples, pears), all created the impression that there was a needless attack on United States interests, coupled in some instances with suspicion that these controls were being manipulated for the benefit of British business interests. Although American opinion was strongly anti-Nazi (and anti-Soviet), it was not all that pro-British or pro-French.

52. Foreign Office Minutes, 28 November 1939, FO 371/22830, pp. 214–16. About the same time, Foreign Office officials worried with reports from the Washington embassy of anti-British broadcasts in New York by British-born commentator Boake Carter, alleging that Chamberlain, Simon, and other leading figures held stock in German armaments companies. It was at length agreed, and reinforced by staff assistants at Downing Street, to ignore these charges as unworthy of contradiction (ibid., pp. 190–91, 197–98). Foreign Office exasperation also appeared in reaction to a French statement of late November that made effusive reference to American attitudes and positions over recent months. "The French can take liberties which we never could without raising isolationist hornets nests round our ears," Scott and Balfour agreed (ibid., pp. 217–18).

Indeed, anti-British feeling had increased, partly out of a bad conscience that while Britain was "pulling her weight" the United States was not, but partly on the feeling that Britain was "keeping the war going while the rest want peace." Again in Lothian's view, the best corrective for all this was the fullest possible publicity, through the best American correspondents, about what the Allies were thinking and doing. To influential private friends (Waldorf Astor and Geoffrey Dawson), Lothian wrote that American opinion had reached a settled position: overwhelmingly for the defeat of Hitler and against Stalin, but equally against involvement in the war. The conflict had developed along unexpected lines, and the United States felt it a purely European concern that did not threaten its own security because the Russian agreement was evidently going to ruin Hitler.[53]

To Lothian's discouraging account, Victor Mallet, counselor in the Washington embassy on leave in London, had more to add. He too detailed the paradoxical sentiments of Americans, attributing the shift in opinion partly to the circumstances of the war itself but also to the resurgence of internal political issues (including fear in some circles that America's involvement would open the way for Roosevelt to assume dictatorial powers). Beyond that, he noted "a quite ridiculous distrust of the Prime Minister." Americans still complained that he had been deceived at Munich; they found his appearance and voice uninspiring and craved for the more "colorful" Churchill. There was really nothing much that Britain could do to correct this: "It is to the mentality of the movie-fan that the appeal has to be made, and the British and American publics do not always admire the same qualities in their political leaders." While visiting Halifax, Mallet was asked what, if anything, would bring America into the war on Britain's side. "Nothing short of a big disaster," such as the destruction of London or of the fleet, he replied—and even then Britain could expect only economic and financial aid. In summarizing his visit in London for Lothian, Mallet wrote:

> I get the impression that the Americans may soon be unpopular over here. People are tired of being preached at by them. The press is restraining itself very well, but people talk . . . and it will be difficult to persuade them that

53. CAB 65/2, 1 December 1939, p. 192; Lothian to Halifax, 14 December 1939, FO 414/276, pp. 167–68; Lothian to Waldorf Astor and Geoffrey Dawson, 18 December 1939, Lothian Papers, GD 40/17/398. See also Lothian to Halifax, 20 December 1939, FO 115/3420, File 1532.

> America is entitled to have *any say whatever* when the peace terms are discussed unless she takes a constructive part in helping us to win the war.[54]

Another assessment of American opinion that caught the attention of Chamberlain and Foreign Office officials was written by Charles des Graz, of the Postal Censorship Department. Beginning with the fundamental isolationism of the United States, it pointed out that indignation at certain European nations rather than sympathy for others was a major factor in the attitude of Americans, "with whom emotion and idealism are driving forces." Fear was the motive underlying American reactions toward events in Europe; haunted by dread of involvement, Americans invented plausible reasons to rationalize their fear and make it appear respectable to themselves. One of these was the notion that this was not a war for democracy, and that America would not have been drawn into the last war if it had not been for the subtlety of British propaganda. Thus fear of falling victim again to British propaganda had become "a positive mania," all the more critical at a time when the United States was entering upon an electoral campaign. Handed directly to an official (Rucker) at 10 Downing Street, this paper was first examined by Chamberlain, who sent it along to the Foreign Office, where it was favorably scrutinized. Possibly one reason for Chamberlain's interest was the unusually positive picture it gave of him. Of Britain's "certain invaluable assets" in the United States, it declared, the first was the prime minister, "now firm in the sympathy and respect of the average American and able, when broadcasting, to draw from their beds thousands across the Atlantic to whom hardly another British statesman is even known by name."[55]

Personal assessments aside, the condition of American opinion was not encouraging to the British. Even Churchill wrote at year's end (in relation to British policy on Jewish immigration into Palestine and the need to conciliate American Jewry and enlist its aid in combatting isolationist and anti-British tendencies in America): "The trend of American opinion since the war has been disappointing, and the movement to interpret neutrality in the strictest manner has gathered unexpected strength." In consequence, accounts such as Lothian's on the "sustained

54. Report by Mallet, 14 December 1939, FO 371/22830, pp. 219–31; Mallet to Lothian, 18 December 1939, FO 800/397. Both Halifax and King George VI expressed to Mallet their irritation with Joseph Kennedy, the former calling him a "lightweight" who was defeatist and dilly about the war, the latter recounting a good talking-to administered in an effort to put some heart into him.

55. FO 371/22830, pp. 302–8.

success" of the British Pavilion at the New York World's Fair, portraying to Americans "the prestige of Great Britain, the dignity of our history and our life and work, and of our industrial achievement," were of small consolation.[56]

Specific issues troubling the Anglo-American relationship in the last months of 1939 included the matter of respective shipping rights, as Britain worked to enforce procedures deemed essential to her belligerent status and the United States tried to maintain its position of legal neutrality. Points of friction inevitably arose over diverging interpretations of international law and focused in particular on contraband control. Recognizing potential difficulties right from the start, and wishing to avoid serious quarrels of the kind that had characterized 1914–17, Hull had summoned Lothian on September 4 and initiated a series of meetings from which evolved an arrangement for taking up specific problems as they arose, through quiet, informal discussions rather than by means of diplomatic protests. This procedure worked well, with the result that few controversies became as acute as those of World War I, and American public sympathy for Britain was never seriously weakened by the impact of shipping disputes. But there were lingering suspicions and some tedious moments.[57]

The late September establishment, by the Panama Conference, of a neutrality zone extending 300 to 1,000 miles (according to the contour of the coastline) off the Atlantic coast of the Americas, in which all belligerent activities would be outlawed, was of great potential benefit to Britain in relieving the Royal Navy of a heavy load of patrol responsibilities and freeing ships for the Atlantic convoy. Roosevelt had arranged for the conference because of his concerns for a joint inter-American neutrality policy and greater economic cooperation to counter the instability in Latin America—fraught with possibilities for Nazi meddling—that a European war would bring. He no doubt realized that this would both aid the Allies and advance the cause of hemispheric defense—while enabling him to maintain open options in rapidly changing circumstances. Of course, Britain wanted to be sure that *all* belligerents would comply and that the safety zone would not become a haven for German vessels. This meant the establishment of effective patrol by the American navy, and Roosevelt responded by assigning eighty ships to duty in the area. This issue was, in fact, the occasion of a direct,

56. NC 7/9/71, 25 December 1939; Lothian to Halifax, 28 December 1939, FO 414/277, p. 7.
57. Hull, *Memoirs,* 1:678–81.

personal exchange between Roosevelt and Churchill. Churchill consulted the war cabinet, but Lothian was not informed—and was consequently embarrassed some time later when Welles pointed to Churchill's letter and October 5 enclosures to Kennedy as Britain's acceptance of the Panama proposals, and Lothian was not aware of them. Nor was the ensuing interpretation of details relating to the security zone an easy matter. Churchill wrote Chamberlain on Christmas Day that he was "worried by the stiff attitude" being taken in Washington on these matters; Roosevelt was certainly Britain's best friend, "but I expect he wants to be re-elected, and I fear that isolationism is the winning ticket."[58]

At the time the arms embargo was repealed, Moffat, of the State Department, could not help feeling that "the British may draw false conclusions from the size of the vote and think they have us in their pocket. As it is, we are getting more frequent indication of the cavalier way in which they are treating us in the blockade." In the following weeks, problems (related to contraband lists, blacklists, and stoppage on the high seas) complicated the daily work of the department, and the operating principle "no help to Germany but no Dominion status for ourselves" emerged with some force. There was sharp division over how to respond to Britain's establishment of a Navicert system (a scheme by which a kind of commercial passport was issued by the British to a shipment destined for a neutral, after the British were satisfied that the consignee would not reship to Germany), which could be abused to the point of permitting Britain to control American exports. The position at length adopted—one of "no comment," reserving all American rights should any abuse develop—stemmed more from a lack of alternative than from good will. Britain's late-November decision to intercept all ships emanating from German ports and to seize goods of German origin wherever found on the high seas drew warnings from Washington against interference in the legitimate neutral trade of the United States. There was increasing irritation over Britain's forcing of American ships into contraband control ports to have their cargoes examined, especially those, such as Kirkwall (Scotland), within the belligerent zone, which they were forbidden by American law to enter. Hull informed Lothian that United States steamship companies operating vessels to Europe had

58. CAB 65/3, 5 October 1939, pp. 92–98; Lothian to Halifax, 16 November 1939, FO 414/276, p. 150; Dallek, *Franklin Roosevelt and American Foreign Policy,* pp. 205–6; Churchill to Chamberlain, 25 December 1939, NC 7/9/69. Roosevelt also telephoned Churchill on the night of 5 October about a German warning that the U.S.S. *Iroquois* would be sunk by the British (CAB 65/1, 6 October 1939, p. 215).

voluntarily agreed to cooperate with British authorities to serve mutual interests, and this spirit of liberality would best be met "by a corresponding degree of accommodation and flexibility" on Britain's part. If Britain persisted, the United States would consider further action and would expect compensation for losses and injuries resulting from the infraction of its rights as a matter of course. He did not press further, however, and Lothian wrote the Foreign Office that Hull's message was "studiously moderate in tone."[59] But more would be heard of this issue in the new year.

Another British irritant for Americans during late 1939 was the censorship of mail. Kennedy, in particular, was angry about what he perceived to be excessive interference with his own correspondence and complained to Halifax in mid-November that it was just this sort of thing that was likely to get Britain into trouble with the United States. On a broader scale, the embassy vigorously protested the removal from British, American, or other neutral ships of mail addressed to neutral countries and the opening of sealed letter mail sent from the United States. The war cabinet was not oblivious to the issue. A late November discussion centered on whether more harm than good was being done by interference with German propaganda sent through the mail and destined for the United States; and a December 21 discussion found the president of the Board of Trade recommending cabinet reconsideration of the censorship of American mails if it was causing additional delays in export trade.[60] But these were matters to which there were no quick and easy solutions.

During the last two months of 1939, the British watched the situation in the Far East very closely, torn by the desire to avoid any deterioration of relations with Japan (if possible, even to resume conversations with her on certain problems) and the need to present a firm image and march in step with United States policy in the area. Halifax clearly explained this position to Kennedy, stressing assurances to President Roosevelt that Britain, in any case, would not depart from "the broad strategy . . . which we sought to follow so far as we could in conformity with that of the United States government." American feeling against Japan had

59. *Moffat Papers*, pp. 276–78; Johnson to Halifax, 8 December 1939, FO 414/276, pp. 160–61; Hull to Lothian, 14 December 1939, FO 115/3420, File 1479; Lothian to Halifax, 20 December 1939, FO 371/22838, pp. 55–57.

60. Halifax to Lothian, 17 November 1939, FO 371/22830, pp. 187–88; Johnson to Halifax, 27 December 1939, FO 414/276, p. 169; CAB 65/2, 29 November, 21 December 1939, pp. 179, 321.

intensified, Lothian reported in mid-November, and the United States apparently meant to hold firm at a time when Britain might be preparing the way for a partial retreat; but this did not connote an American disposition to protect British interests except as a consequence of the maintenance of its own. Collaboration or joint action seemed as far away as ever, and the best that Britain could hope for, Mallet argued in a long memorandum on American policy dated December 8, was that it would benefit from any strong action that the United States might take on its own behalf. Washington realized that, with a European war on its hands, Britain was not able to do much in Asia, and could at times "find a good excuse for parallel action" with London. The United States would not hesitate to pull its own chestnuts out of the fire because a few British chestnuts happened to be there too. But the U.S. administration appeared to be convinced, Mallet added, that China could never really be dominated or colonized by Japan; the Japanese people lacked the essential qualities for colonizing. Nor did the State Department fear a partition of China between Japan and Russia, because any understanding between these two "desperadoes" would not last long.[61] As a result the possibility of effective coordinated action seemed as distant as ever.

Generally, however, 1939 did not close on all that pessimistic a note for the British. Even the Russian attack on Finland was given a positive twist by Chamberlain, who did not think "the allied cause . . . likely to suffer thereby." It had added a great deal to the general feeling that the ways of dictators "make things impossible for the rest of the world" and had infuriated the Americans, who had a sentimental regard for the Finns because they had paid off their war debt. Indeed, Chamberlain saw Russia's action as vindication of Britain's failure (or refusal) to sign an agreement with Moscow the previous August. He "thanked his stars," he told General Pownall in mid-December, that those conversations had collapsed. Otherwise, it would have been Britain, not Germany, that would have had to laugh off Russia's action in the Baltic area. How much useless effort would have been spent in trying to prevent Russia from doing such things, and how the government's prestige would have fallen if it had signed an agreement "with such people."[62] The sort of optimism that prevailed in some quarters is revealed in a letter that

61. Halifax to Lothian, 27 November 1939, FO 414/276, p. 153; Lothian to Halifax, 20 November 1939, FO 115/3420, File 1549; Mallet Memorandum, 8 December 1939, FO 800/397.

62. Neville to Ida, 3 December 1939, NC 18/1/1133A; *Pownall Diaries*, 1:271.

Maurice Hankey, former secretary of the cabinet, wrote to General Smuts at Christmastime:

> Now that four months have passed the picture looks very different. Every day the Italian menace is disappearing. The Japanese threat is also receding, and America is much more assertive in the Far East. Finland, so far, has made Russia look silly. This is strengthening the faint hearts in the Balkans. And above all one begins to feel, if one dares to admit it even to oneself, that the Germany of today is not quite the old Germany of 1914–1918.[63]

In the first four months of the war, the course and nature of which remained uncertain, Anglo-American relationships, especially in terms of greater cooperation and open collaboration, had not improved significantly. Old fears, hesitations, and suspicions remained intact on both sides. But it was also still uncertain how crucial this was to the British, many of whom were asking, at least indirectly, about the Americans: Who needs them anyway?

63. Hankey to Smuts, Christmas, 1939, HNKY 4/31.

IX.
The Welles Mission and Chamberlain's Fall

A FEELING OF OPTIMISM about the war, which resulted in complacency about the need to seek a closer relationship with America—or anyone else, for that matter—continued to pervade the upper echelons of British government until the series of events that prompted Chamberlain's fall from leadership in May 1940. Halifax told the cabinet late in January that a recent speech by Hitler was "a weak one and . . . entirely that of a man on the defensive." The British should simply ignore it. Chamberlain agreed. Two months later, Halifax enumerated "a good many straws blowing that are favorable": the British people definitely seemed to have a more aggressive spirit than the Germans; the British navy, he "suspected," was steadily beating the German submarine; and there were signs of "depression, discomfort and definite shortage" inside Germany. About the same time, a buoyant Chamberlain told the Conservative Central Council that he was now ten times as confident of victory as he had been when the war started, and assured them that (as Halifax recorded it), "by having allowed nothing to happen for the last six months, Hitler had missed the bus." And on April 19, the foreign secretary reported information—obtained through a high official in the U.S. State Department—that the German Army Command was strongly opposed to adventuring in Norway, and if Hitler were now to meet with serious reverses on land in the West, it would probably overthrow the Nazi regime. Moreover, it did not appear that Italy was ready to take any particular action.[1]

1. CAB 65/5, 31 January 1940, p. 139; Halifax Papers, 2, 4 April 1940, A7.8.3, pp. 63, 65–66; Wallace Diary, c. 496, 4 April 1940; CAB 65/6, 19 April 1940, p. 239.

Meantime, the whole range of what, in retrospect, appear to be relatively minor issues that had arisen during the first four months of the war continued to trouble Anglo-American relations. These included the British censorship of mail, British actions in enforcing contraband control (especially the forcible taking of U.S. ships into the combatant zone for inspection), and restrictions placed by Britain on trade with America. In addition, there was confusion during the first weeks of January about a new matter: the operation of the maritime security zone that had been established by the Declaration of Panama several months before, by which belligerent vessels were to refrain from military operations in an imaginary area ranging from 300 to 1,000 miles off the shores of the Americas. Britain had possessions within the zone and needed the right of entry. Germany did not. And Britain feared that ineffective patroling would make the zone a vast sanctuary for enemy vessels to prey upon Allied shipping. Halifax thought "decent interment" of the whole idea the only solution, but Lothian pressed the difficulties of enforcement with the State Department and came away believing both that the problems were understood and that there existed a will to reach some agreement with Britain about them. No particular agreement in fact resulted; but in the weeks that followed, U.S. protests over British violations were generally mild, and the British tried to respect American sensibilities by intercepting enemy vessels as far away from the American coast as possible.[2]

The latter part of January saw a flare-up of resentment against Britain in the State Department—a "minor crisis" in Anglo-American relations, Lothian later called it—that was reflected openly in the press. Lothian reported newspaper accounts of increasing irritation, which he attributed to various things: the inevitable annoyance of any neutral at restrictions imposed by belligerents; a belief in America that Britain was inclined to trade upon Washington's known sympathy for the Allied cause and to pay more attention to the protests of neutrals, such as Italy (who had greater nuisance value), than her own; and a desire to stave off criticism in Congress, now in session again, of failure to protect American rights. Lothian was not greatly alarmed because there was no genuine public protest and no lessening of the administration's desire for Allied success in the war. But he saw "potential danger" and urged

2. *Confidential Dispatches: Analyses of America by the British Ambassador, 1939–1945,* pp. 18–19; Halifax to Gort, 3 January 1940, FO 800/328, p. 404; Lothian to Halifax, 8 January 1940, FO 414/277, p. 6; Foreign Office Minutes, 19 January 1940, FO 371/24234, pp. 290–91. Roosevelt skirted the issue in his press conference of 16 January (*FDR Press Conferences,* 15:85).

that Britain do everything possible to meet the State Department's complaints by transferring the examination of American ships from Kirkwall (Scotland) to St. John (New Brunswick), speeding up the passage of American ships through contraband control points, answering or removing grounds for the charge that Italians and others received better treatment (and facilities) than Americans, and giving "practical evidence" that the examination of mails was vital to the blockade.[3]

Irritation on all these matters had been building up for some time and seemed to peak during the third week of January, triggered perhaps by reports from London that the British were transferring their purchases of tobacco from the United States to Turkey and publicity given the examination of mails on the Pan American Clipper at Bermuda. The British may have taken earlier American protests too lightly. Halifax told the cabinet on January 5, for example, that a recent American note protesting British interference with U.S. mails in American or other neutral ships on the high seas was "not as stiff" as press reports had suggested; and the Foreign Office took the view that Washington "felt bound on formal grounds" to make the protest and to raise the legal argument whether British action involved only contraband examination or censorship. Halifax did not believe the note was "really unfriendly." Indeed, the Foreign Office did not reply until January 16, when it explained that British action was based upon the established practice of 1914–18 and chided Washington that no apparent protest had been directed at Germany for its reckless and indiscriminate destruction of neutral property (including mails) on board ships sunk by the Germans. In contrast, Britain was merely examining mails and forwarding innocent material as soon as its nature was established. Nevertheless, it would try to reduce delays and examine specific complaints in a friendly, accommodating spirit.[4] But Washington *did* take such matters seriously. British action in stopping the Pan American Clipper at Bermuda and removing foreign mail for censorship was a daylong topic of discussion at the State Department, January 19, and Lothian observed that "Americans are notoriously sensitive about their mail." Many persons had told him that it was these "pin-pricks" that made trouble and alienated popular sympathy.[5]

At the same time, the British were by no means insensitive to American

3. Lothian to Halifax, 21 January 1940, FO 414/277, p. 12.

4. CAB 65/5, 5 January 1940, p. 19; Halifax to Johnson (U.S. Embassy), 16 January 1940, FO 414/277, pp. 9–10.

5. *Moffat Papers,* p. 286; Lothian to Halifax, 21 January 1940, FO 414/277, p. 12.

complaints. Although it had not yet been disclosed, a means had been formulated for sparing U.S. ships the visit to a contraband control post within the combat area *if* their cargo was fully covered by Navicerts when eastbound or by certificates of origin when westbound. Such vessels could be examined at sea unless they carried passengers or mail. And the Admiralty was considering the establishment of a base in Canadian waters (probably Halifax, Nova Scotia, or St. John) for the examination of mails and passengers carried on ships leaving or bound for U.S. ports. If the U.S. objection to the Navicert system—on the "somewhat childish ground that it infringes American sovereignty" (as a Foreign Office official put it)—persisted, it was possible that a station would be instituted in Canada for examining goods as well as passengers and mail. On grounds of general policy, the Foreign Office wanted the largest possible number of ships dealt with on "the other side of the Atlantic." It was understood that American objections to Kirkwall were actually in Britain's interest. If an American ship was bombed or mined there, Britain would suffer most from the resulting uproar, not Germany.[6]

A visit to Hull on January 22 left Lothian with mixed reactions. The secretary of state thought developing friction "might become very dangerous" and wondered whether the advantages to be gained by Britain in interfering with American neutral rights was worth the price of alienating American sympathy. He was also agitated about Britain's restrictions on trade and finance, particularly the cessation of tobacco purchase. A sweeping abandonment of purchases of American staple products by its best customer would irritate U.S. exporters and strengthen the arguments of those who held that the war had so dislocated commerce that the trade agreements for which they were still fighting in Congress were useless. In reporting to London, Lothian said that Hull would "soon revert to his usual support of the Allies," and suspected that Roosevelt had calculated that "a little demonstration against Great Britain" would somehow be helpful to his policy of giving all the assistance he could to the Allies within the Neutrality Act. But it would be useful for Halifax or Chamberlain to say something in a public speech about Britain's anxiety not to affect multilateral trade adversely, and important for the British government to provide Roosevelt

6. Foreign Office to Lothian, 6 January 1940; Memorandum to Halifax, 8 January 1940, FO 800/324, pp. 127, 128–29. Lothian was instructed to seek American views on these matters; and Halifax wrote Geoffrey Dawson, editor of the *Times*, warning against premature publicity.

privately with "as complete a statement as is possible of the future as they see it," especially in regard to financial matters involved in pursuing the war.[7]

Hull had his economic adviser expand his views on Anglo-American trade relations to the British commercial counselor a short time later, seeking "earnest and immediate consideration" of practical suggestions, including some that he put forward (several of which dealt with publicity) to remedy or ameliorate the situation. The State Department recognized Britain's problems of financing essential war requirements and providing necessary shipping but nonetheless felt entitled to ask it to purchase tobacco and apples (so Lothian reported), "not as a condition, but in consideration of United States Government facilitating these purchases and maintaining trade agreement." Meantime, Halifax drew the attention of the cabinet to the friction with America and agreed both to consider Lothian's suggestions and to prepare a "long and reasoned reply" to be communicated to Washington. Lothian had more to report on January 26, as a result of conversation with R. Walton Moore (assistant secretary) and Moffat at the State Department. The feeling had been growing for some time, he related, that although the administration had shown the utmost friendship to Britain, the British had not gone out of their way to return that friendship by meeting administration difficulties and had given more regard to nuisance nations like Italy. Further, the conviction had grown that Britain was using wartime necessity to divert trade from America to other countries. Businessmen had been expressing irritation with such things as mail delays, cable interruption, and the long detention of ships, and things gradually built up. The State Department now seemed to feel "rather uncomfortable about the whole business," Lothian added, and Britain should consciously go as far as possible to give the impression that it was seriously trying to meet American views within the constraints imposed by the prime necessity of winning the war.[8]

7. Lothian to Halifax, 22 January 1940, FO 414/277, pp. 20–21; Hull, *Memoirs,* 1:748–49. Lothian also visited Berle, who handed him an aide-mémoire protesting the British delay of American ships at Gibraltar; and when he acknowledged that the Italians had an easier time because they capitalized on their nuisance value, Berle responded that the United States might have to become more of a nuisance to have its rights respected (Berle, *Navigating the Rapids,* p. 285).

8. Lothian to Halifax, 25, 26 January 1940, FO 414/277, pp. 22–24; CAB 65/5, 23, 24 January 1940, pp. 99, 103. The account of Lothian's conversation with Moore and Moffat that appears in the *Moffat Papers,* pp. 287–90, makes the U.S. position appear rather selfish and insufficiently alert to the stakes involved in the war now under way, especially for Britain. For another example of similar sentiment, albeit a month or so later, see *The War Diary of Breckinridge Long,*

Halifax was able to tell the cabinet on February 1 that the situation in relation to America was now "somewhat easier." Lothian had exercised Roosevelt's own suggestion, made early in the war, that, when matters of dispute arose between the two countries, they should avoid diplomatic notes and seek settlement by less formal methods. He had had another long conversation with Hull (which Lothian described as "extremely friendly"), in which all major outstanding problems had been touched upon and Lothian "had taken full advantage of the opportunity offered." The Washington chancery later reported that the "less friendly and more irritated elements" in the State Department, which had earlier decided that the time had come "to demonstrate publicly how jealous the State Department was of United States Government rights and how active it was in protecting United States interests," did not have the support of the American public, which was prepared to bristle at arrogant British interference with its normal rights but not disposed to see itself the victim of British bullying. That too facilitated the reduction of tension.[9]

Thus the "minor crisis" of January 1940 began to wane, but it was not without impact. Lothian wrote Halifax that it marked a "permanent change" in the American attitude: the somewhat humiliating desire to escape the risk of war at almost any price was giving way to a more resolute defense of American rights generally. Feeling an old irritation at Britain's historic command of the seas and sensing acutely that it was now a sea power equal to Britain, the United States wanted to be treated with due consideration and no doubt realized that it could "probably compel us" by threatening retaliation. Britain must face the fact, Lothian said, that "the period of easy going we have enjoyed over here" has ended, and the United States would expect to be consulted a good deal more about British policy on all matters affecting American interests. Britain must hereafter *prove* to America that any action taken that affected its interests was really necessary for winning the war—and this would best be done beforehand. Once that was established, there would be no difficulty. But Britain could no longer impose restrictions and expect Washington to acquiesce.[10]

---

pp. 61, 65–66. Britain's attitude had led Americans to believe that she was not "playing fair," Long recorded. Berle recorded in his diary on January 24: "We have been pretty stiff with the British . . . and had reason to believe they were worried about it" (*Navigating the Rapids,* p. 287).

9. CAB 65/5, p. 144; Lothian to Halifax, 30 January 1940, FO 414/277, pp. 24–25; Washington Chancery to American Dept. (FO), 3 February 1940, FO 371/24248, pp. 254–59.

10. Lothian to Halifax, 27 January 1940, FO 800/324, pp. 132–36. The latter point was

The British ambassador continued to reflect on this for some days. Writing Halifax a week later, and enclosing a 23-page summary of America's present and probable future attitude, he noted that public opinion—which he found "continually decisive"—had gradually shifted from viewing the war as a "football match" to a much more serious consideration of the issues at stake. He repeated the view that Britain must pay much more attention to the effects of its actions on American opinion and prove to American satisfaction that they were essential to victory. Britain must also refrain from offering Americans advice as to what they ought to do. Emotional appeals about common ancestry, language, ideals—anything that looked like propaganda designed to influence American policy—only created "a cold fury" in the American mind. Patience was essential while Britain and America gradually discovered the basis on which they could confidently cooperate for their own and the common good. Halifax was so impressed with this dispatch that he arranged to have a similar assessment of British feelings and problems produced periodically for the information of Lothian and heads of missions elsewhere.[11]

The grievances that traversed the Atlantic during late January 1940 were not, of course, all one way. Minutes by some Foreign Office officials during the first ten days of February revealed considerable exasperation on that side of the ocean too. First Secretary Perowne set forth a list of grievances against the United States government, as they had come to the attention of the American Department, on February 1. In a "shower of notes," he wrote, the State Department had complained about various aspects of contraband control; and even before the ink was dry, they had been given to the press, along with "inspired statements designed to work up feeling and create prejudice against us in the U.S." Such behavior was unjustified and sprang no doubt from perceived electoral necessities. Hull's complaints about agricultural purchase restrictions, calculated to placate purely sectional interests, were "*prima facie* inexcusable . . . sheer effrontery if he troubled to think it out." Americans were prone to "emotional tantrums" and seemed to be "governed to an unusual degree by their irrational faculties," strong among which appeared to be a "fundamental latent hostility" toward Britain—a sort of love-hate complex. To be sure, Britain was guilty of inadequate expla-

reiterated in Washington Chancery to American Dept. (FO), 3 February 1940, FO 371/24248, p. 259.

11. Lothian to Halifax, 3 February 1940, FO 800/324, pp. 141–63, 188–89.

nations of contraband control, but Americans must be told of the negative impression their actions had made; otherwise, they would employ these tactics "over and over again until we are completely down and out." In a summary note the following day, Perowne continued: "The U.S. Gov't are always telling us that they want us to win the war. But with the sole, important, exception of the repeal of arms embargo (which does them no harm and even some good, materially) all that they have *done* or seem to want to do, hampers our efforts." The Panama Zone hindered Britain's prosecution of the war at sea. The Johnson Act prevented the financing of greatly increased war purchases from loans or credits. The Neutrality Act made it expensive and inconvenient for Britain to acquire food and supplies from abroad and to sell British goods to earn dollars and other foreign currencies. By excluding Bergen (Norway), the Combat Zone helped the Germans without providing Britain with any corresponding advantageous port. Thus the United States was looking solely to its own interests, Perowne felt, and had not made any real attempt to think things out. "One would like them to feel less and think more," he concluded.[12]

Other Foreign Office personnel shared Perowne's concerns to varying degrees. Balfour thought Lothian might "indulge in some plain speaking" with the State Department, though he allowed that there was apparently some substance to American complaints about agricultural purchases and contraband control. Scott doubted that Britain was in a position "to start throwing stones," but he saw no harm in plain speaking—though Britain should not be under any illusion about the effect it would have. Cadogan, the under secretary, wrote flatly: "The U.S. are most annoying. It is better not to reflect too much on their tiresomeness." He remembered feeling about America in the last war as Perowne felt now. Lothian might be supplied with a summary of British grievances that he could cite from time to time in order to avoid the danger of "letting it be thought that we do not notice these things," but its use should be left to his discretion. Vansittart disagreed: Lothian should be *instructed* to put Britain's case fully to the president. No political harm ever came from standing up for oneself; it was the failure to do so that was fatal. Yet Britain was in an equivocal position. Americans were "pusillanimous," lacking in any form of "political virility," and "an unattractive hotch-potch in the mass"; but the improvement of relations with them, however remote the chances, was "one of the faint hopes for

12. Minutes by Perowne, 1, 2 February 1940, FO 371/24248, pp. 165–71.

the democratic world." Even Halifax had a say in it all: he wished to retain ambassadorial discretion, but Lothian could be told to speak plainly, and personally, to the president on these matters "in whatever way he judged most effective . . . unless he saw fundamental objection to doing so."[13]

Foreign Office personnel were no more discouraged than the prime minister. Writing to his sister on January 27, he confessed to having "a most depressing week." Abuse of the government by the press—anonymous journalists with only a smattering of the facts and no political experience who deigned to tell him how he should change his methods—filled him "with a sick resentment." Further, the behavior of the neutrals, who went out of their way to pretend that between Germany and the Allies there was little to choose, was "most exasperating."

> The U.S.A. goes right back on us because while we opened all our dollars on buying war stores from them we have none left to buy tobacco. And they declare that they are insulted when we examine the mails which are a vehicle of a carefully organized system of aid and relief to our enemies. Heaven knows I don't want the Americans to fight for us—we should have to pay too dearly for that if they had a right to be in on the peace terms—but if they are so sympathetic they might at least refrain from hampering our efforts and comforting our foes.[14]

By mid-February, however, the Foreign Office had had second thoughts about the idea of a direct protest to Washington or the preparation of a list of grievances to be relayed by Lothian. Instead, it was more inclined to play along with the need for cultivating American public opinion and paying the price necessary to do that. Balfour prepared a long memorandum on Anglo-American relations, as affected by the former's wartime measures and the latter's neutrality, that was temperate in tone and carefully reasoned. It listed ways in which American attitudes and actions had "gravely impeded" Britain's war effort and filled the average Englishman with "intense exasperation." Yet the special problems of America generally, and the Roosevelt administration in particular, were clearly recognized. Allowing that British objections could be summed up in four words, "Stop being so neutral," it weighed the psychological effect of remonstrances and recrimination and concluded that since

13. Foreign Office Minutes, 2–10 February 1940, ibid., pp. 161–64.

14. Neville to Ida, NC 18/1/1140. Feeling a real sense of discouragement, Chamberlain thought there would be "compensations" in relinquishing leadership to someone else, "only I don't see that other to whom I could hand over with any confidence that he would do better than I."

American public opinion was in a position to exercise decisive influence on the outcome of the war, it was to the movement of that opinion rather than dealings with the administration that Britain must look "for possible salvation." In his own minuted explanation of the memorandum, Balfour declared that things had changed over a period of several weeks: American protests had declined, the Welles mission (see below) had been announced, Ashton-Gwatkin (economic adviser) was going to America to explain difficulties in the field of economic warfare, and Lothian had reported that U.S. opinion was slowly moving in the direction of intervention. Thus, it no longer seemed necessary to give expression to Britain's own grievances. Of paramount importance now was "cultivating the good graces of powerful sections of American public opinion, on whose good will we are in the last analysis dependent for victory."[15] After other officials had expressed approval, Under Secretary Cadogan candidly drew the moral:

> What it seems to amount to is this: that at any given moment we shall run out of dollars. We may then, with possibly small chance of success, have to throw ourselves on the mercy of the Americans. We shall advance the date of that unpleasant situation only by a few weeks by squandering bribes [apples and tobacco] on the electors, and that may make all the difference. It may be a good gamble, and perhaps worth taking, however much it goes against the grain.[16]

At least one other important thing had changed too. On January 29, Churchill had given orders to the fleet not to bring any American ships into the combat zone. Explaining this later to the cabinet in terms of deference to Halifax's anxiety lest "anything untoward" should happen to a U.S. vessel, he concurred that it would be a "real calamity" if an incident (German torpedoing of an American vessel with a resultant loss of life) should occur that would touch off anger in the United States against Britain. By mid-February, however, the decision was causing Britain other problems, Halifax told the cabinet: great embarrassment in the administration of contraband control in relation to other neutrals, particularly Italy and Japan, with an attendant danger that "serious inroads" would be made into the whole contraband system. He now thought the

15. Balfour Memorandum and Minute, 19 February 1940, FO 371/24248, pp. 176–95. Foreign Office personnel were divided over the degree to which American agitation had been "artificial," i.e., deliberately worked up by the State Department and lacking public backing. See Minutes by Cowell, Perowne, Balfour, and Scott, 22 February 1940, ibid., pp. 200–202.

16. Cadogan Minute, 1 March 1940, ibid., pp. 172–75.

proper course was to inform Washington frankly of Britain's difficulties and to ask whether America would be "willing" to let Britain take a U.S. vessel into Kirkwall for examination from time to time in order to maintain the principle. The problem was obviously one of striking a balance between serious annoyance to the United States and difficulties with other neutrals caused by a U.S. exemption—and this was causing the British considerable consternation.[17]

Churchill and Roosevelt were in direct, if limited, contact about these matters. The president wrote on February 1 that "our conversation in regard to search and detention of American ships is working out satisfactorily." But he added frankly that there had been much public criticism of Britain's policy in the United States, and the general feeling was that the net benefit to Britain was not worth the annoyance to America. Responding at the end of February, Churchill explained that his order of a month before was still in effect; but real embarrassment resulted when, for example, the Moore-McCormick line actually advertised in Norway that it did not have to worry about Navicerts or Kirkwall, and when Scandinavian countries complained of discrimination in America's favor. He hoped for help in holding the position he had adopted, by way of American shipping lines utilizing the Navicert system—which, he reminded Roosevelt, was an American invention—and not carrying mails for Scandinavia until arrangements at another port of inspection (St. John or elsewhere) could be readied.[18]

So despite the cooling down of irritated feeling about issues relating to shipping, trade, and censorship, these problems by no means disappeared. Nor did the British always feel able to retreat. In response to a January protest against Britain's blockading of German exports to America (which Washington regarded as being in conflict with well-established principles of international law), the Foreign Office felt quite unable to accept the American viewpoint or to admit that the legitimate exercise of her belligerent rights could give rise to claims—although adding that claims put forward on solid ground would receive the fullest consider-

17. CAB 65/5, 17 February 1940, p. 221. Halifax's diary entry for 16 February reflects the problem of "balancing interminable risks on two or three sides" (Halifax Papers, A7.8.3, p. 25).

18. Roosevelt to Churchill, 1 February 1940, *F.D.R.: His Personal Letters,* 2:995; Churchill to Roosevelt, 28 February 1940, FO 800/324, pp. 186–87. Roosevelt had written to Churchill: "I wish very much that I could talk things over with you in person—but I am grateful to you for keeping me in touch, as you do." The question of establishing a contraband control base at St. John had been taken up in the cabinet on 27 February (CAB 65/5, p. 266). Ten days later a draft telegram to the U.K. high commissioner in Ottawa, outlining a scheme for the base and proposing the grounds for a joint approach to Washington, was approved by the cabinet (CAB 65/6, p. 51).

ation.[19] And when the U.S. chargé in London told Halifax, with reference to British restrictions on American agricultural imports, that if the roles of the two countries were reversed, Britain would inevitably take the view that America now held, Halifax pointedly demurred: perhaps so, if the United States was engaged in a local, limited war; but certainly not if it were fighting for its life as Britain was now.[20] There was the issue in stark relief: the British were involved in a struggle for existence, which made American complaints appear petty. America suffered, as the British saw it, from "an acute attack of . . . 'neutromania,'" and was still preoccupied with the legal defense of selfish interests. Between the two positions there was still a considerable, even if slowly lessening, chasm. In any case, a friendly conversation between Lothian and Hull on February 24 seemed to lay the January "crisis" finally to rest. The ambassador explained Britain's readiness to do everything possible to meet U.S. wishes and lessen the inconveniences, short of doing anything that would reduce the effectiveness of its blockade of Germany—its most important weapon at the moment. Hull understood and gave the impression of realizing that the public controversy had been permitted to go too far. The two agreed that the situation "should not be taken too seriously and would not be allowed to affect the fundamental goodwill on both sides."[21]

All of this occurred against a background of concern for the condition of American public opinion that continued to preoccupy British officials at all levels. Even Chamberlain had delayed his appointment of Hore-Belisha, recently removed from the War Office, to the Ministry of Information until he had checked out and dismissed a suggestion that the naming of a Jew would discount the value of the ministry in American eyes.[22] Extensive commentary (through minuting) by Foreign Office personnel (often in response to dispatches from Lothian, reports from the British Library of Information in New York, or State Department press releases) attested to a constant awareness of the matter and the basic issues involved. And Lothian was a veritable wellspring of information and observations, writing regularly on the subject not only to the Foreign Office but to a number of individuals as well.

Foreign Office officials did not always agree, and the opinion of one

19. Johnson (U.S. embassy) to Halifax, 17 January 1940; Halifax to Johnson, 21 February 1940; FO 414/277, pp. 10–11, 37–38.

20. Notes for a Meeting of Ministers, 28, 29 February 1940, FO 800/321, pp. 75, 80.

21. Lothian to Halifax, 24 February 1940, FO 414/277, p. 43.

22. Neville to Ida, 7 January 1940, NC 18/1/1137.

often served as a counterbalance to another on various issues. Several examples will illustrate this. Upon receiving a report from the British Library of Information, New York, January 9, demonstrating great American interest in peace aims and fear that, unless peace came soon, America would be drawn into the war against its will, Crowell expressed impatience with American "idealism"—closing one's eyes to the war and thinking about peace—when "everything which we stand for is threatened by disaster." But Gage noted that moralizing was not an exclusively American habit and that U.S. opinion would likely be swung into the war only by a gradual realization that the Allies must win if life was to be tolerable. The best Britain could do at the moment to improve the tone of American articles was to counter German lies as quickly and effectively as possible. Perowne did not attach much importance to American press rationalizations of fear and guilt complexes. He was "not sure . . . that we, at present, need much more from the U.S. than we are getting." When the need arose, Britain would likely get greater assistance. A similar report on American isolation, several weeks later, also drew varied reactions. There was no point in attempting to combat American isolationist sentiment, Crowell asserted; even a clear statement that Britain did not want America in the war in any circumstances would be interpreted as subtle propaganda. The only practical lesson was that speeches and pronouncements likely to have an American audience should avoid abstract words, and "instead of talking about freedom, justice, and the rule of law it would probably be better to refer to concentration camps, firing squads and armed invasions." But abstract words were Roosevelt's way—and the way of all convincing speakers—Stevenson argued. Whitehead thought the survey gave "an entirely false picture." It was true that Americans had a deep-seated suspicion of Britain's role and were decidedly sensitive about what they regarded as its habit of twisting American statements into pro-Allied gestures, but "they also really rather like us." For Balfour, special interest attached to the fact that American isolationism and anti-British sentiment were essentially the same thing; and though he did not draw the obvious moral, it would have been most difficult to ameliorate the latter so long as the former persisted.[23]

Lothian's long summary of American attitudes (dated February 1 and received at the Foreign Office on February 15), in which he counseled patience with America and said that "the destinies of the two countries

23. Foreign Office Minutes, 9, 25, 27 January, FO 391/24238, pp. 95–98, 129, 138–41.

and of the Dominions are now inextricably involved and . . . the future of our civilization depends upon our gradually discovering the basis on which we can confidently cooperate," prompted diverse reactions. Whitehead and Balfour thought it a "brilliant survey," emphasizing the need to demonstrate clearly to Americans that Britain's actions were essential to winning the war. But effective American intervention would require a long period of development, Perowne noted, and would have to occur well before the moment at which Britain was "in the last ditch," militarily or financially. He hoped that Lothian's optimism about eventual U.S. aid was justified, but he seemed to doubt it. Balfour simply wrote: "Anything we can do to cultivate American good will is worth the price of rubies." That view was shared by Scott: if the United States did not help at the right time and in the right way, Britain might lose the war; and the time, manner, and degree of its help would be related to what it thought Britain deserved by its past conduct and its treatment of American interests. In expanding this view some days later, Scott noted that Britain must "take constant account of [American] public opinion, and within the limits of her legitimate war needs, humour it, educate it, and pre-dispose it even more in our favour." The real problem that Britain had not yet faced up to, he added, was that its wartime purchasing had in fact dislocated the American economy. Cadogan thought Scott right to press these points, but "Americans are the most difficult people on earth to deal with," a fact owing most likely to their political system. There was no way Britain could adjust its wartime purchasing without adversely affecting some segment of the American economy, and though he was all for avoiding trouble and making things easier for the Roosevelt administration, "we shan't succeed in either direction, and we had better therefore seek Divine assistance in resigning ourselves." That drew comment from Halifax: yes, but Scott's diagnosis was valuable nonetheless.[24]

Lothian's letters to individuals during these trying weeks reflected a basic, if sometimes cautious, optimism about the movement of American opinion. America was still friendly to the Allies and vehemently against Hitler and Stalin, he wrote to L. S. Amery; but there would be no abandonment of neutrality until its own vital interests were affected in some

24. Lothian to Halifax, 1 February 1940, FO 414/277, p. 36; Foreign Office Minutes, 15 February and after, 1940, FO 371/24238, pp. 215–18; Scott Memorandum and Foreign Office Minutes, 29 February 1940, ibid., pp. 267–71. Scott had set down his latter observations in view of the impending visit of Sumner Welles. His "Note" was sent to the palace for the king's perusal before seeing Welles.

obvious way. He told Lady Astor that what ultimately counted in America was not the president or secretary of state but public opinion. And the American people were slowly making up their minds, he wrote Sir Samuel Hoare, that in their own and civilization's interest they would have to intervene: "There is a rising feeling that the U.S. is playing an unworthy part in one of the great dramas of history, and is in danger of losing her soul unless she shoulders her share of the burden"; but Britain must not offer advice to Americans about what they ought to do; they must reach their own conclusions. The mass of Americans still believed that Britain and France could win the war without American assistance, he wrote Viscount Samuel, but "the top people are not nearly so confident, especially on the economic side." Presumably this would translate eventually into something practical. Britain was "drifting into difficult waters" with the United States, he wrote Sir Alan Lascelles on February 20, and Americans were extremely sensitive about British propaganda that might drag them into war. But it was still the administration's view that it was in America's own interest to support the Allies by every means short of war. And that fact would, he thought, "steady the boat sufficiently" until the election was over. To Halifax he conceded that Americans were paralyzed by fear of being drawn into war and doubt about what it would achieve in the way of peace and lasting improvement; but "underneath they are hungering in this country for idealism and for sacrifice for a constructive cause"; that hunger might someday precipitate America into vigorous cooperation. So for Lothian at least, hope continued to prevail, although the end that he sought would have to be slowly and carefully nurtured.[25]

To Halifax, on February 27, Lothian posed an interesting question: was the British government contemplating a resummoning of the old Imperial War Cabinet of 1918? "The more the Empire aspect of the war can be visibly represented the better from the American point of view," he believed. There was in America no suspicion of, or antipathy to, the dominions, and the reconstruction of something like the old Imperial War Cabinet would help to strengthen the argument that the Allies were fighting for the freedom of small nations and weaken the German view that this was just a war between two imperialisms. He continued:

25. Lothian to Amery, 9 January 1940, Lothian Papers, GD 40/17/398, p. 166; Lothian to Lady Astor, 27 January 1940, Astor Papers, MS 1416/1/4/59; Templewood, *Nine Troubled Years,* pp. 417–18; Lothian to Samuel, 8 February 1940, Lothian Papers, GD 40/17/404, pp. 339–40; Lothian to Lascelles, 20 February 1940, FO 800/398; Lothian to Halifax, 11 March 1940, ibid.

> If the United States is ever to come out of isolation and move towards cooperation with us, she would be far more likely to do so if the proposal is to cooperate with a British commonwealth of free nations all of whom are obviously taking a hand in formulating policy and wartime decisions than with a Britain which would seem once more to be bossing the show.[26]

No reply appears in the file.

J. C. Smuts, South African prime minister, wrote a letter concerning American—and world—opinion at the end of January that circulated among the highest British officials. Unless the war was shortened by the internal breakdown of Germany, he told Maurice Hankey, "the ultimate issue may once more depend on the U.S.A. and this is strong reason why we should keep neutral world opinion with us." Americans, Smuts reasoned, were susceptible to "that strong force, which will in the end weigh more heavily with them than the isolation of the Middle West." No nation was more capable of sudden and violent changes of public opinion than America, and the more frightful the Germans became and the more dangerous the war to their own interests, the more violently Americans would swing toward Britain, *if* in the meantime she had not lost the support of world opinion. Hankey sent copies of this letter to Chamberlain, Eden, Simon, Halifax, and Churchill. Eden felt "in pretty close agreement with the whole letter," and Halifax found that "it exactly represents my own view as to the imponderable importance of neutral opinion." Though Chamberlain thought Smuts "unduly pessimistic"—presumably about the ultimate issue depending once more on America—he agreed about "the importance of keeping ourselves right in world opinion."[27]

Specific issues that arose in the course of events tended, naturally, to call into question the more abstract theorizing about America and its potential, future role. One such event was the shocking—at least for the British—revelation in early February that President Roosevelt was about to send Under Secretary of State Sumner Welles on a tour of Rome, Berlin, Paris, and London for the purpose of gathering information about the possibility of a negotiated peace. A complex of factors figured in Roosevelt's thinking. In a general sense, there was his lingering Wilsonian outlook, reinforced by elements in the State Department, that still saw a role for the United States in preventing or diverting traditional European power struggles. The idea of a negotiated peace died hard,

26. Lothian to Halifax, 27 February 1940, FO 800/309, pp. 122–24.

27. Smuts to Hankey, 26 January 1940, HNKY 5/1; Hankey to Chamberlain, 23 February 1940; Eden to Hankey and Halifax to Hankey, 24 February 1940, HNKY 4/32.

especially in view of accumulating appeals, which he had thus far ignored, for Roosevelt to play a mediating role. In a more specific way, the president had feared for some time that the Allies were too weak to resist a German assault and was encouraged in that fear by dispatches from Bullitt and Kennedy throughout the fall of 1939. If Britain and France collapsed, the chances of keeping America out of war would be greatly diminished. Further, the president somehow needed to convince himself, as well as the American people and others around the world, that he had made every honorable effort to head off impending catastrophe. If the effort failed to produce positive diplomatic result, it would nonetheless advance the education of the American people in the futility of dealing with Hitler and the difficulty of ultimately keeping out of war. At the very least, it would produce information about important European leaders that would be useful to the president. There were considerations of domestic politics as well. A peace initiative that resulted in serious discussions would greatly enhance his political strength and solidify support for a third term, which he now was clearly contemplating. It would also diminish the challenge of the isolationists to his foreign policy. With all these considerations running through his mind, Roosevelt determined to examine the chances for a peace settlement before a German spring offensive shattered the quiet of the Western front. He fully realized that the odds were slim and that to succeed he would need the combined powers of "the Holy Ghost and Jack Dempsey." But he owed it to the American people, he told Welles—who was instrumental in helping persuade the president to proceed—to leave no stone unturned.[28]

The Welles mission was publicly announced on February 9. Muting its real purpose (to explore the possibilities for peace) in response to warnings that an avowed peace effort would damage the spirit of unity and resolution in London and Paris and provoke a renewed surge of isolationist criticism at home, Roosevelt said it was designed solely to advise himself and Hull "as to present conditions in Europe." Welles was authorized to make no proposals or commitments, and statements made to him by the officials of other governments would be kept in strict confidence and communicated only to the president and the secretary of

28. Dallek, *Franklin Roosevelt and American Foreign Policy,* pp. 215–17; Cole, *Roosevelt and the Isolationists,* pp. 340–41; Reynolds, *Creating the Anglo-American Alliance,* pp. 69–72; Offner, *Origins of the Second World War,* pp. 169–73; Langer and Gleason, *The Challenge to Isolation,* pp. 361–75. Welles relates the story of his mission in *The Time for Decision.*

state.[29] The British had learned of the president's plan a week before, when Roosevelt had summoned Lothian to tell him. (The French were not informed in advance; Roosevelt feared a leak to the press.) In that situation Roosevelt had explained the mission's purpose—so Lothian reported to London—in terms of satisfying himself and American public opinion that every possibility of ending the war had been explored in view of the inevitable Nazi spring offensive against Britain and Britain's need to retaliate. He was not hopeful that Welles would find an acceptable basis for agreement, but that would enable him to declare that Germany was the obstacle to peace and that its people were being made to fight not for national security and integrity but for aggression. If Chamberlain had any comment, the president added, he would gladly receive it upon his return to Washington from a weekend absence. Lothian told Roosevelt that the Welles trip would produce "a profound effect in Europe of mingled hope and anxiety," and might lead to a weakening of Allied morale.[30] His prediction of anxiety in London was on the mark indeed.

The British were considerably less than enthusiastic about Roosevelt's proposal. Cadogan wrote in his diary, February 2: "About lunch-time telegram from Roosevelt about his awful, half-baked, idea of sending Sumner Welles (!) over here with a flourish of trumpets to collect data on which Roosevelt is to proclaim basis of peace!" And he was the primary drafter of Britain's response. The six-page telegram that went to Lothian over Chamberlain's name on February 3 tried to avoid giving the impression that the impulse which inspired the "courageous proposal" was not fully appreciated. But it expressed deep anxiety lest the move embarrass the democracies to Germany's advantage (unconvinced as it was of the failure of the policy of force) and pointed to the "utmost difficulty" with which the British people—and no doubt the French as well—could be persuaded that *any* settlement was worth signing with Hitler or the Nazi regime. It also set forth various points of clarification about the situation in Europe as seen from London. Chief among them

29. Press Conference Announcement, 9 February 1940, PSF, Box 63. In making the announcement, Roosevelt was unusually "short" with the press correspondents, discouraging them from trying "to break it down by impossible questions," telling them just to "stand on the language" of the statement, and warning that "probably anything you add . . . to enlarge on this . . . will be wrong" (*FDR Press Conferences,* 9 February 1940, 15:140–43).

30. Lothian to Halifax, 2 February 1940, FO 800/324, pp. 137–39. Welles told Lothian next day that if the 100-to-1 chance of obtaining agreement did not come off, he thought the only statement Roosevelt could make would be that he regretted that no agreement was in sight (Lothian to Halifax, 3 February 1940, ibid., p. 164).

were these: word of a great German spring offensive was part of a war of nerves directed against neutrals as well as belligerents and not "necessarily conclusive" as to peace being more difficult to attain later on; and any peace settlement must include guarantees against the renewal of aggression "during our lifetimes." Chamberlain felt "considerable diffidence" in making suggestions, but thought that Poland should be included in Welles's tour and perhaps Finland. The mission would prompt a lot of ill-informed discussion in nearly all quarters, and Roosevelt should make clear in his announcement his own conviction "that the first essential purpose to be achieved is durability of any settlement arrived at." One special problem the British foresaw was the encouragement of division within free and open societies, in contrast to the apparent unity into which the German people "will remain dragooned."[31]

The British had been expecting a peace move from either the Italian government, the pope, or President Roosevelt, but had not foreseen that it would be so spectacular as a public mission from Washington, with objectives fully advertised in advance. They could not help suspecting, Lothian was informed, "that what the President now proposed to do is precisely what Hitler hoped he would do." Circulating stories about the irresistibility of Germany's offensive power were a part of German propaganda, they believed, and moves for peace without proper and essential conditions would only play into Hitler's hands. They were also concerned about the influence of defeatist Ambassador Kennedy and "certain [unnamed] American businessmen with dubious political connections" in fixing Roosevelt's policy.[32]

The depth of negative feeling is clear from Foreign Office reactions to an informal conversation of February 4 between Graham Hutton, of the Foreign Office, and Butterworth, of the U.S. embassy. Butterworth, just returned from Washington, reported that American officials really were alarmed at the situation facing Britain. "The boys around Roosevelt" (the architects of the New Deal)—isolationist, autarkic, and fervidly nationalist—foresaw no German collapse and were terribly concerned about being drawn into the war if it dragged on. Their views of what would constitute a sound peace were strongly colored by an underlying pessimism about American involvement, and any chance of peace was

31. *Cadogan Diaries,* p. 250; Chamberlain to Lothian, 3 February 1940, FO 800/324, pp. 165–70.

32. Telegram to Lothian, 4 February 1940, FO 800/324, p. 173. The sender of this telegram is unclear; it appears to be Halifax, acting for the prime minister.

ipso facto a chance for the Democrats, if not Roosevelt, to retain control of American destinies.[33] For Scott this seemed to confirm doubt on Roosevelt's part that the Allies could win; thus the last moment for an attempt at peace was at hand. But even if Britain told him that Welles's mission would damage its interests, he would proceed anyway, feeling that he was saving the British from themselves. So *whatever* impression Welles gained in Europe, he would almost certainly report to Roosevelt in such a way as to make it nearly inevitable that the peace campaign be pushed further. And, since the Germans would promise anything, knowing Britain would not accept their promises, the British would be "pilloried as the obstacle to peace." Sargent agreed with Scott's analysis of Roosevelt's motives; unless he stopped the war quickly, the United States would be called upon to rescue Britain and France—and presumably rescuing them from bankruptcy would be as disagreeable as rescuing them from defeat. Again Cadogan's ire burst forth: "I think this confirms our suspicions about the origins and motives of Mr. Roosevelt's latest half-baked scheme, which we are trying to kill by kindness—and firmness." Halifax thought this record "interesting enough for the P.M. to see," and Chamberlain examined it, without written comment, on February 8. As a sort of postlude, Vansittart suggested that Britain could do a great deal more "to warn President Roosevelt off any undesirable grass, before we have to receive the grass-snake, Mr. Welles."[34]

A further exchange between Chamberlain and Roosevelt took place February 6–8. When Lothian delivered Chamberlain's telegram of February 3, Roosevelt "expressed appreciation and general agreement with it." In any published instructions to Welles, he would avoid use of the word "peace" and simply refer to a tour of inquiry. Welles would be told to inform Berlin that any attack on France and Britain "which showed any prospect of success" would inevitably bring the United States closer to intervention. Feeling the situation to be one "in which a little audacity might have tremendous results," Lothian asked Roosevelt whether Welles could not warn Germany that it was impossible to defeat Britain because before it could succeed, the United States would intervene. This might be the surest way of preventing the kind of attack that would force American intervention; and if Germany could be convinced, then the president might make a proposal for ending the war on terms that would provide security for all. Roosevelt did not dispute that "some

33. Record of Conversation, 5 February 1940, FO 371/24238, pp. 228–32.
34. Foreign Office Minutes, 7–8 February 1940, ibid., pp. 225–27.

such step was the right one to take," Lothian reported, but it was politically impracticable for him to do so. He could probably get 40 percent of the American people to support it, but less than 25 percent of Congress, which he thought more backward than the country. Thus, raising the issue in a presidential election year would only result in a violent campaign and the return of an extremely isolationist Congress. Such a step would be practicable only after events compelled Americans to face realities that it was not yet feasible to place before them.[35]

Chamberlain added a new dimension on February 7. In order to keep Roosevelt acquainted with "the inner movements here," he revealed that Britain and France, as a result of discussions two days earlier, were pressing preparations to send military forces to the aid of Finland (which had been under attack by Russia since late November 1939) "when the critical period approaches," probably not later than the third week in March. They would have to ask Norway and Sweden to provide necessary facilities for the passage of forces and were now worried that announcement of the Welles mission would interfere with the success of that plan. Specifically, if Norway and Sweden got the idea that some sort of peace negotiations were likely, they might refuse the facilities required "to save Finland," excusing themselves on the ground that Finland would no doubt be looked after in the coming negotiations and that, if they should fail and Finland was destroyed, the responsibility would not be theirs.[36] In briefing Lothian about this development, Halifax noted that for this reason and those earlier presented to Roosevelt, "we hope the President will not pursue his plan." But he left to Lothian's judgment how far to go in dissuading him. If he was determined to send Welles, Halifax hoped there would be no public announcement. If there must be a public announcement, it should not be in any form that would suggest that the mission was part of a peace plan.[37]

In relaying Chamberlain's latest concern to the White House, Lothian

35. Lothian to Chamberlain, 6 February 1940; Lothian to Halifax, 7 February 1940; FO 800/324, pp. 175, 181–82. Cadogan thought Roosevelt "shaken" by British arguments (*Cadogan Diaries*, pp. 253–54).

36. Chamberlain to Lothian, 7 February 1940, FO 800/324, pp. 177–78. Chamberlain explained to Roosevelt that Anglo-French intentions to aid Finland grew out of: (1) the potential indictment of the two governments, by their own people, for having betrayed the cause for which they took up arms; and (2) the fact that the conquest of Finland would mean the practical subjugation of Scandinavia to Germany and Russia.

37. Halifax to Lothian, 7 February 1940, ibid., p. 179. Halifax thought it unfortunate that Rome was the first stop on Welles's itinerary. That would give the impression that Roosevelt was acting in concert with the pope, and it would be better if that could be avoided.

was assured by Roosevelt that the procedure he proposed to use would remove the dangers the prime minister feared. He would explain publicly that Welles was not going on a peace mission but merely to assess the situation. He would send personal letters to the kings of Norway and Sweden explaining that there was only a thousand-to-one chance of peace and that the mission was merely one of inquiry. He would make it clear that there was no connection with any Vatican peace plan. Further, Welles would have private instructions that Roosevelt was not interested in a truce or an unstable peace, and that "anything like a successful attack on France or England would inevitably bring the United States nearer war."[38] That is where matters stood when Roosevelt made his February 9 announcement—which Cadogan labeled "not too bad," although "that croaker Cordell Hull also announced talks with neutrals about a 'peace settlement' which 'might be extended to belligerents.'" A further telegram to the president, in draft form, was laid aside by Cadogan (Chamberlain consenting to send nothing) "now that Roosevelt has splashed all his stuff."[39]

By this time Lothian was of the opinion that the Welles mission did not mean much. Roosevelt felt he ought to explore the situation, but did not think that anything practical would come of it. Indeed, shortly after Welles's departure for Europe on February 16, the ambassador wrote to his sister, Roosevelt had gone fishing in the Pacific. Meantime, one of Lothian's regular informants, Sir Samuel Hoare, had written him that there was not the least chance of peace in the near future, and "any attempt to push one would only irritate democratic opinion." Public sentiment in Britain was solidly behind the war effort, and neutrals were coming to the view that Germany could not win. Welles would see that for himself; indeed, his visit to Britain might prove "a useful antidote against the defeatism of people like Kennedy." Halifax too was moderately reassured, writing in his diary: "Roosevelt's announcement . . . has . . . gone tamely, which is all to the good." But the Foreign Office remained wary. To Lothian's suggestion that Welles, as head of the president's unofficial committee on Anglo-American postwar economic cooperation, might meet with Sir George Schuster, his British counterpart,

38. Lothian to Chamberlain, 8 February 1940, ibid., p. 183.

39. *Cadogan Diaries*, p. 254. Although Hull's statement that "diplomatic conversations of an informal character have been commenced with neutral Governments" was generally linked by the press to the Welles mission, the secretary of state explained that their purpose was to determine an equitable economic basis for peace after the war rather than to seek a cessation of hostilities in Europe (Lothian to Halifax, 13 February 1940, FO 414/277, p. 32).

when he was in London, reaction was sharply negative. Among the six officials who so responded, feeling that London must move very carefully until it was much clearer what the president intended, Whitehead warned against providing the State Department with a channel to force consideration of an early peace on Britain; Scott saw "every possibility of complications—and worse"; and Kirkpatrick noted his instinct against initiating any cooperation between the two countries.[40]

The British followed Welles's visits to Rome and Berlin with interest, but received little information about how things were going. Halifax told the cabinet on February 27 of word from Sir Percy Loraine, British ambassador to Rome, that Welles had had "a most satisfactory" interview with Count Ciano, the Italian foreign minister. But Loraine himself had learned "little of interest" in a luncheon conversation with Welles. He did, however, report that Roosevelt's emissary hoped to arrive in Britain between March 8 and 10. British attention was directed toward how to handle Welles when he reached London. Halifax warned his fellow ministers of the danger that Welles might receive from Hitler "a mass of specious material which might take him in." And Scott reminded fellow Foreign Office personnel of two important points constantly to bear in mind about the visit. First, the forthcoming presidential election was regarded by all Americans as an issue of transcendent importance; and whatever the ultimate purpose of Welles's visit, he would inevitably be thinking the whole time of how anything he saw or heard affected that issue. Second, Welles would no doubt cling obstinately to the view that the American continent could safeguard its neutrality by isolating itself behind a neutrality zone. Although the idea was now "wholly fallacious," its roots were deep in American history, and Welles cherished it with "an almost religious fervor."[41]

Attention also turned to the social side of the visit, as Lothian advised that "every attention and courtesy" be paid to Welles, who had "distinct views regarding his own importance," as well as to Pierrepont Moffat

40. Lothian to Lady Astor, 10 February 1940, Astor Papers, MS 1416/1/4/59; Lothian to Lady Minna Butler-Thwing, 22 February 1940, Lothian Papers, GD 40/17/470, p. 10; Hoare to Lothian, 13 February 1940, Templewood Papers, XI:5; Halifax Papers (Diary), 12 February 1940, A7.8.3, p. 19; Foreign Office Minutes, 17–20 February 1940, FO 371/24248, pp. 1–1A. When in London, Welles agreed that the two committees might exchange ideas informally, but there should be no formal connection between them. Some general correspondence followed in April among Welles, Schuster, and Sir Horace Wilson. FO 371/24248, pp. 22–23, 34–50.

41. CAB 65/5, 27, 29 February 1940, pp. 266, 277; Notes of a Meeting of Ministers, 29 February 1940, FO 800/321, p. 80; Foreign Office Minutes, 7 March 1940, FO 371/24254, pp. 1–2.

(traveling with Welles), on whose good offices the Washington embassy was very dependent. Accordingly, Herschel Johnson, chargé at the American embassy, was notified of British readiness both to offer Welles fitting entertainment and to arrange for him to see anyone or anything he wanted to see. Neither proved, at length, to be a problem. There were various private offers to entertain Welles, who indicated through Kennedy—who "blew in" (Halifax's term) to the Foreign Office on the afternoon of March 8—that he did not want any dinner party larger than eight. This prompted Halifax to write in his diary, "It looks, therefore, like being the same dinner every night."[42]

The British sense of courtesy, however, did not extend to an easy sharing of military information. In anticipation of Welles's visit to London, the American military attaché, General Miles, sought from the War Office permission to visit the British Expeditionary Force, a statement of the composition of British forces, and an outline of plans for expansion. On advice from the Foreign Office, all his requests were denied. Although nearly a year before, the U.S. ambassador had been given particulars on British air strength for transmission to Roosevelt, the situation was deemed by the cabinet to be different now that Britain was at war. When Welles reached London, confidential discussions would no doubt touch upon military matters; but until that time, details should wait. As if to reassure his colleagues, Hankey (minister without portfolio) told them that this was consistent with the way Colonel House had been handled as President Wilson's emissary in 1915.[43]

Welles arrived in London on March 10 (and was met at Heston airport by Cadogan). He carried a simple handwritten note from Roosevelt to Chamberlain:

> My dear Chamberlain,
> Sumner Welles, my Under Secretary of State and an old boyhood friend, will give you this. What you tell him will be maintained in the strictest confidence and will be told solely to myself and Cordell Hull on my talk with him on his return. At this grave moment I deeply hope this exchange

42. Lothian to Scott, 29 February 1940, FO 800/324, p. 190; Stevenson Minutes, 1–2 March 1940, ibid., p. 193; Halifax Papers (Diary), 8 March 1940, A7.8.3, p. 143. Among those offering to entertain Welles were Anthony Eden (who described Welles as a "rather stiff dog" who had nonetheless been good to him when he was in Washington a year before), Clement Attlee, and Ronald Tree (Eden to Halifax, about 1 March 1940, FO 800/324, pp. 191, 195).

43. CAB 65/6, 2 March 1940, p. 28.

of views may be of real value towards a peace which is neither "unconclusive nor precarious." Enough said. My warm regards.

Faithfully,
Franklin D. Roosevelt[44]

Conversations with British officials took place over the next few days. Although Cadogan thought Welles "clam-like," and Hoare labeled him "a complacent, well-meaning 'fat,'" other reactions were more positive. Chatfield "liked the look of him" and got "a good impression of honesty of purpose." Halifax found him to be a person whom, "much to my surprise, I liked." Expecting to encounter "a very stiff, unsympathetic creature," he was (he recorded in his diary) "favorably disappointed." Halifax thought Welles "remote from the facts still," and inclined to believe that the European problem could be solved by paper ingenuity in devising arrangements about disarmament. But he found that discussion with him went rather well. Chamberlain reported to his sister that Welles's manner was at first "distinctly stiff," but as he got closer to him, he concluded that he was "the best type of American I have met for a long time." This assessment was perhaps enhanced by Welles's declaration, obviously pleasing to Chamberlain, that the president had a deep admiration for him and would like nothing better than an opportunity of meeting—although he realized that was not possible at present. Some people, Chamberlain continued, thought he and Roosevelt would not understand each other; but Welles "thought we should understand one another perfectly."[45] As the conversations closed, Chamberlain reciprocated Roosevelt's handwritten note (March 13):

My dear Roosevelt,

Your very kind letter . . . was duly handed to me by Sumner Welles, whom it was a great pleasure to me to meet. We have had two frank and intimate talks and he knows exactly how the situation appears to me.

I sincerely hope that his mission may have fruitful results, if not immediately, yet in time to avert the worst catastrophe.

Meanwhile may I say how deeply I admire the courage and humanity with which you are striving to grapple with this last and culminating effort to establish the rule of force.

Yours sincerely,
Neville Chamberlain[46]

44. Roosevelt's handwritten note, dated 14 February, is filed in NC 7/11/33/141.

45. *Cadogan Diaries*, pp. 260–61; Templewood Papers, XI:5; Chatfield to Lothian, 14 March 1940, CHT/6/2, p. 194; Halifax Papers (Diary), 11 March 1940, A7.8.3, pp. 46–47; Neville to Ida, 16 March 1940, NC 18/1/1147.

46. PSF, Departmental Correspondence, Box 63.

Chamberlain gave an account to the cabinet of his discussions with Welles; and the nature of the conversations, as well as his perceptions of them, can be distilled from it. Welles had reached the conclusion, Chamberlain reported, that any successful peace proposal would have to provide the sense of security against further aggression required by the Allies and to permit Hitler to continue in the German government. He thought the necessary sense of security could be obtained by general disarmament of a far-reaching character and the possible creation of an international air force that would act as a sanction to prevent Germany from descending on small nations in the future. Chamberlain responded that Welles "was aiming at the impossible." The Allies had gone into the war to convince Germany and the world that force did not pay, and any solution that would enable Hitler to claim otherwise would be unacceptable. Rejecting the idea that it was possible to secure disarmament first and confidence thereafter, Chamberlain thought it "fantastic to believe" that nations that had lived for so long under terror from Germany could be persuaded to give up the means of defending themselves unless there was "a complete change of heart" in Germany. No doubt the best security for the peace of the world was the united strength of France and Britain. Were disarmament to occur, it would have to be very gradual and qualitative in nature. The United States would never give any guarantee to Europe, Welles had said, but it would participate in the international supervision of disarmament and in economic reconstruction. Chamberlain concluded that Roosevelt would make some attempt to bring the war to an end, even if it should be embarrassing to Britain; so it was important to avoid illusions about Britain's position.[47]

Churchill then reported on his conversation with Welles. The British people had been greatly impressed before the war, he had told Roosevelt's emissary, by the strength of feeling in the United States that Nazism must be crushed. Now that Britain had entered the war, it must fight it to a finish, "even though this meant putting all to the stake." To bring about a peace settlement, Churchill looked to the establishment of some international body on the lines of the League of Nations, an international tribunal for dealing with justifiable disputes, and possibly an international air force. But there was no value in discussing peace terms until Germany had been absolutely defeated; peace propaganda in the United States would only do harm, and Britain's defeat by Germany, he shrewdly warned Welles, might well result in the surrender of its fleet,

47. CAB 65/6, 13 March 1940, pp. 67–68.

which would leave Berlin at once in command of a fleet larger than America's. No disarmament would be satisfactory that did not provide for equality in the means of rearmament, since otherwise an aggressor state could so reorganize its factory system as to enable it to rearm in defiance of the terms of the peace settlement. He flatly denied that the United States would be ruined if the war continued, as some like Kennedy contended; in all countries the standard of life in 1940 was higher than at the time of the last war.[48]

If Britain pursued her course resolutely, it would win the war, Simon and Kingsley Wood (secretary of state for Air) had impressed upon Welles. He must realize, Simon noted, the strength of Britain's resources and not go back to Washington with the impression that peace proposals (the real object of which was to reassure American fears) "would serve also to save us from destruction." Generally, the sense of British resolution must have been conveyed effectively to Welles. Euan Wallace, minister of transport, certainly thought so, recording in his diary: "This gentleman [Welles] appears to have arrived with the idea that since neither side was likely to win the war this summer, it might be just as well to make peace without obliging the Nazis to liberate Austria, Czechoslovakia, and Poland. He left . . . with his point of view very substantially altered."[49]

Upon departing London, Welles revisited Rome before returning to Washington. Chamberlain, thinking more at the moment about a peace initiative from Rome than from Washington, believed that Mussolini would learn from him that "the attitude of the Allies was very stiff." Welles would indicate the conditions essential to any settlement, and Mussolini would then consider whether such terms were likely to be acceptable to Hitler. All this would take time, so Chamberlain did not expect "any spectacular development . . . in the immediate future." At the same time, he drew a curious conclusion from Welles's opinion that there was a very slim chance—1 in 10,000, he had put it—that Hitler could be brought to the point of agreeing to give up "most of what Nazism stands for." Chamberlain thought him mistaken, but knowing Hitler's capacity to put himself temporarily into different or contradictory moods, he could see how a mistake might be made. But then, reverting to his habit of inventing rays of hope, he added: "That Hitler

48. Ibid. Eden also had told Welles that he saw no way out save the defeat of Germany and the establishment of a new regime there. Life in a Europe under German hegemony would not be worth living. Eden, *The Reckoning*, pp. 105–6.

49. CAB 65/6, 13 March 1940, pp. 67–68; Wallace Diary, 9–17 March 1940, p. 135.

should have talked in such a way seems to me significant of a lurking want of confidence at the bottom of his mind." Chamberlain had also told Welles that he was skeptical of a German spring offensive—a view that Welles did not share—and interpreted Welles's shock at Mussolini's appearance to mean the Duce was suffering under severe strain.[50]

Halifax, meantime, was attempting to deal with American journalists, whose main preoccupation seemed to him to be the risk of Britain's accepting a patchwork peace. "I lose no opportunity," he wrote in his diary, "of trying to tell these people politely something of our feeling at being the constant recipients of good advice from them, who themselves take no very active part." Nor was he comforted by a talk with journalist Walter Lippmann, who was apprehensive about what Welles and Roosevelt might do under the pressure of American politics.[51]

As a kind of post-mortem to Welles's visit to London, Vansittart composed, on March 18, a memorandum that, despite the author's penchant for irritation and his long-declining influence in British policy formulation, nonetheless indicates the trail of bitterness that the Welles mission left in certain quarters. Seeing Welles "more and more clearly as an international danger," he thought his idea of security through disarmament "not only a delusion but a deathtrap," adding:

> But . . . Welles' chief crime towards common sense and humanity is that he has now gone so far as to want us to make peace with Hitler. That surely is lunacy for which both he and his chief, President Roosevelt, deserve the highest condemnation. It is now pretty clear . . . that President Roosevelt is ready to play a dirty trick on the world and risk the ultimate destruction of the Western Democracies in order to secure the re-election of a Democratic candidate in the United States. It is not only the Prime Minister who has drawn this deduction; it is the general expectation of everybody that I know who also knows anything of the American situation.

Worried lest "this criminal maneuver" be initiated before Britain could stop it, Vansittart felt that Britain should pressure Roosevelt "to prevent him from selling the world for his own particular mess of pottage." The president should be told that the British were "horrified" at the idea of making peace with Hitler and would have absolutely none of it. If this were not done quickly, Britain would soon be confronted with impossible proposals touched up speciously on paper or designed to push her

50. CAB 65/6, 15 March 1940, p. 81; Neville to Ida, 16 March 1940, NC 18/1/1147.
51. Halifax Papers (Diary), 15 March 1940, A7.8.3, pp. 53–54.

into the dock. And he added as a postscript: Welles knew perfectly well that any peace proposals from Hitler were "pure eyewash."[52]

Vansittart need not have worried quite so much. Roosevelt read a statement to the press on March 29 that Welles had concluded his mission without making any peace proposals in the name of the United States government or receiving proposals from any source. The information he had obtained would be of great value in the conduct of U.S. foreign relations, but there was "*scant immediate prospect*" (Roosevelt's emphasis) for a just and lasting peace in Europe. One week before, Lothian had called upon Hull to express the thanks of the British for his promptness in acting to dispel the "peace at any price" rumors that had arisen from Welles's activity in Europe. And Hull later wrote: "Nothing he [Welles] learned gave us any basis for action. The leaders he talked to offered no real hope for peace." The Welles mission was thus the last peace initiative undertaken by President Roosevelt. It shattered whatever illusions about a negotiated peace that still lingered in Washington and helped prepare the president for the catastrophe about to befall Europe.[53]

If Roosevelt had sent Welles to Europe thinking it could do no harm, even if it did no good, he was not entirely correct in his assessment. Although British concerns were perhaps exaggerated and Welles's visit to London went better than expected, suspicions lingered. Even Halifax's message to Roosevelt, conveyed through Arthur Murray—that it was a great reassurance to know that Roosevelt and the British had "exactly the same values"—seemed as much a message of encouragement to the president as a sign of British confidence. Of course, events initiated by Hitler soon altered everything. If one of Roosevelt's motives in sending Welles had been to delay—even for a week or a month—if not to prevent a pending German offensive, thus giving the British and French more time to prepare, this was not understood in London, where doubt remained that there would be an offensive. And if Welles's visits to Paris and London were only "window-dressing" (inasmuch as Roosevelt already knew the thinking of the French and British) calculated to balance the picture while he got the real "low-down" on Hitler and Mussolini in Berlin and Rome, that too was not appreciated by the British. Indeed, it caused some additional difficulty with Roosevelt's ambassadors in

52. This memorandum is printed in its entirety in Bullitt, *For the President,* pp. 404–5.

53. *FDR Press Conferences,* 15:210–11; Hull, *Memoirs,* 1:740; Langer and Gleason, *The Challenge to Isolation,* p. 375.

Paris and London. Neither had received prior notice of Welles's mission, and Bullitt believed that he had an understanding with Roosevelt that *he* was the chief presidential adviser on European affairs. Sensitivities were exacerbated in a way that adversely affected these relationships—and wartime policymaking—later on.[54]

Kennedy, of course, had long before incurred the displeasure, if not the wrath, of British officials. Nothing had happened during the first months of 1940 to improve the situation. Halifax told the cabinet early in the new year of a report that Kennedy, on leave in Washington, was behind the recent American peace move; and there was suspicion in London, especially at the Foreign Office, that he had a hand in promoting the Welles mission. Foreign Office minutes at the end of January, in relation to a news item about Kennedy's pending return to Britain and his recuperation from an illness brought on by wartime duties in London, clearly show the nature of feeling about him. Perowne, who had heard that Kennedy was spreading it all over the States that the British were "whopped" in this war and did not have an earthly chance of winning, noted sarcastically: "The rigours of life in London in wartime are so considerable that they induce illness in certain ambassadors some 2 months after they have returned to their native lands!" Balfour added: "Gastric trouble contracted no doubt at the dining tables of Mayfair." It was left to Vansittart, sure that Perowne's report was true, to summarize things: "Mr. Kennedy is a very foul specimen of double-crosser and defeatist. He thinks of nothing but his own pocket. I hope that this war will at least see the elimination of his type." Presumably the British would have to take him back, but he should be "estimated at his true value—which is heavily minus—both here and at No. 10." It was agreed all around that there was nothing to be gained in saying anything to Washington about Kennedy at this juncture, or in trying to convert him to a different view upon his return. His outlook seemed to be based "on some fundamental and emotional attitude of mind rather than on reason." Halifax nonetheless volunteered to have a "firm talk" with Kennedy—if he returned to London.[55]

54. Murray to Roosevelt, 5 April 1940, PSF, Diplomatic Correspondence, Box 29; Robert Murphy, *Diplomat among Warriors,* pp. 54–55; Bullitt, *For the President,* p. 403. On Roosevelt's motives, see *The War Diary of Breckinridge Long,* p. 64.

55. CAB 65/11, 8 January 1940, p. 57; Foreign Office Minutes, 18–25 January 1940, FO 371/24251, pp. 54–57; Foreign Office Minutes, 29 January–1 February 1940, FO 371/24248, pp. 145–48; Halifax Minute, 15 February 1940, FO 371/24251, p. 61. The Foreign Office was deeply concerned about Kennedy's request (of the U.S. embassy) for pacifist literature to be for-

As Kennedy sailed for Britain in late February, Lothian reported Kennedy's talks in America to have been pro-Ally but "frightfully defeatist." He saw nothing but gloom ahead, mainly for economic reasons.[56] The ambassador's expected return prompted further Foreign Office commentary. Balfour considered him "malevolent and pigeon-livered" and quoted Hamlet about being one part wisdom and three parts coward. Scott urged that Kennedy no longer be treated like an honorary member of the cabinet, which drew a reaction from Halifax: "I should think it is a diminishing temptation." A serious effort was made by Whitehead to explain Kennedy's attitudes in terms of his political position (as a representative of a Catholic, Irish, anti-English group), his belief that Britain would collapse financially before it could win the war, and the ghost of Walter Hines Page (whom many well-educated Americans considered a traitor, "having handed himself over body and soul to Downing Street" during World War I). But these explanations, Balfour noted, were no excuse for Kennedy's "spontaneous advertisement of defeatism." C. A. Warner's contribution to the discussion was word from a reliable American journalist that neither Roosevelt nor the State Department had any confidence in Kennedy but wanted to get him out of the way, since he was in a position to control 25 million Catholic votes. The ambassador, for his part, was hardly enthusiastic about returning to London, telling another American diplomat that everything he could do there could be done by a $50-a-month clerk, and expressing his desire to quit, except that he did not know how to do it gracefully before the fall elections.[57]

In speaking with Kennedy on March 8, Halifax described the "solid determination" of the British people, imploring him to understand Britain's resolution not to be deceived into trusting any assurances of the present German government, which experience had shown were worthless, and to accept only a settlement that would give complete security against a recurrence of aggression. Kennedy's response—*not* directly to Halifax but in sharing his feelings about British attitudes with other

---

warded urgently; Stevenson wondered whether it was required for Welles's edification before he started on his trip (FO 371/24251, pp. 58–59).

56. Lothian to Halifax, 27 February 1940, FO 800/324, p. 184. Interestingly, Breckinridge Long had found Kennedy much disturbed at the growth of anti-British feeling in America (*The War Diary of Breckinridge Long*, p. 59).

57. Foreign Office Minutes, 3–4 March 1940, FO 371/24251, pp. 85–86; Warner to Balfour, 3 March 1940, ibid., p. 63; Foreign Office Minutes, 6–9 March 1940, ibid., pp. 65–66; Murphy, *Diplomat among Warriors*, p. 58.

Americans in the context of Welles's visit—was paraphrased by Moffat (traveling with Welles) as follows: "For Christ's sake, stop trying to make this a holy war, because no one will believe you; you're fighting for your life as an Empire, and that's good enough." This outlook disturbed not simply the British but some Americans as well, as demonstrated by an altercation between Kennedy and Bullitt at the State Department before Kennedy's return to London. Kennedy had said that Germany would win the war, Britain would "go to hell," and that his one interest was in saving his money for his children. When Kennedy sharply criticized Roosevelt, Bullitt berated him for disloyalty. Kennedy declared he would say what he pleased, Bullitt called him ignorant on foreign affairs, and they parted in anger. A month after Welles's visit to London, Kennedy was urging on Roosevelt congressional legislation to prohibit the purchase of gold—a move that would surely have impaired Britain's capacity to obtain dollars to buy needed war materials. The president had to instruct him to keep his hands out of Treasury policy. Even after Chamberlain gave way to Churchill, Kennedy was still at it, telling the deposed prime minister on May 16 that French morale was broken; and he did not see how Britain could fight on without them. Chamberlain agreed; if France collapsed, Britain's only chance of escaping destruction would be a Roosevelt appeal for an armistice. Kennedy thereupon suggested this to the president so that he could prepare himself for such an appeal were it to be needed on short notice.[58]

In striking contrast to Kennedy's performance in London was the work of Lord Lothian in Washington. Although sometimes inclined to concentrate on particular aspects of questions to the exclusion of other important aspects, and to express in public speeches personal ideas about the postwar world as if they were established government policy (which drew a gentle warning from the Foreign Office at the end of January), his efforts at advancing American understanding of Britain's situation were consistently well received. He had the full confidence of his own government, as well as a close relationship of mutual trust with officials in Washington (even confirmed Anglophobes like Adolf Berle, in the State Department, took a quick liking to him) and an easy and open relationship with the American press. Even when mildly rebuking

58. Halifax to Lothian, 8 March 1940, FO 800/324, p. 200; *Moffat Papers,* p. 298; Ickes, *Diary,* 3:147; Blum, *Roosevelt and Morgenthau,* p. 296; NC 2/24A, 16 May 1940. In mid-May the French embassy in London was thinking about initiating a complaint to Washington about Kennedy's attitude. Halifax thought it all right, if the British were kept out of it. But as always, he doubted it would do any good. FO 371/24251, pp. 79–82A.

him, Halifax raved about the quality of his speeches: his choice of subjects, the manner of presentation, the language used, and so on—finding them all the more remarkable in view of "the throng of isolationists and others waiting all agog to trip you up on the charge of propaganda." Those at home who had doubted the wisdom of his appointment on the grounds of his earlier views toward Nazi Germany or his fondness for "large ideas"—"high-minded ballyhoo," Hugh Dalton called it—to the neglect of essential details, were pleasantly surprised both by the nature and quality of his performance and the success he achieved. This view was corroborated by many Americans, including critical-eyed journalists; Eugene Meyer, of the *Washington Post,* for example, wrote privately to a high-placed English friend that he did not know how London could have sent anyone who would do better work in the circumstances. As previously noted, the tributes to Lothian from both sides of the Atlantic, upon his untimely death in December 1940, went far beyond the requirements of diplomatic protocol and normal standards of civility.[59]

Lothian, who was personally palatable to Americans in ways not always characteristic of Englishmen, had discovered that "Americans . . . like being talked to straight and made to think, always provided you don't tread on one or more of [their] numberless irrational prejudices." He attributed his own success to knowing the American mind and dealing frankly with controversial issues. Thus he was open and candid, always in gentlemanly fashion, trying to portray the exact nature of Britain's predicament—which he freely acknowledged as such—without ever telling the Americans what they were expected to do about it. He had quickly learned that whatever conclusions Americans reached, they must reach them through their own initiatives and on their own terms. This approach was well illustrated in addresses he made to the Chicago Council on Foreign Relations, January 4, and the St. Louis Chamber of Commerce, April 19. On the first occasion, he described the war as a struggle between two conflicting ways of life. Britain was fighting for those ideals of freedom that were most fully realized in the United States, but it was not trying to drag America into the war. No democracy would accept the hideous consequences of military conflict until convinced that its own vital interests, including its ideals, were at stake. "If ever you

59. Perowne Memorandum and Foreign Office Minutes, 20–30 January 1940, FO 371/24246, pp. 36–39, 44–47; Halifax to Lothian, 30 January 1940, FO 800/398; Meyer to Chatfield, 18 January 1940, FO 794/18; David Reynolds, *Lord Lothian and Anglo-American Relations, 1939–1940,* pp. 1–14, 57–60. Reynolds's work gives a detailed assessment of Lothian's service as Britain's ambassador in Washington, with major emphasis on the period after 10 May 1940.

are driven to action," he declared, "it will not be because of propaganda but because of the relentless march of events." Again in St. Louis, he proclaimed that Hitler was attempting to destroy the ideals of liberty upon which the civilization of the modern Western world was based, whereas a British victory would lay the foundations for the free and liberal world that the democracies had believed in but had failed to establish. Britain was no longer able to sustain, by itself, on the basis of her naval power, the international system of the nineteenth century that had brought order and unity to the world. The United States must now share in control of the seas. But "we would only ask you, in considering our actions, to realize that our people . . . are submitting to hardships which are already very formidable and will certainly become more so, and to weigh the troubles we cause you against the tremendous issues which are at stake in this war." Interference with normal peacetime rights was bound to cause irritation, and were America's and Britain's positions reversed, the British would surely feel similar aggravation. But the alternative was the "Dark Age" that would follow extension of the Nazi system to Europe and the world.[60]

International suspicions and irritations—to say nothing of resistance to change in procedures—seldom dissipate quickly, however. And in the weeks between Welles's mission and Chamberlain's fall from power, they continued to persist on both sides of the Anglo-American relationship, sometimes appearing in simple but nonetheless telling form. Indeed, among British officials, increasingly preoccupied with developments in Europe, there was a surprising degree of doubt whether anything could be done about it, save in a cautionary, preventive way. Foreign Office personnel endorsed a late February request by the *New York Times* that correspondent Harold Callender be granted an interview with Chamberlain in order to prepare an article designed to counteract prejudice against the prime minister still lingering in many American quarters. Scott wrote Sir Horace Wilson to suggest that it would "afford an excellent opportunity, which has hitherto been lacking, for a better under-

60. Lothian to Halifax, 11 March 1940, FO 800/324, pp. 205–10; Lothian, *American Speeches*, pp. 49–62, 71–78. Lothian's references to "federalism" in the St. Louis speech again concerned F.O. officials, and Halifax sent him another warning about the need for caution in implying peace objectives that had not been determined. But several weeks later, after reading the full text of Lothian's speech, Halifax wrote that it was "exactly the right sort of way in which to talk to our American friends," and hoped that Lothian would have "further opportunities of educating them." Halifax to Lothian, 30 April, 14 May 1940, FO 371/24246, pp. 68–70, 78–79, 109; also FO 800/398.

standing of the Prime Minister's personality and point of view" and encouraged Chamberlain to agree to the request. Wilson, however, feared "dangerous possibilities," particularly in view of Welles's impending visit. But the Foreign Office was reluctant to take "no" for an answer. Whitehead allowed that the granting of such interviews was not in the English tradition, but the great importance of capturing the good will and imagination of the American public made it time perhaps for leading members of the government to increase their accessibility to American press representatives. Lack of such contacts was one reason the American public found it so hard to appreciate British policies and purposes. Perowne suggested that the Press Department at No. 10 might try to evolve some technique for dealing with applications of his kind systematically; and Balfour was intrigued by Walter Lippmann's idea that the prime minister should give an occasional luncheon party to half a dozen of the best American journalists in London. But Charles Peake, of the Foreign Office News Department, was squarely against a Chamberlain interview with Callender. No such interviews were given to British correspondents, who would be incensed at privileges granted to others that they did not enjoy. And so the matter fizzled.[61]

About the same time, B. E. F. Gage, of the Foreign Office, suggested the establishment of an allowance for entertaining members of the U.S. embassy and press correspondents in private homes, believing that much could be learned in this way about what Americans in London were thinking and reporting. He had been taking embassy members to the Marlborough Club and arranging with an American friend to host cocktail parties "where touched by powerful dry martinis their tongues began to wag." The practice might be rewarding, Perowne observed, although Americans should not be courted so suddenly as to cause suspicion or embarrassment. And there was always the danger that the scheme would become known, with unfortunate consequences. As for Gage's presence at a party hosted by a U.S. embassy secretary, Perowne could only lament: "I have toiled for years in similar vineyards without achieving so much as a cup of tea!" Balfour thought Gage's efforts commendable and was willing to defray the cost of Marlborough Club entertaining out of his own modest allowance. It was unwise, however, to subsidize American hosts and hostesses, thus exposing them to the charge of being propaganda agents. But Scott squelched the whole idea. The views of

61. Foreign Office Minutes and Correspondence, 27 February–18 March 1940, FO 371/24238, pp. 233–47.

embassy members were already pretty well known; and whatever they thought would have little effect on the American electorate or the State Department. It was far more important to be sure that embassy members and correspondents knew what the British were thinking and how the actions of the U.S. government struck them.[62] This is an insignificant episode, to be sure; but it reveals a broader problem: a perceived need for greater Anglo-American exchange of information, however informal, and yet doubt as to whether it would make much difference anyway.

The issue of growing anti-American feeling in Britain also commanded the attention of Foreign Office personnel. General Miles, the U.S. military attaché, had brought this to Gage's attention in early March, expressing a hope for more articles in the British press explaining American attitudes in a sympathetic manner. Walter Lippmann made the same point to Scott a few days later. The feeling was well-known in America and could seriously affect Anglo-American relations, Whitehead asserted, in suggesting that a major Foreign Office official discuss the matter with several leading British editors; they might in turn have Raymond Swing, Walter Lippmann, or some other prominent Americans contribute articles explaining American attitudes to the English. Perowne preferred to see American journalists explain British difficulties to the U.S. public, but, realizing this was not a practical possibility, agreed that contact about Whitehead's suggestion could be made with the *Times* and the *Daily Telegraph*. Such articles would not so much enlighten the British public, he believed, as prepare the way for comparable articles in the American press explaining Britain's position and difficulties. Balfour and Scott concurred with the idea, the former doubting, however, that such articles would do much to dispel anti-American feeling, "which must necessarily increase in proportion to the extent to which we suffer in a war from which the U.S.A. elects to remain aloof." It was a big problem requiring a professional touch, Scott added, expressing an interest in having Peake's views. Peake saw it as a matter of sentiment: Britain could aptly be compared to a man struggling for his life in a stormy sea who knew himself to be in view of a man on the pier with a life belt behind him who contented himself with shouting good advice. Feeling in such circumstances was not likely to be cordial. He discussed the matter with others, including the press lord, Viscount Camrose, and thought it might be raised at an April 11 Dartmouth House dinner with a score of editors and diplomatic correspondents. But, it was later re-

62. Foreign Office Minutes, 2–5 March 1940, FO 371/24248, pp. 265–67.

ported, the subject was hardly touched upon at the dinner, where it was generally agreed that there was no prospect of putting more U.S. news into British papers[63]; thus, a problem was recognized and delineated but no solution found.

The condition of American opinion continued to concern the British, especially the Foreign Office, throughout the spring of 1940. When Lothian complained about unnecessary friction caused by British government announcements—affecting United States interests that were made public before he, or anyone else, had an opportunity to prepare the ground for them—Whitehead recognized a real danger that the emotional tone of the United States could become set in an attitude of hostility; and it was hard to imagine a more dangerous point on which Britain could fail. The departments whose actions tended to disturb Anglo-American relations were the Treasury and the ministries of Food, Supply, and Shipping. All were aware of the importance of the matter, Perowne observed; but warning notes, over Cadogan's signature, could be addressed to all of them. With Sargent's and Cadogan's approval, this was done late in March—a signal that the Foreign Office would no longer let itself be ignored by other departments in matters affecting America, a practice that had heretofore been all too common. And Lothian was informed that "the Departments concerned have again been warned to be circumspect." The ambassador, in turn, reemphasized that "one very important way of helping us here is the intelligent management of the American press men in London whenever—preferably before if possible—any matters of controversy arise."[64] But progress was slow in this arena.

Considerable agitation arose in the Foreign Office early in May when word circulated that Sir Nevile Henderson was going to lecture in the United States. No worse form of propaganda could be devised, Vansittart warned Halifax. Munich was Britain's greatest handicap in America and its authors "*anathema maranatha.*" To stir the whole thing up again by exporting Henderson at a time like this would be sheer folly. Lothian likewise thought it would be a bad mistake. Few would believe that he was not officially sponsored; and if his tour were not regarded as British propaganda to get the United States into the war, it would be seen as mere money-making, also an unfortunate impression to convey in the

63. Foreign Office Minutes, 8–14 March, 20 April 1940, ibid., pp. 273–78.

64. Foreign Office Minutes, 20–26 March 1940, ibid., pp. 282–85, 293; Butler to Balfour, 9 April 1940, FO 371/24249, pp. 46–47.

circumstances. Neither Cadogan nor the American Department had any knowledge of Henderson's intentions, so Halifax contrived to contact him directly, commenting first on his recently published "intensely interesting" book (*Failure of a Mission: Berlin, 1937–1939*), then mentioning rumors that he had been invited to do a lecture tour in the United States and advising strongly against accepting such an invitation. It was Britain's considered policy, Halifax explained, to avoid all forms of propaganda in the United States, where "propaganda phobia has reached a terrific pitch." Every Englishman who set foot there was automatically regarded as the mouthpiece, if not the direct emissary, of the government, and Henderson would be no exception.[65] No tour was made.

Meantime, Lothian tried to review the state of American opinion both for the Foreign Office and private friends. A report to Halifax, April 29, described the United States as 95 percent anti-Hitler but also 95 percent determined to keep out of the war unless American vital interests—which included her ideals—were directly challenged. The German invasion of Denmark and Norway, which had begun on April 9, had revitalized the old feeling that sooner or later the United States would be dragged into the war. It was almost universally appreciated that the Allies were standing between Hitler and the United States, so if the need became obvious, loans, credit, or even gifts to the Allies to help them fight would certainly be forthcoming. But what the United States would not do—any more than Britain had done—was to take farsighted defensive action. He summarized that Americans were still dominated by fear of involvement and incapable of positive action. On the other hand, the war was steadily drifting closer, and they knew it. The point at which they would be driven to say—as Britain had done after Prague—"thus far and no farther" depended mainly on the dictators and events that they precipitated. Roosevelt and Hull were anxious to take vigorous action on the principle "everything short of war." But it was an election year, and all other candidates for election, especially the Republicans, unfamiliar with international affairs, were paralyzed by fear of being charged with a desire to get America into war. If elected, they would no doubt deal with the situation in a "practical and realist manner"; but for now they were "completely mesmerized by fear of the great god, 'the American Electorate.'" Lothian also predicted that if the United States

65. Vansittart Memorandum, 2 May 1940; Lothian to Halifax, 4 May 1940; Halifax to Henderson, 6 May 1940; FO 794/10. At an Eden Group dinner in London on 17 April, Harold Nicolson found Duff Cooper's account of the propaganda-consciousness of the United States "terrifying" (Nicolson, *Diaries,* 3:72).

entered the war, it would be by methods altogether different from the last time. There would be no great demonstration in Congress led by a Wilson proclaiming that America was not only defending her own rights but crusading for a new world. "It will begin from exactly the opposite end."[66]

In letters to friends, Lothian made similar, and additional observations. "I don't believe the United States will ever formally declare war," he wrote one of them in late April; it was too difficult constitutionally. It was much more likely to come in by practical movements, such as fleet operations in the Pacific, and carry the policy of helping Britain further until really taking an active part in the war. Roosevelt had to be very careful not to give the isolationists an electoral cry that would lead to the return of a completely isolationist Congress. But he was a good politician and would not fall into the trap. America, in no sense pacifist if her own vital interests were challenged, would "fight like blazes," he assured another. And there was a growing conviction among thinking Americans that the United States would inevitably be drawn in by some act of Hitler or the Japanese, he wrote to several more. Meantime, he did not feel critical of the United States. It stood very much where Britain had stood during the era of Baldwin, who later confessed he had not told the electorate the truth about German rearmament for fear of losing the next election. "We cannot really throw stones at the United States, because we adopted almost the same policy ourselves in the two or three years preceding the war."[67]

There was also another response to British criticism of America that Lothian thought important: "The United States is really holding the baby for us in the Pacific." It had "moved up into the front line," and so long as it maintained its present policy, British interests in the Pacific were secure. Actually, the Foreign Office was somewhat concerned about "a certain divergence" in British and American policy toward Japan, exacerbated by the situation in Europe. Whereas there was a powerful inducement for Britain to refrain from antagonizing the Japanese, a long Foreign Office analysis of mid-April noted, the United States was free from this deterrent and "professedly at least . . . readier to risk the consequences of a policy which implies putting on the 'screw.'" It was

66. Lothian to Halifax, 29 April 1940, FO 414/277, pp. 65–66; also FO 800/324, pp. 223–28.

67. Lothian to: Josiah Wedgwood, 27 March; Sir Alan Lascelles, 22 April; Percival Witherby, 30 April; Captain Victor Cazelet and Viscount Samuel, 4 May 1940; Lothian Papers, GD 40/17/399, 404, 406, 514; Lothian to Sir Gerald Campbell, 20 April 1940, FO 800/398.

a cardinal point of British policy to keep in step with the United States in the Far East at a time when it was generally giving the lead; but it was "all-important to know how great is the risk of the United States Government drawing back in a crisis and leaving her associates 'out on the end of the branch.'" The grounds for fearing such an event were implicit in a long-term review of American policy in Asia, which revealed a record of oscillation between strength and weakness; and the course that would be followed depended very largely on the state of public opinion and the play of party politics. Further, American interests in the Far East were perceived in London to be "less vital" than Britain's, both in terms of territory and commodities. If American "repression" of Japan was evidently essential to saving the British Commonwealth from destruction, there could be no doubt of America's willingness to exert itself. But short of that, "there must be very considerable doubt as to how much public support there will be for the Far Eastern policy laid down by the State Department if this policy seems to be leading to a serious danger of war."[68]

One of the specific issues at stake was that of contraband control, and London was not sure what to expect from Washington. The general plan for dealing with the leakage of goods into Germany through Russia was to restrict the export to Russia of goods from the British and French empires. An important corollary was to try to get Japan to agree to a strict limitation of goods carried in Japanese ships or on Japanese-controlled railways and destined for Russia, and to induce the United States to do likewise. Halifax did not think the latter would be easy, since the attitude of Washington in this matter had recently been "unhelpful." The Supreme War Council at length decided to arrange for stricter control and was willing to "buy" Japanese acquiescence, if necessary, by facilitating Japanese purchases of raw materials in British colonies. The United States clearly would not like this, since it considered Japan to be an aggressor nation. But Britain would have to explain the "practical character" of such an arrangement to the State Department and also ask its agreement to Britain's stopping United States exports to the Far East that might be reexported to Germany. Lothian, who believed the proposed negotiations with Japan would require delicate handling—were

68. Lothian to Captain Victor Cazelet, 11 March 1940, Lothian Papers, GD 40/17/399; Lothian to Lady Astor, 20 March 1940, Astor Papers, MS 1416/1/4/59; Foreign Office Memorandum, 13 April 1940, FO 414/277, pp. 58–60. Chatfield reinforced Lothian's view, writing him on 14 March that "the very much more prominent part the United States is tending to play" in the Far East was "of enormous importance" (CHT 6/2, p. 199).

Washington not to be exasperated—recommended that the U.S. government be consulted in advance on these matters. The Supreme War Council agreed that negotiations with Japan should not begin without prior notification to Washington, and there the matter dangled as new developments in Europe commanded full attention. The British were gratified to learn (through a published statement by Cordell Hull) that in the event of a German invasion of Holland, the United States was interested in maintaining the integrity of the Netherlands East Indies; and Churchill was authorized to let Roosevelt know, through the U.S. naval attaché in London, that if Washington ordered its fleet to the Philippines, Britain would be willing to provide all possible repair and docking facilities at Singapore.[69]

As for America's perception of its vital interests, for which Lothian believed she would "fight like blazes," Roosevelt was not at all forthcoming in his definition of them. In an April 18 session with 275 members of the American Society of Newspaper Editors, for example, while rambling expansively over a number of topics (including U.S. defense and how and where to draw the line on defending interests and territory vital to the United States) the president's clear implication was that America's vital interests lay much farther afield than was often recognized. He also clearly implied that he understood the British, whose way of life was not a threat to America's way or to her security, whereas one of the "new-fangled countries [Nazi Germany or Bolshevik Russia] might cause me trouble in my old age if they were my neighbors." Underneath all this was the clear suggestion that Britain's interests were America's interests, punctuated by the observation that every man, woman, and child in America needed to ask what would happen to the United States if dictatorship won in Europe and Asia. But it all was merely suggestive, and any comfort the British might have derived was no doubt neutralized by the overtones in Roosevelt's further observation that he knew the British well and was onto all their tricks. When they tried to slip something over on him, he caught them and told them—and that was one reason they liked him. They now knew they could not fool him, he asserted—a good position for him to be in.[70]

At the same time, there were some indications of a growing awareness in America that Britain's interests were closely related to its own. Frank

69. CAB 65/6, 27 March, 17, 18, 20 April 1940, pp. 121, 266a, 231, 245; Halifax Notes, 11 April 1940, FO 800/321, p. 84. Halifax was not disturbed by the idea of taking a strong line with Russia. His principal preoccupation was to keep out of trouble with Japan.

70. *FDR Press Conferences,* 15:274–81.

Ashton-Gwatkin, a Foreign Office economic expert visiting Washington to discuss questions relating to economic warfare, observed a significant change in the outlook of the State Department. Whereas only a month or two before the lawyers had exercised a determining influence on the discussions to which he was a party, the department had now put aside legalistic arguments and "the situation was developing rapidly in [Britain's] favor." Lothian described for Halifax the manner in which Roosevelt had recently cut off a potentially embarrassing congressional investigation into Allied purchases of aircraft in America by making it known in unequivocal language that the administration was determined to facilitate such purchases and had no fear of repercussions on America's own rearmament efforts. In fact, General George C. Marshall (army chief of staff) had gone so far as to declare administration policy in this regard a matter of vital importance for America's national defense. So the agitation in Congress came quickly to nothing, an outcome generally welcomed by the press, which saw the administration's decision as serving American interests and assisting the Allies at the same time. And the Anglo-French Purchasing Board, acting on the basis of a British proposal accepted by the French late in March, began to make good progress with its arrangements for the purchasing of aircraft.[71]

Behind-the-scenes contacts between Roosevelt and leading Englishmen were also warmer in tone. Arthur Murray wrote Halifax that his recent letters from the president showed that Roosevelt "felt it very keenly that all he can be is 'belligerent in thought'"; he violently disliked everyone and everything connected with the Nazi regime and was not likely to do anything that would "let Hitler off." As the war expanded in Europe, Roosevelt wrote to King George VI, May 3, relating "how very much you have been in our thoughts," and adding: ". . . You must not hesitate to call on me for any possible thing if I can help or lighten your load."[72] No such message was sent to Chamberlain, however, and it was only after his fall from power that Britain, under Churchill's leadership, began to "call on Roosevelt" in significant ways.

With the pressure of events in Europe (especially the Norway campaign) and criticism at home (much of it from inside his own government) weighing heavily on him in late April, Chamberlain felt a strong inclination "to take my head out of the collar and let someone else do

71. CAB 65/6, 3 April 1940, p. 142; Lothian to Halifax, 4 April 1940, FO 115/3422, File 860.

72. Elibank, "Roosevelt: Friend of Britain," p. 368; *F.D.R.: His Personal Letters*, 2:1020–21.

the donkey work." With reference to the war in general and Norway in particular, the most common question, "chronic in the U.S.A.," he wrote his sister, was why Britain was always too late. Why did it let Hitler take the initiative? Why didn't it have some plan that would take him by surprise? The answer was simple, he added; Britain was not yet strong enough. But the questioners would rather not believe it. If Britain could weather the year and remove its worst deficiencies, it "might look round the world for diversions and start a new war in any locality which suited us and not the Germans." But he doubted that he would be able to hold things quiet for the rest of the year.[73]

How right he was! Britain's failure to halt the German advance into Norway—responsibility for which inevitably fell on the prime minister—brought to a head, particularly in Parliament but also in the nation at large, a gradually deepening crisis of confidence in Chamberlain's ability—and will—to lead the nation in arms. The Commons debate of May 7–8 was decisive. Not only was Chamberlain's defense of the conduct of Norwegian operations, the structure of the war cabinet (which excluded Labour because the party was simply unwilling to work with Chamberlain) and other issues (related to equipping Britain for total war) unconvincing and lacking inspiration; the prime minister seriously damaged his own position when, hearing the call for a division on the second day, he rose in anger and besought "his friends" to support him in the lobby. Such an appeal to party or personal loyalty was altogether misplaced in the circumstances of peril confronting the nation. This was devastatingly illustrated by the call of Leo Amery, a lifelong Chamberlain friend and colleague, for a "real National Government" to replace the one that (in Cromwellian terms) had already sat too long. When the vote was taken, Chamberlain's majority was drastically reduced, and it was clear to all that he did not have the kind of support required to face the deepening crisis. Hasty contact with Labour leaders reaffirmed their unwillingness to serve in a government under Chamberlain's leadership. A meeting of the prime minister, Halifax, Churchill, and David Margesson (chief Conservative whip), made all the more tense by the opening of the German attack on Holland (May 10), resulted in the withdrawal of Halifax from consideration as Chamberlain's successor—largely on

73. Neville to Ida, 27 April 1940; Neville to Hilda, 4 May 1940; NC 18/1/1152–53. With regard to the British failure at Trondheim, Chamberlain thought the effort had to be made; otherwise Norway and Sweden would have fallen at once into German hands. But success would have been costly, entangling the British in an enterprise that in the end "would have drained our strength dangerously in the effort to maintain our position."

his own initiative, but certainly with encouragement from Churchill—and Churchill's emergence as the man of the hour.[74]

There was considerable question on both sides of the Atlantic about the new man in charge of Britain's fate. When Lothian told Welles on May 5 that the Chamberlain government might well go under, he added, ruefully, that "there was no one who could act as Premier." Welles recalled that Churchill was drunk on the first of the two evenings he had been with him in London, and saw in his peregrinations no indication of clearcut leadership. Although Hull wrote in his memoirs years later that "the President and I welcomed the change," inasmuch as a resolute man was required in the position, and Churchill's ideas had paralleled his own for several years, Roosevelt was sufficiently uncertain that he solicited the views of various associates as to what kind of man Churchill really was. And the best he could do, when word arrived in Washington that the change had occurred, was to muse to his cabinet colleagues that he supposed Churchill was the best man England had.[75] In London, Maurice Hankey, longtime secretary of the cabinet and confidant of prime ministers and politicians, wrote Sir Samuel Hoare that he was "aghast" at the cabinet changes:

> God help the country which, at the beginning of the supreme crisis of its fate, suddenly replaces half of the eight key leaders by men without experience of war, or of public affairs (other than very sordid politics), or of administration. . . . And which commits its future existence to the hands of a dictator whose past achievements, even though inspired by a certain amount of imagination, have never achieved success!

He doubted that "the wise old elephants will ever be able to hold the Rogue elephant" in check.[76]

The Rogue Elephant, however, did act swiftly in relation to the United States. He told the cabinet on May 13 that, with its consent, he proposed to send an urgent personal message to President Roosevelt to inform

74. See Rock, *Chamberlain*, pp. 197–200, for more detail on the circumstances surrounding Chamberlain's resignation and Churchill's assumption of leadership.

75. Berle, *Navigating the Rapids*, p. 310; Hull, *Memoirs*, 1:764; Frances Perkins, *The Roosevelt I Knew*, p. 80; Ickes, *Diary*, 3:176. Ickes recorded (12 May) his own pleasure that Chamberlain was out: "I had no hope in my own heart so long as this inept man was at the head of the British Government." A week before he had labeled Chamberlain "the evil genius not only of Great Britain but of Western civilization." Ibid., 3:171, 176.

76. Hankey to Hoare, 12 May 1940, HNKY 4/32. Several days earlier Hankey had written Chamberlain that he was "well nigh indispensable as Prime Minister." Churchill was, Hankey conceded, "amazingly valuable," but his judgment was not fully reliable (ibid., May 9, 1940).

him of the seriousness of the situation confronting Britain. The idea met with immediate approval, discussion ensued as to what action Roosevelt might take to help the Allies, and the service ministers and the minister of supply were invited to communicate at once, for inclusion in Churchill's message, any suggestions "as to particular types of war material which they were especially anxious to obtain from the United States." Churchill's appreciation of the situation was dispatched to the president on May 15.[77] The story of the Churchill-Roosevelt relationship that developed thereafter, spawned of mutual need and a common ability to appreciate the drama of history and to share the burdens of those who must make it, is admirably chronicled elsewhere. So are Anglo-American relations more generally in the period prior to Pearl Harbor.[78]

77. CAB 65/7, 13 May 1940, p. 73; *Roosevelt and Churchill: Their Secret Wartime Correspondence*, pp. 94–95.

78. See Lash, *Roosevelt and Churchill,* and Reynolds, *The Creation of the Anglo-American Alliance, 1937–1941.*

X.
A Summing Up

FEW WOULD DISPUTE the contention that the years 1937–40—when Neville Chamberlain was prime minister of Britain and Franklin Roosevelt was president of the United States—were crucial times in the history of Europe and the world. These were the years in which the peace—or at least the truce—that ended the Great War of 1914–18 was shattered, when fascist aggression threw the world into a second conflagration of unprecedented dimensions and changed the face of Europe and the world in ways nearly unimaginable a few years before. They were years of crisis, of near-constant tension, uncertainty, and anxiety. They were years in which the determination of policy and action (seldom as easy as those with simplistic solutions to human problems suggest) was made doubly difficult by the unresolved issues of World War I, the sharp impact of economic depression upon political affairs, the new and not-well-understood forces and ideologies at work in the world, and the increasing complexity of international relationships generally. In short, recognition of the difficult problems confronting leaders in Britain and America is an appropriate starting point for a summary appraisal of their policies during the period. It was not a pretty world that they confronted, and the problems that prevailed were sufficient to challenge the most talented and experienced statesmen.

Certainly Chamberlain and Roosevelt were talented and experienced statesmen although their greatest strengths may have lain outside foreign affairs. However, it may be asked how much experience counted, inasmuch as the nature and ultimate direction of the fascist movements (from which most of the trouble sprang) were still open to debate, and the major fascist leaders were men of quixotic personality whose shifts of mood and behavior made prediction and consistency of reaction to them impossible. Of the two, Roosevelt seemed to grasp the dangerous nature of Nazism earlier and more fully than Chamberlain and to sense that something must be done to keep the aggressive tendencies of Germany under control. But he was farther from the scene than Chamberlain and thus not moved by as great a sense of urgency or constrained by as great a fear of direct threat to his own nation. Chamberlain, inclined to distinguish between "good" and "bad" Germans and to seek for means to ensure the influence of the former over the latter, never seemed to grasp fully the extent to which Hitler was the symbol and spearhead of a vast new force in German life. He kept waiting—in vain—for the "good" Germans somehow to come to their senses, to exercise a restraining influence on Hitler and the Nazis—perhaps even to overthrow them. This inevitably tempered his perception of policy.

Looking back from the vantage point of later years, it is clear that the closest possible Anglo-American cooperation was essential to the vital interests of both nations as well as to any chance of diverting or precluding the onset of World War II. Whether such cooperation would have made any substantial difference in Hitler's European policy must remain an open question. The odds are against it seeing that Hitler's regard for the United States, especially for the fighting qualities of what he described as "a mass of immigrants," was very low; and his respect for Britain, which was surprisingly high so long as he thought it no threat or barrier to his own ambitions, had certainly begun to deteriorate sharply by early 1938. It is equally impossible to calculate the effect that closer Anglo-American cooperation might have had on Japanese policy in the Pacific. Surely the Japanese would have been slow to confront Britain and America head-on, had their attention and energies not been diverted elsewhere. But events in Asia were clearly influenced by developments in Europe, and the Japanese took full advantage of opportunities presented to them by the European distractions of the major adversaries of their drive for power and influence in the Pacific. It seems unlikely, then, that a much closer Anglo-American working relationship could actually have prevented World War II—although the possibility will always be present to titillate the imaginations of those who like to ponder "what might have been." But it would surely have given aggressors greater pause for thought; and greater mutual understanding between London and Washington would have advanced more effective preparation for war, thereby materially shortening the conflict that ensued and saving Europe and the world untold suffering.

But the thirties were a curious time in Britain for relations with the

United States—and conversely. Among political leaders there was an overabundance of suspicion, some of which was firmly grounded in historical experience; but a significant portion of it resulted from myth, prejudice, or ignorance. Few American politicians knew much about the realities of British and European politics—and worse still, showed little desire to learn. Their opposite numbers in Britain did not understand the springs of American behavior and were quick to dismiss it as crude and immature. In America, in particular, there was a strong desire to avoid the company of foreigners, lest this provide a basis for isolationist criticism. In Britain there was honest doubt about the usefulness of keeping company with Americans. It was almost unthinkable that the leaders of the two countries should actually meet and get to know one another. Indeed, it seems hardly credible in these present days of rapid transportation that during the latter 1930s no member of the British government visited America, and American officials seemed no more anxious to visit Britain. Instead, there was a marked and unfortunate reliance on go-betweens, many of whom simply did not serve their purpose well.[1]

The historical record of Anglo-American relations during Neville Chamberlain's prime ministership reveals that during the first half of 1937, Franklin Roosevelt showed a more intensive interest in, and concern about, European affairs than has often been suggested, and that he made some effort to demonstrate this interest to the British.[2] This was the result of genuine alarm about the direction of developments and attitudes in Nazi Germany, in which Roosevelt early perceived a clear and dangerous threat—however indirect and distant at the time—to traditional Anglo-American interests and values. He extended a tentative hand of friendship to Britain that Ambassador Lindsay thought "full of gifts" and worthy of grasping. There was nothing very specific in Roosevelt's initiative, and Lindsay's appraisal was no doubt overly optimistic. But the president's actions betokened the desire for friendship and for the development of a closer relationship between the two nations than had heretofore existed, and that was a new element of potentially great importance. Historians of American foreign relations will argue

1. See Nicholas, *The United States and Britain,* p. 86; Victor Mallet's Memoir, pp. 60–61.

2. In an article entitled "Franklin Roosevelt's Diplomatic Debut: The Myth of the Hundred Days," Frederick W. Marks III shows that Roosevelt was much more active in foreign affairs during his first 100 days in office in 1933 than historians have generally believed. A parallel can no doubt be drawn with 1937.

ad infinitum about the extent to which Roosevelt was free to pursue initiatives with Britain, given the state of opinion in America (about which there is more below), but at least it appears that Roosevelt was prepared to try. And in view of his resounding electoral victory in late 1936, he was in the strongest possible position to do so.

In extending an invitation to Chamberlain to visit Washington, Roosevelt clearly revealed a desire to "get to know" the new prime minister better. The clumsy handling of the invitation was unfortunate indeed, for it added greater cause for reticence to British doubt about the value of such a meeting that was already present. It was characteristic of Roosevelt that he should approach the issue in a manner that can only be called informal. It was equally characteristic of Chamberlain that he should respond with something less than enthusiasm to such an approach. Chamberlain, of course, was busy with affairs at home and could see no particular value in such a meeting with the president at that juncture. Roosevelt's persistent questioning about preparatory steps that might expedite a meeting was met by Chamberlain's asserting that the European situation was now "less menacing" and the prospect of improving the Far Eastern situation by action on the part of the Western powers nil. This gave Roosevelt precious little to go on, and is especially puzzling in view of Chamberlain's seeming conviction (in the months immediately prior to his assumption of leadership) that Germany was the main source of danger to peace in Europe and that nothing but the threat of meeting superior force if it attempted aggression would deter it. Certainly there were no illusions about American participation in a threat of force in 1937, but the tightening of bonds in any potential anti-Nazi coalition would have seemed a useful endeavor. The fact is that Chamberlain's outlook had changed upon his assumption of leadership. Whereas previously he had said that only force would influence Germany, he now began to believe that timely concessions to meet legitimate German grievances—appeasement—constituted the most effective approach for dealing with the German danger. Not much had happened in Germany to change his outlook. Rather, the shift is better explained in terms of the weight of responsibility, which now rested on his shoulders alone, and his growing confidence in his own ability—indeed, his sense of mission—to resolve the problems threatening Europe and thus ensure peace for the Continent. There is no indication that this important shift in Chamberlain's position was conveyed to Roosevelt or that he understood it had occurred.

This is not to say that the idea of appeasement appealed any less to

Roosevelt than it did to Chamberlain. If it could have been demonstrated that such a policy would have had the desired effect, there is little question that Roosevelt would have supported it—certainly up to a point. Indeed, a case can be made, as D. C. Watt has done, that there were considerable parallels between Roosevelt's position and Chamberlain's. Had their places been reversed, there would surely have been differences in the course of action taken. But whether, in the end, there would have been any substantial difference of basic policy—"whether Roosevelt would have trod the path of Churchill"—is another matter entirely.[3] Even so, this would appear to be as strong an argument in favor of a closer relationship as against it. If there were important parallels in their policy orientation, a cooperative reinforcement of each other's position and initiatives, as well as a kind of comparative double-check on the successes and failures achieved by each, would surely have been useful and instructive. It was the decision to go it alone on the basis of one's own perception, and to approach appeasement piecemeal rather than on a more general ground (that is, without any guarantees that specific concessions would result in the easing of tensions through the resolution of broader international issues) that resulted in so much grief later on—through the transformation of appeasement from an honorable policy posture into a formula for surrender. That decision, which was taken during the second half of 1937 and bore bitter fruit in the year that followed, was essentially Chamberlain's.

Roosevelt's policy was tentative and uncertain. Historians still debate the motive and meaning of his famous "Quarantine Speech" in October 1937. Surprisingly forthright in enunciating an attitude toward aggressors, it fell far short of proposing a program to deal with them. And the evasiveness with which he responded to later questions about the meaning of his remarks did nothing to inspire confidence that a clear, new policy was emerging. Indeed, the Brussels Conference, which followed shortly thereafter, provided a good opportunity for taking a lead in attempting to mobilize peaceful forces against Japanese aggression in the Pacific. Unmistakable hints from London and Paris indicated that those nations would go as far as the United States in taking action in the Far East. But a wary Roosevelt now held back, and American policy quickly degenerated into the initiating of platitudes that had no particular effect. Certainly Anthony Eden, British foreign secretary, tried to get more from the Americans than that, but to no avail. His efforts were

3. Watt, "Roosevelt and Chamberlain," pp. 203–4.

hindered by the posture of his own government, which feared the potential repercussions of vigorous action. The episode no doubt discouraged him, but it also reinforced his conviction that America's strength was the unexploited reserve that had to be tapped "if the world was to be saved." This conditioned his reaction to Roosevelt's initiative of January 1938, that resulted in his resignation, and thus removed from Chamberlain's cabinet the one person who, above all others, advocated a closer tie with the United States as a fundamental cornerstone of British policy.

The Roosevelt proposal of January 1938 and Chamberlain's handling of it appear to have been very important in the development—or non-development—of Anglo-American relationships. Again, historians have been divided in their estimate of its significance, but its importance can be established on a number of counts. Above all else, a change in Roosevelt's attitude toward Britain is clearly apparent. The year before, he had taken a certain initiative with Britain, in recognizing the importance of a closer relationship and making various moves—however halting and ill-considered—to promote it; but thereafter he was much more aloof and inclined to sit back and watch while Chamberlain pursued his own policy in his own way. Genuine Roosevelt initiatives in European affairs, as they related to Britain's interests, came to an end, and his policy became largely one of defensive reaction to European developments and the interjection of opinions and pleas at points in time when the weight of American opinion seemed to be potentially valuable. The degree of disappointment that Roosevelt felt over Chamberlain's rebuff of his proposal—about which there has been considerable argument—is difficult to establish. But his disappointment is not the crucial issue. Inasmuch as Roosevelt's decision to set the proposal in motion in the first place had been drawn out and hesitant, and clearly emanated from a feeling that "something must be tried" (rather than a conviction that his proposal constituted the true and obvious solution to the problems bedeviling Europe), he might even have been relieved when Chamberlain turned it down. That took him "off the hook." Roosevelt had acted out of a sense of responsibility, of duty to the world community, and at least his conscience was clear for having tried to move. Far more important is the effect of the rebuff on Roosevelt's later outlook. He became a spectator rather than a participant in European affairs and was inclined to say to Britain: "O.K., have it *your* way, and we'll see what happens."

Given the background of experience and attitudes within which

Chamberlain operated, it is easy to see why he reacted as he did to Roosevelt's initiative. Doubting that the president really understood the subtleties of the European situation (and completely confident that *he* did), or that he was in a position to take effective action even if he knew what it were, Chamberlain was loathe to let Roosevelt's "woolly" initiative get in the way of his own by now well-calculated effort. Further, Chamberlain's mind was prone to concentrate on short-term effects. Thus he saw the potential weaning of Italy from the Axis as more important than cultivating the American connection. In this he was simply mistaken, for he not only failed to separate Italy from Germany but, in his readiness to accept the recognition of Italian Abyssinia as a condition to improving relations with Rome, he alienated American opinion by approving the fruits of aggression. Perhaps the symbolic importance of the issue was more important than the practical aspect, but with Washington "principle" counted for much. Chamberlain's readiness to disregard it was probably more important in relation to American attitudes than any personal pique that Roosevelt may have felt over the rejection of his initiative. Had Italy been won over, the price may have been forgivable. But Chamberlain had a way of making deals for which he got little in return. This hardly enhanced American confidence.

It seems increasingly clear that the issue of Britain's relations with America was more basic to Eden's resignation from the cabinet (February 1938) than the opening of negotiations with Italy. Eden simply saw the former as more important than the latter, whereas Chamberlain did not. But since Roosevelt's initiative was secret, he could not at once resign on that account. The prime minister's determination to have it his way, supported by a large majority in the cabinet, gave Eden little choice but to resign. His loss was clearly detrimental to British relations with the United States.

After the *Anschluss*, Chamberlain felt entirely vindicated for having aborted the Roosevelt proposal. In view of Hitler's action, he believed he had saved the president from looking like a fool. The possibility that pursuit of the Roosevelt initiative, implying a certain American involvement in the affairs of Europe, might have helped change the course of events in Austria did not seem to enter his mind. Although London was not unmindful of American sensitivities in regard to the negotiations with Italy, such considerations played no real part in British deliberations.

As the Czech crisis developed during the summer of 1938, Roosevelt was busy with domestic problems and, having agreed to defer to Chamberlain's preferred approach to European affairs, maintained a discreet silence about developments in central Europe. Chamberlain, for his part, envisaged no role for the United States in the extension of his efforts to appease Hitler and proceeded entirely without reference to America. Indeed, the near total absence in British policy deliberations of any reference to the United States—and any influence it might have wielded in helpful directions—is a powerful indicator of the degree to which America was dismissed from Britain's European calculations. It was almost as if Roosevelt's earlier expressions of interest in European affairs were of no consequence whatsoever. The president had earlier offered to help Britain however he could if a crisis arose, but the offer was either entirely forgotten (which is difficult to believe) or was deemed so useless that it precluded any effort to discover what help Roosevelt might afford. At length the September crisis heated up to the point where an anxious Roosevelt again felt a need to try something that might be beneficial: thus his appeal for a peaceful settlement. But he was not called upon by Chamberlain to help; indeed, the prime minister made no contact with him throughout the height of the crisis. It is impossible to measure the extent of Roosevelt's influence—if any—on the "peaceful" settlement at Munich. Certainly other things were more important, including the intervention of Mussolini. Chamberlain and Hitler agreed on at least one thing: the Czech issue was to be settled by the major European powers—Russia excluded; the intervention of "outsiders," however well-meaning, was not welcome. The prime minister would no doubt have appreciated Roosevelt's stamp of approval on the Munich settlement, but Roosevelt chose to keep silent.

Chamberlain's own appraisal of Munich is difficult to determine. Clearly his "peace in our time" statement was made in a moment of high emotion and did not represent his settled judgment about what had been accomplished. Yet it is equally evident that he was hopeful, if not genuinely optimistic, about the future possibilities of appeasement. This is difficult to understand, in view of the brutal treatment he had received at Hitler's hands. But with Chamberlain hope was a major component of personality, and it sometimes led him to impose a construction on events that did not correspond with reality. Roosevelt was clearly discouraged—and frightened—by Munich. Substantial American efforts to strengthen its military forces, especially air power, are directly related to the Munich settlement; and Roosevelt began to look around thereafter for ways to strengthen British (and French) will. This disparity of outlook did not augur well for improving Anglo-American relations, and it is not surprising that the months from Munich to the German occupation of Prague in March 1939 constitute a real "down" period in relations between the two nations.

Nothing seemed to draw Britain and America closer together during that period. On the contrary, there was much that kept them apart. There was no unity of action or attitude toward Japan's limiting the freedom of navigation on the Yangtze or the vicious anti-Semitic pogrom in Germany. British efforts to put the Anglo-Italian agreement of April 1938 into force reopened the wounds of the previous spring in relation to recognizing control of territory gained by force. Even the signing of the Anglo-American trade agreement in November seemed no great cause for rejoicing after the long, hard bargaining that had preceded it and British resentment over concessions required by Washington at a time when Britain was hard-pressed in world affairs. The apparent success of Eden's year-end visit to America, remarkable in that he successfully avoided saying anything critical of the British government, was resented by Chamberlain. And the initial visit of Lord Lothian, ambassador-designate to Washington, with Roosevelt left the president disheartened at British irresolution. A variety of little issues seemed to divide them and cause irritation out of proportion to their significance. These included the question of economic retaliation against Japan, the issue of economic assistance to China, the continuing matter of Britain's war debt, the possession of certain Pacific islands, and ambassadorial representation. The two countries did not move closer together during this time. Right up to the German action against Prague, Chamberlain seemed to find cause for increasing optimism about the solidification of peace. The extent to which this was genuine, as compared to contrived for the purpose of increasing confidence by talking it into being, will probably never be known. In any case, it did not bespeak a need for closer cooperation with America.

In the weeks that followed Prague, the British showed considerable concern about the effects of their contemplated actions on feeling and opinion in the United States. But there was certainly no consultation about policy and no request for help of any kind. There was a certain amount of indirect American influence in the guarantees to Poland and Greece, in the sense that the British were clearly concerned, throughout those trying days, that Americans think that Britain was reacting appropriately to the German threat, which now appeared in sharper focus than ever before. Washington's hope for a stronger British stance had been unmistakable at least since the time of Munich. There is, of course, no way to measure the precise extent of American influence, especially since Chamberlain and his colleagues were also keenly concerned that their own countrymen think they were reacting appropriately to the German threat. Put another way, the unrelenting pressure in Parliament and press for a new British initiative to meet the radically changed circumstances was a major—perhaps the primary—element in forcing a reluctant Chamberlain to make so drastic a departure in British foreign policy—a move that he later described in Parliament as "a portent . . . so momentous that I think it safe to say it will have a chapter to itself when the history books come to be written."[4] American reaction merely reinforced this.

For his part Roosevelt hoped for some lead from the British that would both demonstrate their own resolution and help him with the continuing education of his own people. He thought the British guarantee to Poland an excellent move and believed that it would have "a very great effect," although there was no communication with Chamberlain or the Foreign Office about it. American reaction to the guarantee was generally positive. Then two weeks later Roosevelt made a move of his own that he no doubt hoped would help restrain the dictators, though his confidence in such an outcome was slight. His April 15 messages to Hitler and Mussolini, in which he sought assurances of nonaggression against thirty-one explicitly named nations, took Chamberlain completely by surprise. The prime minister's public and private reactions were both favorable, though the Foreign Office seriously doubted promises of nonaggression from Hitler.

During the summer months of 1939, there was no significant change in Anglo-American relations. Prolonged and tortured discussion in America of the need for neutrality revision seemed to get nowhere and was certainly not encouraging to the British; however, the royal visit to the United States proved to be a greater success than might have been anticipated. The warmth of the public reaction to Their Majesties was especially gratifying; Roosevelt handled the visit in such a way as to indicate that he attached real significance to it; and the personal relationship established between king and president clearly showed mutual confidence and respect. The total effect of the visit on both sides of the Atlantic is impossible to measure, but the episode constituted a refreshing oasis in the desert of Anglo-American relations at the time. That

4. *Parl. Debs., HC,* 3 April 1939, 345:2481–86. For a discussion of the intense public pressure on Chamberlain between 15–31 March, see Rock, *Appeasement on Trial,* chap. 8.

Chamberlain showed no apparent interest in what the king had learned in his talks with Roosevelt bespeaks a lack of concern that is difficult to fathom. British difficulties with Japan in China during the summer months found the United States holding back from any direct involvement and thus offered no basis for cooperative efforts. Indeed, as war loomed ever larger in relation to the Polish crisis, there was no meaningful communication, let alone cooperation, between London and Washington. Each was still content to go its own way and see how things would develop.

When the war began, neither Britain nor the United States had any clear appreciation of what it would ultimately become, and this certainly influenced their attitudes in relation to each other. Roosevelt and Chamberlain communicated by letter, the former inviting the prime minister to write him (outside of normal diplomatic channels) about any problems that arose, the latter responding appreciatively but without any sense of urgency. Chamberlain's outlook toward the war—that it could be won without decisive victory in the field, through a collapse of the German home front—obviously lessened the importance in his mind of any role the United States might play. Toward the end of 1939, the British placed aircraft orders totalling $110 million in America; but their concern to preserve their dollar balances (understandable enough in normal conditions) and their doubt about the quality of American machines suggest again a genuine lack of perception about the scope of the struggle confronting them. Roosevelt's establishment of direct contact with Churchill shortly after the start of the war proved to be the beginning of a personal relationship that would become invaluable to both nations later on. At the time it mainly revealed the president's need for a contact in the cabinet beyond the prime minister. This did not speak well for the Chamberlain-Roosevelt relationship. Indeed, Chamberlain, still very much caught up in the toils of partisan politics and the superiority of his own judgment, seemed incapable of leading a great national effort of the kind that was now required.

The revision of American neutrality law in November 1939, which ended discrimination against the victims of aggression and was clearly favorable to Britain, was seen as a hopeful sign by the British and others in Europe. But Roosevelt's harping (as the British saw it) on the need for London to admit the errors of empire as a means of influencing American public opinion was not kindly received in Britain. Neither was the singularly defeatist attitude of Ambassador Kennedy toward the war in general. A host of lesser irritations, shipping problems among them, further compounded ill feeling.

The "minor crisis" in Britain's relations with America that developed during the third week of January 1940 indicated the wide divergence of perspective that still separated the two countries. American sensitivity about a variety of British actions that affected American interests, but that were deemed by London essential to the pursuit of the war, suggested both a lack of appreciation in Washington for the scope of the struggle confronting Britain and a commensurate British insensitivity to earlier American protests. The British did become greatly concerned about American public opinion and came to recognize that it would be the decisive factor in ultimate U.S. participation in the war. Consequently, great care was taken to avoid offending it. Little could be done to influence it; that would depend on the course of developments in the war.

The Welles mission of March 1940, apparently a genuine effort on Roosevelt's part to test the possibilities of a negotiated peace before the anticipated spring escalation of the war (as well as a demonstration to Americans that he was exhausting whatever chances for peace that remained), only irritated and exasperated the British, who by now had discarded all idea of negotiating with Hitler. Their distrust of the president's and Welles's intentions proved to be unfounded. But there was distrust; and the absence of clear communication between Washington and London once again exacerbated the situation unnecessarily. In the final crisis of confidence (May 1940) that brought Chamberlain down, there was no contact between London and Washington initiated by either side. When Churchill took over, he moved at once to give Roosevelt a full appraisal of the European situation and to seek American aid. A new chapter in British relations with the United States was thus opened.

Neither Chamberlain nor Roosevelt operated in a political vacuum, of course, and any assessment of their policies and actions during 1937–40 must take into account the broader political milieus in which they worked. Historians will no doubt go on debating the extent to which the freedom of decision and action of both men was limited by the particular circumstances of the times and the sociopolitical forces that played upon them. No real consensus is likely to emerge, but some observations on these matters are in order here.

The validity of appeasement, as pursued by the Chamberlain government, has long been the subject of intense debate and continuing disagreement. That Chamberlain's early efforts were representative of, and gave expression to, a sentiment that ran strong and deep among the English people seems quite beyond dispute. The policy involved a certain defiance of probabilities, inasmuch as the dictators were hardly distinguished for the generosity and reasonableness of their actions and attitudes in previous years. Yet any practical estimate of the diplomatic situation in 1937 seemed to suggest that appeasement, at least of a limited and exploratory nature, was worth a try. Men and movements have been known to change; and if many Germans long misjudged the nature of Hitler and Nazism (which seems an established fact), it is easy to see how Englishmen, further removed from the scene and viewing things from a wholly different perspective, might do so as well. But it is not Chamberlain's early commitment to appeasement that is at issue here. It is the method and manner by which he chose to pursue it and the tenacity with which he clung to the policy despite the accumulation of a substantial body of evidence to suggest that it was not accomplishing the peaceful objectives he had in mind but was, in fact, encouraging further acts of aggression. Both these considerations pertain, directly or indirectly, to Britain's relations with the United States, and that is the crucial issue here.

The growing concern of British policymakers about the dangerous disparity between the nation's commitments and its capabilities, as well as the recognized need to reduce the number of potential enemies and to gain the support of potential allies, has already been noted. A major difficulty in Chamberlain's policy arose from his concentration on the reduction of enemies to the exclusion of gaining support from allies. Had the appeasement of Germany and Italy "worked," this may have been no particular problem, but since it failed—abjectly—he was left with nothing to go on save British honor and courage. Put another way (if tritely), Chamberlain simply put too many eggs in one basket. What he might have been able to accomplish by way of gaining support from potential allies will always remain uncertain. Skeptics, like Chamberlain himself, who distrusted not only the United States but France and Russia as well (albeit in varying degrees and for different reasons), would argue that the chances of promoting useful relationships with allies were very slim indeed. But the point is that no real effort was ever made.[5]

5. See Rock, *British Appeasement in the 1930s*, pp. 44–45, 50–51, for a discussion of the

One reason for Chamberlain's lack of effort was a conviction that he should go it alone and tackle appeasement piecemeal (issue by issue) rather than advancing on a broader front, which would have encompassed a range of issues that were troubling international relations. Again, this might have made some sense had his early initiatives met with some positive response from those whom he was attempting to appease. But they did not, and instead of discouraging him, the negative results convinced him that greater efforts in the same direction were required for success. If one dose of appeasement would not cure the dictators' ailments, then surely additional doses would do the job.

Because he viewed the prospects of appeasement this way, a closer relationship with the United States was simply not high on his list of priorities. Far from believing he needed its support, he thought it would only interfere with his own efforts. Nor was he pressured effectively, either from within his government (after Eden resigned) or outside it, to look at things differently. Occasionally, a dissident Conservative, a Liberal, or a Labour M.P. would call in Parliament for Britain to make strenuous efforts to "draw her friends closer to her," and mention the United States by name. Or an editorial in a newspaper with similar political leanings would do the same.[6] But these were voices without substantial political clout—the voices of "mavericks" such as Churchill or Lloyd George, or of Labour and Liberal leaders, such as Attlee, Greenwood, and Sinclair, for whom Chamberlain and his supporters had come to feel, on a variety of counts, only disdain or contempt. They were generally heard politely but not taken seriously. In this sense, the failure to grasp the need for Britain to broaden its base of friends and potential allies was a failure not simply of Chamberlain and his cabinet but the British government and people at large.

Put another way, Chamberlain's approach to policy was supported by a large majority of the British people longer than some might have wished, later on, to admit. But this does not mean that Chamberlain's policy options were drastically limited by British opinion. It often has

---

Chamberlain government's perception of France and Russia. In the instance of France, Chamberlain had no confidence in its willingness or ability to deal with Germany in any effective way and worried lest French ministers, in a moment of tension and mounting pressure to "do something," might do something very silly, thus dashing his own hopes and destroying his own efforts at appeasement. In the case of Russia, Chamberlain not only felt deep ideological misgivings, but thought it weak militarily and unstable politically. Russia was simply not a worthy ally whose assistance would be crucial.

6. See Rock, *Appeasement on Trial,* passim.

been argued that Chamberlain had no real choice to do other than what he did in the pursuit of appeasement, given the peace psychosis of the British people. This is a highly debatable proposition. It may be true up to the time of Munich, but certainly not thereafter. The sense of profound relief that followed hard upon the signing of that settlement quickly gave way to widespread feelings of guilt and humiliation. The undercurrent of anxiety that stemmed from the frightening recollection of digging slit trenches in public parks and trying on gas masks in anticipation of a German air attack created an opportune atmosphere for the development of a new policy orientation, a new initiative to meet a threat that by now should have been obvious. But the nation was left devoid of constructive leadership and lulled back to the slumber of false security at a time when it should have been awakening to stark reality. Whatever the judgment on Chamberlain's behavior in the period from Munich to Prague, it was *not* dictated by the force of British opinion, whether in Parliament, press, or general public. After Munich the British were a confused and troubled people. Far from pushing the government in any particular direction, they were more inclined to follow flaccidly. And many of them sensed a need for something different, even when they could not articulate clearly what it should be.[7] It is altogether possible, of course, that initiatives in new and different directions would have failed. Specifically, it is possible that efforts to draw closer to potential allies, especially to the United States, would have failed. But we shall never know because no efforts in such directions were undertaken.

After Prague—or more particularly after the British guarantee to Poland—Chamberlain reluctantly undertook to open negotiations with Russia, looking toward its inclusion in a possible peace front. This was clearly forced upon him, much against his judgment, by pressure in Parliament, press, and public as a means of reinforcing the new departure heralded by the guarantee and giving practical effect to it.[8] This halfhearted endeavor failed, not least because the Russians found themselves in the fortuitous position of being wooed simultaneously by the Germans and were thus enabled to cast their lot with the highest bidder—or the side from which they thought they stood to gain the most in terms of assuring their own security. The point here is that various pressures in Britain were pushing the government in the direction of

7. Ibid., chaps. 6–7.

8. See William R. Rock, "Grand Alliance or Daisy Chain: British Opinion and Policy toward Russia, April–August, 1939."

seeking friends and allies in the worsening international situation, but it had no apparent effect on Britain's posture toward the United States. In the period from Prague to the outbreak of war, there was no particular effort to improve the working relationship (whatever its dimensions) between Britain and America that even vaguely resembled the effort—however halfhearted—toward Russia. The way was certainly open for new initiatives, but none of major proportion was forthcoming.

Nor did the situation change substantially after the outbreak of hostilities. Mesmerized by the notion that the war need not be pursued with genuinely extraordinary effort and would somehow end without developing into an all-out conflict (once the Germans came to realize what they were up against), and consequently believing that American assistance (save in terms of material aid in as yet undetermined dimensions) would be unnecessary to the Allied cause—indeed, believing that direct American involvement would only complicate things in unfortunate ways for those in Europe who would at length be called upon to negotiate a peace—Chamberlain remained cool and cautious in his relationship with Roosevelt and America. Precisely how much of this was attributable to his lack of confidence in America's reliability and the view that Americans could not be cajoled or influenced but must come to their own conclusions in due course, rather than to his estimate of Britain's ability (along with France) to manage things alone, is difficult to measure. These factors surely worked in inextricable combination.

Just as it has been customary to hold that Chamberlain's options and actions were severely circumscribed by British public opinion, it has long been argued that Roosevelt's foreign policy was hamstrung by the isolationist sentiment of the American Congress and people. Certainly there is truth in this. It has been abundantly demonstrated by American diplomatic historians that the isolationist element in Congress was both large and vocal, and that Roosevelt, the consummate politician, was ultrasensitive to its bellowings; but as a flat statement it falls short of the mark. It makes the isolationist forces out to be more cohesive and all-pervasive than they actually were and gives no credit to Roosevelt's considerable ability to maneuver within the broader parameters of policy available to him whenever he wanted to do so. Roosevelt's resounding electoral victory in November 1936 gave him a base from which to exert some genuine initiative, and his actions during 1937 indicate a willingness on his part to take a very active interest in foreign affairs—indeed, to get involved in certain ways that might have been helpful. His desire to establish a closer rapport with Britain was especially evident, as was his wish to do something that might have assisted in alleviating tensions with Germany. That he went about this in largely unspectacular ways suggests that he clearly understood the need to avoid provoking unnecessarily those who were thoroughly isolationist in their outlook, but it does not suggest that he felt condemned to impotence by their presence. The "Quarantine Speech" in Chicago, and the real possibility that it was motivated at least in part by a certain demand *in favor of* a more vigorous American stance against aggression, support this contention. Roosevelt himself was merely testing the waters in certain ways and feeling his way along through the intricate uncertainties of foreign affairs. There were no doubt times when there was something of an isolationist element in his thinking about the world, and on those occasions it was convenient to use the strength of isolationist sentiment across America as an explanation for his own hesitancy—just as Chamberlain frequently used the strong desire of the British people for peace as a pillar of support for appeasement. This is not to deny that strong isolationist sentiment existed. It is merely to say that it need not have hamstrung Roosevelt completely, unless he wanted it to do so.[9]

After the rebuff of his January 1938 proposal—which, had it been approved by Chamberlain and executed by the president, would surely have exposed him to considerable isolationist criticism—Roosevelt *chose* to withdraw, as it were, from further initiatives in European affairs. Though momentarily repulsed by Chamberlain's initial negative reaction, he had plenty of opportunity, in the context of Chamberlain's subsequent messages of retreat, to push ahead with his idea had he been really intent upon doing so. Rather, he surrendered his initiative meekly, and thus betrayed something less than complete conviction that it was the right direction in which to move and that he must take the lead. The waverings and uncertainties that had preceded Roosevelt's decision to issue his proposal in the first place, and the lack of consensus among his chief foreign policy advisers about it (Sumner Welles pushed strongly for the proposal, in various forms, over a period of time; Cordell Hull

9. For a thorough examination of Roosevelt and American isolationism, see Cole, *Roosevelt and the Isolationists, 1932–1945*. Cole declares that during World War II American isolationists were crushed nearly as completely as the Axis powers. A new way of life and mode of thinking were emerging, and Roosevelt was closely in tune with what the United States was becoming. As for the autumn of 1937, Cole writes: "For years he [Roosevelt] had been groping for methods . . . that might enable the United States to play a larger and more positive role in trying actively to preserve peace and security. Both the intractable problems abroad and isolationist strength at home made that groping difficult in the extreme. But Roosevelt was trying" (p. 246).

showed great reluctance) make it possible to believe that Roosevelt was content—even relieved—to have the proposal die a quick death. There is nothing in the written record to substantiate this view beyond question, but neither is there anything flatly to deny it. In short, one is tempted to say that Roosevelt's withdrawal from involvement in the European scene in 1938 was as much—or more—the result of conclusions he reached upon the rejection of his January initiative and his own feelings about the wisdom of a hands-off posture while Chamberlain tried to see what he could do to improve the European situation, as it was the result of deference to isolationist pressures in the American Congress and public. Not that he approved entirely of Chamberlain's method and manner or was as optimistic about the chances for success as was Chamberlain; but had the prime minister succeeded in his efforts to appease the dictators and thus improve the general atmosphere in Europe, it is likely that Roosevelt would have been among the first to applaud him.

The circumstances and outcome of Munich clearly frightened the president, as well as the American people, and hardened his conviction that war was coming. A new sense of urgency in American military preparations—albeit for defensive purposes—was one important upshot of this. A second was the renewed determination of American public opinion to stay clear of the vortex of war and prevent the wily Europeans from drawing them into their own senseless internecine struggles. The more the latter sentiment grew, the greater the difficulty Roosevelt encountered in conveying his own opinion that the fates of America and Europe were inextricably intertwined: he talked at length about America being able to stay out of European conflict, but it is doubtful that he really believed it. One cannot have it both ways. If Roosevelt is given credit for perceiving earlier than most the ultimate nature of the fascist menace and the indivisibility of security among democratic nations—as surely seems appropriate—then his protestations of American noninvolvement can hardly be taken at face value. Here the politician was at work saying what his constituents wanted to hear.

Distressed but not entirely surprised by the German attack on Prague, Roosevelt was heartened by the British guarantee to Poland. So was American opinion generally, for it finally appeared that Britain was prepared to take a stand against further Nazi aggression. Interest in bolstering Britain's military preparations grew—mainly from the conviction that the stronger Britain was, the greater was the likelihood that America would not be drawn into a conflict. But this did not mean that the way was now open for further moves by Roosevelt. Hitler's confidence had reached its apex, and little that the president could do would have much effect upon him. During these months the desire of Americans to stay out of war was expressed with increasing intensity. This no doubt weighed heavily on Roosevelt. But the absence of opportunity to do anything effective to alter the course of events and the difficulty of knowing what effective action might entail are at least equally good explanations of Roosevelt's noninvolvement as Europe wound down to war.

Once the fighting began, Roosevelt was trapped between his own understanding of America's importance to the Allied war effort and his equally clear perception that the American people (and Congress) were determined to remain aloof from the whole despicable thing. This might have created a very unhappy situation for him had the military course of the war taken a different direction and had Britain (and France) been forced to call upon him for substantial aid much sooner than they did. But the actual course of the war, reinforced by Chamberlain's puzzling conviction that it would somehow come to an end before Germany undertook a full-scale attack in the West—thus precluding the need for open American involvement—kept him free from all but moderate pressures. He was not required to make really critical decisions on the issues of war and peace because nothing in the course of events compelled him to do so, and no Allied leader sought (at that stage) more support than the United States was willing to give. It was this situation that permitted a number of tedious little issues—matters of troublesome dimensions but certainly not great issues in the broader context of the war that was to come—to dominate and bedevil Anglo-American relations during the fall and winter of 1939–40. It was not until Chamberlain had been ousted and Churchill had taken his place that Roosevelt's ability to provide the kind of aid that could compromise his posture of safety with the American people was put to the test. By that time, of course, new and frightening developments in the war itself—namely, the German attack on the Low Countries and France—had put a completely different complexion on things.

The central dilemma of British policy in the years of Neville Chamberlain's prime ministership was how to defend British interests in three areas of the world—Europe, the Mediterranean, and the Far East—at the same time. From the vantage point of history, it is apparent that the dilemma could not be resolved without the full participation of the United States in efforts to keep the peace, and after the fighting had begun, to win the war. But this was not understood or appreciated by British policymakers in the Chamberlain government—or, if there was, at times, a subtle undercurrent of understanding, they could not bring themselves to draw the conclusion openly and to act upon it. Emotional factors with strong historical bases, ranging from a belief in their own superiority and ability to handle things alone to a genuine distrust of a politically immature America, often took precedence in their thinking. So did their underestimation of both the danger confronting them and the ability of the United States to help materially, even if its spirit were willing. As late as July 20, 1940, Chamberlain wrote his sister: "We mustn't forget that it will be a long time before they [the Americans] can give us any material aid to speak of. Their neglect of their defences has been even greater than ours and they haven't even the potential capacity to produce what is needed to fill the gaps."[10] As has been noted previously, Roosevelt, for his part, seemed to perceive the common dangers to both nations earlier than most. But he was not encouraged toward meaningful cooperation, at least in Europe, by the British. Harold Macmillan, British prime minister in the 1960s, declares in his memoirs that the most decisive feature of the Allied collapse in the twenty years after 1918 was the retirement of the United States into isolation. He then adds:

> During the whole of my life, the main problem confronting the Old World has been somehow or other to induce the New World to accept the responsibilities of its growing material and moral strength. The chief anxiety of far-seeing statesmen, like Eden or Churchill, has been to achieve this end. Chamberlain was too provincial and too self-centered to understand its importance.[11]

One particular factor that troubled British policymakers in the years preceding World War II was the fear that economic expansion at the expense of Great Britain was a primary motive of American leaders. There was much concern in London about the American image of British wealth and how increasing dependence upon the United States, in circumstances wherein Washington could drive a hard bargain, would adversely affect Britain's world position. American leaders clearly understood the potential leverage they wielded in this regard; but there is little basis for concluding that aggressive economic expansion was a

10. Neville to Ida, NC 18/1166.
11. Macmillan, *Winds of Change*, p. 522.

key motive in Anglo-American affairs in the late 1930s, however much American leaders may have been tempted by it. Considerations of national security, fear of war, and a community of interest with Britain (in the sense of recognizing that Britain's continued independence and vitality were essential to the security of the United States) were stronger American motives. Before the outbreak of war, American economic coercion would probably have had the effect of driving Britain toward Germany—so long as the barest prospect of appeasement remained; until Pearl Harbor, economic policy in Washington sprang largely from Henry Morgenthau and the Treasury, whose primary concerns were restraining Nazism and pacifying public opinion.[12] So British suspicions in this regard were exaggerated, if not unwarranted, and led to a defensive posture that was largely unnecessary.

This is not to say that American attitudes toward Britain were always wholly constructive, insofar as the British were concerned. Roosevelt himself seemed to harbor certain prejudices that made him suspicious of the British. Behind his sincerity, charm, and outward show of friendship, there lurked a feeling of hostility—perhaps of jealousy—toward the great imperial history of Great Britain. He was no particular friend of the British Empire, and the idea of its liquidation was certainly more pleasing than frightening to him—as the history of later wartime diplomacy clearly shows. Indeed, according to Oliver Lyttelton (Lord Chandos), whose views are authentically British whatever their accuracy, Roosevelt held "some innate suspicions of the British which are a pathological tradition of Americans." He believed to the end of his life that Britain intended to use American power to pull British chestnuts out of the Balkans and Europe more generally, that the British levied taxes upon their colonies and battened upon their riches, all the while oppressing the people and allowing them no sort of progress. (At the same time, he admired the courage and stubbornness of the British race.) Roosevelt's personal emissary, Harry Hopkins, once told an all-party meeting of British MP's that "there . . . always has been and always will be" about twenty-five percent of Americans who dislike Britain. This feeling stemmed from racial origins and historical factors, but "personal grievances and prejudices also bear a part." There was nothing that could be done about it—but that gave no reason for despair about Anglo-Amer-

12. See Warren F. Kimball, "Lend-Lease and the Open Door: The Temptation of British Opulence, 1937–1942." John M. Blum writes that Roosevelt, for his part, was suspicious of the New York financial community, which was long opposed to the New Deal, and of Wall Street's ties to London (*Roosevelt and Morgenthau,* p. 290).

ican friendship. Further, the British were often exasperated by the American tendency to moralize—to preach interminably, often without thought of action. As D. C. Watt has put it: to the British government, and especially to Chamberlain, Roosevelt seems to have appeared as "an unreliable windbag."[13]

If Chamberlain and his colleagues made certain unfortunate miscalculations, so, too, did Roosevelt. Despite his clear understanding of the Anglo-American community of interest—the relationship of Britain's continued vitality and independence to the security of the United States—he seemed to underestimate the power that the aggressors would be able to mobilize and to overestimate the ability of Britain, with its French and other allies, to restrain them. It was probably not until the fall of France—some weeks after Neville Chamberlain had relinquished office—that a full realization of Allied weakness and Axis strength dawned upon him. If this is so, it was not simply the change in British leadership that began to influence Roosevelt's outlook—though the impact of Churchill's personality and realism is undeniable—but also the drastic change in the course and nature of the war.

Where American public opinion was concerned, there persisted suspicion that so long as Chamberlain remained prime minister, the discredited policy of appeasement would prevail—even after war had been declared. The comparative inactivity of the "phony war" fed the feeling that Britain was not in earnest.[14] But Chamberlain's change of heart and attitude was remarkable. After September 3, 1939, there was no serious consideration of compromise peace. The proponents of appeasement, having gone to the utmost limits of their policy and failed, were now driven with equal resolution to the opposite extreme: nothing would suffice save the disappearance of the Nazi regime. Nor did Chamberlain's commitment to this new outlook falter, although he was genuinely at a loss as to how to pursue the war and at length felt it possibly "providential" that his fall from power "coincided with the entry of the real thing."[15]

If there was any lesson to be learned from 1914–18, it was that future war against an aggressive Germany would require the combined efforts of Britain, the United States, and other nations as well. Nothing less

13. See Harold Macmillan, *The Blast of War, 1939–1945*, pp. 120–21; Oliver Lyttelton (Lord Chandos), *The Memoirs of Lord Chandos: An Unexpected View from the Summit*, p. 298; Watt, "Roosevelt and Chamberlain," p. 185; Earl Winterton, *Fifty Tumultuous Years*, p. 168.

14. See Lothian's annual report to Halifax, 3 September 1940, in Hachey, *Confidential Dispatches*, pp. 5–6.

15. Neville to Ida, 17 May 1940, NC 18/1/1156.

would do. But the interwar period saw very little of the warmth and intimacy that is so vital, in their own self-interest, to relations between the two great English-speaking nations. And if there is any moral to be drawn from the historical account presented in these pages, it is that the first and foremost need of both Britain and America in the conduct of foreign affairs is to keep on close and intimate terms with each other at all times in order to promote the solid, united front required by their extensive common interests.[16] The shift in their power relationships relative both to each other and the rest of the world has not substantially changed this. In the period from mid-1937 to mid-1940, the two nations acted more like selfish, suspicious rivals than like patient, protective brothers. The result was a vicious circle of doubt that materially reduced their effectiveness in confronting the challenge of Hitler in Europe—to say nothing of the Japanese threat in the Pacific. If the Churchill-Roosevelt combination at length became "the partnership that saved the West"—as Joseph Lash attests in the subtitle to his compelling volume on the two statesmen[17]—the Chamberlain-Roosevelt *non*partnership during the period came very close to losing it.

16. See Douglas-Home, *The Way the Wind Blows*, p. 68. Douglas-Home was an aide to Chamberlain during the late 1930s and much later on foreign secretary and prime minister.

17. Lash, *Roosevelt and Churchill, 1939–1941*.

Bibliography

I. Unpublished Documents

Great Britain. Public Record Office, Kew.
  Air Ministry (AIR 19)
  Cabinet Office (CAB 2, 23, 27, 53, 63, 65)
  Foreign Office (FO 115, 371, 414, 794, 800)
  Prime Minister's Office (PREM 1)
United States
  President's Secretary's File. Franklin D. Roosevelt Library, Hyde Park, New York.
  State Department Manuscripts. National Archives, Washington, D.C.

II. Published Documents

Complete Presidential Press Conferences of Franklin D. Roosevelt. Vols. 9–15. New York, 1972.
Confidential Dispatches: Analyses of America by the British Ambassador, 1939–1945. Edited by Thomas E. Hachey. Evanston, Ill., 1974.
Documents on British Foreign Policy, 1919–1939. Edited by E. L. Woodward and Rohan Butler. Third Series. London, 1949–55.
Documents on German Foreign Policy, 1918–1945. Series D. Washington, D.C., 1949–54.
Foreign Relations of the United States: Diplomatic Papers. 1937–40. Washington, D.C., 1954–63.
Parliamentary Debates (Great Britain), *House of Commons.* Fifth Series.
———. *House of Lords.* Fifth Series.

III. Private Papers

Sir John Anderson Papers. India Office Library, London.
Lady Nancy Astor Papers. University of Reading Library.
Clement Attlee Papers. Churchill College, Cambridge.
Adolf A. Berle Papers. Franklin D. Roosevelt Library, Hyde Park, New York.
Neville Chamberlain Papers. Birmingham University Library.

Lord Chatfield Papers. National Maritime Museum, Greenwich.
Lionel Curtis Papers. Bodleian Library, Oxford.
Hugh Dalton Papers and Diary. British Library of Political and Economic Science, London.
J. C. C. Davidson Papers. Bodleian Library, Oxford.
Norman Davis Papers. Library of Congress.
Walter Elliot Papers. National Library of Scotland, Edinburgh.
Lord Halifax Papers. Borthwick Institute, York.
Maurice Hankey Diaries and Correspondence. Churchill College, Cambridge.
Harry Hopkins Papers. Library of Congress.
Cordell Hull Papers. Library of Congress.
Harold Ickes Papers. Library of Congress.
Sir Thomas Inskip Diaries. Churchill College, Cambridge.
Breckinridge Long Papers. Library of Congress.
Lord Lothian Papers. Scottish Record Office, Edinburgh.
Victor Mallet Memoir. Churchill College, Cambridge.
David Margesson Correspondence. Churchill College, Cambridge.
Jay Pierrepont Moffat Papers. Houghton Library, Harvard University.
Henry Morgenthau, Jr. Papers. Franklin D. Roosevelt Library, Hyde Park, New York.
Eric Phipps Papers. Churchill College, Cambridge.
Franklin D. Roosevelt. Franklin D. Roosevelt Library, Hyde Park, New York.
  Map Room Files
  Official Files
  President's Personal Files
Walter Runciman Papers. University of Newcastle Library.
Sir John Simon Diaries. Bodleian Library, Oxford.
Lord Stanhope Papers. Kent Archives Office, Maidstone.
Lord Swinton Papers. Churchill College, Cambridge.
Lord Templewood Papers. Cambridge University Library.
David Euan Wallace Diary. Bodleian Library, Oxford.
Earl of Woolton Papers. Bodleian Library, Oxford.

IV. Published Correspondence, Diaries, Memoirs, Papers, Speeches

Acheson, Dean. *Present at the Creation: My Years in the State Department*. New York, 1969.
Amery, L. S. *My Political Life*. 3 vols. London, 1953–55.
Attlee, Clement R. *As It Happened*. New York, 1954.
Avon, Earl of (Anthony Eden). *The Memoirs of Anthony Eden: Facing the Dictators*. Cambridge, Mass., 1962.
———. *The Memoirs of Anthony Eden: The Reckoning*. Cambridge, Mass., 1965.
Berle, Adolf A. *Navigating the Rapids, 1918–1971: From the Papers of Adolf A. Berle*. Edited by Beatrice B. Berle and Travis B. Jacobs. New York, 1973.
Biddle, A. J. Drexel, Jr. *Poland and the Coming of the Second World War: The Diplomatic Papers of A. J. Drexel Biddle, Jr., United States Ambassador to Poland, 1937–1939*. Edited by Philip Cannistraro, Edward Wynot, Jr., and Theodore Kovaleff. Columbus, Ohio, 1976.
Blum, John M. *From the Morgenthau Diaries*. 3 vols. Boston, 1959–67.
Bohlen, Charles E. *Witness to History, 1929–1969*. New York, 1973.
Bullitt, William C. *For the President: Personal and Secret. Correspondence between*

Franklin D. Roosevelt and William C. Bullitt. Edited by Orville H. Bullitt. Boston, 1972.
Butler, Lord. *The Art of the Possible: The Memoirs of Lord Butler*. London, 1971.
Cadogan, Alexander. *The Diaries of Sir Alexander Cadogan, 1938–1945*. Edited by David Dilks. London, 1971.
Chamberlain, Neville. *In Search of Peace*. New York, 1940.
Chatfield, Lord. *It Might Happen Again* (London, 1947).
Churchill, Winston S. *The Gathering Storm*. Boston, 1948.
———. *Winston S. Churchill: His Complete Speeches, 1897–1963*. Edited by Robert R. James. 8 vols. London, 1974.
Citrine, Lord. *Men and Work: An Autobiography*. London, 1964.
Colville, Sir John Rupert. *The Fringes of Power: 10 Downing Street Diaries, 1939–1955*. London, 1985.
Dalton, Hugh. *The Fateful Years: Memoirs, 1931–1945*. London, 1957.
Douglas-Home, Alec. *The Way the Wind Blows: An Autobiography*. New York, 1976.
Duff Cooper, Alfred. *Old Men Forget: The Autobiography of Duff Cooper*. London, 1954.
Gladwyn, Lord. *The Memoirs of Lord Gladwyn*. New York, 1972.
Gore-Booth, Paul. *With Great Truth and Respect*. London, 1974.
Halifax, Lord. *Fullness of Days*. New York, 1957.
Harvey, Oliver. *The Diplomatic Diaries of Oliver Harvey, 1937–1940*. Edited by John Harvey. London, 1970.
Hull, Cordell. *The Memoirs of Cordell Hull*. 2 vols. New York, 1948.
Ironside, General Sir Edmund. *The Ironside Diaries, 1937–1940*. Edited by Colonel Roderick Macleod and Denis Kelly. London, 1963.
Ismay, General Lord. *The Memoirs of General Lord Ismay*. New York, 1960.
Ickes, Harold L. *The Secret Diary of Harold L. Ickes*. 3 vols. New York, 1954.
James, Robert R. *Memoirs of a Conservative: J. C. C. Davidson's Memoirs and Papers, 1910–1937*. New York, 1969.
Jones, Thomas. *A Diary with Letters, 1931–1950*. London, 1954.
Kirkpatrick, Ivone. *The Inner Circle: Memoirs of Ivone Kirkpatrick*. London, 1959.
Lee, General Raymond E. *The London Journal of General Raymond E. Lee, 1940–1941*. Edited by James Leutze. Boston, 1971.
Liddell Hart, Basil L. *The Liddell Hart Memoirs*. 2 vols. New York, 1965.
Lockhart, Sir Robert Bruce. *The Diaries of Sir Robert Bruce Lockhart*. Edited by Kenneth Young. 2 vols. London, 1973.
Long, Breckinridge. *The War Diary of Breckinridge Long*. Edited by Fred L. Israel. Lincoln, Neb., 1966
Lothian, Lord. *The American Speeches of Lord Lothian, July 1939 to December 1940*. New York, 1941.
Low, David. *Low's Autobiography*. New York, 1957.
Lukasiewicz, Juliusz. *Diplomat in Paris, 1936–1939: Papers and Memoirs of Juliusz Lukasiewicz, Ambassador of Poland*. Edited by Waclaw Jedrzejewicz. New York, 1970.
Lyttelton, Oliver (Lord Chandos). *The Memoirs of Lord Chandos: An Unexpected View from the Summit*. New York, 1963.
Macmillan, Harold. *Winds of Change, 1914–1939*. New York, 1966.
———. *The Blast of War, 1939–1945*. New York, 1967.
The Moffat Papers: Selections from the Diplomatic Journals of Jay Pierrepont Moffat, 1919–1943. Edited by Nancy H. Hooker. Cambridge, Mass., 1956.
Morrison, Herbert. *Herbert Morrison: An Autobiography*. London, 1960.
Murphy, Robert. *Diplomat among Warriors*. London, 1964.

Nicolson, Harold. *Diaries and Letters, 1930–1962*. Edited by Nigel Nicolson. 3 vols. London, 1966–68.
Perkins, Frances. *The Roosevelt I Knew*. New York, 1946.
Pownall, Sir Henry. *Chief of Staff: The Diaries of Lieutenant-General Sir Henry Pownall*. Edited by Brian Bond. 2 vols. Hamden, Conn., 1973.
Roosevelt, Eleanor. *This I Remember*. New York, 1949.
Roosevelt, Franklin D. *Franklin D. Roosevelt and Foreign Affairs*. Edited by Edgar B. Nixon. 3 vols. Cambridge, Mass., 1969.
Roosevelt and Frankfurter: Their Correspondence, 1928–1945. Edited by Max Freedman. Boston, 1967.
F.D.R.: His Personal Letters, 1928–1945. Edited by Elliott Roosevelt. 2 vols. New York, 1950.
Roosevelt and Churchill: Their Secret Wartime Correspondence. Edited by Francis Loewenheim, Harold D. Langley, and Manfred Jonas. New York, 1975.
Simon, Viscount. *Retrospect: The Memoirs of the Rt. Hon. Viscount Simon*. London, 1952.
Slessor, Sir John. *The Central Blue: The Autobiography of Sir John Slessor, Marshal of the RAF*. New York, 1957.
Stimson, Henry L., and McGeorge Bundy. *On Active Service in War and Peace*. New York, 1948.
Templewood, Viscount. *Nine Troubled Years*. London, 1954.
Tully, Grace. *F.D.R.: My Boss*. New York, 1949.
Welles, Sumner. *The Time for Decision*. New York, 1944.
Willert, Sir Arthur. *Washington and Other Memories*. Boston, 1972.
Winterton, Earl. *Fifty Tumultuous Years*. London, 1955.
———. *Orders of the Day*. London, 1953.

V. Secondary Works

Adams, Henry H. *Harry Hopkins: A Biography*. New York, 1977.
———. *Years of Deadly Peril: The Coming of the War, 1939–1941*. New York, 1969.
Adamthwaite, Anthony. *France and the Coming of the Second World War, 1936–1939*. London, 1977.
Allen, H. C. *Great Britain and the United States: A History of Anglo-American Relations, 1783–1952*. New York, 1955.
Allen, H. C., and Roger Thompson, eds. *Contrast and Connection: Bicentennial Essays in Anglo-American History*. Athens, Ohio, 1976.
Aster, Sidney. *1939: The Making of the Second World War*. New York, 1973.
Barker, Elisabeth. *British Policy in South-East Europe in the Second World War*. London, 1976.
Barron, Gloria J. *Leadership in Crisis: FDR and the Path to Intervention*. Port Washington, N.Y., 1973.
Bell, Coral. *The Debatable Alliance: An Essay in Anglo-American Relations*. London, 1964.
Beloff, Max. "The Special Relationship: An Anglo-American Myth." In Martin Gilbert, ed., *A Century of Conflict, 1850–1950: Essays for A. J. P. Taylor*. New York, 1967.
Beschloss, Michael. *Kennedy and Roosevelt: The Uneasy Alliance*. New York, 1980.
Birkenhead, Earl of. *Halifax: The Life of Lord Halifax*. London, 1965.
Blum, John M. *Roosevelt and Morgenthau*. Boston, 1970.
Borg, Dorothy. *The United States and the Far Eastern Crisis of 1933–1938*. Cambridge, Mass., 1964.

———. "Notes on Roosevelt's 'Quarantine' Speech." *Political Science Quarterly* 72 (1957): 405–33.
Branson, Noreen, and Margot Heinemann. *Britain in the 1930's*. New York, 1971.
Burns, James McGregor. *Roosevelt: The Lion and the Fox*. New York, 1956.
Butler, J. R. M. *Lord Lothian, 1882–1940*. London, 1960.
Carroll, F. M. "A Double-Edged Sword: Anglo-American 'Special Relations,' 1936–1981." *International History Review* 6 (1984): 454–64.
Coit, Margaret L. *Mr. Baruch*. Boston, 1957.
Cole, Wayne S. *Roosevelt and the Isolationists, 1932–1945*. Lincoln, Neb., 1983.
———. *America First: The Battle against Intervention, 1940–41*. New York, 1953.
Colvin, Ian. *The Chamberlain Cabinet*. London, 1971.
———. *Vansittart in Office: An Historical Survey of the Origins of the Second World War Based on the Papers of Sir Robert Vansittart*. London, 1965.
Cowling, Maurice. *The Impact of Hitler: British Politics and British Policy, 1933–1940*. Chicago, 1975.
Dallek, Robert. *Franklin D. Roosevelt and American Foreign Policy, 1932–1945*. New York, 1979.
Dennis, Peter. *Decision by Default: Peacetime Conscription and British Defence, 1919–1939*. Durham, N.C., 1972.
Dilks, David. *Neville Chamberlain*. Vol. I: 1869–1929. Cambridge, 1984.
Divine, Robert A. *Roosevelt and World War II*. Baltimore, 1969.
———. *The Illusion of Neutrality*. Chicago, 1962.
Douglas, Roy. *The Advent of War, 1939–1940*. London, 1978.
———. "Chamberlain and Eden, 1937–1938." *Journal of Contemporary History* 13 (1978): 97–116.
———. *In the Year of Munich*. London, 1977.
Dreifort, John E. *Yvon Delbos at the Quai D'Orsay: French Foreign Policy during the Popular Front, 1936–1938*. Lawrence, Kan., 1973.
Drummond, Donald F. *The Passing of American Neutrality, 1937–1941*. Ann Arbor, Mich., 1955.
Elibank, Viscount. "Franklin Roosevelt: Friend of Britain." *Contemporary Review* 1074 (1955): 362–68.
Esthus, Raymond A. "President Roosevelt's Commitment to Britain to Intervene in a Pacific War." *Mississippi Valley Historical Review* 50 (1963): 28–38.
Eubank, Keith. *Munich*. Norman, Okla., 1963.
Fehrenbach, T. R. *F.D.R.'s Undeclared War, 1939 to 1941*. New York, 1967.
Feiling, Keith. *The Life of Neville Chamberlain*. London, 1947.
Feis, Herbert. *The Road to Pearl Harbor: The Coming of War between the United States and Japan*. Princeton, 1950.
Freidel, Frank. *Franklin D. Roosevelt*. 4 vols. Boston, 1952–73.
Fuchser, Larry W. *Neville Chamberlain and Appeasement: A Study in the Politics of History*. New York, 1982.
George, Margaret. *The Warped Vision: British Foreign Policy, 1933–1939*. Pittsburgh, 1965.
Gilbert, Martin. *Winston S. Churchill*. Vol. 5: *The Prophet of Truth, 1922–1939*. Boston, 1977.
———. *The Roots of Appeasement*. London, 1966.
———, and Richard Gott. *The Appeasers*. London, 1963.
Haight, John M. *American Aid to France, 1938–1940*. New York, 1970.
———. "Roosevelt and the Aftermath of the Quarantine Speech." *Review of Politics* 24 (1962): 233–59.

Henson, Edward L., Jr. "Britain, America, and the Month of Munich." *International Relations* 2 (1962): 291–301.

Herzog, James H. *Closing the Open Door: American-Japanese Diplomatic Negotiations, 1936–1941*. Annapolis, Md., 1973.

Hilton, Stanley E. "The Welles Mission to Europe, February–March, 1940: Illusion or Realism?" *Journal of American History* 58 (1971): 93–120.

Hinsley, F. H., et al. *British Intelligence in the Second World War: Its Influence on Strategy and Operations*. Vol. I. New York, 1979.

Hyde, H. Montgomery. *Neville Chamberlain*. London, 1976.

Iriye, Akira. *Across the Pacific: An Inner History of American-East Asian Relations*. New York, 1967.

James, Robert R. *Churchill: A Study in Failure, 1900–1939*. Cleveland, 1970.

Jonas, Manfred. *Isolationism in America, 1935–1941*. Ithaca, N.Y., 1966.

Kaiser, David E. *Economic Diplomacy and the Origins of the Second World War: Germany, Britain, France, and Eastern Europe, 1930–1939*. Princeton, 1980.

Kennedy, Paul. *The Realities behind Diplomacy: Background Influences on British External Policy, 1865–1980*. London, 1981.

Kimball, Warren F. "Churchill and Roosevelt: The Personal Equation." *Prologue* 6 (1974): 169–82.

———. "Lend-Lease and the Open Door: The Temptation of British Opulence, 1937–1942." *Political Science Quarterly* 86 (1971): 232–59.

Kimball, Warren F. *The Most Unsordid Act: Lend-Lease, 1939–1941*. Baltimore, 1969.

Koskoff, David E. *Joseph P. Kennedy: A Life and Times*. Englewood Cliffs, N.J., 1974.

Kottman, Richard N. *Reciprocity and the North Atlantic Triangle, 1932–1938*. Ithaca, N.Y., 1968.

Lafore, Laurence. *The End of Glory: an Interpretation of the Origins of World War II*. Philadelphia, 1970.

Lammers, Donald. *Explaining Munich: The Search for Motive in British Policy*. Stanford, 1966.

Langer, William L., and S. Everett Gleason. *The Challenge to Isolation, 1937–1940*. New York, 1952.

Lash, Joseph. *Roosevelt and Churchill, 1939–1941: The Partnership That Saved the West*. New York, 1976.

Lee, Bradford E. *Britain and the Sino-Japanese War, 1937–1939: A Study in the Dilemmas of British Decline*. Stanford, 1973.

Leigh, Michael. *Mobilizing Consent: Public Opinion and American Foreign Policy, 1937–1947*. Westport, Conn., 1976.

Leutze, James R. *Bargaining for Supremacy: Anglo-American Naval Relations, 1937–1941*. Chapel Hill, N.C., 1977.

———. "The Secret of the Churchill-Roosevelt Correspondence: September 1939–May 1940." *Journal of Contemporary History* 10 (1975): 465–91.

Louis, W. Roger. *British Strategy in the Far East, 1919–1939*. Oxford, 1971.

Lowe, Peter. *Great Britain and the Origins of the Pacific War: A Study of British Policy in East Asia, 1937–1941*. Oxford, 1977.

Macdonald, C. A. *The United States, Britain, and Appeasement, 1936–1939*. New York, 1981.

———. "Economic Appeasement and the German 'Moderates,' 1937–1939: An Introductory Essay." *Past and Present* 56 (1972): 105–35.

Macleod, Iain. *Neville Chamberlain*. London, 1961.

Marks, Frederick W. III. "Franklin Roosevelt's Diplomatic Debut: The Myth of the Hundred Days." *South Atlantic Quarterly* 84 (1985): 245–63.

May, Ernest R. *"Lessons" of the Past: The Use and Misuse of History in American Foreign Policy.* New York, 1973.
Medlicott, W. N. *British Foreign Policy since Versailles, 1919–1963.* London, 1968.
Megaw, M. Ruth. "The Scramble for the Pacific: Anglo-United States Rivalry in the 1930s." *Historical Studies* 17 (1977): 458–73.
Middlemas, Keith. *Diplomacy of Illusion: The British Government and Germany, 1937–1939.* London, 1972.
Mommsen, Wolfgang J., and Lothar Kettenacher, eds. *The Fascist Challenge and the Policy of Appeasement.* London, 1983.
Morley, James W. *The Fateful Choice: Japan's Advance into Southeast Asia, 1939–1941.* New York, 1980.
Mowat, R. B. *The American Entente.* London, 1939.
Murfett, Malcolm. *Fool-Proof Relations: The Search for Anglo-American Naval Cooperation during the Chamberlain Years, 1937–1940.* Singapore, 1984.
Murray, Williamson. *The Change in the European Balance of Power, 1938–1939: The Path to Ruin.* Princeton, 1984.
Namier, Lewis B. "Munich Survey: A Summing Up." *Listener* 40 (1984): 835–36.
Newman, Simon. *March 1939. The British Guarantee to Poland: A Study in the Continuity of British Foreign Policy.* Oxford, 1976.
Nicholas, H. G. *The United States and Britain.* Chicago, 1975.
Northedge, F. S. *The Troubled Giant: Britain among the Great Powers, 1916–1939.* London, 1961.
Offner, Arnold A. "Appeasement Revisited: The United States, Great Britain, and Germany, 1933–1940." *Journal of American History* 64 (1977): 373–93.
———. *The Origins of the Second World War: American Foreign Policy and World Politics, 1917–1941.* New York, 1975.
———. *American Appeasement: United States Foreign Policy and Germany, 1933–1938.* Cambridge, Mass., 1969.
Ovendale, Ritchie. *"Appeasement" and the English-Speaking World: Britain, the United States, the Dominions, and the Policy of "Appeasement," 1937–1939.* Cardiff, 1975.
Parkinson, Roger. *Peace for Our Time: Munich to Dunkirk—The Inside Story.* London, 1971.
Peden, G. C. *British Rearmament and the Treasury, 1932–1939.* Edinburgh, 1979.
Pelling, Henry. *Winston Churchill.* New York, 1974.
Pogue, Forrest C. *George C. Marshall, Education of a General, 1880–1939.* New York, 1963.
Porter, David L. *The Seventy-sixth Congress and World War II, 1939–1940.* Columbia, Mo., 1979.
Postan, M. M. *British War Production.* London, 1952.
Pratt, Julius W. *Cordell Hull, 1933–1944.* 2 vols. New York, 1964.
Pratt, Lawrence R. *East of Malta, West of Suez: Britain's Mediterranean Crisis, 1936–1939.* Cambridge, 1975.
———. "The Anglo-American Naval Conversations on the Far East of January 1938." *International Affairs* 47 (1971): 745–59.
Range, Willard. *Franklin D. Roosevelt's World Order.* Athens, Ga., 1959.
Rauch, Basil. *Roosevelt. From Munich to Pearl Harbor: A Study in the Creation of Foreign Policy.* New York, 1950.
Reynolds, David. *Lord Lothian and Anglo-American Relations, 1939–1940.* Philadelphia, 1983.
———. "FDR's Foreign Policy and the British Royal Visit to the U.S.A., 1939." *Historian* 45 (1983): 461–72.

———. *The Creation of the Anglo-American Alliance, 1937–1941: A Study in Competitive Cooperation.* Chapel Hill, N.C., 1982.
Rhodes, Benjamin D. "The British Royal Visit of 1939 and the 'Psychological Approach' to the United States." *Diplomatic History* 2 (1978): 197–211.
Rock, William R. *British Appeasement in the 1930s.* London, 1977.
———. *Neville Chamberlain.* New York, 1969.
———. *Appeasement on Trial: British Foreign Policy and Its Critics, 1938–1939.* Hamden, Conn., 1966.
———. "The British Guarantee to Poland, March, 1939: A Problem in Diplomatic Decision-Making." *South Atlantic Quarterly* 65 (1966): 229–40.
———. "Grand Alliance or Daisy Chain: British Opinion and Policy toward Russia, April–August, 1939." In Lillian P. Wallace and William C. Askew, eds. *Power, Public Opinion, and Diplomacy.* Durham, N.C., 1959.
Roskill, Stephen. *Naval Policy between the Wars.* 2 vols. London, 1968, 1976.
———. *Hankey, Man of Secrets.* Vol. III. London, 1974.
Rostow, Nicholas. *Anglo-French Relations, 1934–1936.* New York, 1984.
Rowse, A. L. *Appeasement: A Study in Political Decline, 1933–1939.* New York, 1961.
Russett, Bruce M. *Community and Contention: Britain and America in the Twentieth Century.* Cambridge, Mass., 1963.
Shay, Robert P., Jr. *British Rearmament in the Thirties: Profits and Politics.* Princeton, 1977.
Sherwood, Robert E. *Roosevelt and Hopkins: An Intimate History.* New York, 1948.
Storry, Richard. *Japan and the Decline of the West in Asia, 1894–1943.* London, 1979.
Sykes, Christopher. *Nancy: The Life of Lady Astor.* London, 1972.
Taylor, A. J. P. *The Origins of the Second World War.* London, 1961.
———. *Englishmen and Others.* London, 1956.
Taylor, Telford. *Munich: The Price of Peace.* New York, 1979.
Thompson, Neville. *The Anti-Appeasers: Conservative Opposition to Appeasement in the 1930s.* Oxford, 1971.
Thorne, Christopher. *Allies of a Kind: The United States, Britain, and the War against Japan, 1941–1945.* Oxford, 1978.
———. *The Limits of Foreign Policy: The West, the League, and the Far Eastern Crisis of 1931–1933.* New York, 1972.
———. *The Approach of War, 1938–1939.* London, 1967.
Trotter, Ann. *Britain and East Asia, 1933–1937.* New York, 1975.
Turner, Arthur C. *The Unique Partnership: Britain and the United States.* New York, 1971.
Vieth, Jane K. "Joseph P. Kennedy at the Court of St. James's: The Diplomacy of a Boston Irishman." In Kenneth P. Jones, ed., *U.S. Diplomats in Europe, 1919–1941.* Santa Clara, Calif., 1981.
Wallace, William V. "Roosevelt and British Appeasement in 1938." *Bulletin of the British Association for American Studies* 5 (1962): 4–30.
Watt, Donald C. *Succeeding John Bull: America in Britain's Place, 1900–1975.* Cambridge, 1984.
———. "Roosevelt and Chamberlain: Two Appeasers." *International Journal* 28 (1973): 185–204.
———. *Personalities and Policies.* London, 1965.
Weinberg, Gerhard L. *The Foreign Policy of Hitler's Germany.* Vol. II: Starting World War II, 1937–1939. Chicago, 1980.
Welles, Sumner. *Seven Major Decisions.* London, 1951.
Wendt, Berndt Jürgen. *Economic Appeasement: Handel und Finanz in der britischen Deutschland Politik, 1933–1939.* Düsseldorf, 1971.

Wheeler-Bennett, Sir John W. *Special Relationships: America in Peace and War.* London, 1975.
———. *King George VI: His Life and Reign.* New York, 1965.
———. *Munich: Prologue to Tragedy.* London, 1948.
Wiltz, John E. *From Isolation to War, 1931–1941.* London, 1969.
Wolfers, Arnold. *Britain and France between Two Wars: Conflicting Strategies of Peace since Versailles.* New York, 1940.
Woodward, Sir Llewellyn. *British Foreign Policy in the Second World War.* Vol. I. London, 1970.
Wrench, John Evelyn. *Geoffrey Dawson and Our Times.* London, 1955.

VI. Dissertations

Gilman, Ernest. "Economic Aspects of Anglo-American Relations in the Era of Roosevelt and Chamberlain, 1937–1940." University of London, 1976.
Harrison, Richard A. "Appeasement and Isolation: The Relation of British and American Foreign Policy, 1935–1938." Princeton University, 1974.

Index

WILLIAM R. ROCK is Professor of History at Bowling Green State University in Ohio. He is the author of *British Appeasement in the 1930s*, *Neville Chamberlain*, and *Appeasement on Trial*.

This book is set in Sabon by Brevis Press

*

Jacket design by Jane Forbes